Global Value Chains and Global Production Networks

The global economic system is experiencing a profound period of rapid change. The emergence of globalized production and distribution systems, which bring together diverse constellations of economic actors through a complex regime of global corporate governance, state regulation and new international divisions of labor, demands corresponding and innovative explanatory models. Global value chains (GVCs) and global production networks (GPNs) have been particularly useful as conceptual frameworks for understanding the global market engagement of firms, regions and nations. This book examines the rise of GVCs and GPNs as dominant features of the international political economy. It brings together leading thinkers in the field and sets out new directions for future scholarship in understanding the contemporary global economic system. In doing so, this book makes a significant contribution to our understanding of the international political economy and the global economic system in the post-Washington Consensus era of contemporary capitalism.

This book was published as a special issue of the *Review of International Political Economy.*

Jeffrey Neilson is Senior Lecturer in economic and environmental geography at the University of Sydney, where he researches economic development and natural resource management in Southeast Asia, with a primary focus on Indonesia.

Bill Pritchard is an Associate Professor in human geography at the University of Sydney, where he specialises in agriculture, food and rural places. Professor Pritchard is interested in the ways that global and local processes are transforming places, industries and people's lives.

Henry Wai-chung Yeung is a Professor of economic geography at the National University of Singapore. His research interests cover, broadly, theories and the geography of transnational corporations, global production networks and global value chains, East Asian firms and developmental states in the global economy.

Global Value Chains and Global Production Networks

Changes in the International Political Economy

Edited by

Jeffrey Neilson, Bill Pritchard and Henry Wai-chung Yeung

Routledge
Taylor & Francis Group
LONDON AND NEW YORK

First published 2015 by Routledge

2 Park Square, Milton Park, Abingdon, Oxon OX14 4RN
711 Third Avenue, New York, NY 10017, USA

Routledge is an imprint of the Taylor & Francis Group, an informa business

First issued in paperback 2017

British Library Cataloguing in Publication Data
A catalogue record for this book is available from the British Library

ISBN 13: 978-1-138-84956-3 (hbk)
ISBN 13: 978-1-138-05914-6 (pbk)

Typeset in Palatino
by RefineCatch Limited, Bungay, Suffolk

Publisher's Note
The publisher accepts responsibility for any inconsistencies that may have arisen during the conversion of this book from journal articles to book chapters, namely the possible inclusion of journal terminology.

Contents

Citation Information

The chapters in this book were originally published in the *Review of International Political Economy*, volume 21, issue 1 (February 2014). When citing this material, please use the original page numbering for each article, as follows:

Chapter 1

Global value chains and global production networks in the changing international political economy: An introduction
Jeffrey Neilson, Bill Pritchard and Henry Wai-chung Yeung
Review of International Political Economy, volume 21, issue 1 (February 2014) pp. 1–8

Chapter 2

Global value chains in a post-Washington Consensus world
Gary Gereffi
Review of International Political Economy, volume 21, issue 1 (February 2014) pp. 9–37

Chapter 3

Value chains, neoliberalism and development practice: The Indonesian experience
Jeffrey Neilson
Review of International Political Economy, volume 21, issue 1 (February 2014) pp. 38–69

Chapter 4

Governing the market in a globalizing era: Developmental states, global production networks and inter-firm dynamics in East Asia
Henry Wai-chung Yeung
Review of International Political Economy, volume 21, issue 1 (February 2014) pp. 70–101

Chapter 5

The role of the state as an inter-scalar mediator in globalizing liquid crystal display industry development in South Korea
Yong-Sook Lee, Inhye Heo and Hyungjoo Kim
Review of International Political Economy, volume 21, issue 1 (February 2014) pp. 102–129

Chapter 6

Market rebalancing of global production networks in the Post-Washington Consensus globalizing era: Transformation of export-oriented development in China
Chun Yang
Review of International Political Economy, volume 21, issue 1 (February 2014) pp. 130–156

Chapter 7

Global models of networked organization, the positional power of nations and economic development
Matthew C. Mahutga
Review of International Political Economy, volume 21, issue 1 (February 2014) pp. 157–194

Chapter 8

Explaining governance in global value chains: A modular theory-building effort
Stefano Ponte and Timothy Sturgeon
Review of International Political Economy, volume 21, issue 1 (February 2014) pp. 195–223

Chapter 9

Missing links: Logistics, governance and upgrading in a shifting global economy
Neil M. Coe
Review of International Political Economy, volume 21, issue 1 (February 2014) pp. 224–256

Please direct any queries you may have about the citations to clsuk.permissions@cengage.com

Global value chains and global production networks in the changing international political economy: An introduction

Jeffrey Neilson[1], *Bill Pritchard*[1] *and Henry Wai-chung Yeung*[2]

[1]*School of Geosciences, University of Sydney, Sydney, Australia*
[2]*National University of Singapore, Singapore*

The emergence of global production and distribution systems, which bring together diverse constellations of economic actors through an increasingly complex regime of global corporate governance, widespread outsourcing of productive functions, and new international divisions of labour, has stimulated the rise of corresponding conceptual models to explain these developments in International Political Economy (IPE). Global value chains (GVCs) and global production networks (GPNs) have been particularly useful as explanatory frameworks for understanding the global market engagement of firms, regions and nations. These interrelated approaches explain geographical patterns of value creation, retention and capture in the global economy primarily through the conceptual architecture of chain *governance* and network *dynamics* – crucial theoretical shorthands for the ability of lead firms to coordinate the value-added activities of a multitude of economic actors (Gereffi, 1994; Henderson et al., 2002; Gereffi et al., 2005). Through these theoretical frameworks, global market engagement is reconceptualized from a passive process involving the reaction of independent actors to market signals, as in international trade theories (e.g. Grossman and Rossi-Hansberg, 2008), to a set of industrial transformations constructed within system-wide dynamics of coordination and control by economic and non-economic actors.

A key feature of global economic reorganization presented in these conceptual models is the progressive outsourcing by lead firms in developed countries of their peripheral, and frequently low-value, productive functions to low-cost countries and regions, while maintaining control of core nodes of value creation and retention in their home countries. Despite spatially diverse production systems and the fragmented ownership of different productive functions, lead firms have continued to dictate the terms and conditions of participation in networks and chains through different types of governance that act upon participants 'at-a-distance'. The generalized trend, highlighted two decades ago in a seminal book chapter by Gereffi (1994), was the increasing prominence of buyer-driven commodity chains in the global economy. The US retail behemoth Wal-Mart (along with its European counterparts Tesco from the UK, Carrefour from France, and Metro from Germany) was emblematic of this emergent form of economic organization, reflecting the massive transformation of the retail sector in North America and Western Europe, and the enhanced purchasing power of advanced economies, while simultaneously off-shoring production to other countries – primarily those in East Asia, Latin America, and Africa (see also Hamilton *et al.*, 2011). These dual processes of continued high rates of consumption in the affluent world and expanding economic opportunities for value chain participation elsewhere in the world have provided the bedrock for the attendant models of global economic organization. Indeed, the phenomenal economic rise of East Asia over the last quarter century was predicated upon these exact processes.

Since Gereffi's (1994) initial work, academic research on GVCs and GPNs has grown substantially and entered into a mature phase in the 2010s. This journal has published two of the most influential theoretical papers in this genre of research in the social sciences (Henderson *et al.*, 2002; Gereffi *et al.*, 2005). In recent years, the lexicons of global value chains and global production networks have also received significant attention from major international organizations such as the World Bank (Cattaneo *et al.*, 2010a), UNCTAD (2013), World Trade Organization (Elms and Low, 2013), OECD (OECD-WTO-UNCTAD, 2013), and elsewhere. A 2010 World Bank report on the post-2008 world economy further claims that 'given that production processes in many industries have been fragmented and moved around on a global scale, GVCs have become the world economy's backbone and central nervous system' (Cattaneo et al., 2010b: 7). The time is now ripe for a critical reappraisal of the conceptual development and the empirical manifestations of GVCs and GPNs as the core feature of the international political economy. In December 2011, we organized a workshop in Singapore bringing together many of the leading researchers in the GVC-GPN platform that led to this special issue of *Review of International Political Economy*. The eight articles in this special issue reinforce our assertion that now is a critical moment to ask major questions about state functionality in the context of fundamentally restructured global production systems, changing international political economy in the face of significant market shifts, and future prospects for theory development in this genre of IPE research. In what follows, we discuss each of these three major questions in light of the papers in this special issue.

First, the conceptual prisms of GVCs and GPNs have long prefigured central questions about the role of the state in shaping the international political economy. To date, however, explicit theorization of the state's role has been somewhat lacking in the GVC and GPN literatures. State action and inaction is often a key aspect of GVC/GPN research narratives (about firms, regions, nations), but is rarely placed in the foreground, and even more rarely, given due theoretical consideration. While the original GVC formulation tends to treat the state as a context for firm-specific action, GPN researchers are more explicit in their incorporation of state institutions in shaping the constitution of global production networks. We argue that global economic change is increasingly demanding a greater prominence of such considerations. The state is clearly not a unitary entity, but a constellation of functions and capacities. Importantly for the subject at hand, the enactment of these functions does not always crystallize in consistent signals for global engagement and potential upgrading. State action, and inaction, inherently comprises the contradictions that are intrinsic to the complex exercise of sovereign powers. The absence, as much as the presence, of the state might be a crucial shaper of the (dis)enabling environments for articulation into GVCs and GPNs. In particular, state action and inaction creates the enabling conditions that shape whether and how firms, regions and nations are able to engage with global markets, and their capacities to *upgrade* these engagements. Most obviously, this includes such policy arenas as wage-setting, tariffs, taxes (and tax concessions), infrastructure provision, education, training and research, and spatial planning (such as the establishment of free trade zones and business hubs).

On the one hand, GVCs/GPNs are emergent artefacts from state action: they always 'touch down' somewhere, and in every 'somewhere', there is always the hand of the state (either in its presence or its relative absence). Yet also, GVCs/GPNs impact recursively within the arenas in which they are connected. Processes of global competition associated with participating in GVCs and GPNs may place pressures on the state to dilute or liberalize wages policies; may inspire the state to beef up research or training capacities; or may entice states into entrepreneurial strategies such as provisioning firms with tax holidays or even taking a direct equity stake in these firms, in the attempt to capture a 'better slice' of a GVC/GPN. Normative stances on the appropriate role of the state have, of course, featured prominently within ongoing debates around development models, as with the Washington Consensus and the perceived need for a post-Washington Consensus. In this special issue, the papers by Gereffi (2014), Neilson (2014) and Yeung (2014) offer a useful reinterpretation of the state's role in GVCs and GPNs. While Gereffi's paper argues that the emergence of contending centres of political institutions and power in the post-Washington Consensus era has led to a more diffuse role of state capacity, Yeung argues for a fundamental shift in partnership between economic actors and state institutions in favour of non-state actors in global production networks. Neilson questions the way that GVC theory and practice have, perhaps unwittingly, repositioned the role of the state as an agent of development. Taken together, these conceptual papers point to the changing role of the state in a global economy coordinated through GVCs and GPNs. Empirically, Lee *et al.*'s (2014) paper provides a nuanced analysis of the reconstituted role of the South Korean state in supporting the articulation of its domestic LCD industry into global production networks. Instead of the all powerful developmental state cajoling domestic firms – the dominant leitmotif in earlier studies of East Asian development (e.g. Amsden, 1989; Evans, 1995), Lee *et al.* argue that the South Korean state plays an intermediary role in facilitating the strategic coupling of domestic economic actors with global lead firms.

Second, rapid market shifts have fundamentally reshaped the international political economy in recent years, particularly since the 2008 global financial crisis. The relationship between economic development models and the changing realities of global economic organization has been a feature of much research using the frames of GVCs and GPNs. Accelerating globalization in the 1990s and 2000s was reflected in GVC/GPN research into international subcontracting networks in sectors such as clothing and footwear, electronics, consumer goods, automobile assembly and agri-food systems. These complexes were sectoral expressions of the geo-economic shifts in the trade balances of countries in the global North (especially the US). The rise of China as 'factory to the world' and, to a lesser extent, India as the 'world's back office' were contingent upon the global expansion of captive forms of chain/network governance in manufacturing and services. As lead firms headquartered in the global North ruthlessly relocated upstream activities to lower cost production sites in the global South, they manufactured the global conditions of debt and imbalance that, arguably perhaps, lay at the heart of recent global economic turmoil. A vital question at the current moment is how global-scale shifts in consumption and production relations (particularly if and when the Chinese Renminbi is re-valued against the US dollar) will reverberate upon GVCs/GPNs.

The global financial crisis of 2008, ongoing economic stagnation in many parts of Western Europe and Japan, the rapidly growing economic (and geopolitical) influence of China, and the end of Washington Consensus development models have raised new questions about whether the organization of the global economy is entering a new phase. Perhaps most significant in this regard is the shifting end-markets for consumer goods as the balance of purchasing power shifts towards Asia and other emerging economies (e.g. Brazil, South Africa, Russia, and elsewhere). This shift is characterized by the widespread expectations that Chinese demand will be the prime catalyst capable of leading the world out of economic stagnation. If this is indeed to occur, then the corresponding shifts in corporate and geopolitical power are profound, and we would argue, have not yet been fully conceptualized in IPE. As long as the architecture of global economic organization aligned with the political priorities of developed states, there was little cause for friction: but this may be changing. In this special issue, Yang's (2014) article tackles specifically how China's shift from export-oriented industrialization to growing its own domestic market may have significant implications for understanding how foreign and domestic firms rearticulate and reconfigure value-adding activity in their production networks. At the international level, Gereffi's (2014) paper observes that such a geo-economic shift towards very large economies in the Global South may reshape the power relations between global lead firms and their suppliers. Some of the latter have grown significantly to become major producers in their own right, partnering rather than depending on the former to succeed in global competition. Both papers point to the cascading effects of how market shifts are transmitted through value chains and production networks in different industries.

Third, theoretical advancement in GVC-GPN research seems to be lagging behind a large number of empirical studies of different value chains and production networks in the global economy. While several of the pioneering papers are highly influential in empirical research, they remain fairly typological and categorical. One group of these papers (Gereffi, 1994; Gereffi *et al.*, 2005) tends to focus specifically on the governance of different types of value chains; another group of theory papers (Henderson *et al.*, 2002; Coe et al., 2004; Yeung, 2009) offers a range of conceptual categories such as territorial embeddedness and strategic coupling for understanding economic development. Still, none of these provides the necessary causal explanation of why and how economic development takes place in different regional and national economies. In this regard, two papers by Mahutga (2014) and Ponte and Sturgeon (2014) seek to advance theory development in GVC-GPN research. In particular, Mahutga's paper develops an exchange-theoretic conceptualization of inter-firm power in order to explain the different configurations of global production and, by implications, the diverse developmental trajectories of national economies. Going beyond inter-firm exchange relations, Ponte and Sturgeon propose a modular theory development process that incorporates both inter-firm relations and broader institutional, regulatory and societal processes to arrive at a more comprehensive theory of GVC governance.

While these two papers by Mahutga (2014) and Ponte and Sturgeon (2014) help refine our existing theoretical understanding of inter-firm power dynamics and chain governance, they remain broadly confined to a 'productionist' understanding of GVCs and GPNs. Seeking to break new theoretical ground, Coe's (2014) paper shifts our conceptual and empirical attention away from manufacturing industries to logistics both as a service industry with its own distinctive value-generation networks and as a critical link enabling value activity in different global industries. This expanding conception of 'production' in GVC-GPN thinking beyond mere manufacturing activity is a welcome move to underscore the critical importance of intermediaries in such chains and networks. Apart from providers of logistics, these intermediaries refer to traders, financiers, standards-setters, and other providers of advanced business services such as management consultants, legal services, recruitment agencies, and others. These firm and non-firm intermediaries not only bridge and connect different value chains and production networks, but also offer unique inputs, mostly intangible in nature, to make these networks work.

Coe's contribution, moreover, alerts us to the unfinished business that defines GVC-GPN research. As noted at the outset of this introductory article, this field of enquiry has entered a mature phase in the 2010s. However, mainstream recognition of GVCs-GPNs as an intellectual modality for thinking about the global economy should not be equated with complacency from researchers that the approach is cut-and-dried. Even beyond the new empirical insights and conceptual foci presented in this special issue, this is a field that warrants ongoing renovation and renewal. The theoretical and methodological toolkit of the GVC-GPN approach needs to be as restless as the global economy it serves to study.

If the past is any guide to the future, we foresee two arenas of ongoing contestation that will define the ways that the GVC-GPN approach is insinuated within ensuing debates about the global economy. First, the papers in this special issue highlight the ongoing tension within GVC-GPN studies between what Peck (1999) labelled as 'deep' and 'shallow' research objectives. In the GVC-GPN field there is an obvious, and it appears to us, widening, disjuncture between the use of this approach to generate broad-based critical analysis on the dynamics of capitalism, and as a technocratic means to 'solve' industry problems. These tensions have been aggravated by the very success of the approach. As Gereffi's (2014) contribution to this issue suggests, with the discourse of value chains and production networks permeating international organizations and national and local development agencies, the resultant diffusion of ideas leads to a reformulation of established development paradigms. But as shown in Neilson's (2014) paper in this special issue, this 'translation' of academic thinking into policy practice may be highly selective and politicized, leading to significant loss of the critical thinking in the original theory development, such as the state's mediating role, power asymmetries, and historical-geographical contexts. These ongoing struggles over the ways that GVC-GPN efforts are framed will require continued scrutiny from researchers.

The second arena of contestation we see relates to the politics of GVC-GPN research. As numerous researchers in this area have previously suggested, it is impossible to study a GVC-GPN from 'nowhere'. Researchers are inevitably socially and territorially positioned, and through this positioning, come to see the functionalities and implications of GVC-GPN processes with distinctive emphases and purposes in mind. This point is important to note, because in the history of this field, GVC-GPN analysis has been deployed for extremely varied, and indeed, oppositional, political intents. A notable feature of this approach is that key elements and concepts translate across the lexicon of business interests and efficiency paradigms, and civil society interests and rights-based paradigms. A GVC-GPN analysis of the textiles sector in Bangladesh undertaken by a labour-rights organisation will look very differently from one done by a management consultancy, yet common terminologies and conceptual frameworks may flow through both studies.

In summary, the rise of global value chains and global production networks as a dominant feature of the international political economy has now received substantial academic and policy attention. However, there is clearly a strong rationale for more sustained research into the theory of these chains and networks and their politics and practice in the empirical realm. We hope this special issue makes a modest contribution to such a critical step in understanding the international political economy in the post-Washington Consensus era of contemporary capitalism.

REFERENCES

Amsden, Alice H. (1989) *Asia's Next Giant: South Korea and Late Industrialization*, New York: Oxford University Press.

Cattaneo, Olivier, Gereffi, Gary and Staritz, Cornelia (eds) (2010a) *Global Value Chains in a Postcrisis World: A Development Perspective*, Washington, DC: World Bank.

Cattaneo, Olivier, Gereffi, Gary and Staritz, Cornelia (2010b) 'Global value chains in a postcrisis world: resilience, consolidation, and shifting end markets', in Olivier Cattaneo, Gary Gereffi and Cornelia Staritz (eds) *Global Value Chains in a Postcrisis World: A Development Perspective*, Washington, DC: World Bank, pp. 3–20.

Coe, Neil M., Hess, Martin, Yeung, Henry Wai-chung, Dicken, Peter and Henderson, Jeffrey (2004) '"Globalizing" regional development: a global production networks perspective', *Transactions of the Institute of British Geographers*, New Series, 29(4), pp. 468–84.

Elms, Deborah K. and Low, Patrick (eds) (2013) *Global Value Chains in a Changing World*, Geneva: World Trade Organization.

Evans, Peter (1995) *Embedded Autonomy: States and Industrial Transformation*, Princeton, NJ: Princeton University Press.

Gereffi, Gary (1994) 'The Organization of Buyer-Driven Global Commodity Chains: How US Retailers Shape Overseas Production networks', in Gary Gereff and Miguel Korzeniewicz (eds) *Commodity Chains and Global Capitalism*, Westport, CT: Praeger, pp. 95–122.

Gereffi, Gary, Humphrey, John and Sturgeon, Timothy (2005) 'The Governance of Global Value Chains', *Review of International Political Economy*, 12(1): pp. 78–104.

Grossman, Gene and Rossi-Hansberg, Esteban (2008) 'Trading Tasks: A Simple Theory of Offshoring', *American Economic Review*, 98(5), pp. 1978–97.

Hamilton, Gary G., Petrovic, Misha and Senauer, Benjamin (eds) (2011) *The Market Makers: How Retailers Are Reshaping the Global Economy*, Oxford: Oxford University Press.

Henderson, Jeffrey, Dicken, Peter, Hess, Martin, Coe, Neil M. and Yeung, Henry Wai-chung (2002) 'Global Production Networks and the Analysis of Economic Development', *Review of International Political Economy*, 9(3), pp. 436–64.

OECD-WTO-UNCTAD (2013) *Implications of Global Value Chains for Trade, Investment, Development and Jobs*, Report Prepared for the G-20 Leaders Summit, September 2013, http://unctad.org/en/PublicationsLibrary/unctad_oecd_wto_2013d1_en.pdf, accessed on 9 September 2013.

Peck, Jamie (1999) 'Editorial: Grey Geography?', *Transactions Institute of British Geographers*, NS, 24, pp. 131–5.

UNCTAD (2013) *World Investment Report 2013: Global Value Chains: Investment and Trade for Development*, New York: United Nations.

Yeung, Henry Wai-chung (2009) 'Regional Development and the Competitive Dynamics of Global Production Networks: An East Asian Perspective', *Regional Studies*, 43(3), pp. 325–51.

Global value chains in a post-Washington Consensus world

Gary Gereffi

Department of Sociology, Duke University, Durham, NC, USA

ABSTRACT

Contemporary globalization has been marked by significant shifts in the organization and governance of global industries. In the 1970s and 1980s, one such shift was characterized by the emergence of buyer-driven and producer-driven commodity chains. In the early 2000s, a more differentiated typology of governance structures was introduced, which focused on new types of coordination in global value chains (GVCs). Today the organization of the global economy is entering another phase, with transformations that are reshaping the governance structures of both GVCs and global capitalism at various levels: (1) the end of the Washington Consensus and the rise of contending centers of economic and political power; (2) a combination of geographic consolidation and value chain concentration in the global supply base, which, in some cases, is shifting bargaining power from lead firms in GVCs to large suppliers in developing economies; (3) new patterns of strategic coordination among value chain actors; (4) a shift in the end markets of many GVCs accelerated by the economic crisis of 2008–09, which is redefining regional geographies of investment and trade; and (5) a diffusion of the GVC approach to major international donor agencies, which is prompting a reformulation of established development paradigms.

I. VIEWING THE GLOBAL ECONOMY THROUGH A VALUE-CHAIN LENS

Globalization has given rise to a new era of international competition that is reshaping global production and trade and altering the organization of industries (Gereffi, 2011). Since the 1960s, international companies have been slicing up their supply chains in search of low-cost and capable suppliers offshore. The literature on 'the new international division of labor' traced the surge of manufactured exports from the Third World to the establishment of labor-intensive export platforms set up by multinational firms in low-wage areas (Fröbel *et al.*, 1981). This was typified by the American production-sharing or 'twin plant' program with Mexico and the German export-processing zones for apparel assembly in Central and Eastern Europe. The pace of offshore production soon accelerated dramatically and took new organizational forms (Dicken, 2011). In the 1970s and 1980s, US retailers and brand-name companies joined manufacturers in the search for offshore suppliers of most categories of consumer goods, which led to a fundamental shift from what had been 'producer-driven' commodity chains to 'buyer-driven' chains. The geography of these chains expanded from regional production-sharing arrangements to full-fledged global supply chains, with a growing emphasis on East Asia (Gereffi, 1994, 1996).

In the 1990s and 2000s, the industries and activities encompassed by global supply chains grew exponentially, covering not only finished goods, but also components and subassemblies, and affecting not just manufacturing industries, but also energy, food production and all kinds of services, from call centers and accounting to medical procedures and research and development (R&D) activities of the world's leading transnational corporations (Engardio *et al.*, 2003; Engardio and Einhorn, 2005; Wadhwa *et al.*, 2008). Since the early 2000s, the global value chain (GVC) and global production network (GPN) concepts gained popularity as ways to analyze the international expansion and geographical fragmentation of contemporary supply chains (Gereffi *et al.*, 2001; Dicken *et al.*, 2001; Henderson *et al.*, 2002; Gereffi, 2005).

There are numerous reviews of the distinctive features of the global commodity chain (GCC) and the GVC and GPN approaches to analyzing global supply chains.[1] In general, they all characterize the global economy as consisting of complex and dynamic economic networks made up of inter-firm and intra-firm relationships. However, it is equally true that there are national and international political underpinnings to the shifts in global supply chains that have taken place over the past four decades. In the 1960s and 1970s, the key players in most international industries were large, vertically integrated transnational corporations (Vernon, 1971) and their link to the growing markets of developing countries was primarily via the import-substituting industrialization (ISI) model of growth that had been well established in Latin America, Eastern Europe and parts of Asia since the 1950s. The 'East Asian miracle' (World Bank, 1993), based on the rapid economic advance of Japan and the so-called East Asian tigers (South Korea, Taiwan, Hong Kong and Singapore) since the 1960s, highlighted a contrasting development model: export-oriented industrialization (EOI) (Gereffi and Wyman, 1990). Buttressed by the neoliberal thrust of the Reagan and Thatcher governments in the US and the UK, respectively, export-oriented development became the prevailing orthodoxy for developing economies around the world. This model came to be known as the 'Washington consensus,' and EOI was lauded for giving many small economies in the developing world the opportunity to benefit from scale economies and to learn from exporting to much larger trade partners, thereby overcoming the bias of the ISI model toward the limited number of developing countries with large domestic markets.

The death knell for ISI, especially in Latin America, came from the oil shock of the late 1970s and the severe debt crisis that followed it (Urquidi, 1991). The ISI approach had devised no way to generate the foreign exchange needed to pay for increasingly costly imports, and escalating debt service payments led to a net outflow of foreign capital that crippled economic growth. When many developing countries, under pressure from the International Monetary Fund (IMF) and the World Bank, made the transition from ISI to EOI during the 1980s (Gereffi and Wyman, 1990), there was an equally profound reorientation in the strategies of transnational corporations. The rapid expansion of industrial capabilities and export propensities in a diverse array of newly industrializing economies in Asia and Latin America allowed transnational corporations to accelerate their own efforts to outsource relatively standardized activities to lower-cost production locations worldwide. It is precisely this change in the strategies of transnational companies that enabled the shift from ISI to EOI in developing economies, and it corresponds to the shift from producer-driven to buyer-driven commodity chains at the level of global industries (Gereffi and Korzeniewicz, 1994).[2]

However, the development story for East Asia and other newly industrializing economies cannot be captured solely through a contrast of the ISI and EOI models, since the shift from ISI to EOI was not total or uncontested in either East Asia or Latin America. Indeed, elements of both strategies were intertwined since countries tended to move from relatively easy to more difficult phases of both ISI and EOI over time (Gereffi and Wyman, 1990). In addition, the growth of GPNs has been linked to rising levels of income inequality, within and between countries, which can be explained in large measure by the dynamics of rents in GVCs, which are increasingly determined by intangible assets (such as copyrights, brand names and design) as more tangible barriers to entry in manufacturing have tended to fall (Kaplinsky, 2000). In the wake of the 2008–09 global economic crisis, the rapid growth of productive capabilities in China, India and other large emerging economies has created a profound shift in global demand for both finished goods and intermediates from North to South, with both positive and negative implications for developing country exporters (Kaplinsky and Farooki, 2011).

Today, the organization of the global economy is entering a new phase, or what some have referred to as a 'major inflection point' (Fung, 2011), which could have dramatic implications for economic and social upgrading and downgrading among countries, firms and workers. The role of the 'Washington consensus' as a paradigm for developing countries has been severely weakened (Gore, 2000) and no alternative development strategy has taken its place. Thus, our analysis of GVCs in this post-Washington Consensus world must not only take account of changes in the organization of production and trade on a global scale, but also examine the role of emerging economies as new sources of demand and production competencies in the global economy. The increasing importance of GVCs in the current era challenges the traditional way of measuring countries' export performance and international competitiveness, and it suggests that the post-crisis futures of advanced industrial and developing economies are interdependent to a hitherto unprecedented degree.

The remaining sections of this paper are organized as follows. First, recent trends in GVC governance reveal a growing consolidation in the supply base among both countries and firms, and we argue that geographic consolidation is facilitating the co-evolution of more concentrated lead firms, suppliers and intermediaries in GVCs. Second, the evolution of GVCs has altered our basic notions of how and where economic development occurs, which is illustrated by the growing importance of value-added trade and shifting end markets for GVCs, which are giving rise to new patterns of regionalization in the global economy. Third, the GVC framework has become increasingly prominent in the development agendas of a diverse array of bilateral and multilateral donor organizations, which is leading to a greater focus on showing how vertically coordinated trade and investment patterns in the global economy can be linked to employment outcomes and a renewed concern with social upgrading. Conclusions will be drawn about how these interrelated changes are likely to shape economic and social welfare in emerging models of global development.

II. GOVERNANCE STRUCTURES AND INCREASING CONCENTRATION IN GLOBAL VALUE CHAINS

The GVC framework focuses on globally expanding supply chains and how value is created and captured therein. By analyzing the full range of activities that firms and workers perform to bring a specific product from its conception to its end use and beyond, the GVC approach provides a holistic view of global industries from two contrasting vantage points: top down and bottom up. The key concept for the top-down view is the 'governance' of GVCs, which focuses mainly on lead firms and the organization of global industries; the main concept for the bottom-up perspective is 'upgrading,' which focuses on the strategies used by countries, regions and other economic stakeholders to maintain or improve their positions in the global economy (Gereffi and Fernandez-Stark, 2011). Recent trends related to GVC governance will be discussed in this section of the paper, and the links between economic and social upgrading and new forms of value-added trade and shifting end markets in GVCs will be the focus of the next section.

Governance is a centerpiece of GVC analysis. It shows how corporate power can actively shape the distribution of profits and risks in an industry, and it identifies the actors who exercise such power. Within the chain, power at the firm level can be exerted by lead firms or suppliers. In 'producer-driven' chains, power is held by final-product manufacturers and is characteristic of capital-, technology- or skill-intensive industries. In 'buyer-driven' chains, retailers and marketers of final products exert the most power through their ability to shape mass consumption via dominant market shares and strong brand names.[3] They source their products from a global network of suppliers in cost-effective locations to make their goods. The most notable form of 'supplier power' comes via platform leadership (e.g., firms that exhibit marketing or technological dominance, which allows them to set standards and get higher returns for their products), although supplier power typically is not associated with the explicit coordination of buyers or other downstream value chain actors (Frederick and Gereffi, 2009; Sturgeon, 2009).

The role played by lead firms is highlighted in various typologies of GVC governance. The initial distinction between producer-driven and buyer-driven commodity chains was introduced in the mid-1990s in order to mark the rise of global buyers in the 1970s and 1980s as retailers and brand marketers began to set up international sourcing networks to procure consumer goods directly from offshore suppliers, mainly in East Asia (Gereffi, 1994, 1999). These 'full-package' production networks based on local suppliers supplanted many of the assembly-oriented production networks initially set up by multinational manufacturers based in the developed economies (Bair and Gereffi, 2001). However, as the case studies of GVCs proliferated, and more industries and countries were incorporated into the analysis, it was clear that the dichotomous categories of buyer-driven and producer-driven commodity chains were too broad to capture the full complexity of the GVC governance structures that were emerging in the world.

In addressing this challenge, a new typology of GVC governance structures was elaborated, which sought both to describe and explain in a parsimonious way the significant differences between various types of value chains. Between the two extremes of classic markets and hierarchies (i.e., vertical integration), three network forms of governance were identified: modular, relational and captive (Gereffi *et al.*, 2005). In these network forms of GVC governance, the lead firm exercises varying

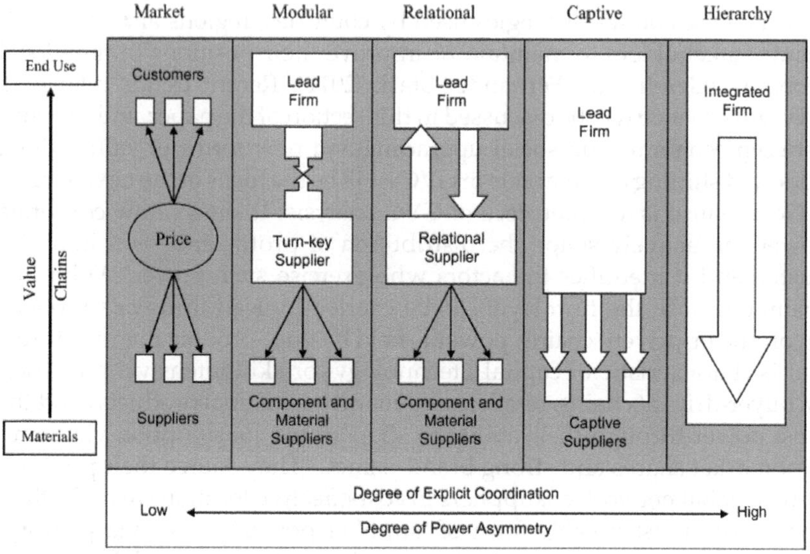

Figure 1 Five types of global value chain governance.
Source: Gereffi, Humphrey and Sturgeon (2005: 89).

degrees of power through the coordination of suppliers without any direct ownership of the firms (Figure 1).

The five-fold typology of GVC governance published by Gereffi, Humphrey and Sturgeon (2005) has been very widely utilized and extensively cited, and it has become a mainstay of our conceptual toolkit on GVC governance. One of the reasons for the popularity of this approach is that it allows us to show quite easily how the form of governance can change as an industry evolves and matures, and indeed how governance patterns within an industry can vary from one stage or level of the chain to another. For example, in the offshore services value chain, all five types of GVC governance structures identified in the typology coexist, but their role in upgrading varies according to the characteristics of suppliers in developing countries, the requirements of lead firms and the kinds of international professional standards utilized in these chains (Fernandez-Stark *et al.*, 2011). The impact of multiple and shifting forms of GVC governance on the ability of local producers to upgrade within global chains has been particularly notable in the agrifood sector (Dolan and Humphrey, 2004; Gereffi *et al.*, 2009; Lee *et al.*, 2012), although the phenomenon exists in other industries as well (Gereffi and Fernandez-Stark, 2011; Gereffi *et al.*, 2011).

Today, we are entering a very different era. By the mid-2000s, the Washington Consensus development model was already beginning to unravel. US hegemony was eroding and the large emerging economies, led by China and India, were altering the organization of production and how rules were made that affected the global economy. Consolidation was growing at both the country and supply chain levels in a number of hallmark global industries, such as apparel (Frederick and Gereffi, 2011; Staritz and Frederick, 2012), automobiles (Sturgeon *et al.*, 2008; Sturgeon and Van Biesebroeck, 2011) and electronics (Sturgeon and Kawakami, 2011; Brandt and Thun, 2011). When the global economic recession hit in 2008–09, this ended all prospects of a return to the old order. As the consumption of advanced industrial economies was curtailed, developing countries around the world began to look for alternatives to declining or stagnant northern markets. Large emerging economies turned inward and redirected production to their domestic markets and regional neighbors, and industrial policy has become more prominent.

In this context, the governance structures of GVCs are changing as well. The problem is no longer one of coordinating far-flung, fragmented and highly specialized global supply chains through triangular production networks orchestrated by East Asian intermediaries (Gereffi, 1999). The question increasingly posed by the transnational lead firms of GVCs is, 'How can we "rationalize" our supply chains from 300–500 suppliers to 25–30 suppliers?' The new suppliers are expected to be bigger, more capable and strategically located to access large markets. In this new environment, the extreme asymmetries of power in favor of lead firms that characterized the buyer-driven and producer-driven chains are shifting in many cases toward the top manufacturers located in emerging economies such as China, India, Brazil and Turkey. These countries have well-organized domestic supply bases and they have moved up the value chain to incorporate key input suppliers, as well as pre-production (design, R&D and purchasing) and post-production (logistics, marketing and branding) services.

Even in this post-Washington Consensus world, the established GVC governance structures from prior decades still exist, and they will continue to play an important role in shaping development agendas. However, new governance structures are being created that reflect the realities of GVCs today. This can be seen in the links between the organizational consolidation occurring within GVCs and the geographic concentration associated with the growing prominence of emerging economies as key economic and political actors.

After 1989, the breakup of the Soviet Union, the opening of China to international investment and trade, and the liberalization of India brought a number of very large economies onto the global stage, known initially as BRICs (Brazil, Russia, India and China).[4] This influenced the globalization process, as GVCs began to concentrate in these giant countries that offered seemingly inexhaustible pools of low-wage workers, capable manufacturers, abundant raw materials and sizeable domestic markets. Thus, China became the 'factory of the world,' India the world's 'back office,' Brazil had a wealth of agricultural commodities, and Russia possessed enormous reserves of natural resources plus the military technologies linked to its role as a Cold War superpower. These emerging economies became major production centers worldwide, although their specific role in GVCs varied according to their openness to trade and foreign investment and other strategic considerations.

Since 2000, the shift in production from North to South in the global economy has accelerated and an expanding number of high-growth economies are playing prominent roles in a wide variety of industries as exporters and also new markets (Staritz *et al.*, 2011). This reflects multiple factors, including the growing significance of emerging economies, the decline in export orders due to the global economic crisis of 2008–09, and the explicit efforts of GVC lead firms to rationalize their supply chains in order to deal with smaller numbers of highly capable and strategically located suppliers.

One noteworthy consequence of global consolidation is the growth of big GVC producers and intermediaries, which tend to offset to some degree the power of global buyers. China became the world's dominant supplier of apparel, footwear and consumer electronics products, especially after the termination of the Multi-Fibre Arrangement (MFA) for apparel in 2005, and giant contract manufacturers and traders (such as Foxconn in electronics, Yue Yuen in footwear and Li & Fung in apparel) have considerable clout. India and Brazil have also generated their own manufacturing multinationals, such as Tata and Embraer.

Lead firms themselves are getting bigger through mergers, acquisitions and the decline of many rivals and, thereby, they are also increasing their global market shares.[5] At the same time, there is growing awareness of the strategic vulnerabilities of global supply chains in terms of the access of lead firms to critical raw material supplies (Lynn, 2005). This is particularly apparent in the agrifoods sector, where consumer goods firms such as Cadbury, Coca-Cola, Unilever and others are expanding their direct involvement in the procurement and sustainability of the raw material sides of their value chains, such as cocoa, coffee and sugar. This is also evident in autos and electronics, where concern over the availability of raw materials, such as lithium and coltan (Nathan and Sarkar, 2011), respectively, are introducing greater engagement between GVC lead firms and host country suppliers and governments. Thus, the long-term trend toward specialization and fragmentation in GVCs is being supplanted by a greater emphasis on strategic collaboration.

In summary, concentration is growing across different segments of GVCs, and this co-evolution of concentrated actors appears to have two main implications for GVC governance: in at least some cases, a shift of bargaining power toward large domestic producers vis-à-vis global buyers; and an affinity between geographic concentration in large emerging economies such as China and India and organizational consolidation in GVCs. Novel patterns of industrial organization in emerging economies seem to fit this pattern, including China's supply chain cities, which integrate all aspects of GVCs from input suppliers to final goods manufacturers, and design centers to showrooms, for global buyers within specialized production locations (Gereffi, 2009); India's pioneering workforce development strategies to train local engineers and information technology specialists for global R&D hubs (Wadhwa *et al.*, 2008); and Brazil's 'industrial condominium' and 'modular consortium' concepts for automobile production that recruit GVC lead firms and their top suppliers to set up coordinated manufacturing facilities in the same factory complex, such as Volkswagen's truck and bus chassis plant in Resende (Neto and Pires, 2010).

III. ECONOMIC UPGRADING AND THE NEW GEOGRAPHY OF GLOBAL PRODUCTION AND TRADE

While governance issues have attracted a good deal of attention among GVC scholars, the research on economic upgrading has been at least as important because many of the people who use the GVC framework have a very strong development focus. The GVC paradigm links scholarly research on globalization with the concerns of international organizations, policy makers and social activists who are trying to harness the potential gains of globalization to the pragmatic goals of economic growth, including more and better jobs and improved competitiveness for numerous regions, countries and social groups that feel increasingly vulnerable in the global economy. In both developed and developing countries, there is growing concern that the economic gains of participating in global supply chains do not necessarily translate into good jobs or stable employment and, in the worst case, economic upgrading may be linked to a significant deterioration of labor conditions and other forms of social downgrading. A key research question is: Under what conditions can participation in GVCs contribute to both economic and social upgrading in developing countries? (Barrientos *et al.*, 2011a, 2011b; Lee *et al.*, 2011).

The emergence of GVCs has redefined how we conceptualize economic development. For most early industrializers, including the US, Germany and Japan, industrialization meant building relatively complete supply chains at home. The core idea was that no nation could become globally competitive without a broad and deep industrial base, and thus considerable effort was dedicated to bring together the capital, technology and labor needed to create new industries. The ISI model of development, as previously noted, attempted to replicate the feat of these initial industrializers by enlisting transnational corporations in producer-driven GVCs to build modern industries in relatively big developing countries, step by step, working from final products back to key components and subassemblies (such as engines in cars) under the watchful eye of interventionist developmental states.

The current era of export-oriented industrialization, which is sometimes called 'globalization's 2nd unbundling' (Baldwin, 2011), has opened up a radically new development path. Today, nations seek to industrialize by simply joining a supply chain to assemble final goods or make specialized inputs; they no longer try to build single-nation supply chains from scratch. For Baldwin, globalization's first unbundling was that railroads and steamships made it feasible to spatially separate production and consumption, and once the separation was feasible, scale economies and comparative advantage made it inevitable. The second unbundling was linked to the information and communication technology revolution, which allowed production stages that were previously performed in close proximity to be geographically dispersed in order to reduce production costs. The spatial scale of the second unbundling is not fixed, however; it could be regional or global, and thus the geographical configuration of GVCs can and does change over time.

In short, while industrialization under the EOI model became easier and faster (countries could just 'join' supply chains by performing specialized tasks, rather than 'build' them), it may also be less meaningful. If countries are only engaged in the simplest forms of EOI, such as assembling imported parts for overseas markets in export-processing zones, then they would develop neither the institutions, nor the know-how, nor the consumer markets needed to create and sustain entire industries. Indeed, for many of the small and least developed countries in the global economy, the gains associated with traditional forms of industrialization in terms of high-income jobs, forward and backward linkages, and wealth creation and innovation have been limited and uneven at best under the EOI model. Furthermore, there is growing concern that the extensive global outsourcing associated with globalization's second unbundling may have alarming implications for innovation and the international competitiveness of even the advanced industrial economies.[6]

The challenge of economic upgrading in GVCs, therefore, is precisely to identify the conditions under which developing as well as developed countries and firms can 'climb the value chain' from basic assembly activities using low-cost and unskilled labor to more advanced forms of 'full package' supply and integrated manufacturing. 'Economic upgrading' is defined as the process by which economic actors – firms and workers – move from low-value to relatively high-value activities in GVCs (Gereffi, 2005: 171). Within the GVC framework, four types of upgrading have been identified (Humphrey and Schmitz, 2002):

1. Product upgrading, or moving into more sophisticated product lines;
2. Process upgrading, which transforms inputs into outputs more efficiently by reorganizing the production system or introducing superior technology;
3. Functional upgrading, which entails acquiring new functions (or abandoning existing functions) to increase the overall skill content of the activities; and
4. Chain upgrading, in which firms move into new but often related industries.

The ability or inability of countries and firms to upgrade in these various ways has been the focal point of numerous GVC studies, but novel aspects related to the upgrading process have been introduced in the post-Washington Consensus era. First, there has been growing interest by the World Trade Organization (WTO), the Organisation for Economic Co-operation and Development (OECD) and other international organizations to establish new metrics of value-added trade that will clarify the extent to which successful export-oriented economies use domestic or imported inputs to fuel their growth. Second, in the wake of the 2008–09 global economic crisis, economic diversification through shifting end markets appears to be reconfiguring the growth opportunities for GVCs in ways that may shift their orientation toward the domestic markets of large emerging economies and toward more regionally oriented, rather than global, supply chains. We will consider each topic below.

A new metric for GVC analysis: Value-added trade

In a world characterized by a predominance of GVCs, exports of final products are increasingly composed of imports of intermediate inputs. As supply chains go global, therefore, more intermediate goods are traded across borders, and more parts and components are imported for use in exports (Feenstra, 1998). In 2009, world exports of intermediate goods exceeded the combined export values of final and capital goods, representing 51 per cent of non-fuel merchandise exports (WTO and IDE-JETRO, 2011: 81). Governments and international organizations are taking notice of this emerging pattern of global trade, which is called a shift from 'trade in goods' to 'trade in value added,' 'trade in tasks' and 'trade in capabilities'[7] (OECD, 2011; WTO and IDE-JETRO, 2011).

Emerging economies have clearly improved their position in GVCs, surging ahead of the advanced industrial countries in terms of export performance. Between 1995 and 2007, the global export market shares of the US and Japan fell by 3.8 and 3.7 percentage points, respectively, while China more than doubled its market share from 4 per cent in 1995 to 10.1

per cent in 2007, making it the world export leader (ahead of Germany, the US and Japan). South Korea, Mexico, Turkey, South Africa and the former transition countries in central Europe also increased their export market shares during this period (Beltramello *et al.*, 2012: 9–10). Potentially more impressive is the fact that emerging economies made their most significant gains in high- and medium-technology industries, which were previously the stronghold of OECD countries.[8] This phenomenon was mainly driven by China, whose share of exports of goods in high-tech industries soared by 13.5 percentage points during the period, 1995–2007, moving it ahead of the US as the world's largest exporter of high-tech products (Beltramello *et al.*, 2012: 10).

While most intermediate goods are still traded within large regional economic blocks, such as the European Union, rather than across them (OECD, 2011), Asia's linkages to the European Union and North America represented the two highest inter-regional import flows of intermediate goods in 2008. Asia imported more intermediate goods than it exported, indicating the region's high level of integration within global supply chains (WTO and IDE-JETRO, 2011: 83–5). The geographical concentration of supply chains is also obvious at the country level. In 2000–08, China accounted for 67 per cent of the world's processing exports,[9] followed by Mexico with 18 per cent (WTO and IDE-JETRO, 2011: 21).

China has benefited greatly from this form of participation in global supply chains. One-third of China's imports are destined for export processing zones, which account for almost half of the country's exports (WTO and IDE-JETRO, 2011: 21). China's 'supply chain cities' are a perfect illustration of how China is turning scale-driven specialization into a persistent competitive advantage for the country. From foreign direct investment-driven clusters in Guangdong to single-product clusters in Zhejiang, China's sheer size has allowed it to set up broad manufacturing clusters at the regional level. These specialized clusters are linked, on the one hand, to East Asian suppliers of key parts and components and, on the other hand, to global buyers to bring Chinese products to the world market (Gereffi, 2009).

Paradoxically, China does not create or capture most of the value generated through its value chain exports. In fact, as more types of intermediate goods are traded within global supply chains, the discrepancy is growing between where final goods are produced and exported and where value is created and captured. For example, Apple's iPhones are entirely assembled in China by a Taiwanese contract manufacturer (Foxconn) and exported to the US. When a traditional measure is used, which assigns the gross export value of the product to the exporting country, the unit export value of iPhones from China is $194.04. Of this, only $24.63 is imported content from the US, meaning that every iPhone imported into the US results in a US balance of payments deficit of $169.41 (Figure 2). However, this does not mean that China benefits from a trade surplus of $169.41 for each

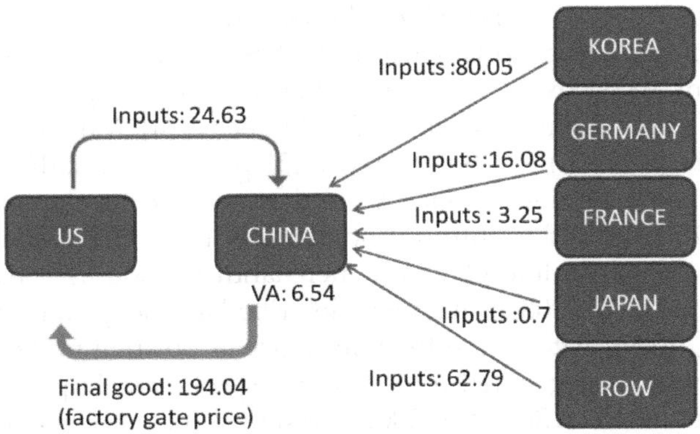

US trade balance with	CHINA	KOREA	GERMANY	FRANCE	JAPAN	ROW	WORLD
Gross	-169.41	0	0	0	0	0	-169.41
Value added	-6.54	-80.05	-16.08	-3.25	-0.7	-62.79	-169.41

Figure 2 US bilateral trade balance with China for one unit of iPhone4 (US$). *Source:* OECD (2011: 40).

iPhone it exports, since the value added in China is only $6.54 per phone. The balance of China's iPhone production costs is made up of imports from Korea ($80.05), Germany ($16.08) and diverse other countries.[10]

These advances in GVC metrics related to value creation and value capture are a propitious development for policy-oriented research (OECD, 2011; WTO and IDE-JETRO, 2011; UNCTAD, 2013). As showcased by the iPhone study, existing trade statistics are unable to grasp the changing patterns of global production and trade. This is an area where GVC analysis and supply chain management research can be mutually beneficial.[11] Sophisticated value chain data disaggregated by business functions can complement existing country-level trade statistics and industry-level input-output data, providing a clear picture of who is gaining and losing in GVCs (Sturgeon and Gereffi, 2009). When combined with data on employment, they will greatly advance our understanding of both economic and social development opportunities in the global economy.

Shifting end markets and the regionalization of GVCs

As world trade bounces back from the 2008–09 economic crises, emerging economies are becoming a main engine of world economic recovery. Tepid growth in the global North since the mid-1980s was slowed even further by the latest crisis, whereas demand is quickly growing in the global South, particularly in large emerging economies such as China, India and

Brazil (Staritz *et al.*, 2011). Over the period, 2005–10, the merchandise imports of the European Union and the US increased by 27 per cent and 14 per cent, respectively, while emerging economies expanded their merchandise imports much faster: Brazil (147 per cent), India (129 per cent), China (111 per cent) and South Africa (51 per cent). In 2010, 52 per cent of Asia's manufactured exports were destined for developing countries (WTO, 2011), indicating shifting end markets in the global economy.

The dramatic decline of world merchandise trade as a result of the economic crisis of 2008–09 has been described as 'the great trade collapse' (Baldwin, 2009). After more than six years of positive trade growth, all OECD countries registered a decline in exports and imports exceeding 10 per cent between 2008 and 2009, reaching a record negative growth of -37 per cent in April 2009 (Beltramello *et al.*, 2012: 27). The trade collapse was much larger in intermediates than in final consumption goods, which underscores the existence of a 'bullwhip' effect in GVCs – namely, lower demand for final consumption goods (downstream) is amplified in more dramatic demand reductions for intermediates that are upstream in the value chain (Altomonte *et al.*, 2012).

The 'great trade collapse' accelerated the shift in end markets from the North to the South in GVCs (Kaplinsky and Farooki, 2011) and it also encouraged lead firms from developing countries to regionalize their supply chains. In sub-Saharan Africa, for instance, the recent entry of South African clothing manufacturers in neighboring countries such as Lesotho and Swaziland has led to the rise of regional value chains driven by South African retailers. Compared to the US buyer-driven chain, these regional chains focus on shorter production runs and quick response with higher fashion content, and are based on direct relationships to large South African clothing retailers (Morris *et al.*, 2011). Similarly, South African supermarkets are expanding via regional supply chains and spearheading the rise of supermarkets across sub-Saharan Africa (Weatherspoon and Reardon, 2003).

The GVC literature shows that value chains oriented to different end markets often entail distinct upgrading opportunities (Palpacuer *et al.*, 2005; Gibbon, 2008). For example, the demand in lower-income countries for less sophisticated products with regard to quality and variety can have major upgrading implications (Kaplinsky *et al.*, 2011). On the one hand, lower entry barriers and less stringent product and process standards in emerging markets can facilitate the participation of developing country firms in global supply chains. They can engage in higher value-added activities, such as product development and design, which they would have little chance to do in the global chains. With more intimate knowledge of local and regional markets vis-à-vis multinational firms, they can generate 'frugal' innovations that are suitable to resource-poor environments (Clark *et al.*, 2009). On the other hand, solely focusing on low-income markets could lock suppliers into slimmer margins and cutthroat competition. Their knowledge advantage in local markets often evaporates quickly when multinational firms catch up in learning the markets, as found in the Chinese mobile phone industry (Brandt and Thun, 2011).

IV. THE IMPACT OF GVC ANALYSIS ON THE DEVELOPMENT AGENDAS OF INTERNATIONAL DONORS

GVC studies are pervasive in academic publications that examine a wide range of global industries,[12] and the framework has been adopted by many of the major international donors and peak organizations concerned with economic development, including the World Bank (Webber and Labaste, 2009; Cattaneo *et al.*, 2010), the WTO (WTO and IDE-JETRO, 2011), the OECD (OECD, 2011; Beltramello *et al.*, 2012), the International Labour Organization (ILO) (Gereffi, 2006), the US Agency for International Development (USAID, 2012), the US International Trade Commission (USITC, 2011), the World Economic Forum (2012), and the UN Conference on Trade and Development (UNCTAD, 2013).

The international institutions that have provided the underpinning for the Washington Consensus, such as the World Bank, the IMF and the WTO, along with major bilateral donors, such as USAID and the UK's Department for International Development (DFID),[13] have embraced new heterodox models of development thinking, with an emphasis on sectoral analysis that allows macro issues such as international trade and investment to be linked more closely with the micro development issues of employment, gender dynamics and sustainable livelihoods (M4P, 2008). In addition, new alliances have emerged among diverse UN and other international agencies (such as the World Bank and the ILO) to promote joint research agendas that explore the links between economic and social upgrading, explicitly using the GVC framework (Cattaneo *et al.*, 2010; Barrientos *et al.*, 2011a).

Unlike most social science theories and paradigms, which have only a limited impact on specific international organizations and development policy settings, the GVC framework is unusual in that it has diffused very rapidly during the past decade and been adopted by a wide range of economic, social and cultural organizations, as well as action-oriented non-governmental organizations (NGOs) in the labor and environmental arenas. Table 1 identifies some of these international donor organizations and recent projects or studies that are informed by the GVC approach.

While this topic merits a far more detailed discussion, two aspects of the use of GVC analysis in these organizations will be touched on below. First, what are the similarities and differences in how GVC analysis is used in these organizations? For example, most of these international donors have development programs that emphasize pro-poor growth, the protection of

Table 1 Use of Global Value Chain Analysis in Selected International Organizations

Organization	Illustrative GVC Publications	Content Description	2012						
			GVC	LED	Clusters	PSD	TVET	Poverty	Micro
World Bank	Cattaneo et al. (2010).	This book uses a GVC perspective to analyze the impact of the global financial crisis of 2008-09 on global trade, production and demand in several sectors. Particular attention is paid to opportunities for developing countries to enter into GVCs post-crisis.	x		x	x		x	x
IDB	Flores and Vaillant (2011).	This paper compares the upgrading performance of Latin American countries in terms of export sophistication in a variety of industries.	x	x	x	x		x	x
DFID	Capturing the Gains (2012).	This three-year research project brings together an international network of experts to gain information on the employment and wellbeing of workers and small producers in GVCs.	x		x	x		x	
USAID	Value Chain Development Wiki (2012).	This website gathers information from various projects and draws on research conducted under USAID's Microenterprise Development Team to codify good practice in value chain development, with an eye to linking SMEs into global, national and local value chains.	x		x	x	x		x
GTZ/GIZ	Will (2011).	This manual considers information from GTZ-funded pilot projects in developing countries in order to draw lessons about the various processes by which smallholders can receive GLOBALGAP certification, which is required by many European food retailers.	x	x		x	x	x	

WTO	WTO (2011).	This publication uses a GVC framework to consider changing trade patterns in East Asia. It proposes a new trade statistic - trade in value added - to complement traditional trade statistics.	x						
OECD	OECD (2011).	This report to the OECD Working Party on Globalization of Industry and the Committee on Innovation, Industry and Entrepreneurship uses the GVC framework to provide policy advice to OECD countries with a focus on maintaining competitiveness and identifying new sources of growth.	x		x	x			
ILO	Herr and Muzira (2009).	This guide for development practitioners, governments and private actors outlines strategies for upgrading within value chains while maintaining or improving labor standards for workers.	x	x			x	x	

Notes:
GVC: The Global Value Chain framework focuses on the placement of firms and localities within the global organization of trade and production within particular sectors or industries.
LED: The Local Economic Development framework focuses on initiatives geared towards the local or sub-national public sector as an enabler or instigator of economic development.
Clusters: The Cluster framework focuses on initiatives geared towards the local or sub-national private sector.
PSD: Private Sector Development strategies focus on the concept of "making markets work."
TVET: Technical and Vocational Education and Training strategies focus on improving the quality and quantity of workers' marketable skills through vocational training initiatives.
Poverty: Poverty Alleviation programs are those that seek the reduction, alleviation or eradication of poverty.
Micro: Microfinance programs make very small "microloans" to entrepreneurs or households that are otherwise unable to access financial markets under favorable terms.

small and medium enterprises and local stakeholders, and a private sector-oriented, market-led model. However, they differ in other respects, such as the weight given to economic growth in relation to poverty reduction as well as geographic regions and sectors of particular interest. Second, what are the other development models or frameworks that are being used in each organization and to what degree are these complementary or antagonistic with the GVC approach? One of the key reasons for the turn to GVC and GPN approaches may be that their emphasis on global industries offers a meso-level, sectoral and actor-oriented approach to the global economy, which provides multi-scalar options to link global and local levels of analysis, in contrast to macro models, which focus on general economic trends and broad policy prescriptions, or the micro and localized approach of clusters, which aren't connected to the broader structures at the national, regional or global levels.

Value chain analysis is used widely today as an instrument of private sector development by virtually all major bilateral and multilateral donor agencies. Altenburg (2007) highlights two main reasons for the increasing popularity of the GVC approach within the international donor community since the end of the 1990s: first, the accumulating evidence of a link between economic growth driven by the private sector and poverty reduction; and second, the fact that global integration of trade and production through GVCs transmits the pressures of global competition to domestic markets in developing economies, leaving less space for local firms to design, produce and market on their own. As Altenburg (2007: 04) puts it, 'The question is thus not *if*, but *how* to integrate in value chains in a way that allows for incorporation of a growing number of the workforce and increasing levels of productivity and outcomes. This calls for a balanced approach which takes both competitiveness and equity issues into account.'

There is no simple way to connect GVC analysis to private sector development, since the firms in a value chain range from transnational corporations to microenterprises, and the institutional context and geographic scope of value chains vary enormously. In order to provide some guidance for interventions by donors, Humphrey and Navas-Alemán (2010) distinguish four different objectives of donor interventions: strengthening the weakest link to address potential bottlenecks; improving flows of knowledge and resources to make all firms in the chain more productive; working on specific links between firms to improve efficiency; and creating new or alternate links in the chain to promote diversified outcomes.

An alternative to this bottom-up approach to value chain development is targeting lead firms rather than local suppliers – i.e., working with the strongest link in the chain, rather than the weakest. This lead-firm-centered, top-down GVC approach has been used effectively for very different purposes, whether it be the World Bank's revitalized 'Aid for Trade' initiative, which sees the private sector as the engine that powers global trade and urges GVC lead firms to play a greater role in building trade capacity in developing countries (World Bank, 2011), or the confrontational stance of NGOs such as Oxfam (2004), which mobilizes international campaigns against lead firms to improve the conditions of women workers in global supply chains.

The reality is that most bilateral and multilateral donors use GVC analysis in combination with other diagnostic tools they have tried in the past (Table 1) to address a variety of broad development goals, including poverty reduction, economic growth, employment creation and income generation, enterprise development, and environmental stability and cleaner production (UNIDO, 2011). One of the most comprehensive reviews of the approaches of seven UN agencies to value chain development concludes, however, that there is considerable 'fuzziness' about how the concept is adopted: '... [value chain]-related activities sometimes seem to be rather the outcome of "re-labelling" former private sector development interventions. In other cases, activities that could clearly be subsumed under the value chain approach are not labeled accordingly .... These observed shortcomings in knowledge management, transparency and the lack of defined unique selling positions make inter-agency cooperation in [value chain] promotion difficult' (Stamm and von Drachenfels, 2011: 30). In short, much of the literature that uses the GVC moniker misses the point and doesn't apply the framework consistently.

The widespread adoption of the GVC framework by international donors during the past decade represents a remarkable convergence around a single paradigm, notwithstanding the differing emphases across UN and bilateral agencies. Skeptics might argue that the neoliberal fundamentals of the Washington Consensus model of development remain entrenched in many of these organizations (Neilsen, 2013), even if GVC analysis is rooted in assumptions that are highly critical of the neoliberal paradigm (see Gereffi and Korzeniewicz, 1994; Kaplinsky, 2005; Bair, 2009; Hamilton and Gereffi, 2009; Sturgeon, 2009; Lee, 2010). The counterargument made throughout this article is that the GVC perspective highlights the power dynamics in global industries, embodied in the role of lead firms and the institutions that underpin the global economic order, and this introduces broader and more heterodox views of development that challenge the mainstream.

During the past decade, the global economy has seen a transfer of production, technological capabilities, growth potential, consumption and political clout from the North to the South. One of the major reasons for the popularity of the GVC framework is that it allows us to analyze many of these shifts with greater precision than prior paradigms. While interpretations of the direction and impact of these trends will vary, the contributions of GVC analysis should not be discounted because the donor organizations have multiple and sometimes discordant agendas. Furthermore, as more international organizations employ the GVC paradigm, its methodological rigor and policy relevance are likely to increase.

V. CONCLUSIONS

What will replace the globalization model? This is the question posed in a recent newspaper article, which contends: 'The globalization model of the past 30 years is cracking up. And there appears to be no new model to replace it' (Smick, 2012). While we concur that globalization as we know it is undergoing a series of fundamental shifts, many elements of the future system are there for us to see. The international competitiveness of advanced industrial economies has gradually been eroded, at least in terms of traditional measures of export performance. Emerging economies now play a more prominent role in international trade, and they have expanded their export market shares of high technology and medium technology products, with China playing a particularly prominent role (Beltramello *et al.*, 2012). The emergence of GVCs cautions against an overreliance on simple export measures of competitiveness, however, and this paper has sought to unpack various insights from the GVC perspective to better understand some of the new features of the post-Washington Consensus global economy.

The Washington Consensus model of development, which held sway from the mid-1980s through the mid-2000s, is a nation-state-centered view of the global economy, in which countries are the primary units of analysis in international production and trade. The main topics of debate involved the extent to which economic policies were 'market-friendly' or overly interventionist (World Bank, 1993), and the nature of the stabilization programs and market access agreements that would be imposed on recalcitrant developing economies by the IMF, the World Bank and other international financial and trade institutions to bring them in line with the dominant model.

The GVC framework fundamentally challenges this view of the global economy and it provides a different interpretation of the key drivers of change over the past four decades. The sector-based approach of the GVC perspective is premised on the structural diversity of global industries, which are major entry points for developing nations in the global economy. The major analytical categories used to examine global value chains include:

1. The role of *lead firms* in setting performance requirements and standards that condition entry and mobility within GVCs;
2. The evolving nature of *production and trade networks* that link large and small suppliers to the global economy as well as to domestic economies;
3. Trajectories of social and economic *upgrading and downgrading*, and patterns of *access and exclusion*, which help describe the connections

between the development of firms and countries within the international system;

4. Multiple *governance structures* (international and domestic, public and private, chain-based and civic) that link different components of the system together;
5. The shift from trade in goods to *trade in value added, tasks and business functions* in looking at key economic activities related to upgrading and competitiveness; and
6. *Interventions and pressure points* that allow for change in this system.

Economic globalization is a byproduct of international production and trade networks organized by transnational firms and it is embedded in various kinds of regulation, including rules of the game established by international institutions, national government policies, and varied forms of private governance used by non-state actors to manage activities in GVCs (Mayer and Gereffi, 2010). One potential outcome of the current situation is that public governance will be called upon to play a stronger role in supplementing and reinforcing corporate codes of conduct, product certifications, process standards and other voluntary, non-governmental types of private governance that have proliferated in the last two decades, and that multi-stakeholder initiatives involving both public and private actors will arise to deal with collective action problems.

While the contours of a new international economic order are still in flux, several features are already having an impact on development agendas. The most dynamic growth poles in the global economy are constituted by an expanding number of rising powers that combine relatively large domestic markets, skilled workforces, capable producers and a push toward indigenous innovation. These include the original BRIC countries as well as South Korea, Mexico, Turkey and Indonesia, among others (O'Neill, 2011). As the EOI development strategy is replaced by more inward-looking approaches focusing on domestic and regional markets, industrial policy in the leading economies of the South is likely to become more significant. While policy priorities at the macro level of the global economy seek new ways to channel trade and investment patterns toward more robust employment outcomes (OECD, 2012), the challenge will be to link economic upgrading and social upgrading in terms of both material conditions of work and the quantity and quality of jobs created in contemporary GVCs (Barrientos *et al.*, 2011a, 2011b).

ACKNOWLEDGEMENTS

The author would like to thank Andrew Guinn, Rebecca Schultz and Jackie Xu for their research assistance on this paper.

NOTES

1 For recent reviews of GCC and GVC literature, see Bair (2009), Lee (2010), and Gereffi and Lee (2012).

2 In the original 1994 article that introduced the concepts of producer-driven and buyer-driven GCCs, there is a section on 'The Role of State Policies in Global Commodity Chains,' which makes the link between GCCs and development strategies very clear: 'An important affinity exists between the ISI and EOI strategies of national development and the structure of commodity chains. Import substitution occurs in the same kinds of capital- and technology-intensive industries represented by producer-driven commodity chains ... In addition, the main economic agents in both cases are [transnational corporations] and state-owned enterprises. Export-oriented industrialization, on the other hand, is channeled through buyer-driven commodity chains where production in labor-intensive industries is concentrated in small to medium-sized private domestic firms located mainly in the Third World. Historically, the export-oriented development strategy of the East Asian [newly industrializing countries] and buyer-driven commodity chains emerged together in the early 1970s, suggesting a close connection between the success of EOI and the development of new forms of organizational integration in buyer-driven industrial networks' (Gereffi, 1994: 100).

3 Knowing if the lead firm in a chain is a buyer or a producer can help to determine the most likely upgrading opportunities for suppliers. For example, buyer-driven chains tend to provide more opportunities to their suppliers in product and functional upgrading because the core competence of the buyers is in marketing and branding, not production, whereas lead firms in producer-driven chains often require varied forms of process upgrading and international certifications among their suppliers due to strict quality and performance standards that affect the entire chain.

4 Jim O'Neill (2011), the Goldman Sachs executive who coined the catchy acronym BRIC in 2001 to refer to Brazil, Russia, India and China, now argues that there is a much larger number of 'growth economies' (BRICs plus 11) that fall into this category. These include the MIST nations (Mexico, Indonesia, South Korea and Turkey), and other periodic high-performers such as Bangladesh, Egypt, Pakistan, the Philippines, and Vietnam (Martin, 2012). The original BRIC classification was extended to BRICS with the addition of South Africa in 2010. For purposes of this paper, the origin of these acronyms is less important than the collective effect of this set of so-called emerging economies, which are reshaping both supply and demand in many GVCs.

5 Li & Fung, the largest trading company in the world, has around 30,000 suppliers globally and operates in 40 countries (Fung, 2011).

6 Pisano and Shih (2009), for example, argue that the US is in danger of losing its 'industrial commons,' which includes not just suppliers of advanced materials, production equipment and components, but also R&D know-how, engineering and processing skills, and a wide range of other manufacturing competencies. Because manufacturing is closely tied to the capacity for innovation, offshore manufacturing can undermine the capabilities of the US economy to remain competitive in existing high-tech industries, which often depend in critical ways on the industrial commons of mature sectors, and also impede its ability to move into new industries. This helps explain why Apple does not manufacture its iPhone in the US. While labor costs are obviously much lower and a certain class of skilled workers more abundant in China, where all US-sold iPhones are assembled, perhaps the biggest limitation is that the vast majority

of suppliers needed to make the hundreds of parts that go into every iPhone are located in East Asia, and not North America. This could hinder the ability of US companies to remain innovative (see Duhigg and Bradsher, 2012; Shih, 2009; Pisano and Shih, 2012).

7 There are conceptual difficulties, however, in using individual tasks or capabilities as a unit of analysis in determining how easy it is to fragment and relocate work in GVCs. It is more likely that larger sets of activities associated with 'business functions' will be outsourced, rather than individual jobs and capabilities (Sturgeon and Gereffi, 2009).

8 Since these figures refer to gross exports, we need more detailed information about the degree of domestic or foreign value added to assess the extent to which these numbers reflect the local assembly of high tech imports or significant national technology content.

9 Processing exports refer to exports that use duty-free imports for subsequent processing and re-exports.

10 This is not an uncommon pattern in China. Domestic content accounts for only about half of China's manufacturing exports and it is even smaller (18 per cent) in its processing exports, mostly done by foreign-owned firms (Koopman *et al.*, 2008).

11 Note that the iPhone study and other similar studies (e.g., Linden *et al.*, 2009; Dedrick *et al.*, 2010) are based on tear-down analysis generated by supply chain management consultancies such as iSuppli.

12 Around 680 publications and 570 authors were listed on the Global Value Chains website (http://www.globalvaluechains.org) as of 20 February 2013.

13 DFID changed the name of its bilateral economic aid program to the UK Agency for International Development (UKaid) in 2012.

NOTES ON CONTRIBUTOR

Gary Gereffi is Professor of Sociology and Director of the Center on Globalization, Governance & Competitiveness at Duke University. He has published numerous books and articles on globalization, global value chains, and economic and social upgrading in various parts of the world, including: *The New Offshoring of Jobs and Global Development* (International Institute of Labour Studies, 2006); *Global Value Chains in a Postcrisis World: A Development Perspective* (co-edited with Olivier Cattaneo and Cornelia Staritz) (The World Bank, 2010); and *Shifting End Markets and Upgrading Prospects in Global Value Chains* (co-edited with Staritz and Cattaneo) (special issue of *Int. J. of Technological Learning, Innovation and Development*, 2011).

REFERENCES

Altenburg, T. (2007) 'Donor Approaches to Supporting Pro-Poor Value Chains', Report prepared for the Donor Committee for Enterprise Development, Working Group on Linkages and Value Chains, <www.deza.admin.ch/ressources/resource_en_162916.pdf> (accessed 20 February 2013).

Altomonte, C., Di Mauro, F., Ottaviano, G., Rungi, A. and Vicard, V. (2012) 'Global Value Chains During the Great Trade Collapse: A Bullwhip Effect?', European Central Bank, Working Paper Series No. 1412, <http://papers.ssrn.com/sol3/papers.cfm?abstract_id=1973497> (accessed 20 February 2013).

Bair, J. (ed.) (2009) *Frontiers of Commodity Chain Research*, Stanford, CA: Stanford University Press.

Bair, J. and Gereffi, G. (2001) 'Local Clusters in Global Chains: The Causes and Consequences of Export Dynamism in Torreon's Blue Jeans Industry', *World Development*, 29(11): 1885–1903.

Baldwin, R. (2009) 'The Great Trade Collapse: What Caused It and What Does It Mean?', in R. Baldwin (ed.) *The Great Trade Collapse: Causes, Consequences and Prospects*, London: Centre for Economic Policy Research, pp. 1–14.

Baldwin, R. (2011) 'Trade and Industrialisation after Globalisation's Second Unbundling: How Building and Joining a Supply Chain are Different and Why It Matters', Working Paper 17716, December, Cambridge, MA: National Bureau of Economic Research, <http://www.nber.org/papers/w17716> (accessed 20 February 2013).

Barrientos, S., Gereffi, G. and Rossi, A. (2011a) 'Economic and Social Upgrading in Global Production Networks: A New Paradigm for a Changing World', *International Labour Review*, 150(3–4): 319–40.

Barrientos, S., Mayer, F., Pickles, J. and Posthuma, A. (2011b) 'Decent Work in Global Production Networks: Framing the Policy Debate', *International Labour Review*, 150(3–4): 299–317.

Beltramello, A., De Backer, K. and Moussiegt, L. (2012) 'The Export Performance of Countries within Global Value Chains (GVCs)', *OECD Science, Technology and Industry Working Papers*, 2012/02, OECD Publishing, <http://dx.di.org/10.1787/5k9bh3gv6647-en> (accessed 20 February 2013).

Brandt, L. and Thun, E. (2011) 'Going Mobile in China: Shifting Value Chains and Upgrading in the Mobile Telecom Sector', *International Journal of Technological Learning, Innovation and Development*, 4(1–3): 148–80.

Capturing the Gains (2012) 'Programme Overview', <http://www.capturingthegains.org/about/index.htm> (accessed 20 February 2013).

Cattaneo, O., Gereffi, G. and Staritz, C. (eds) (2010) *Global Value Chains in a Postcrisis World: A Development Perspective*, Washington, DC: The World Bank.

Clark, N., Chataway, J., Hanlin, R., Kale, D., Kaplinsky, R., Muraguri, L., Papaioannou, T., Robbins, P. and Wamae, W. (2009) 'Below the Radar: What Does Innovation in the Asian Driver Economies Have to Offer Other Low Income Economies?', INNOGEN Working Paper No. 69, Milton Keynes, UK, <http://oro.open.ac.uk/15241/> (accessed 20 February 2013).

Dedrick, J., Kraemer, K.L. and Linden, G. (2010) 'Who Profits from Innovation in Global Value Chains? A Study of the iPod and Notebook PCs', *Industrial and Corporate Change*, 19(1): 81–116.

Dicken, P. (2011) *Global Shift: Mapping the Changing Contours of the World Economy*, 6th edn, New York: Guilford.

Dicken, P., Kelly, P.F., Olds, K. and Yeung, H. (2001) 'Chains and Networks, Territories and Scales: Towards a Relational Framework for Analyzing the Global Economy', *Global Networks*, 1(2): 89–112.

Dolan, C. and Humphrey, J. (2004) 'Changing Governance Patterns in the Trade in Fresh Vegetables between Africa and the United Kingdom', *Environment and Planning A*, 36(3): 491–509.

Duhigg, C. and Bradsher, K. (2012) 'How the U.S. Lost Out on iPhone Work', *The New York Times*, 21 January, < http://www.nytimes.com/2012/01/22/business/apple-america-and-a-squeezed-middle-class.html?_r=1&src=me&ref=general> (accessed 20 February 2013).

Engardio, P., Bernstein, A. and Kripalani, M. (2003) 'Is Your Job Next?', *BusinessWeek*, 3 February, pp. 50–60.

Engardio, P. and Einhorn, B. (2005) 'Outsourcing Innovation', *BusinessWeek*, 21 March, pp. 47–53.

Feenstra, R. C. (1998) 'Integration of Trade and Disintegration of Production in the Global Economy', *Journal of Economic Perspectives*, 12(4): 31–50.

Fernandez-Stark, P. Bamber, P. and Gereffi, G. (2011) 'The Offshore Services Value Chain: Upgrading Trajectories in Developing Countries', *International Journal of Technological Learning, Innovation and Development*, 4(1–3): 206–34.

Flores, M. and Valliant, M. (2011) 'Global Value Chains and Export Sophistication in Latin America', *Integration and Trade*, 32(15): 35–48.

Frederick, S. and Gereffi, G. (2009) 'Value Chain Governance', US-AID Briefing Paper, <http://microlinks.kdid.org/library/value-chain-governance-briefing-paper> (accessed 20 February 2013).

Frederick, S. and Gereffi, G. (2011) 'Upgrading and Restructuring in the Global Apparel Value Chain: Why China and Asia are Outperforming Mexico and Central America', *International Journal of Technological Learning, Innovation and Development*, 4(1–3): 67–95.

Fröbel, F., Heinrichs, J. and Kreye, O. (1981) *The New International Division of Labor*, New York: Cambridge University Press.

Fung, V. (2011) 'Global Supply Chains – Past Developments, Emerging Trends', <http://www.fungglobalinstitute.org/publications/speeches/global-supply-chains–past-developments-emerging-trends-193.html> (accessed 20 February 2013).

Gereffi, G. (1994) 'The Organization of Buyer-Driven Global Commodity Chains: How U.S. Retailers Shape Overseas Production Networks', in Gary Gereffi and Miguel Korzeniewicz (eds) *Commodity Chains and Global Capitalism*, Westport, CT: Praeger, pp. 95–122.

Gereffi, G. (1996) 'Commodity Chains and Regional Divisions of Labor in East Asia', *Journal of Asian Business*, 12(1): 75–112.

Gereffi, G. (1999) 'International Trade and Industrial Upgrading in the Apparel Commodity Chain', *Journal of International Economics*, 48(1): 37–70.

Gereffi, G. (2005) 'The Global Economy: Organization, Governance, and Development', in Neil J. Smelser and Richard Swedberg (eds) *The Handbook of Economic Sociology*, 2nd edn, Princeton, NJ: Princeton University Press, pp. 160–82.

Gereffi, G. (2006) *The New Offshoring of Jobs and Global Development*, ILO Social Policy Lectures, Geneva, Switzerland: International Institute for Labour Studies and International Labor Organization.

Gereffi, G. (2009) 'Development Models and Industrial Upgrading in China and Mexico', *European Sociological Review*, 25(1): 37–51.

Gereffi, G. (2011) 'Global Value Chains and International Competition', *The Antitrust Bulletin*, 56(1): 37–56.

Gereffi, G. and Fernandez-Stark, Karina (2011) 'Global Value Chain Analysis: A Primer', Center on Globalization, Governance and Competitiveness, Durham, NC: Duke University, <http://www.cggc.duke.edu/pdfs/2011-05-31_GVC_analysis_a_primer.pdf> (accessed 20 February 2013).

Gereffi, G., Fernandez-Stark, K. and Psilos, P. (eds) (2011) *Skills for Upgrading: Workforce Development and Global Value Chains in Developing Countries*, Center on Globalization, Governance and Competitiveness, Durham, NC: Duke University, <http://www.cggc.duke.edu/gvc/workforce-development/> (accessed 20 February 2013).

Gereffi, G., Humphrey, J., Kaplinsky, R. and Sturgeon, T.J. (2001) 'Introduction: Globalisation, Value Chains and Development', *IDS Bulletin*, 32(3): 1–8.

Gereffi, G., Humphrey, J. and Sturgeon, T. (2005) 'The Governance of Global Value Chains', *Review of International Political Economy*, 12(1): 78–104.

Gereffi, G. and Korzeniewicz, M. (eds) (1994) *Commodity Chains and Global Capitalism*, Westport, CT: Praeger.

Gereffi, G. and Lee, J. (2012) 'Why the World Suddenly Cares about Global Supply Chains', *Journal of Supply Chain Management*, 48(3): 24–32.

Gereffi, G., Lee, J. and Christian, M. (2009) 'U.S.-Based Food and Agricultural Value Chains and Their Relevance to Healthy Diets', *Journal of Hunger and Environmental Nutrition*, 4(3–4): 357–74.

Gereffi, G. and Wyman, D. L. (eds) (1990) *Manufacturing Miracles: Paths of Industrialization in Latin America and East Asia*, Princeton, NJ: Princeton University Press.

Gibbon, P. (2008) 'Governance, Entry Barriers, Upgrading: A Re-Interpretation of Some GVC Concepts from the Experience of African Clothing Exports', *Competition and Change*, 12(1): 29–48.

Gore, C. (2000) 'The Rise and Fall of the Washington Consensus as a Paradigm for Developing Countries', *World Development*, 28(5): 789–804.

Hamilton, G. G. and Gereffi, G. (2009) 'Global Commodity Chains, Market Makers, and the Rise of Demand-Responsive Economies', in Jennifer Bair (ed.) *Frontiers of Commodity Chain Research*, Stanford, CA: Stanford University Press, pp. 136–61.

Henderson, J., Dicken, P., Hess, M., Coe, N. and Yeung, H. (2002) 'Global Production Networks and the Analysis of Economic Development', *Review of International Political Economy*, 9(3): 426–64.

Herr, M. L. and Muzira, Tapera J. (2009) *Value Chain Development for Decent Work: A Guide for Private Sector Initiatives, Governments and Development Organizations*, Geneva, Switzerland: ILO.

Humphrey, J. and Navas-Alemán, L. (2010) 'Value Chains, Donor Interventions and Poverty Reduction: A Review of Donor Practice', IDS Research Report 63, Brighton, UK: Institute of Development Studies, University of Sussex.

Humphrey, J. and Schmitz, H. (2002) 'How Does Insertion in Global Value Chains Affect Upgrading in Industrial Clusters?', *Regional Studies*, 36(9): 1017–27.

Kaplinsky, R. (2000) 'Globalisation and Unequalisation: What Can be Learned from Value Chain Analysis?', *Journal of Development Studies*, 37(2): 117–46.

Kaplinsky, R. (2005) *Globalization, Poverty and Inequality: Between a Rock and a Hard Place*, Malden, MA: Polity Press.

Kaplinsky, R. and Farooki, M. (2011) 'What are the Implications for Global Value Chains When the Market Shifts from the North to the South?', *International Journal of Technological Learning, Innovation and Development*, 4(1–3): 13–38.

Kaplinsky, R., Terheggen, A. and Tijaja, J. (2011) 'China as a Final Market: The Gabon Timber and Thai Cassava Value Chains', *World Development*, 39(7): 1177–90.

Koopman, R., Zhi, W. and Shang-Jin, W. (2008) 'How Much of Chinese Exports is Really Made in China? Assessing Domestic Value-Added when Processing Trade is Pervasive', Working Paper No. 14109, Cambridge, MA: National Bureau of Economic Research, <http://www.nber.org/papers/w14109> (accessed 20 February 2013).

Lee, J. (2010) 'Global Commodity Chains and Global Value Chains', in Robert A. Denemark (ed.) *The International Studies Encyclopedia*, Oxford, UK: Wiley-Blackwell, pp. 2987–3006.

Lee, J., Gereffi, G. and Barrientos, S. (2011) 'Global Value Chains, Upgrading and Poverty Reduction', Capturing the Gains Briefing Note No. 3,

November, <http://www.capturingthegains.org/pdf/ctg_briefing_note_3.pdf> (accessed 20 February 2013).

Lee, J., Gereffi, G. and Beauvais, J. (2012) 'Global Value Chains and Agrifood Standards: Challenges and Possibilities for Smallholders in Developing Countries', *Proceedings of the National Academy of Sciences of the United States of America*, 109(31): 12326–12331.

Linden, G., Kraemer, K.L. and Dedrick, J. (2009) 'Who Captures Value in a Global Innovation Network? The Case of Apple's iPod', *Communications of the ACM*, 52(3): 140–4.

Lynn, B. C. (2005) *End of the Line: The Rise and Coming Fall of the Global Corporation*, New York: Doubleday.

Martin, Eric (2012) 'Move over, BRICs. Here Come the MISTs', Bloomberg BusinessWeek, August 9, <http://www.businessweek.com/articles/2012-08-09/move-over-brics-dot-here-come-the-mists> (accessed 20 February 2013).

M4P (Making Markets Work Better for the Poor) (2008) *Making Value Chains Work Better for the Poor: A Toolbook for Practitioners of Value Chain Analysis*, London: UK Department of International Development.

Mayer, F. and Gereffi, G. (2010) 'Regulation and Economic Globalization: Prospects and Limits of Private Governance', *Business and Politics*, 12(3), Article 11, <http://www.bepress.com/bap/vol12/iss3/art11/> (accessed 20 February 2013).

Morris, M., Staritz, C. and Barnes, J. (2011) 'Value Chain Dynamics, Local Embeddedness, and Upgrading in the Clothing Sectors of Lesotho and Swaziland', *International Journal of Technological Learning, Innovation and Development*, 4(1–3): 96–119.

Nathan, D. and Sarkar, S. (2011) 'Blood on Your Mobile Phone? Capturing the Gains for Artisanal Miners, Poor Workers and Women', Capturing the Gains Briefing Note No. 2, February, <http://www.capturingthegains.org/pdf/ctg_briefing_note_2.pdf> (accessed 20 February 2013).

Neilson, J. (forthcoming) 'Value chains, neoliberalism and development practice: The Indonesian experience', *Review of International Political Economy*, 20.

Neto, M. S. and Pires, S. R. I. (2010) 'Modular Consortium and Industrial Condominium: Analyzing Two Contemporary Forms of Inter-Firm Governance in the Brazilian Automotive Industry', Gerpisa Colloquium, Berlin, Germany, <http://gerpisa.org/en/print/677> (accessed 20 February 2013).

OECD (2011) 'Global Value Chains: Preliminary Evidence and Policy Issues', DSTI/IND(2011)3, Paris: OECD, <http://www.oecd.org/dataoecd/18/43/47945400.pdf> (accessed 20 February 2013).

OECD (2012) *Policy Priorities for International Trade and Jobs*, Douglas Lippoldt (ed.), <www.oecd.org/trade/icite> (accessed 20 February 2013).

O'Neill, J. (2011) *The Growth Map: Economic Opportunity in the BRICs and Beyond*, New York: Penguin.

Oxfam (2004) *Trading Away Our Rights: Women Working in Global Supply Chains*, Oxford, UK: Oxfam International.

Palpacuer, F., Gibbon, P. and Thomsen, L. (2005) 'New Challenges for Developing Country Suppliers in Global Clothing Chains: A Comparative European Perspective', *World Development*, 33(3): 409–30.

Pisano, G. P. and Shih, W. C. (2009) 'Restoring American Competitiveness', *Harvard Business Review*, 87(7/8): 114–25.

Pisano, G. P. and Shih, W. C. (2012) 'Does America Really Need Manufacturing? Yes, When Production is Closely Tied to Innovation', *Harvard Business Review*, 90(3): 94–102.

Shih, W. C. (2009) 'The US Can't Manufacture the Kindle and That's a Problem', *Harvard Business Review* Blog, <http://blogs.hbr.org/hbr/restoring-american-competitiveness/2009/10/the-us-cant-manufacture-the-ki.html> (accessed 20 February 2013).

Smick, D. M. (2012) 'What Will Replace the Globalization Model?', *The Washington Post*, 16 October <http://articles.washingtonpost.com/2012-10-16/opinions/35500171_1_global-trade-chinese-banks-euro-zone> (accessed 20 February 2013).

Stamm, A. and von Drachenfels, C. (2011) 'Value Chain Development: Approaches and Activities by Seven UN Agencies and Opportunities for Interagency Cooperation', Geneva: ILO, <http://www.ilo.org/empent/Publications/WCMS_170848/lang–en/index.htm> (accessed 20 February 2013).

Staritz, C. and Frederick, S. (2012) 'Summaries of the Country Case Studies on Apparel Industry Development, Structure, and Policies', in Gladys Lopez-Acevedo and Raymond Robertson (eds) *Sewing Success? Employment, Wages, and Poverty Following the End of the Multi-Fibre Arrangement*, Washington, DC: World Bank, pp. 211–497.

Staritz, C., Gereffi, G. and Cattaneo, O. (eds) (2011) Special Issue on 'Shifting End Markets and Upgrading Prospects in Global Value Chains', *International Journal of Technological Learning, Innovation and Development*, 4(1–3).

Sturgeon, T. J. (2009) 'From Commodity Chains to Value Chains: Interdisciplinary Theory Building in an Age of Globalization', in Jennifer Bair (ed.) *Frontiers of Commodity Chain Research*, Stanford, CA: Stanford University Press, pp. 110–35.

Sturgeon, T. J. and Gereffi, Gary (2009) 'Measuring Success in the Global Economy: International Trade, Industrial Upgrading, and Business Function Outsourcing in Global Value Chains', *Transnational Corporations*, 18(2): 1–36.

Sturgeon, T. J. and Kawakami, M. (2011) 'Global Value Chains in the Electronics Industry: Characteristics, Crisis, and Upgrading Opportunities in Firms from Developing Countries', *International Journal of Technological Learning, Innovation and Development*, 4(1–3): 120–47.

Sturgeon, T. J. and Van Biesebroeck, J. (2011) 'Global Value Chains in the Automotive Industry: An Enhanced Role for Developing Countries?', *International Journal of Technological Learning, Innovation and Development*, 4(1–3): 181–205.

Sturgeon, T.J., Van Biesebroeck, J. and Gereffi, G. (2008) 'Value Chains, Networks and Clusters: Reframing the Global Automotive Industry', *Journal of Economic Geography*, 8: 297–321.

UNCTAD (2013) 'Global Value Chains and Development: Investment and Value Added Trade in the Global Economy – A Preliminary Analysis'. Geneva: UNCTAD, <http://unctad.org/en/PublicationsLibrary/diae2013d1_en.pdf> (accessed 28 February 2013).

UNIDO (2011) *Diagnostics for Industrial Value Chain Development: An Integrated Tool*, Vienna, Austria: UNIDO, <http://www.unido.org/fileadmin/user_media/MDGs/IVC_Diagnostic_Tool.pdf> (accessed 20 February 2013).

Urquidi, V. L. (1991) 'The Prospects for Economic Transformation in Latin America: Opportunities and Resistances', *LASA Forum*, 22(3): 1–9.

USAID (2012) 'Value Chain Development', MicroLINKS wiki, <http://microlinks.kdid.org/good-practice-center/value-chain-wiki> (accessed 20 February 2012).

USITC (2011) *The Economic Effects of Significant US Import Restraints: Seventh Update 2011*, Special Topic: Global Supply Chains. Publication 4253, Washington, DC: USITC.

Vernon, R. (1971) *Sovereignty at Bay: The Multinational Spread of US Enterprises*, New York: Basic Books.

Wadhwa, V., De Vitton, U.K. and Gereffi, G. (2008) 'How the Disciple Became the Guru: Workforce Development in India's R&D Labs', Report prepared for the Ewing Marion Kauffman Foundation, <http://papers.ssrn.com/sol3/papers.cfm?abstract_id=1170049> (accessed 20 February 2013).

Weatherspoon, D. D. and Reardon, T. (2003) 'The Rise of Supermarkets in Africa: Implications for Agrifood Systems and the Rural Poor', *Development Policy Review*, 21(3): 333–55.

Webber, C. M. and Labaste, P. (2009) *Building Competitiveness in Africa's Agriculture: A Guide to Value Chain Concepts and Applications*, Washington, DC: World Bank.

Will, M. (2011) 'Integrating Smallholders into Global Supply Chains', GTZ Division Economic Development and Employment and Division Agriculture, Fisheries and Food, April, <http://www.giz.de/Themen/en/dokumente/gtz2010-en-globalgap-group-certification.pdf> (accessed 20 February 2013).

World Bank (1993) *The East Asian Miracle*, Oxford: Oxford University Press.

World Bank (2011) *The Role of International Business in Aid for Trade: Building Capacity for Trade in Developing Countries*, Washington, DC: World Bank.

World Economic Forum (2012) 'The Shifting Geography of Global Value Chains: Implications for Developing Countries and Trade Policy', Global Agenda Council on the Global Trade System, WEF, <http://www3.weforum.org/docs/WEF_GAC_GlobalTradeSystem_Report_2012.pdf> (accessed 20 February 2013).

WTO (2011) *International Trade Statistics 2011*, Geneva, Switzerland: WTO.

WTO and IDE-JETRO (2011) 'Trade Patterns and Global Value Chains in East Asia: From Trade in Goods to Trade in Tasks', World Trade Organization and Institute of Developing Economies, Geneva and Tokyo, <http://www.ide.go.jp/English/Press/pdf/20110606_news.pdf> (accessed 20 February 2013).

Value chains, neoliberalism and development practice: The Indonesian experience

Jeffrey Neilson

School of Geosciences, University of Sydney, Sydney, Australia

ABSTRACT

This paper provides a critical analysis of the emergence of an approach within the practice of international development that adopts a 'value chain' discourse, and traces the conceptual underpinnings of this discourse and practice through its translation from scholarly literature. This practical application of value chain theory has involved the selective application and interpretation, by development practitioners, of key scholarly ideas on global commodity chains, development strategies and industrialization. The specific application of value chains in Indonesian development practice, however, is silent on other aspects of the global value chain framework, such as the role of the state in mediating development strategies, power asymmetries within chains, and world-historical circumstances that shape upgrading possibilities. Despite foundational roots in critical analyses of global capitalism, recent 'value chains for development' applications appear to be perpetuating a neoliberal development agenda, which is facilitating the enhanced penetration of multinational capital into the economy and lives of the rural and urban poor.

INTRODUCTION

This article problematizes the widespread adoption of diverse value chain approaches to development practice that has taken place over the last decade. In doing so, it highlights several conceptual inconsistencies associated with the policy uptake of the approach. This case study of how an idea, emanating from critical political economy, has been translated and subsequently employed by international development agencies demonstrates the persistent ability of dominant actors and organizations to co-opt critical social theory and perpetuate prior commitments to a neoliberal development project. Critically engaged reflection on this matter is timely, with both value chain theory and value chain practice vying for influence in the post-Washington Consensus development world of the early twenty-first century.

The article calls for heightened sensitivity towards what were previously key tenets of the scholarly framework for Global Commodity Chain (GCC) and Global Value Chain (GVC) studies: the institutional settings of the chain and the role of the state; industrial upgrading as a development strategy; processes of establishing and exerting power throughout the chain; and a concern for world-historical processes that shape opportunities for inclusion and exclusion in global development. This need for re-engagement with critical value chain theory has assumed strategic importance in recent years, as international development agencies have increasingly adopted a value chain discourse within their programmatic applications and have tended to interpret aspects of the framework in ways that perpetuate neoliberal economic prescriptions for development. This article examines the dialectical relationship between development strategies and the evolution of the GCC/GVC framework over the past 25 years – a relationship that has involved an uneasy oscillation of value chain thinking between the two meanings of the term, 'development'. Underlying the key arguments in this paper, therefore, is a concern for the relationship between development as a post-World War II project of intervention in the 'third world' and development as a geographically uneven, profoundly contradictory set of historical processes (Hart, 2001: 650).

There has been an explosion of interest in 'value chains for development' over the last decade, as evident from the 27 'Value Chain Strategy Papers' published by 18 different international development agencies that are listed in Appendix A. These are documents (handbooks, working papers, policy documents, reviews and guides) with a primary thematic focus on value chains as an intervention strategy. The first such document we could identify was published by the United Nations Conference for Trade and Development (UNCTAD) in 2000 and, of the 27 documents, only six were published before 2005, suggesting a particularly rapid uptake of value chain thinking within development agencies in the second half of the decade. In July 2010, seven UN agencies joined together to create the United Nations Value Chain Development Group (UN VCD Group) in an initiative that highlights the broadening appeal of value chain approaches across a number of UN agencies (Stamm and von Drachenfels, 2011).

This widespread developmental uptake presents an apparent contradiction. Despite drawing conceptual inspiration from an analytical framework derived from intellectual foundations in critical, and even radical, political economy, value chain applications have been embraced by many agencies still enamoured of Washington Consensus policy prescriptions (or at least what Rodrik (2006) has labelled an 'Augmented Washington Consensus'). In this article, I explain this apparent contradiction by analysing the disjunctures occurring at three critical moments of translation: the preparation of a policy-ready conceptual framework from the scholarly literature that occurred around the time of the 'Bellagio Workshop' in 2000; the in-house interpretation of this framework by leading development agencies from around 2005; and then the programmatic application by international donors in the latter half of the decade using Indonesia as a case study.

This article is correspondingly organized into five sections. Following this initial brief introduction, the second section briefly charts the intellectual foundations of the global value chain framework from its cradle in dependency theory through to its transformation into a conceptual framework for development interventions. The aim of this section is to identify the key conceptual foundations of the GVC framework that have contributed to its subsequent adoption and interpretation by development practitioners and to highlight elements of the conceptual framework that have subsequently influenced donor practices. The third section presents evidence for the claim that a value chains discourse has been widely adopted by the international development community and presents an argument for why value chain approaches have been so readily absorbed within a post-Washington Consensus world of development theory. The fourth section presents the case study of Indonesia, where value chain interventions have featured prominently amongst various donor programmes since around 2005. This commences with a review of Indonesian economic development, followed by an analysis of how three leading donor agencies have applied value chain thinking programmatically within Indonesia. The final section concludes with an explanation of how the processes of interpretation and practical application have ensured the perpetuation of a neoliberal development agenda.

TOWARDS A CONCEPTUAL FRAMEWORK FOR VALUE CHAIN DEVELOPMENT INTERVENTIONS

Global value chain (GVC)[1] analysis has developed an influential set of conceptual tools to understand the operations of industry systems across world geography, thereby providing an informed analysis of how capitalist processes generate opportunities and constraints for different people and places in the global economy. Kaplinsky and Morris (2001: 4) explain this deceptively straightforward notion thus:

> The *value chain* describes the full range of activities which are required to bring a product or service from conception, through the different phases of production (involving a combination of physical transformation and the input of various producer services), delivery to final consumers, and final disposal after use.

The intellectual origins of the GCC framework can be firmly traced back to the institutionalist and world-historical structural analyses of global capitalism that emerged during the 1970s in close association with the ideas of dependency theory (Frank, 1969; Furtado, 1970; Cardoso and Faletto, 1979). The influence of dependency theory was evident in the early work of Gary Gereffi (a highly influential contributor to value chain thinking) on the pharmaceuticals industry in Latin America (Gereffi, 1983). Indeed, the term, 'commodity chains', was initially introduced in conjunction with the offshoot of dependency theory known as world-systems theory[2] (Hopkins and Wallerstein, 1977, 1986). Wallerstein (2004) presents world-systems theory as a specific critique of modernization theory's optimistic view that global unevenness would dissolve over time as long as undeveloped states followed the advice and prescribed economic, political and social policies of more developed states. Importantly, the policy applications inspired by world-system theory tended towards state intervention in markets and import-substituting industrialization (ISI), rather than laissez-faire and export-oriented industrialization (EOI). While the implications for development strategies resulting from GCC analyses moved beyond this oversimplified binary towards a more contingent assessment (Gereffi, 1989), Gereffi (1989: 525) still explained: '[F]or semi-periphery countries to ascend in the world economy, they will have to find new ways to move to the most profitable end of commodity chains.'

Two important dimensions that have emerged within GCC analysis are 'governance' and the 'institutional framework' (commonly presented alongside 'territoriality' and the 'input-output structure' of a chain). The early interest in world-historical processes dovetailed with the increased scholarly attention afforded to the role of transnational companies in the global economy throughout the 1970s (Vernon (1971) and numerous studies by the United Nations Commission on Transnational Corporations (UNCTC), as listed in UNCTAD (2004)). Indeed, these UNCTC studies were important forerunners for subsequent commodity chain research. The ability of transnational corporations to exert a global influence was subsequently articulated by Gereffi through the concept of chain 'governance', which depicted the relationship between core and periphery nodes in the chain (Gereffi, 1994). The term, 'lead firm', subsequently emerged to designate those firms with the capacity to govern chains (Gereffi, 1999), replacing the earlier reference to 'core companies' (Gereffi, 1994). Along with governance, the institutional framework was also considered a pivotal dimension of a global commodity chain and was presented by Gereffi (1995: 113) as 'how local, national, and international conditions and policies shape the globalization process as each stage of the chain'. The renewed interest in the role of the state signified by this reference to institutions also seemed to encourage the later acceptance of value chain approaches within post-Washington Consensus debates, as discussed below.

The shift in the literature from 'commodity chains' to 'value chains' played an important role in facilitating the subsequent uptake of 'value chains' terminology by development agencies. This shift, attributed by Hess and Coe (2006) to scholars from the Institute for Development Studies (IDS) at Sussex, has been described elsewhere by Bair (2005, 2009) as reflecting much more than a simple terminological adjustment. Bair argues that it reflects a deeper conceptual turn away from the earlier world-systems theory orientation. It was also a deliberate strategic move to increase its appeal for donors. An important moment in the emergence of an implementation-ready 'value chains for development' discourse, associated with the shift from 'commodity' to 'value', was a workshop held at Bellagio, Italy, in 2000, sponsored by the Rockefeller Foundation (papers from which were presented in a special issue in the *IDS Bulletin,* 2001: Vol. 32). According to some Bellagio participants, 'Value chains' was considered more appropriate to a larger set of products (Sturgeon, 2009) and had established associations with the prior work of Michael Porter (as explained by Ponte and Gibbon (2005)). A further contributing factor to the terminological shift appeared to be the associations between 'commodity chains' and its roots in 'fatalistic' structuralist development economics (as argued by Cramer (1999)), which drew defensive responses from commodity chain scholars (such as Gibbon (2001)), who sought to play down these intellectual influences.

Porter's work on value chains was indeed already well known as a theory on the competitive advantage of firms within business studies literature (Porter, 1998, first published in 1985). Porter, however, applied the value chain concept far less liberally in his subsequent study on the competitiveness of nations (Porter, 1990), which he essentially associates with the national attributes that foster competitive advantage in particular industries. Porter (1988) was primarily concerned with how an individual firm can create and sustain competitive advantage by outperforming its rivals, and he used the value chain as the primary heuristic device to analyse firm competitiveness. For Porter (1998: 33):

> The value chain disaggregates a firm into its strategically relevant activities in order to understand the behavior of costs and the existing and potential sources of differentiation.

It is significant that the work of Porter is identified just as frequently as the work of Gereffi as a key intellectual influence within the development agency strategy papers (Appendix A). Porter's explicitly firm-centric orientation of value chains became a powerful analytical tool for corporate strategic planning, but has also gained considerable traction within the development practitioner community, where I argue it has been applied somewhat problematically.

As discussed in the following section, the analytical concept of 'upgrading' has become the defining process through which value chain development applications have found fertile inspiration from the scholarly literature. Gereffi (1999: 52–3) described 'industrial upgrading' as a 'process of improving the ability of a firm or an economy to move to more profitable and/or technologically sophisticated capital and skill-intensive economic niches'. Here, Gereffi (1999: 39) is influenced by the work of Porter (1990), who also presented upgrading as the process of firms moving into more sophisticated product types, especially the shift from OEM (original equipment manufacturer) towards global marketing strategies for products sold under own brand identities. The key contribution made by GCC/GVC analyses of upgrading was the importance afforded to the nature of relationships with lead firms that shape upgrading opportunities for other chain participants.

GCC theory, moreover, provides a clear analytical framework that describes, based on empirical evidence, the organizational processes through which upgrading takes place. Gereffi (1999: 39) explains:

> Participation in global commodity chains is a necessary step for industrial upgrading because it puts firms and economies on potentially dynamic learning curves.

This claim draws primarily on the experiences of the high-performing Asian economies, whose rapid economic development was made possible through specific articulations of global commodity chains and the off-shoring of US and European manufacturing (Gereffi, 1999). Under this explanation, East Asian firms evolved from simple equipment assembling through to component suppliers to foreign multinationals, and then ultimately developed capacity to design, manufacture and brand their own goods for export. Hamilton and Gereffi (2009) refer to this process as 'demand-responsive economic development'. Similarly, Kaplinsky (2000: 126–7) claims that 'the more powerful actors in the chain are increasingly required to induce (and assist) their suppliers and customers to change their own operating procedures'. The causal relationship between firm-level upgrading and the supportive role of overseas buyers willing to facilitate and encourage the upstream transfer of skills and knowledge was a core element of the conceptual model developed through the Bellagio process.

The *Handbook for Value Chain Research* (Kaplinsky and Morris, 2001) facilitated the uptake of value chain ideas by development practitioners by presenting a coherent conceptual framework for intervention. Of the strategy papers listed in Appendix A, it has probably been the most influential. This handbook was one of several products from the Bellagio workshop and was infused with policy implications and written for both researchers and development practitioners. The underlying policy question addressed in the handbook, and in a number of other associated outputs from Bellagio (such as the *IDS Bulletin*'s 2001 special issue), was:

> If the issue is not *whether* one engages in globalisation but *how*, then where should one place the policy emphasis to ensure that how one engages with [globalisation] spreads the gains from globalisation? (Kaplinsky and Morris, 2001: 102)

A conceptual model for value chain interventions was thereby constructed around the initial integration of local firms and individuals within global value chains, usually followed by institutional supports (potentially from government, non-governmental organizations (NGOs) or development agencies). These supports could assist firms to acquire new competencies and take on new functions associated with high value-adding segments of the chain. The higher rents appropriated by virtue of the firm's new location within the chain could result in higher incomes and, it is widely assumed, broader development benefits. Importantly, however, this paper argues that the adoption of the value chain discourse did not necessitate the wholesale abandonment of previous development strategies built around the Washington Consensus. Mainstream econometric convictions about comparative advantage, competitiveness, transaction costs and the neoliberal scepticism towards an interventionist state could be easily accommodated within the global value chain rubric, at least as it was being translated by development practitioners.

DONOR EMBRACE OF VALUE CHAIN MODELS OF DEVELOPMENT

Almost all major international development agencies have articulated a 'value chains for development' approach to programme delivery during the last decade (Appendix A). These handbooks, working papers, policy documents and guides provide important insights into the appeal of value chains from a practitioner's perspective and reveal the intellectual traditions from which they draw inspiration. The works of both Gereffi and Porter are frequently cited in these documents as being influential in shaping the development approach, notwithstanding their somewhat divergent intellectual concerns, as noted above.

Altenburg (2007), writing for the Donor Committee for Enterprise Development (DCED), provides a useful overview of what he considers to be the conceptual foundations of value chain applications to development practice. Altenburg attributes recent applications primarily to the 'management sciences', including the work of Porter (1990), in addition to earlier work on growth poles and linkages (Perroux, 1955; Hirschman, 1958), on offshoring (Fröbel, Heinrichs and Kreye, 1980) and on clusters (Schmitz, 1995). Variants of the growth pole theory that embrace the stimulating role of transnational corporations (Dunning, 1992) appear to have inspired the adoption of 'lead firms' as conduits of development intervention (discussed below). Far from being a fully coherent theory of development practice in its own right, the value chain developmental discourse draws on ideas emanating from sometimes quite disparate disciplinary roots and traditions.

One of the first donor agencies to adopt value chains as a conceptual framework for its activities was the United Nations Industrial Development Organization (UNIDO), with its UN mandate to promote industrial development in developing countries and its special focus on the promotion of small- and medium-sized enterprises (SMEs). UNIDO was attracted by the potential to facilitate SME development in developing countries by working together with the supplier networks of multinational companies. To this end, it hosted a series of meetings of experts from the public and private sectors, and academic researchers, to explore this theme throughout 2000. A UNIDO publication, *Integrating SMEs in Global Value Chains: Towards Partnership for Development* (Kaplinsky and Readman, 2001), along with the UNCTAD report, *Strategies for Diversification and Adding Value to Food Exports* (Humphrey and Oetero, 2000), appear to be the first publicly available reports published by major donors explicitly promoting value chains as a development approach. Subsequent policy papers, authored, like the UNIDO report, by independent researchers rather than by in-house agency staff, were published by the Inter-American Development Bank (Pietrobelli and Rabellotti, 2004), Deutsche Gesellschaft für Technische Zusammenarbeit (GTZ) (Stamm, 2004; Humphrey, 2005) and the International Labour Organization (ILO) (Schmitz, 2005).

It was not long before the value chain approach was adopted and articulated through donor publications effectively authored 'in-house', such as *Globalization and the Small Firm: A Value Chain Approach to Economic Growth and Poverty Reduction* (Kula, Downing and Field/USAID, 2006) and *Moving Towards Competitiveness: A Value Chain Approach* (FIAS/World Bank, 2007). As we will see, the World Bank Group (primarily through the International Finance Corporation (IFC)) and the US Agency for International Development (USAID) have also been at the forefront of value chain applications in Indonesia. These two documents focus on the applicability of value chains as a lens to analyse underlying policy constraints in industry competitiveness (what Kula, Downing and Field (2006) refer to as the 'business enabling environment'). Similarly, the World Bank document (FIAS, 2007: 36) presents a sample policy recommendations framework, purportedly

Table 1 Use of GCC/GVC terminology within the donor publications adopting a value chain framework listed in Appendix A

	Upgrading	Governance	Lead firm	TNCs/ MNCs	Institutions or institutional
Term appears as a section heading within the report	16	12	6	1	2
Average occurrences within text report	55	21	9	9	15

as a result of a value chain analysis, which lists a somewhat standard set of conventional policy prescriptions: privatization, facilitation of foreign direct investment (FDI), promotion of tax reductions and liberalization of trade. In both documents, the donor agencies demonstrate their receptiveness to the language of value chains while maintaining adherence to prevailing core neoliberal beliefs with respect to policy interventions.

The analytical concept of 'upgrading' has been embraced almost unanimously by development agency actors establishing conceptual foundations for the approach (Table 1) and has been instrumental in chaperoning value chain theory along its transformation from a critical social science through to an action framework for development interventions. According to Gereffi *et al.* (2001: 5), 'firm upgrading involves insertion into local and global value chains in such a way as to maximise value creation and learning'. Policymakers subsequently embraced the idea that participation in global value chains and production networks was the key to economic growth.

Donor interpretations have also been associated with the loss of the adjective, 'industrial', to specify the type of upgrading, and have been encouraged by a substantial broadening of 'upgrading' to encompass a more diverse array of engagement with value chains (as presented by Kaplinsky, 2000; Gereffi *et al.*, 2001; and Gibbon, 2001). These scholarly analyses led to the now widely-recognized four-fold classification of upgrading typologies presented by Kaplinsky and Morris (2001) as product, process, functional and chain (inter-sectoral) upgrading – where only functional upgrading relates specifically to industrialization. Bair (2005), however, argues that the narrow focus on upgrading as an issue of firm-level competitiveness (following a Porter-inspired analysis) ignores broader structural questions of how inequality is produced and reproduced in the global economy. In the donor interpretations, there is apparently little room for industrialization as a national development strategy, and 'upgrading' tends to embrace 'product' and 'process' upgrading, while neglecting concerns over 'functional upgrading'. Reflecting this apparent reluctance to address functional upgrading, Kula, Downing and Field (2006: 14) define firm-level upgrading as 'changes made by firms to improve their competitiveness through product development and improvements in production techniques or processes'. As will be demonstrated in the case of Indonesia, the narrow interpretation of value chain upgrading in agricultural regions as 'market engagement' has even conflicted with the broader development objectives proposed by the Government of Indonesia with respect to industrialization.

Why have donors been so willing to adopt value chain discourse within their programming over the last decade? Gereffi (2013, in press) attributes this to its emphasis on a 'meso-level, sectoral and actor-oriented approach to the global economy, which provides multi-scalar options to link global and local levels of analysis'. While the benefits of such 'joined-up policies' (Kaplinsky, 2000) are clearly important, it is also prudent to recognize both the conceptual and political space for the incursion of 'value chain' approaches that had been created due to intellectual turmoil within development theory and practice over the last decade. The Washington Consensus, with its commitment to a dramatically reduced role for the state, provided a core conceptual basis for development practice throughout the 1980s and 1990s before widespread evidence of policy failures began to unsettle its foundations (high-profile critiques include Rodrik (1997, 1999); and Easterly (2001)). Most disturbing of all was the empirical reality that a number of countries in East and Southeast Asia, which had experienced remarkable economic growth, and which had made substantial gains in terms of poverty reduction in preceding decades, had effectively ignored these same policy descriptions (Wade, 1990). This evidence was acknowledged – albeit somewhat begrudgingly – in the *East Asian Miracle* (World Bank, 1993) and led to some serious soul-searching within the World Bank, and across the international development community more broadly.

Joseph Stiglitz became a key instigator for what he referred to as the need for a 'post-Washington Consensus' (PWC) (Stiglitz, 1998). At the same time, the World Bank published *Beyond the Washington Consensus: Institutions Matter* (Burki and Perry, 1998), and the *World Development Reports* of 2001 and 2002 (World Bank, 2001; 2002) signalled a cautious nod towards reforming the 'vital role' that governments and institutions play in the development process.

The appeal of value chain approaches, therefore, needs to be properly assessed against this particular historic moment within developmental thinking, which also coincided with the Bellagio meeting in 2000. The GVC framework was well-suited to this broader shift towards institutional explanations of development successes and failures. Value chain thinking satisfies an empirical need to explain economic phenomena in a way that is attentive simultaneously to the potentially supportive role of the state, to explanations of inter-firm relationships that avoid conflating all transactions as predominately market-based, and to historical contingency and differential diagnosis. The GVC framework had also contributed empirically-based insights, drawn primarily from the East Asian experience, into processes of upgrading within the global economic system and, therefore, responds, at least partially, to the theoretical challenges posed to development economics by the *East Asian Miracle*. Finally, the GVC framework provides a powerful diagnostic tool to identify significant constraints on economic growth and development in a particular geographic setting (an important aspect of an augmented Washington Consensus, according to Rodrik (2006)). These factors, collectively, help explain the rapid uptake at a conceptual level by development agencies in the latter part of the decade.

In light of the considerable policy interest in value chains for development, surprisingly little research has been conducted on how these policies have been implemented in practice and whether they have been effective 'on the ground'. Two recent assessments, however, have attempted to critically engage with, and to analyse the effectiveness of, value chains for development interventions. A working paper commissioned by UNIDO (Henriksen *et al.*, 2010) analyses six value chain interventions across Asia based on different forms of intervention. Amongst other findings, the paper emphasizes the generally unacknowledged role of institutional path dependencies in shaping intervention design, the general lack of concern for broader development goals, and the dangers of relying on a single lead firm for delivery. Another report, published as an IDS Research Report (Humphrey and Navas-Alemán, 2010), was based on a review of 30 donor-led value chain interventions, and drew a sharp distinction between those projects that specifically targeted poverty reduction, and those categorized as lead firm projects. They also emphasized that despite ample anecdotal evidence from donors about the efficacy of a value chain approach to development, the lack of systematic impact assessments was a serious cause for concern.

THE INDONESIAN DEVELOPMENT EXPERIENCE AND VALUE CHAINS

This paper will now examine the specific programmatic application, by international donors, of value chain approaches within Indonesia. Indonesia is the world's fourth most populous nation, rich in natural resources and the major regional power in Southeast Asia. While Indonesia has experienced periods of strong economic growth in recent decades (Figure 1), accompanied generally by falling poverty levels, serious challenges remain to convert this enormous human and natural potential into sustained

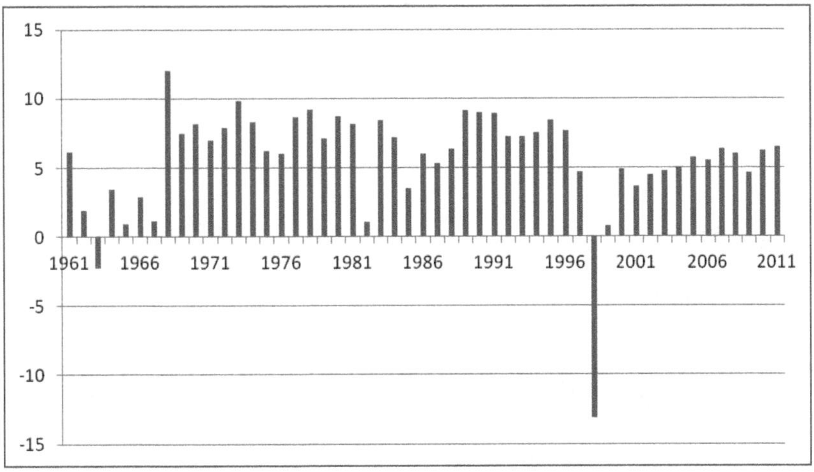

Figure 1 Annual GDP growth in Indonesia (1961–2011). *Data source:* World Bank (2012a).

prosperity for the majority of the population. In 2011, average per capita gross domestic product (GDP) (purchasing power parity, or PPP) was $4,667 with 18 per cent of the population still living on less than $1.25 per day (World Bank, 2012a).

Since proclaiming independence from the Dutch in 1945, Indonesia has experimented with extreme economic nationalism and anti-imperialism under President Sukarno in the 1950s and early 1960s, then with large-scale foreign investment in natural resource exploitation during the initial years of Suharto's New Order regime. The 1973 oil boom made possible a decade-long experiment with ISI policies, helping Indonesia to develop enhanced industrial capacity. A series of balance of payments and fiscal crises in the 1980s forced structural adjustment reforms and a shift towards manufacturing-led export-oriented industrialization (Figure 2), as Indonesia benefitted from the outsourcing strategies of firms from first tier Asian economies, and was identified as a second tier Newly Industrializing Economy (NIE) within the World Bank's *East Asian Miracle* – despite limited upgrading towards high-rent activities in global production networks.

Strong export-oriented growth, however, ended spectacularly with the Asian economic crisis of 1997–98. The rupiah went into free fall, the economy contracted dramatically, millions were thrown into poverty, and the social turmoil extracted a high political price as a 32-year dictatorship ended. Since the crisis, comparative advantage has shifted back slowly towards raw material exports, as reflected in their mildly increased

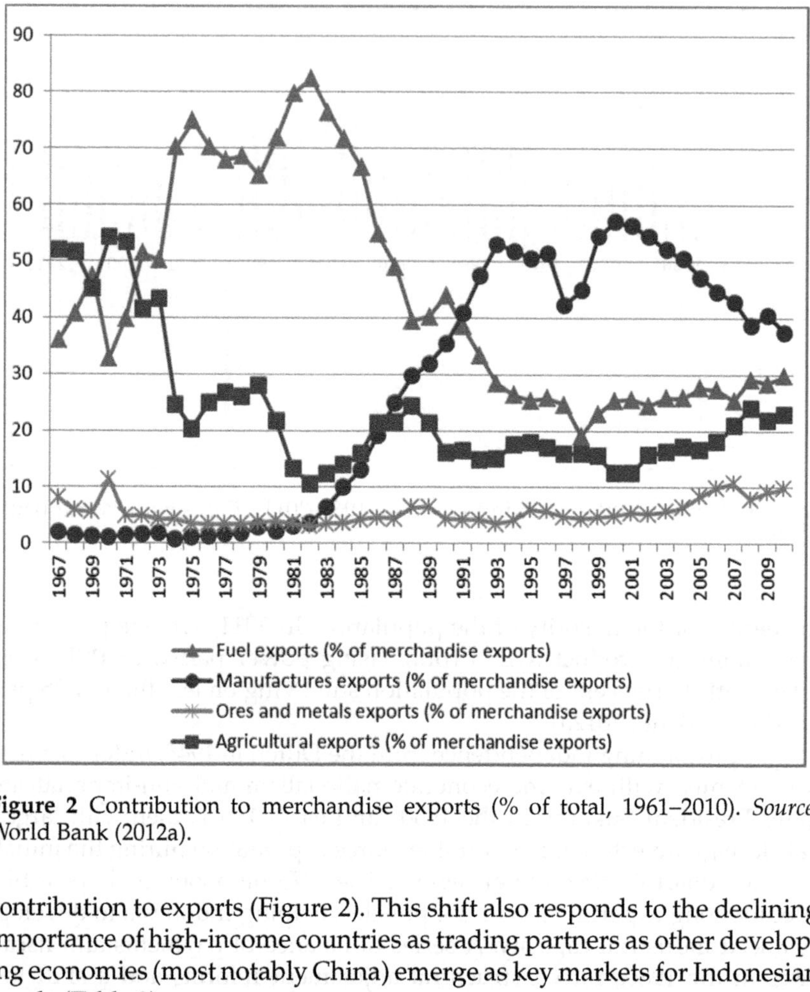

Figure 2 Contribution to merchandise exports (% of total, 1961–2010). *Source:* World Bank (2012a).

contribution to exports (Figure 2). This shift also responds to the declining importance of high-income countries as trading partners as other developing economies (most notably China) emerge as key markets for Indonesian goods (Table 2).

The international donor community played an active role in the post-crisis economic recovery, although the importance of Overseas Development Assistance (ODA) has declined (Figure 3). Within Indonesia,

Table 2 Changing destination of Indonesian merchandise exports (% of total)

	1980	1990	2000	2010
High-income economies	97	91	81	63
Developing economies in East Asia and Pacific	1	6	11	23
Developing economies outside region	2	3	8	14

Source: World Bank (2012a).

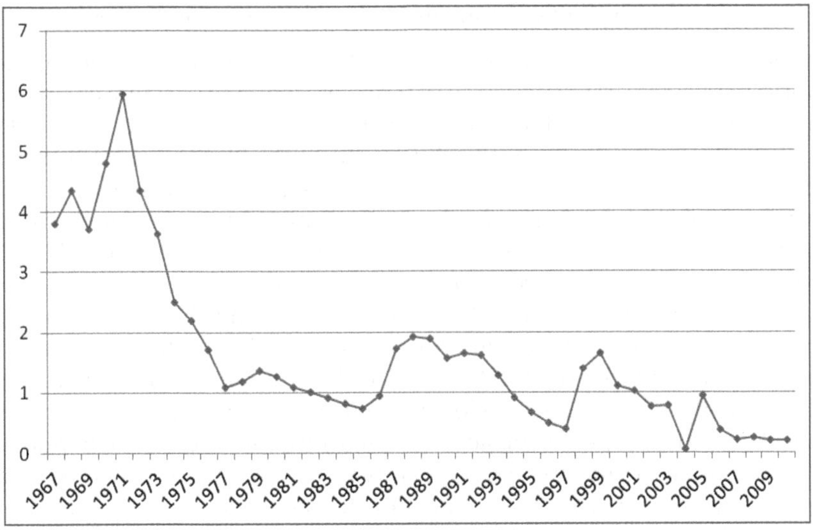

Figure 3 ODA to Indonesia as a percentage of GNI (1967–2010). *Source:* World Bank (2012a).

moreover, scepticism towards bilateral and multilateral development organizations has remained strong following the International Monetary Fund (IMF) mismanagement of the 1998 crisis and associations between the World Bank and the corrupt Suharto government.

The World Bank continues to be the dominant international development agency operating in Indonesia, with gross annual disbursements of around US$2 billion in recent years (World Bank, 2012b). The Indonesian government has, however, made a number of repayments to the Bank (most notably during the period, 2002–07), which reduced the annual net flows of ODA from the Bank indicated in Table 3. Much of the Japanese ODA programme has been provided as loan aid and with a focus on infrastructure development in the energy, transport and irrigation sectors, with little interest in the development of the domestic private sector (Embassy of Japan, 2012). Similarly, the Asian Development Bank focuses on environment, infrastructure, education and finance in Indonesia (ADB, 2012a), although a recent knowledge evaluation report (ADB, 2012b) suggests that it may adopt a value chain approach in the coming years. Three of the next most important development agencies operating in Indonesia – the World Bank Group, USAID and the Australian Agency for International Development (AusAID) – have all explicitly adopted value chain approaches in their programming during the last decade.

The World Bank Group and value chains in Indonesia

In its 2003 Country Assistance Strategy (CAS) paper for Indonesia, the World Bank (2003) refers to the critical role of 'commodity value chains' in linking agricultural producers with the agri-processing sector. The World Bank strategy document specifically identifies the FEATI project (Farmer Empowerment through Agricultural Technology and Information), then in the initial design phase, to be complemented by the IFC's Program for Eastern Indonesia (PENSA), in achieving this objective. The FEATI loan was initially proposed with a focus on strengthening farmer linkages with the private sector (World Bank, 2005), and the accompanying suggestion that a supply chain approach be developed through 'public-private partnerships' (EASRD, 2005). Such an approach, however, was subsequently rejected by the Government of Indonesia due to concerns that it would effectively subsidize (foreign) private sector development within Indonesia, and the FEATI loan was eventually implemented as a more conventional farmer extension development programme. The value chain and industry partnership components of the initial proposal were instead pursued independently through the IFC (through its support for the industry-dominated Cocoa Sustainability Partnership, through AusAID's Smallholder Agricultural Development Initiative (SADI) programme, and then through its own Agribusiness programme).

Since its inception in 1956 as the private sector arm of the World Bank, the IFC has maintained a core mandate to promote private sector development in developing countries. Following the Foreign Investment Advisory Service (FIAS) (2007), however, the IFC has increasingly adopted value chain terminology for its programming. A country review of the IFC in

Table 3 Major sources of ODA to Indonesia (2001–10) (annual average)

	Country	Net ODA ('000 US$ current)
1	ADB	245, 444
2	Japan	239, 546
3	Australia	210, 647
4	IDA (World Bank)	154, 052
5	USA	152, 630
6	Netherlands	80, 827
7	EU institutions	73, 797
8	France	54, 246
9	UK	52, 312
10	IBRD (World Bank)	−264, 209
	Total net ODA	1, 309, 875

Data source: World Bank (2012a).

Indonesia (IEG, 2008: xxii) states the organization's apparently unequivocal commitment to the approach:

> IFC will expand its focus on value chain approaches in all International Development Association (IDA) countries in East Asia starting with Vietnam, but extending to Indonesia and Cambodia, as the benefits both in terms of development impact and investment are clear.

Utilizing a 'supply chain linkage' approach, the IFC's PENSA programme (2003–08) was already promoting market relationships between SMEs and larger core businesses in the extractive industries, handicraft and furniture manufacturing, and agribusiness sectors. While strongly supportive of a value chain approach, the Independent Evaluation Group's (IEG's) (2008) review was critical of the limited links between the IFC's technical advisory services and its investment portfolio in Indonesia (remembering that the IFC's core function is to provide investment services for private sector companies). The IEG review suggested that this was caused, at least in part, by the funding of IFC activities (including PENSA and SADI) by bilateral donors who held diverging priorities (such as targeted poverty reduction).

According to the World Bank's Country Partnership Strategy for Indonesia (2008: 34), the IFC expected to spend US$300 million annually on 'finance, infrastructure and commodity-based supply chains'. This final component has manifested in activities that aim to incorporate farmers within the agribusiness supply chains of lead firms where the IFC already has an investment interest. Within the Indonesian donor community, this has become known as the 'lead firm model'. Following the IEG review in 2008, and driven by concerns over cost and sustainability, the IFC moved away from the earlier 'PENSA model' of direct assistance to local producer groups towards the provision of technical assistance via lead firms, who acted as important development partners (Fargher and Konishi, 2010). For example, the IFC has an established investment relationship with one of the world's largest commodity trading companies, Ecom Agroindustrial Corp. Ltd, which has resulted in the provision of technical advisory services for the company's coffee operations in northern Sumatra, most notably through the establishment of a farmer training centre. The programme, and others like it in Central America and Vietnam, is designed to address the supply chain issues faced by Ecom, to encourage farmers to advance towards certification and to develop longer-term supply contracts with Ecom (IFC, 2012). The lack of strategic targeting for poverty reduction impacts, however, is a recognized weakness of the IFC's global operations, which tends to prioritize investment outcomes and financial returns (IEG, 2011).

In Indonesia, the other key application of a value chain approach by the IFC is what it identifies as support for the Business Enabling Environment (BEE) – initially introduced in the PENSA programme to focus on policy reform and deregulation. This draws on the earlier FIAS policy paper (2007: 36), which claimed encouragingly: 'The World Bank Group has conducted a number of value chain studies, and in one way or another, they have led to substantial policy changes.' The IFC has implemented the BEE approach with respect to the Indonesian cocoa industry, helping to lobby (unsuccessfully) against a controversial export tax on raw beans designed by the government to encourage domestic value-adding (functional upgrading) through new investment in processing. It was claimed that '[s]uch a tax would be passed back to farmers, lowering their returns and ability to implement productivity and quality improvement technologies even further' (EASRD, 2005: x).

USAID and value chains in Indonesia

For USAID, value chain approaches fall within its focus on 'increasing employment' in Indonesia and respond to a stated US Department of State strategic goal to 'expand opportunities for U.S. businesses and ensuring economic security for the [US] nation' (USAID, 2004). Significantly, the 2004 *USAID Strategic Plan for Indonesia* for the period, 2004–09, emphasizes enhanced support for private sector actors:

> To a much greater extent than before, USAID will support business, academia, and civil society as key constituents responsible for creating the demand for economic reform needed to sustain Indonesia's economic growth (USAID, 2004: 44).

This resulted in a programmatic application in Indonesia that was, at times, considered antagonistic towards the state, which USAID apparently viewed as untrustworthy (not an entirely unreasonable standpoint, given that Indonesia ranked 122 out of 133 countries in Transparency International's Corruption Perception Index in 2003). This private sector oriented delivery approach was well suited to USAID's application of value chain industry interventions, which were embraced even more forthrightly in its subsequent strategy paper for Indonesia (USAID, 2009). The centrepiece programme of USAID's employment development programme has been the Agribusiness and Market Support Activity (AMARTA, 2006–11, Phase II, 2011–2016), which specifically adopts the use of value chain terminology: '[T]he project will utilize and strengthen the private sector-led agribusiness environment across the [coffee, cocoa and horticulture] value chains.' AMARTA facilitated value chain linkages through support packages to both producers' organizations and through a grant scheme paid directly to private sector actors. Within the cocoa sector, AMARTA built on a decade-long engagement with farmer training programmes in Sulawesi, but sought to deliver farmer support within the supply base of selected international cocoa trading companies (such as Olam and Armajaro, rather than through the industry-wide Cocoa Sustainability Partnership). With cocoa prices doubling between 2005 and 2008, amidst serious supply constraints affecting international cocoa buyers, AMARTA support for the establishment of up-country buying stations and farmer supply networks was understandably well-received by those industry actors partnering with the programme (Neubert, 2011).

The direct financial support provided to private sector actors as part of a value chain intervention, as occurred in the AMARTA programme, can be contentious. Following the 2004 Indian Ocean tsunami, for example, USAID 'partnered' with a US-based organization, the National Cooperative Business Association (NCBA), to establish a coffee processing plant and associated supplier networks in Aceh province (USAID, 2007). Development support (part of a US$10 million project) was channelled towards the coffee facility and associated producer base, drawing concern from existing industry actors that the programme was providing an unfair advantage to what was widely considered to be a US business interest. This activity involves the purported establishment of producer cooperatives as an integral institutional form, despite the reality that cooperatives – in the Indonesian coffee sector at least – are tightly embedded within, and frequently co-located with, private sector business operations (Neilson, 2008). Notwithstanding the alleged implications for unfair competition, this model of financially supporting the establishment of business entities responsible for sourcing agricultural products, applied previously by USAID in the East Timor coffee industry, has been identified as an 'excellent model' for future value chain activities (Neubert, 2011). The fractious relationship between the AMARTA programme and the Indonesian state, however, was a key reason for the premature cessation of the programme's second phase in early 2013.

AusAID and value chains in Indonesia

While AusAID's 2003 country strategy paper for Indonesia (Ausaid, 2003) does not explicitly refer to value chains, or to private sector led economic development, the 2008 Australia Indonesia Partnership (AIP) Country Strategy (Ausaid, 2008) is clearer. 'Sustainable growth and economic management' is the 'foundation of the AIP', within which rural growth is to be supported through providing 'value-added activities', improving the 'business-enabling environment', and through 'private-sector involvement'. Programmatically, these aspirations were to be achieved through AusAID's Smallholder Agricultural Development Initiative (SADI, 2006–10), which sought to 'build competitive advantage by improving the efficiency of ... supply chains from farmer groups/producer organizations to end-users'. SADI was designed as a 10-year initiative, but was ended after four years of implementation due to poor administrative coordination between its constituent sub-programmes. The proposal for its successor programme, the Australia Indonesia Partnership for Decentralisation – Rural Economic Development (AIPD–Rural, currently proposed for 2013–17), is also couched in terms of 'interventions along the value chain'.

SADI sought to build on, and more effectively integrate, three existing donor initiatives in Indonesia: the World Bank's Kecamatan Development Program (KDP, which was later adopted by the Government of Indonesia as the Program Nasional Pemberdayaan Masyarakat (PNPM)) as a locally-driven rural development activity; the IFC's PENSA programme, referred to as the 'lead firm model' within SADI; and the research programmes of the Australian Centre for International Agricultural Research (ACIAR).[3] Conflicting priorities, however, soon emerged within and amongst these implementing agencies. This was most notably the case between the IFC lead firm model, which was increasingly concerned with assisting IFC's larger investment partners, and the PNPM programme, which targeted poor communities, which then identified their own development priorities through a highly participatory process. Local development priorities in these communities rarely coincided with the commercial supply chain priorities of lead firms. For example, communities identifying coffee improvement as a development priority were frequently unable to satisfy the commercial requirements (due to prevailing environmental conditions or poor accessibility) of specialty coffee buyers partnering as lead firms. The rigid application of the lead firm model in SADI was believed to have reduced the responsiveness of the programme to local needs (Fargher and Konishi, 2010: iv). These differing priorities also reflect the distinction made by Humphrey and Navas-Alemán (2010) between 'lead firm' approaches and 'value chain linkage' activities, where the latter was considered more effective in targeting poor communities and achieving poverty reduction outcomes.

The implementation of SADI also highlighted another potential limitation of the value chain application in rural poverty alleviation, related to the realities of household livelihoods (Fargher and Konishi, 2010). Many rural households in Indonesia manage integrated farm systems with a considerable portfolio of farm-based and off-farm livelihood activities. They are rarely single commodity producers, such that commodity-specific value chain interventions will only impact a small component of their overall livelihood and may, therefore, have limited ability to contribute to broader poverty alleviation. Many farmers felt that an integrated system approach would have responded more effectively to their poverty and livelihood concerns. This concern was raised in the independent completion report for SADI (Fargher and Konishi, 2010: 17) and through ACIAR research funded by SADI (Neilson *et al.*, 2011). Indeed, the challenge of integrating a livelihoods approach within a global value chain framework has become a critical concern within the recent scholarly literature on value chains (for example, Challies and Murray (2011) and also Bolwig *et al.* (2010) in their attempt to integrate value chain models with poverty reduction).

CONCLUSION

If the widespread adoption of value chain discourse within development practice in a post-Washington Consensus world suggests a place for value chain theory in the newer development economics, then it is worth asking to what extent Fine's (2006: 17) accusation that other theories dependent on market imperfections – 'new trade theory', 'new growth theory' and 'social capital' – have been readily turned towards pro-market and minimalist state perspectives is equally applicable to value chain theory?

I raise the possibility that rather than heralding a victory for the inclusion of critical social science within mainstream policy-making circles, the adoption of a value chains for development discourse reflects the persistent ability of mainstream neo-classical economics, and the organizations that embody such thinking, to co-opt critical theory and perpetuate long-held commitments to neoliberal development approaches. As expressed by Hart (2001: 653), 'Even though the fortress walls [of the Washington Consensus] have been breached, there is still vigilant policing.' This claim is presented based on an analysis of, first, how development agencies have selectively interpreted the framework through strategy papers and, second, how the approach has been applied in specific development interventions, as presented here through a study of their application in Indonesia. Two aspects of this process are worth elaborating upon by way of conclusion.

Institutional settings are interpreted as a business enabling environment

The 'institutional settings' of the value chain have been widely interpreted as a 'business enabling environment' by development practitioners. Many GVC models tend to emphasize the role of international trade agreements and domestic regulatory settings (marketing boards and quasigovernmental producer associations) in determining chain governance, where politically-mediated institutions and chain governance are mutually constituted through reiterative processes (Neilson and Pritchard, 2009). The dominant USAID frameworks for a value chain approach (such as Kula, Downing and Field (2006:.12) and Campbell (2008)), however, substitute the institutional settings of the chain with the terminology of the Business Enabling Environment. This is similarly defined as the norms and customs, laws, regulations, policies, international trade agreements and public infrastructure that either facilitate or hinder the movement of a product or service along its value chain. USAID's Business Enabling Environment Program (BEEP), however, interprets this in a more ideologically-driven way, whereby the programme:

> promotes free market reforms to remove barriers to business creation and operation, freeing the individual from unnecessary government restraints on economic activity. (USAID, 2013)

By presenting the institutional framework of a GVC approach as a BEE, USAID and the World Bank have ensured adequate space within their value chain applications to pursue a policy reform agenda aligned with ideological commitments to a minimalist role for state intervention. In the Indonesian case, this has manifested as lobbying against the introduction of an export tax aimed at encouraging industrialization in the cocoa sector, for the easing of foreign investment restrictions for international trading companies, and support for privatized agricultural extension services. While for Kula *et al.* (2006), the BEE encompasses 'the array of laws and regulations that can hinder or expedite business and trade', there are clear differences, both semantically and in the political intent behind 'hindering business' and 'shaping power relations' as presented in many GCC/GVC scholarly accounts. There appears to be an urgent need for development applications to re-engage conceptually with some of the more nuanced institutionalist analyses of economic development emanating from the GCC/GVC literature (for example, Neilson and Pritchard (2009)).

The Indonesian development experience over recent decades has been characterized by pervasive political influences into the policy-making sphere, with the most recent emergence of a still relatively embryonic democratic, party-based political system. In contemporary Indonesia, it is meaningless to assume that policy-making and programme delivery can occur within a protected technocratic realm and, yet, the depoliticized nature of recent value chain applications tend to make this assumption. Publicly-voiced concerns over economic imperialism and a revival in resource-based industrialization policies (as expressed mostly clearly in GOI (2011)) require greater attention if the value chain framework is to meaningfully inform the economic development process. The lack of historical perspective and contingency is another uncomfortable feature of these more recent developmental applications, contrasting with the emphasis this was afforded in earlier GCC studies (such as Gereffi (1994)). Sensitivity towards the shifting end-markets for global value chains

(Kaplinsky, Terheggen and Tijaja, 2011; Gereffi, 2013, in press), as evident in the changing composition of Indonesian exports, is likely to present a different set of upgrading policy prescriptions than those currently advocated through value chain interventions in Indonesia, informed as they are by pre-existing global trade structures.

The role of lead firms as conduits of development assistance

In the Indonesian applications of value chain interventions, lead firms have emerged as strategic development partners. This tendency appears to reflect the ambiguity inherited from the diverse conceptual influences within the construction of value chain developmental discourse. Some donor agencies seamlessly conflate the supply chain management concerns of individual firms with public policy imperatives designed to deliver development benefits to otherwise impoverished chain participants. A number of the pre-project value chain analyses conducted in Indonesia would present a now widely used conceptual model of value chains borrowed from Porter (1998: 37). This visual model presents the value chain from the perspective of a business manager, with 'primary activities' along a lower axis, encompassing inbound logistics, operations, outbound logistics, marketing and sales, and service, and with 'support services' along an upper axis, including procurement, human resource management, technological development, and infrastructure. Working from this model, donor interventions into the value chain can easily confuse the 'supply chain' challenges of particular lead firms with the broader development priorities of target communities.

Under this lead firm model, the implementing agency frequently seeks out large, preferably multinational, firms as partners in the intervention, and then works with those firms in developing their supply chain back to the farm-gate (as particularly evident in the IFC and USAID examples from Indonesia). The potential implications of providing donor support to selected lead firms on local (unfair) competition dynamics are rarely considered in such value chain interventions and, yet, the needs of lead firms are frequently, and often unrealistically, conflated with the needs of target communities during initial design activities. In many instances, value chain approaches to development are being rolled out as institutional support systems that facilitate little more than the enhanced penetration of multinational capital into the economy and lives of the rural and urban poor. An implication of this is an implicit tendency to play down the importance of the power dynamics embedded within modes of chain governance and the role this has in shaping market relationships and upgrading prospects for chain participants in developing countries. This concern echoes the broader critique of the post-Washington Consensus presented by Öniş and Senses (2005), which highlights the continued protection and support of transnational companies in the world economy under the new consensus.

The related issues of competition and competitiveness then hint at a final observation of value chain interventions – that of exclusion. By its very nature, enhancing the competitiveness of firms or chains or even regions through upgrading processes will result in the creation of winners and losers and the reproduction of spatial unevenness. The interventions adopting a lead firm model in Indonesia were particularly susceptible to exacerbating local inequality by inevitably collaborating with farmer groups with heightened levels of capacity to satisfy the quality, process, traceability or financial requirements of the lead firm. This suggests a general lack of concern for broader systemic processes of uneven economic development within recent value chains for development applications.

The analysis in this paper suggests the need for a reinvigorated focus within the developmental applications of GVC frameworks on what were previously key tenets of the framework: the institutional settings of the chain and the developmental role of the state; processes of establishing and exerting power throughout the chain; and a concern for global-scale processes that shape processes of inclusion and exclusion for states, communities and individuals. Earlier GCC research stressed the contingent nature of development strategies – shaped by world economic conditions, national histories, resource endowments, institutions and culture – and so would suggest a need for greater caution when advocating a one-size-fits-all value chain approach to development. This is particularly used when the approach is used as a diagnostic tool to further ideologically-driven reform agendas. The earlier focus on industrialization as a development path, and the normative repositioning of actors and regions in 'core' sites of the chain, brings into question the developmental benefits of simply building stronger links between lead firms and poor farmers (who, it should be noted, have already been participating in global commodity chains for many years, albeit in a disadvantageous way). Critical examination, through detailed empirical studies, of the practices of donor interventions as the discursive practice of value chain developmentalism, offers an exciting, and as yet still relatively understudied, subject for analysis.

ACKNOWLEDGEMENTS

This paper draws on research conducted in Indonesia funded by the Australian Centre for International Agricultural Research (ACIAR). ACIAR's on-going financial support for this research is appreciated, as is the co-operation of development agencies such as AusAID, the International Finance Corporation and USAID. This paper was initially presented at the 'Value Chains, Production Networks, and the Geographies of Development' workshop held at the National University of Singapore, 1–2 December 2011. I would like to express my thanks to the University of Sydney and the National University of Singapore for jointly funding this workshop, and especially to Henry Yeung for hosting it. The paper benefitted enormously from discussion at the workshop and feedback from all the participants and, in particular, I acknowledge the specific assistance provided by Gary Gereffi and Tim Sturgeon. This paper was also presented at a *Cadenas de Valor* workshop at Universidad Nacional del Litoral (UNL) in Santa Fe, Argentina, in November 2012, and the helpful feedback provided by Jennifer Bair at that workshop is acknowledged. Fiona McKenzie at the University of Sydney provided valuable assistance in preparing the database of publications presented in Appendix A. The feedback and direction provided by the anonymous referees of *RIPE* were highly constructive in suggesting necessary revisions. I am, of course, fully responsible for all errors that still remain within this paper.

NOTES

1 The distinction between the terms, 'commodity chain' and 'value chain', used throughout this paper reflects either the terminology used by cited authors in their original texts, or connote clear associations, respectively, with a world-historical analytical approach and an applied developmental or business studies approach. When the distinction is less clear, I have tended to use 'value chain' due largely to the broader acceptance within the development practitioner community, which constitutes the focus of this paper. This decision, however, suggests a coherence of conceptual thought and intellectual continuity throughout the historical development of the 'value chains project' that is problematic. While the conceptual lineages within the literature are self-evident, this paper supports the generally unacknowledged conceptual cleavages between these two terms and the earlier world-system inspired commodity chain research agenda, as highlighted earlier in Bair (2005).

2 However, the earlier work of Bill Friedland (Friedland, Barton and Thomas, 1981; Friedland, 1984) had already established the closely aligned framework of 'commodity systems analysis' within the rural sociology literature.

3 The author's on-going research programme in the coffee and cocoa sectors in Indonesia is funded by ACIAR.

REFERENCES

ADB (2012a) *Country Partnership Strategy Indonesia 2012–2014*, Manila: Asian Development Bank.

ADB (2012b) *Support for Agricultural Value Chain Development, Evaluation Knowledge Study*, Manila: Asian Development Bank.

Altenburg, T. (2007) *Donor Approaches to Supporting Pro-poor Value Chains*, Cambridge Donor Committee for Enterprise Development.

AusAID (2003) *Indonesia Country Program Strategy from 2003*, Canberra: AusAID.

AusAID (2008) *Australia Indonesia Partnership (AIP) Country Strategy 2008–2013*, Canberra: AusAID.

Bair, J. (2005) 'Global Capitalism and Commodity Chains: Looking Back, Going Forward', *Competition and Change*, 9(2): 153–80.

Bair, J. (2009) 'Global Commodity Chains: Genealogy and Review', in Jennifer Bair (ed.) *Frontiers of Commodity Chain Research*, Stanford, CA: Stanford University Press, pp. 1–34.

Bolwig, S., Ponte, S., Du Toit, A., Riisgaard, L. and Halberg, N. (2010) 'Integrating Poverty and Environmental Concerns into Value-chain Analysis: A Conceptual Framework', *Development Policy Review*, 28(2): 173–94.

Burki, S.J. and Perry, G. (1998) *Beyond the Washington Consensus: Institutions Matter*, Washington, DC: World Bank Publications.

Campbell, R. (2008) The Value Chain Framework, USAID Briefing paper, <http://microlinks.kdid.org/library/value-chain-framework-briefing-paper> (accessed 23 January 2013).

Cardoso, F.H. and Faletto, E. (1979) *Dependency and Development in Latin America*, Berkeley, CA: University of California Press.

Challies, E.R. and Murray, W.E. (2011) 'The Interaction of Global Value Chains and Rural Livelihoods: The Case of Smallholder Raspberry Growers in Chile', *Journal of Agrarian Change*, 11(1): 29–59.

Cramer, C. (1999) 'Can Africa Industrialize by Processing Primary Commodities? The Case of Mozambican Cashew Nuts', *World Development*, 27(7): 1247–66.

Dunning, J.H. (1992) *Multinational Enterprises and the Global Economy*, London: Addison Wesley.

EASRD (2005) *Public Private Partnerships for Agriculture in Eastern Indonesia: A Comparative Study of the Beef Cattle and Cocoa Industries*, Technical Note 37874, East Asia Social and Rural Development unit (EASRD, World Bank), Jakarta: World Bank.

Easterly, W. (2001) *The Elusive Quest for Growth: Economists' Adventures and Misadventures in the Tropics*, Cambridge, MA: The MIT Press.

Embassy of Japan (2012) 'Data and Statistics – Official Development Assistance from Japan to Indonesia', www.id.emb-japan.go.jp/oda/en/datastat_01.htm (accessed 20 December 2012).

Fargher, J. and Konishi, Y. (2010) *Smallholder Agribusiness Development Initiative Independent Completion Report*, Jakarta: AusAID, www.ausaid.gov.au/Publications/Documents/sadi-icr.pdf (accessed 7 November, 2011).

FIAS (2007) *Moving toward Competitiveness: A Value Chain Approach*, Washington, DC: The Foreign Investment Advisory Service (FIAS) of The World Bank Group.

Fine, B. (2006) 'The New Development Economics', in K.S. Jomo and B. Fine (eds) *New Development Economics: After the Washington Consensus*, London: Zed Books, pp. 1–20.

Frank, A.G. (1969) *Latin America: Underdevelopment or Revolution: Essays on the Development of Underdevelopment and the Immediate Enemy*, Vol. 165, New York: Monthly Review Press.

Friedland, W.H. (1984) 'Commodity Systems Analysis: An Approach to the Sociology of Agriculture', in Harry K. Schwarzweller (ed.) *Research in Rural Sociology and Development: A Research Annual*, Greenwich, CT: JAI Press, pp. 221–35.

Friedland, W.H., Barton, A.E. and Thomas. R.J. (1981) *Manufacturing Green Gold: Capital, Labor, and Technology in the Lettuce Industry*, New York: Cambridge University Press.

Fröbel, F., Heinrichs, J. and Kreye, O. (1980) *The New International Division of Labour*, Cambridge: Cambridge University Press.

Furtado, C. (1970) *Economic Development of Latin America: Historical Background and Contemporary Problems*, Cambridge: Cambridge University Press.

Gereffi, G. (1983) *The Pharmaceutical Industry and Dependency in the Third World*, Princeton, NJ: Princeton University Press.

Gereffi, G. (1989) 'Rethinking Development Theory: Insights from East Asia and Latin America', *Sociological Forum*, 4(4): 505–33.

Gereffi, G. (1994) 'The Organization of Buyer-driven Global Commodity Chains: How U.S. Retailers Shape Overseas Production Networks', in G. Gereffi and M. Korzeniewicz (eds) *Commodity Chains and Global Capitalism*, Westport, CT: Praeger, pp. 95–122.

Gereffi, G. (1995) 'Global Production Systems and Third World Development', in B. Stallings (ed.) *Global Change, Regional Response: The New International Context of Development*, New York: Cambridge University Press, pp. 100–42.

Gereffi, G. (1999) 'International Trade and Industrial Upgrading in the Apparel Commodity Chain', *Journal of International Economics*, 48(1): 37–70.

Gereffi, G. (2013, in press) 'Global Value Chains in a Post-Washington Consensus World: Shifting Governance Structures, Trade Patterns and Development Prospects', *Review of International Political Economy*.

Gereffi, G., Humphrey, J., Kaplinsky, R. and Sturgeon, T. (2001) 'Introduction: Globalisation, Value Chains and Development', *IDS Bulletin*, 32(3): 1–8.

Gereffi, G. and Korzeniewicz, M. (1990) 'Commodity chains and footwear exports in the semiperiphery', in W. Martin (ed.), *Semiperipheral States in the World Economy*, Westport, CT: Greenwood Press, 45–68.

Gereffi, G. and Korzeniewicz, M. (eds) (1994) *Commodity Chains and Global Capitalism*, Westport, CT: Praeger.

Gibbon, P. (2001) 'Upgrading Primary Production: A Global Commodity Chain Approach', *World Development*, 29(2): 345–63.

GOI (2011) Masterplan for Acceleration and Expansion of Indonesia Economic Development, Coordinating Ministry for Economic Affairs, Government of Indonesia, Jakarta, www.depkeu.go.id (accessed 23 January 2013).

Hamilton, G. and Gereffi, G. (2009) 'Global Commodity Chains, Market Makers, and the Rise of Demand-responsive Economies', in J. Bair (ed.) *Frontiers of Commodity Chain Research*, Stanford, CA: Stanford University Press, 136–61.

Hart, G. (2001) 'Development Critiques in the 1990s: Culs de Sac and Promising Paths', *Progress in Human Geography*, 25(4): 649–58.

Henriksen, L.F., Riisgaard, L., Ponte, S., Hartwich, F. and Kormawa, P. (2010) *Agro-food Value Chain Interventions in Asia: A Review and Analysis of Case Studies*: Vienna: UNIDO.

Hess, M. and Coe, N. (2006) 'Making Connections: Global Production Networks, Standards, and Embeddedness in the Telecommunications Industry', *Environment and Planning A*, 38(7): 1205–27.

Hirschman, A. (1958) *The Strategy of Economic Development*, New Haven, CT: Yale University Press.

Hopkins, T. and Wallerstein, I. (1977) 'Patterns of Development of the Modern World-system', *Review*, 1(2): 11–145.

Hopkins, T. and Wallerstein, I. (1986) 'Commodity Chains in the World Economy Prior to 1800', *Review*, 10(1): 157–70.

Humphrey, J. (2005) *Shaping Value Chains for Development: Global Value Chains in Agribusiness*, Eschborn: Deutsche Gesellschaft für Technische Zusammenarbeit (GTZ).

Humphrey, J. and Navas- Alemán, L. (2010) 'Value Chains, Donor Interventions and Poverty Reduction: A Review of Donor Practice', IDS Research Report 63, Sussex: Institute for Development Studies.

Humphrey, J. and Oetero, A. (2000) *Strategies for Diversification and Adding Value to Food Exports: A Value Chain Approach*, Geneva: UNCTAD.

IDS Bulletin (2001) Issue 32(2): 1–136.

IEG (2008) *IFC in Indonesia: 1990–2006: An Independent Country Impact Review*, Washington, DC: Independent Evaluation Group, International Finance Corporation.

IEG (2011) *Assessing IFC's Poverty Focus and Results*, Washington, DC: Independent Evaluation Group, World Bank.

IFC (2012) *Ecom Coffee: Increasing Productivity of Smallholder Coffee Farmers*, IFC Publications, June, www.ifc.org (accessed 18 April, 2013).

Kaplinsky, R. (2000) 'Globalisation and Unequalisation: What Can Be Learned from Value Chain Analysis?' *Journal of Development Studies*, 37(2): 117–46.

Kaplinsky, R. and Morris, M. (2001) *Handbook for Value Chain Research*, Ottawa: IDRC.

Kaplinsky, R. and Readman, J. (2001) *Integrating SMEs in Global Value Chains: Towards Partnership for Development*, Vienna: UNIDO.

Kaplinsky, R., Terheggen, A. and Tijaja, J. (2011) 'China as a Final Market: The Gabon Timber and Thai Cassava Value Chains', *World Development*, 39(7): 1177–90.

Kula, O., Downing, J. and Field, M. (2006) *Globalization and the Small Firm: A Value Chain Approach to Economic Growth and Poverty Reduction*, AMAP BDS Knowledge and Practice microREPORT #42, Washington, DC: USAID.

Neilson, J. (2008) 'Global Private Regulation and Value-chain Restructuring in Indonesian Smallholder Coffee Systems', *World Development*, 36(9): 1607–22.

Neilson, J., Arifin, B., Fujita, Y. and Hartatri, D.F.S. (2011) 'Quality Upgrading in Specialty Coffee Chains and Smallholder Livelihoods in Eastern Indonesia: Opportunities and Challenges', Proceedings of the 23rd International Conference on Coffee Science, Bali, 3–8 October 2010, Bussigny: Association for Science and Information on Coffee, pp. 454–62.

Neilson, J. and Pritchard, B. (2009) *Value Chain Struggles: Institutions and Governance in the Plantation Districts of South India*, Oxford: Blackwell.

Neubert, D. (2011) *The Agribusiness and Market Support Activity (AMARTA): Final Evaluation*, Produced for review by USAID, Washington, D.C.

Öniş, Z. and Şenses, F. (2005) 'Rethinking the Emerging Post-Washington Consensus', *Development and Change*, 36(2): 263–90.

Perroux, F. (1955) 'Note sur la notion de pôle de croissance', *Economie appliquée*, 7(1–2): 307–20.

Pietrobelli, C. and Rabellotti, R. (2004) *Upgrading in Clusters and Value Chains in Latin America: The Role of Policies*, Washington, DC: Inter-American Development Bank.

Ponte, S. and Gibbon, P. (2005) 'Quality Standards, Conventions and the Governance of Global Value Chains', *Economy and Society*, 34(1): 1–31.

Porter, M.E. (1990) *The Competitive Advantage of Nations/Michael E. Porter*, London and New York: Macmillan.

Porter, M.E. (1998 [1985]) *Competitive Advantage: Creating and Sustaining Superior Performance*, New York: Free Press.

Rodrik, D. (1997) *Has Globalization Gone Too Far?*, Washington, DC: Institute of International Economics.

Rodrik, D. (1999) *The New Global Economy and Developing Countries: Making Openness Work*, Vol. 24, Washington, DC: Overseas Development Council.

Rodrik, D. (2006) 'Goodbye Washington Consensus, Hello Washington Confusion? A Review of the World Bank's Economic Growth in the 1990s: Learning from a Decade of Reform', *Journal of Economic literature*, 44(4): 973–87.

Schmitz, H. (1995) 'Collective Efficiency: Growth Path for Small-scale Industry', *The Journal of Development Studies*, 31(4): 529–66.

Schmitz, H. (ed.) (2004) Local Enterprises in the Global Economy: Issues of Governance and Upgrading, Cheltenham, Elgar.

Schmitz, H. (2005) *Value Chain Analysis for Policy-makers and Practitioners*, Geneva: ILO.

Springer-Heinze, A. (2007) ValueLinks Manual: The methodology of value chain promotion, GTZ, Eschborn.

Stamm, A. (2004) *Value Chains for Development Policy: Challenges for Trade Policy and the Promotion of Economic Development*, Concept Study, Eschborn: Deutsche Gesellschaft für Technische Zusammenarbeit (GTZ) GmbH.

Stamm, A. and von Drachenfels, C. (2011) *Value Chain Development: Approaches and Activities by Seven UN Agencies and Opportunities for Interagency Cooperation*, Geneva: ILO, http://www.ilo.org/empent/Publications/WCMS_170848/lang–en/index.htm (accessed 26 June, 2012).

Stiglitz, J. (1998) *More Instruments and Broader Goals: Moving Beyond the Washington Consensus*, 2nd Annual Wider Lecture, Helsinki: UNU-WIDER.

Sturgeon, T. (2009) 'From Commodity Chains to Value Chains: Interdisciplinary Theory Building in an Age of Globalization', in Jennifer Bair (ed.) *Frontiers of Commodity Chain Research*, Stanford, CA: Stanford University Press, pp. 110–35.

UNCTAD (2004) *List of Publications on Foreign Direct Investment and Transnational Corporations (1973–2003)*, New York and Geneva: United Nations, http://archive.unctad.org/en/docs/ite20041_en.pdf (accessed 1 June 2012).

USAID (2004) *Strengthening a Moderate, Stable and Productive Indonesia: USAID Strategic Plan for Indonesia 2004–2008*, Jakarta: USAID.

USAID (2007) *Gala Celebrates Revitalized Coffee Industry in Gayo Highlands*, Press Release, 12 February, http://jakarta.usembassy.gov/pr_02122007.html (accessed 3 May, 2007).

USAID (2009) *A Partnership for Prosperity: USAID Strategy Indonesia 2009–2014*. Jakarta: USAID.

USAID (2013) *Welcome to USAID Business Enabling Environment Program*, http://www.usaidbeep.org/ (accessed 23 January 2013)

Vernon, R. (1971) *Sovereignty at Bay: The Multinational Spread of U.S. Enterprises*, New York: Basic Books.

Wade, R. (1990) 'Industrial Policy in East Asia: Does It Lead or Follow the Market?', in G. Gereffi and D.L. Wyman (eds) *Manufacturing Miracles: Paths of Industrialisation in Latin America and East Asia*, Princeton, NJ: Princeton University Press, pp. 231–66.

Wallerstein, I. (2004) 'World-systems Analysis', in George Modelski (ed.) *World System History, in Encyclopedia of Life Support Systems (EOLSS)*, developed under the auspices of UNESCO, Oxford: EOLSS Publishers, http://www.eolss.net (accessed 19 October, 2011).

World Bank (1993) *East Asian Miracle: Economic Growth and Public Policy*, Washington, DC: World Bank.

World Bank (2001) 'Entering the 21st Century: The Changing Development Landscape', *World Development Report 1999/2000*, Washington, DC: World Bank.

World Bank (2002) 'Building Institutions for Markets', *World Development Report 2000/2001*, Washington, DC: World Bank.

World Bank (2003) *Indonesia – Country Assistance Strategy*, Washington, DC: World Bank.
World Bank (2005) 'Farmer Empowerment through Agricultural Technology and Information Project Information Document (PID) Concept Stage', Report No. AB478. Washington D.C.: World Bank.
World Bank (2008) *Investing in Indonesia's Institutions: Country Partnership Strategy FY09–12*, Washington, DC: World Bank.
World Bank (2012a) *World Development Indicators*, http://data.worldbank.org/data-catalog/world-development-indicators (accessed November 9, 2012).
World Bank (2012b) *Country Lending Summaries – Indonesia*, http://web.worldbank.org (accessed 20 December 2012).

APPENDIX A Strategy papers published by international development agencies with a principal 'value chains' focus

	Year	Publishing agency	Report title	Author(s)	Academic credit for the VC approach?	Google Scholar citations (December 2012)
1	2000	UNCTAD	*Strategies for Diversification and Adding Value to Food Exports: A Value Chain Perspective*	J. Humphrey & A. Oetero	Porter (1990); Gerrefi (1994);	21
2	2001	IDRC	*Handbook for Value Chain Research*	R. Kaplinsky & M. Morris	Porter (1998)	885
3	2001	UNIDO	*Integrating SMEs in Global Value Chains: Towards Partnership for Development*	R. Kaplinsky & J. Readman	Not attributed	58
4	2004	GTZ	*Value Chains for Development Policy: Challenges for Trade Policy and the Promotion of Economic Development*	A. Stamm	Porter (1998)	16
5	2004	IADB	'Upgrading in Clusters and Value Chains in Latin America: The Role of Policies'	C. Pietrobelli & R. Rabellotti	Gereffi (1999); Kaplinsky and Readman (2001)	167
6	2004	UNIDO	*Inserting Local Industries into Global Value Chains and Global Production Networks: Opportunities and Challenges for Upgrading with a focus on Asia.*	O. Memedovic	Not attributed	15
7	2005	GTZ	*Shaping Value Chains for Development: Global Value Chains in Agribusiness*	J. Humphrey.	Gereffi and Korzeniewicz (1990); Gereffi (1994)	90
8	2005	ILO	*Value Chain Analysis for Policy-makers and Practitioners*	H. Schmitz	Schmitz (2004)	77
9	2005	USAID	*Competitive Strategies for Agriculture-related MSES: From Seeds to Supermarket Shelves*	C. Steen, R. Magnani & L. Goldmark	Refers to Porter, but no reference given until later, refers to Porter (1998)	2

10	2005	USAID	*Trade, Micro and Small Enterprises, and Global Value Chains: microREPORT #25*	L. Goldmark & T. Barber	Not attributed	2
11	2006	SDC	*Compilation of Insights of the Online Debate Value Chains in Rural Development (VCRD)*	D. Roduner & A. Gerrits	Not attributed	4
12	2006	SNV	*Using the Value Chain Approach for Pro-poor Development: Experiences from SNV in Asia*	E. Baan & N. Janssen	Not attributed	0
13	2006	USAID	*Globalization and the Small Firm: A Value Chain Approach to Economic Growth and Poverty Reduction*	O. Kula, J. Downing & M. Field	Not attributed	15
14	2007	GTZ	*ValueLinks: The Methodology of Value Chain Promotion*	*Not available*	Not attributed	
15	2007	GTZ	*Pro-poor Services in Value Chain Promotion*	Braun (editor)	Springer-Heinze (2007)	0
16	2007	SDC	*Donor Interventions in Value Chain Development*	D. Roduner	Not attributed	11
17	2007	USAID	*Value Chain Program Design: Promoting Market-based Solutions for MSME and Industry Competitiveness*	F. Lusby & H. Panliburton	Not attributed	7
18	2007	World Bank/FIAS	*Moving Toward Competitiveness: A Value Chain Approach*	A team led by U. Subramanian	Porter (1998); Gereffi (1994)	3

(Continued on next page)

APPENDIX A Strategy papers published by international development agencies with a principal 'value chains' focus *(Continued)*

	Year	Publishing agency	Report title	Author(s)	Academic credit for the VC approach?	Google Scholar citations (December 2012)
19	2008	DFID/MP4	*Making Value Chains Work Better for the Poor: A Toolbook for Practitioners of Value Chain Analysis (Version 2)*	M. van den Berg *et al.*	Porter (1998); Kaplinsky (2000); Gereffi (1994, 1999, 2005); Gereffi and Korzeniewicz (1994)	5
20	2009	ILO	*Value Chain Development for Decent Work: A Guide for Development Practitioners, Government and Private Sector Initiatives*	M.L. Herr & T.J. Muzira	Kaplinsky (2004)	8
21	2009	ODI	*Trading Up: How a Value Chain Approach Can Benefit the Rural Poor*	J. Mitchell, J. Keane & C. Coles	Kaplinsky and Morris (2001)	15
22	2009	UNIDO	*Value Chain Diagnostics for Industrial Development: Building Blocks for a Holistic and Rapid Analytical Tool*	F. Hartwich & P. Kormawa	Porter (1985); Gereffi (1994, 2001, 2003)	0
23	2009	USAID	*Gender and Pro-poor Value Chain Analysis: Insights from the Gate Project Methodology and Case Studies*	S. Gammage, C. Manfre & K. Cook	Kaplinsky (2000)	3
24	2010	World Bank	*Building Competitiveness in Africa's Agriculture: A Guide to Value Chain Concepts and Applications*	C.M. Webber & P. Labaste	Kaplinsky and Morris (2001)	13
25	2011	ILO	*ILO Value Chain Development Portfolio Analysis: A Stocktaking of ILO Value Chain Related Activities*	D. Núñez & M. Sievers	Gereffi and Korzeniewicz (1994)	0
26	2011	ILO	*ILO Value Chain Development: Approaches and Activities by Seven UN Agencies and Opportunities for Interagency Cooperation*	A. Stamm & C. von Drachenfels	Gereffi and Korzeniewicz (1994)	1
27	2011	FAO	*Gender and Agricultural Value Chains: A Review of Current Knowledge and Practice and Their Policy Implications*	C. Coles & J. Mitchell	Not Attributed	5

Governing the market in a globalizing era: Developmental states, global production networks and inter-firm dynamics in East Asia

Henry Wai-chung Yeung

National University of Singapore, Singapore

ABSTRACT

This paper focuses on the changing governance of economic development in a globalizing era in relation to the dynamics of global value chains and global production networks. Based on recent development in such East Asian economies as South Korea, Taiwan and Singapore, I examine how, since the 1990s, the embedded relation between one variant of state institutions, known as the developmental state, and national firms, well integrated into global chains and networks spanning different territories and regions, has evolved. Because of the deepening strategic coupling of these national firms with lead firms in global industries, the developmental state's attempt to govern the market and to steer industrial transformation through direct policy interventions has become increasingly difficult and problematic. Through this process of strategic coupling, national firms have been gradually disembedded from state apparatuses and re-embedded in different global production networks that are governed by competitive inter-firm dynamics. While the state in these East Asian economies has actively repositioned its role in this changing governance, it can no longer be conceived as the dominant actor in steering domestic firms and industrial transformation. The developmental trajectory of these national economies becomes equally, if not more, dependent on the successful articulation of their domestic firms in global production networks spearheaded by lead firms. In short, inter-firm dynamics in global production networks tend to trump state-led initiatives as one of the most critical conditions for economic development. This paper theorizes further this significant role of global value chains and global production networks in the changing international political economy of development.

INTRODUCTION

After several decades of successful state-led industrialization, the three East Asian 'tiger' economies of South Korea, Taiwan and Singapore have produced a large number of highly competitive national firms in different global industries. From their often humble origin as small-scale and low-tech establishments, some of them have even emerged as the dominant global players in their respective industries. By the early 2010s, these multibillion-dollar East Asian firms had dwarfed their siblings in the Global South and outpaced their competitors in advanced industrialized economies. In 2011, South Korea's Samsung Electronics had sales of US$149 billion and market capitalization of US$118 billion.[1] Hyundai Motor was about half of Samsung Electronics in sales and one-third in market capitalization. Taiwan's largest provider of electronics manufacturing services, Hon Hai Precision (known as Foxconn Technology in China), had sales of US$117 billion and market capitalization of US$37 billion, whereas Quanta Computer, Acer Inc. and Taiwan Semiconductor Manufacturing (TSMC) achieved, respectively, sales of US$37 billion, US$16 billion and US$14 billion. These four Taiwanese firms are global market leaders in contract manufacturing, brand name computers and semiconductor foundry services. Singapore's two world-leading offshore oil-rig builders, Keppel Corp. and Sembcorp Industries, had sales of US$8.2 billion and US$7.4 billion, respectively. Given their relatively small domestic markets, these leading East Asian firms have succeeded in today's global industries, not just in terms of their enormous size measured in sales or assets in their home economies, but, more importantly, they have become world leaders in their respective market segments and industries that are highly *globalized* today.

For over two decades in the political economy studies of development, this anomaly of globally dominant firms emerging from relatively modest latecomer economies in East Asia has been accounted for by a particular variant of state institutions – the developmental state. Widely considered a necessary factor for understanding industrial transformation in these East Asian economies, the strategic role of the developmental state seems to have fallen short of accounting for the unprecedented success of the above leading East Asian firms in today's highly globalized industries, such as information and communications technology (ICT), automobiles and shipbuilding. This explanatory anomaly is attributed primarily to the central analytical focus of these earlier studies of East Asian development on state capacity and their variations across different political economies. In this enormous literature, state types and capacities, as an independent variable, are used to explain the pace and pattern of industrialization and, more broadly, economic development (e.g., Amsden, 1989; Wade, 1990; Evans, 1995; Kohli, 2004). In the earlier historical periods of this model of state-led development, the growth and evolution of domestic firms tends to be viewed as *outcomes* of state action in selecting 'national champions' and focusing on export-oriented industries. Hobday (2001: 25) is quite right to argue that 'because of the dominance of this debate, there are few studies which derive "bottom-up" policy conclusions from firm-level studies. The activities and strategies of firms in engaging with international production networks cannot be properly accounted for within theories of the developmental state, as latecomer firm behaviour tends to be treated (usually implicitly) as an automatic response to policy and economic circumstances, rather than as a shaping influence in its own right.' By the same token, the more recent and successful articulation of these national firms into global production networks spearheaded by global lead firms is still commonly viewed from this statist perspective.[2] These 'revisionist' scholars argue that state initiatives such as active industrial policy and financial support have enabled these national champions to venture into and compete successfully in the global economy. Even though the state in these three East Asian economies has been undergoing significant structural and institutional transformations at the same time, these neo-statist scholars continue to argue for the significant or even central role of the developmental state in governing the market in today's globalizing world economy.

This statist approach to the globalization of East Asian firms and their home economies, however, has underestimated the complex and dynamic evolutionary nature of state-firm relations within the changing context of economic globalization.[3] In this conceptual paper, I aim to demonstrate how the emergence of globally significant East Asian firms cannot be explained solely by state-led initiatives; rather, we need to pay as much analytical attention to the dynamic process through which these East Asian firms articulate into global production networks, defined as an inter-firm organizational nexus of interconnected functions and operations through which goods and services are produced, distributed and consumed in different territories and regions in the global economy. Here, I develop the concept of 'strategic coupling' to argue for a firm-oriented approach as a revision to the dominant state-centric view of industrial transformation and economic development in these East Asian economies. By using the word 'strategic', I afford greater analytical significance to firm-specific strategies in explaining evolutionary state-firm relations and industrial transformation in these economies. In using 'coupling', I refer to the dynamic processes through which national firms decouple partially or completely from their domestic political-economic structures – developmental states or otherwise – over time *and* re-couple with lead firms in global production networks. This analytical approach, broadly known as the global production networks framework, is particularly germane in the recent literature in international political economy.[4] It calls for a revision of the developmental state thesis and the consideration of *more* independent variables that incorporate both micro-firm-specific activities and macro-political economy (as in the developmental state approach). Adding to this micro-macro link is the changing context of the global economy – the emergence of new forms of economic organization and governance such as global production networks and global value chains. This paper thus echoes Gereffi's (2013) call for acknowledging multiple governance structures – international and domestic, public and private, network-based and civic – that link together different territories and economies of the global economy.

As a contribution to the growing literature on the *international* political economy of development, I argue for placing at the centre of our analysis of industrial transformation these new inter-firm dynamics among domestic firms and lead firms in global production networks. In her more recent book, the late Alice Amsden (2007: 153) seemed to have recognized the importance of these East Asian national firms in the global economy, although she did not recast her developmental state ideas to accommodate this new phenomenon:

> National firms in Asia grew brick by brick, machinery supplier by machinery supplier, subsidy by subsidy, entrepreneurial decision by entrepreneurial decision. The creation of professionally managed, family-owned firms, with an entrepreneurial dynamo on top, was probably the hardest step to make in modern economic development, and became the joint effort between business and government. Only with nationally owned firms was globalization possible in the form of outward foreign investment. Thus were born fresh competitors for the multinational Cadillacs of this world.

My argument is situated in the changing governance of economic development since the 1990s in these East Asian economies. Because of the deepening strategic coupling of these national firms with lead firms in global production networks, the developmental state's attempt to govern the market and to steer industrial transformation through direct policy interventions has become increasingly difficult and problematic. This process of strategic coupling has led to an evolutionary change in state-firm relations from one of structural dependence in the early phase of industrialization to increasing autonomy and independence in recent decades, as these national firms participate actively in globalization through their firm-specific integration into different global production networks. Here, I see globalization as a set of tendencies providing 'external shocks' in the selection environment that compels states and firms to reposition themselves, not just internally within their domestic political economies, but, more importantly, also externally in the much more open and competitive global economy of the 21st century. In their reassessment of the developmental state theory, Underhill and Zhang (2005: 53) have indeed anticipated this dynamic shift and linked the rise of East Asian firms to the changing selection environment in an era of globalization:

> The 1980s and 1990s witnessed dramatic changes in the state-market ensemble of industrial governance in East Asia. The sustained process of economic transformation increased the weight of private business in aggregate economic activity. In parallel with their increased structural power, private-sector actors were able to enhance their organizational resources and effectively employ these resources for economic and political purposes. The increasing integration of the national economy with the international financial and trade systems only served to reinforce the position of private industrialists as crucial economic agents and deepened the dependence of the state upon them for national development in an era of globalization.

One important caveat is necessary here. My argument for the evolutionary state-firm relations in these East Asian economies does not imply a zero-sum relationship in which state power declines *because of* the rise of national firms. Instead, I argue that the strategic coupling of these national firms in global production networks cannot be exclusively explained by state power. Coincidentally, during this same historical period of strategic coupling, starting in the late 1980s, the developmental state itself underwent significant political transformations that led to its relative decline in internal cohesiveness and bureaucratic rationality. The two processes have occurred concurrently, but due to different dynamics at work: strategic coupling of national firms in relation to changing inter-firm dynamics in global production networks, and transformation in state roles in response to domestic political and economic liberalization. While the state in these East Asian economies has actively repositioned its role in this changing governance, it can no longer be conceived as the dominant actor in steering domestic industrial transformation. The developmental trajectory of these national economies becomes equally, if not more, dependent on the successful articulation of their domestic firms in global production networks spearheaded by lead firms. In short, inter-firm dynamics in global production networks tend to trump state-led initiatives as one of the most critical conditions for economic development.[5]

The paper is organized into five sections. The next section revisits the developmental state debate in order to situate East Asian development historically within the changing dynamics of economic globalization. This brief critical review points to the historical specificity in which the embeddedness of East Asian firms in their home states should be understood. In other words, the embedded state-firm relations in East Asia should be viewed as a historical construct, rather than a permanent fixture; it is, therefore, subject to change and adjustments in an era of accelerated globalization. The next two sections proceed with a theoretically informed analysis of the changing dynamics of globalization through which East Asian firms have emerged to become dominant players in global industries. Beginning with a re-evaluation of Evans' (1995) concept of 'embedded autonomy', section three explains the gradual unravelling of the state-led model of industrialization since the late 1980s in the three economies. The penultimate section draws important insights from the global production networks perspective to analyse the strategic disembedding of East Asian firms from state governance and their re-embedding processes in inter-firm dynamics. Some important implications for industrial policy and economic governance are offered in the concluding section.

GOVERNING THE MARKET: THE DEVELOPMENTAL STATE REVISITED

In many ways, the meteoric rise of many East Asian firms described at the beginning of this paper would not have happened without the developmental state – some of them such as TSMC, Keppel and Sembcorp were former state-owned enterprises that were the cornerstone of the developmental state's industrialization programme. Revisiting developmental state literature, therefore, enables a more historically grounded understanding of the rise of these national firms. It also prevents us from suffering from what Woo-Cumings (1999a: 2–3) calls the 'presentism of social science accounts and the prescriptive, future-oriented nature of policy studies... [that] tended to peak when Japan and other East Asian economies did well, and then to fall when they were perceived to have slid into the doldrums – as in the early 1990s or in the aftermath of the "financial crisis" of 1997–98. In other words, a nasty case of attention deficit disorder has plagued a coherent account that would link past with present, yielding a lamentable misunderstanding of what the whole enterprise of the "developmental state" was about.'[6] Based on the successful experience of the state in guiding economic development in Japan and, later, South Korea, Taiwan and Singapore, leading proponents of the developmental state such as Johnson (1982, 1995), Deyo (1987), White (1988), Amsden (1989, 2001), Haggard (1990), Wade (1990), Woo (1991), Evans (1995), Woo-Cumings (1999b) and Kohli (2004) have consistently argued that deliberate state interventions via active industrial policy and selective financial allocation have enabled 'national champions' to overcome their latecomer disadvantages and to achieve economies of scale in domestic and international competition. Instead of pursuing market-based price mechanisms, the developmental state has intentionally distorted the market by, as Amsden (1989: 13–4, 2007: 87) famously termed it, 'getting the prices wrong' through its highly selective industrial and financial policies. In this sense, the developmental state can be seen as 'governing the market' (Wade, 1990). With hindsight, this statist approach has provided very important insights into the unique pathways to industrialization and economic growth in East Asian economies; it has adequately explained the institutional legacies of some leading East Asian firms. This intellectual achievement is particularly notable in light of the dominance of the neoclassical and dependency schools of economic development prior to the onset of the developmental state theory in the early 1980s (see a recent review in Stubbs, 2009; Hayashi, 2010).

Given these well-known attributes of the developmental state in Japan and the three East Asian 'tiger' economies, how then did the developmental state go about steering economic development and governing the market? One of the most powerful policy instruments of the developmental state must be its highly interventionist and yet controversial *industrial policy* – the deliberate choice of developing specific industries initially via import-substitution programmes and later through export promotion. This blunt policy instrument was widely practised in Japan and all three East Asian economies against the then prevailing economic orthodoxy of market liberalization and price-based competition. If anything, the developmental state deliberately 'got the prices wrong' by offering cheap credit and other subsidies and incentives to induce private entrepreneurs to participate in this state-led industrialization programme. In return, these entrepreneurs were subject to very stringent performance and standards monitoring by state agencies. Amsden (1989: 94, also 2001) thus argues that '[w]hat lay behind successful postwar industrialization was a monitored system of controls on subsidies. Neither import substitution nor export-led growth was a free-for-all. In many cases, especially that of Korea and Taiwan, exporting was made a condition for domestic protection.' If these entrepreneurs were not forthcoming or capable enough, the state took on the role of entrepreneur and readily stepped in to establish state-owned enterprises that subsequently socialized the market or the industry in the hands of the public sector.

Now that we know a great deal more about the central role of the developmental state in governing the market and industrialization in these East Asian economies during much of the 1960s–1980s period, does the developmental state theory inform us much about the increasingly complex articulation of these national economies into the global economy since the late 1980s and the early 1990s, when economic globalization began to take shape in East Asia? The answer to this question is an important one because there are two interrelated issues at stake here – one concerning the epistemology of state-centrism and the other relating to the empirical realm of changing state-firm relations. First, the primacy of the state as *the* analytical lens in the developmental state theory has compelled most scholars in this genre to focus almost exclusively on the *domestic* nature of state-firm relations. In this theory, private and public firms are analytically important only insofar as they matter to the state's grand strategy of industrialization and economic growth; the former has, therefore, become the latter's 'objects of desire', very much akin to the pawns (firms) in the hands of skilful grandmasters (states) vying for world chess championships.[7] As argued by Boyd and Ngo (2005: 9), this state-centric approach to East Asian industrialization has put too much analytical weight on the state as an independent variable explaining economic growth, the dependent variable. The capitalist firm has mostly dropped out of the analytical theorem of the developmental state. Reflecting on his 1990 classic, *Governing the Market*, Wade (2003: xvii) wrote in the paperback edition, 'Missing, though, is analysis of the external economies of human capital that are a major source of increasing returns to production in Taiwan and other East Asian countries – microanalysis of firm capabilities and corporate governance, and mesoanalysis of interfirm input-output networks, factor markets, and tacit knowledge.' In fact, this auto-critique can also be found in his earlier work with White (1988).

> What none of the chapters on Taiwan and South Korea say much about is the basis of state power, the way it is organized and the micro principles based on which officials make allocation decisions. Still less do they talk about the organizational arrangements that coordinate activities within business firms, and those that link them to government. These are exceedingly important questions (White and Wade, 1988: 12).

I argue that it is precisely these missing *micro-* and *meso*-elements of national firms and their production networks that have since the 1990s come to the forefront of evolutionary change in the development trajectories of East Asian economies. This dynamic change requires a revision to and a reorientation of the developmental state approach – a revision of its claim of strong state influence on national firms and a reorientation of its analytical focus away from state policies and capacities to national firms and other non-state institutions – known in Amsden's (1989: 8–9, emphasis omitted) work as 'the agent of expansion in all late-industrializing countries' *below* the level of the state. To Berger and Lester (2005: xviii), this (re)focus on firms as capitalist actors in the study of East Asian industrialization is important:

> . . . if we start from firms understood as actors with legacies built up out of previous experiences and strongly shaped by the particular societies in which they were born, if we conceive these legacies as resources or lenses – resources for developing new strategies and implementations, lenses for identifying familiar and new aspects of problems and seeing novel options – then we are likely to discover a far greater diversity in the behaviors of firms than any that we might have deduced from their contexts.

Second, if capitalist national firms are indeed important enough now and should be *more* important in the study of the changing position of these East Asian economies in the global economy today, we are immediately confronted with the thorny empirical issue of how these East Asian firms relate to competitive dynamics in global industries. Is it still the developmental state at home and/or new inter-firm relations that are critical to the articulation of these East Asian firms into global production networks? Before I attempt to unpack these changing dynamics of state-firm relations, let me briefly probe further into the analysis of national firms in the developmental state literature. While Johnson's (1982) original contribution focuses primarily on one particular state institution in Japan, the Ministry of International Trade and Industry, the national firm does get some attention from the subsequent protagonists of the theory. Cognizant of the shop-floor level operationalization of state industrialization policies, Amsden (1989: 112, italics in original) notes in her *Asia's Next Giant*, 'The translation of high growth rates of output into high growth rates of productivity depends on what happens *inside the unit of production*. Closing the loop between growth and productivity, therefore, involves an analytical shift, a change in the center of gravity from the state to the other key institution of industrialization, the firm.' However, even if the capitalist firm is sometimes counted and analysed in the developmental state literature, it tends to be read off from the state's policy regimes. Amsden (2001: 193, italics in original), thus, describes the essence of national firms in the Global South, including those from the three East Asian economies, as by-products of the developmental state:

> National leaders in 'the rest', private or public, all shared one characteristic: they tended to be a product of government promotion ('targeting'). In the case of the private leader, it tended to be either an affiliate of a *diversified business group* with a history of government patronage, or a *'state spin-off'*.

To sum up, the developmental state theory can no longer fully account for the dynamic articulation of East Asian economies into the global economy. Its excessive focus on state initiatives and capacities in early industrialization has rendered itself 'locked-into' a conceptual path dependency premised on seeing the economy and its key agents (firms) through the state and its political choice. Its ability to provide insights into the rise of East Asian firms in the global economy becomes handicapped by its analytical baggage of state-centrism. To Jayasuriya (2005: 386), this statist view of East Asian development 'now shows all the hallmarks of a degenerating research programme that is no longer capable of setting out an interesting or relevant agenda'. His view is echoed by Beeson (2006: 451), who argues that 'the relative long-term decline of the state may be inevitable and not a bad thing'. Similarly, O'Riain (2004: 27) argues for understanding the constitutive role of globalization in state-driven development because 'under the globalization project, transnational firms, networks and flows of money, information, and resources have deeply penetrated the most successful localities and nations – the global is no longer a context for developmental strategies but rather a constitutive element of them'.

FROM EMBEDDED AUTONOMY TO GLOBAL CHAINS AND NETWORKS

With hindsight, it is clear that the developmental state literature has focused on the earlier historical period of late industrialization in East Asian economies, when economic globalization was still in its embryonic phase and industrial production in most sectors remained vertically integrated within national boundaries. The then weak integration of these East Asian economies into the emerging global economy allowed for large-scale state-led development initiatives to induce private capital to enter into new industries and to discipline their performance in export markets. In this earlier period up to the late 1980s, the state was able to govern the market by steering the developmental trajectory of national firms through market protection, cheap credits and technology transfer. Economic governance was about rapid catching up with advanced industrialized economies in terms of export production volumes and technological knowhow. A developmental state can be most efficacious in this mode of industrial transformation because of its capacity to provide the necessary capital and centralized industrial planning to effect collective action at the national level.

This state-led industrialization is necessarily predicated on the bureaucratic rationality and internal coherence of the state, without which the state governance of collective action would not be possible and successful industrial transformation would not occur. Put in a more conceptual way, Evans (1995) argues that 'embedded autonomy' is a necessary condition for the efficacy of the developmental state in carrying out its developmental roles as either 'midwifery' or 'husbandry' of domestic industries. To him, the state must enjoy some independence and autonomy from the domestic élites, particularly those in business and industries, in order for it to avoid rent-seeking behaviour by these élites and to exercise its institutional capacity for promoting economic development. This insulation of the state from economic actors and other interest groups, however, needs to be grounded in an embedded relationship between the autonomous state and domestic business élites because the former plans its industrial policies in consultation with the latter and implements such policies with the cooperation of the intended recipients. The success of industrial transformation is, therefore, dependent on both autonomy and capacity of state institutions such that embedded autonomy 'provides the underlying structural basis for successful state involvement in industrial transformation' (Evans, 1995: 12). This structural conception of the developmental state can be quite static, as it does not really explain the dynamics of bureaucratic rationality or consider the evolutionary relationships between the developmental state and national firms over time. In particular, national firms are inadvertently conceived as passive actors in this structurally determined state-market governance model.

Starting in the late 1980s, three important dynamics began to unravel this state-led model of industrialization in the three East Asian economies. As argued by Wong (2011: 95), 'the state is increasingly incapable of directly shaping large firm behavior. By the 1990s, the balance of power and the nature of the relationship between the state and industry had been reversed, and the state no longer commanded industry as it had during the postwar developmental stat period. The development state's ability to steer industry had waned.' First, the state itself underwent significant internal transformations since the early phase of industrialization. In the 1980s, South Korea and Taiwan experienced major political upheavals and regime change. Democratization in the late 1980s began to loosen the strong grip of the developmental state in steering domestic economic governance. In South Korea, inter-agency conflicts and rivalries began to reduce the internal cohesiveness of the developmental state and political freedom led to reduced insulation of state bureaucrats from private interests (Chibber, 2002; Kang, 2002). In the automobile sector, Ravenhill (2003) shows evidence of the state's failure to rationalize different *chaebol* in the nascent industry between 1962 and the 1990s. In Taiwan, similar factionalism and intrastate rivalry could be observed in the leading state bureaucracy in charge of industrial planning and economic development (Ngo, 2005; Chu, 2007; Greene, 2008). Wu (2005) argues that the penetration of nationalist politics into the bureaucracy further subordinated economic policies to political manoeuvre and economic policymaking agencies to politicians, which, in turn, produced paralysing conflicts and reduced dramatically bureaucratic independence and monitoring capabilities. In Singapore, while the state achieved fairly consistent internal coherence and bureaucratic rationality between the 1960s and the 1980s, a significant challenge to its embedded autonomy was the rather unclear demarcation of the boundary between the ruling party and the state bureaucracy, and between the state and the private sector (Rodan, 1989; Hamilton-Hart, 2000; Worthington, 2003). The domination of foreign investment in Singapore's industrialization also reduced the state's autonomy in industrial planning and policy implementation.

Second, the 'market' was transformed simultaneously with the advent of late industrialization in these East Asian economies. At the beginning of their industrialization during the 1960s, the domestic market did not really exist and the primordial goal of the developmental state was exports. When import substitution was practised in South Korea and Taiwan, it targeted heavy and chemical industries that fed into the export-oriented light industries. By the late 1980s, the successful development of these industries led to the much greater integration of domestic industries into global markets. At the same time, many of these industries experienced vertical disintegration and production fragmentation on a global scale due to rapid technological change and changing business strategies and organizational processes (Piore and Sabel, 1984; Gereffi, 2005; Dicken, 2011). This changing organization of industrial production represented an important global shift through which national markets were increasingly integrated into global production networks. In short, the very market that had been governed by the developmental state was no longer confined to national boundaries. Instead, these national markets were incorporated into different value chains and production networks coordinated by global lead firms and spanning different national and regional economies.

The third dynamic, and most important in the context of this paper, was the 'graduation' of national firms from the tutelage of the developmental state. As key beneficiaries of state-led industrialization, these East Asian firms had accumulated significant dynamic capabilities through firm-specific assets and organizational processes such as learning from production for exports, acquiring technologies in the international markets, building firm-specific capabilities through reverse 'brain drain' and intensifying in-house R&D activity. The changing domestic and international financial markets also allowed these national firms to gain much better access to capital and thereby to cut the 'umbilical cord', as coined by Woo (1991: 66), which had previously nurtured them. As these national firms had benefited from favourable state policies, they grew rapidly in the domestic economy and performed well in the export markets. Having developed firm-specific dynamic capabilities, these East Asian firms became less dependent on their developmental state 'parents'.

Taken together, the developmental role of the state was challenged by this market shift from domestic economies towards global production networks. Governing the market in this globalizing era began to give way to economic governance through inter-firm dynamics in these global production networks. What does this evolutionary change leave us with when it comes to understanding the international political economy of East Asian development? The classic works on the developmental state have not dealt with this question because of their primary focus on the nurturing or directive role of the developmental state. But Evans (1995) has anticipated this evolutionary change in relation to what he terms 'the new internationalization'. To him, economic globalization simultaneously brings such significant windows of opportunity for domestic firms and challenges the embedded autonomy of the developmental state:

> The new internationalization clearly complicates the politics of state involvement. Once enmeshed in alliances with transnational firms,

> local entrepreneurs no longer comprise a political constituency as they did under the old greenhouses. Their interests are much less clearly bound up with the growth of local demand and the enhancement of local productive capacity. Getting some share of the proprietary rents generated by their partner's global technological and marketing assets is increasingly important. Consequently, embeddedness is more problematic. At the same time, the political vacuum that allowed early 'guerrilla' initiatives from inside the state has been filled. Once local firms have established themselves, the sector is no longer an empty space politically. The kind of autonomous action that propelled the initial development of the sector is no longer possible. What this analysis suggests, then, is that the new internationalization places new demands on the state yet leaves it less politically able to pursue transformative ends (Evans, 1995: 205–6).

In retrospect, Evans' embedded autonomy seems to work well in the three East Asian economies up to the late 1980s primarily due to the developmental state's authoritarian control and weak social groups. Because of their dependence on subsidies and incentives, domestic firms and state-owned enterprises were often under the control of the developmental state in these economies. Embedded autonomy was, therefore, conditional on the weaknesses and inadequacies of domestic economic agents and social groups. My evolutionary perspective, however, points to changing state-firm relations over time in response to new generative rules associated with intensified global economic integration and the reconfiguration of developmental coalitions since the late 1980s. As argued forcefully by Beeson (2006: 451), 'once the development state has effectively done its job and "caught up" with established industrial economies at the leading edge of production and knowledge, it is far from clear that state planners are any wiser about the course of future technological development than the private sector. In other words, there are limits to what states can do, specific circumstances in which planning development seems to be effective, and a danger of entrenching a counterproductive institutional inertia where the relationships between political and economic elites are inadequately monitored and transparent, or where they linger on past their expiry dates.' While such 'institutional inertia' might be less effective in steering the continual growth of East Asian firms since the late 1980s, what comes to their rescue seems to be the even more complex and open organization of the global economy on the basis of global production networks.

ECONOMIC GOVERNANCE THROUGH INTER-FIRM DYNAMICS IN GLOBAL PRODUCTION NETWORKS

The above lacuna in the developmental state approach to explaining market development after the initial phase of industrialization becomes more obvious because some of the most dynamic and export-oriented business firms from these East Asian economies are newly developed through strong external linkages with lead firms in global production networks. While they might have benefited indirectly from the earlier phase of state incentives and industrial policies, these East Asian firms have grown out of intentional firm-specific strategies that connect locally based actors and lead firms in global production networks. To couple with lead firms in these global production networks, actors in these latecomer economies pull together their resources, learning capacities and strategic efforts to attain what Schmitz (1999) calls 'collective efficiency'. As argued by Pietrobelli and Rabellotti (2011: 1261), '[f]or firms in developing countries inclusion in GVC [global value chains] not only provides new markets for their products, it also plays a growing and crucial role in access to knowledge and enhanced learning and innovation'. To understand the formation and rationality behind these 'externally-induced' industrial changes, we need to incorporate a broader global production networks perspective that takes into account both firm-specific strategies *and* the external linkages and joint action of key actors in global networks.

What then are global production networks? How are they organized and how do they emerge in different industries? A brief reprise is useful here. Since the 1960s, lead firms from advanced industrialized economies have increasingly been taking production activity across borders. Through this process of internationalization, they have become transnational corporations (TNCs). These TNCs are not autonomous and vertically integrated organizations; rather, they resemble a form of intra-firm and inter-firm networks comprising a large assortment of other actors and organizations (Ghoshal and Bartlett, 1990; Gulati, 2007). As TNCs become much more global in their scale and scope of operations, their networks are also concomitantly global in nature, leading to the emergence of global production networks. Coe *et al.* (2008: 272, italics in original) argue that these networks 'reflect the fundamental *structural* and *relational* nature of how production, distribution and consumption of goods and services are – indeed always have been – organized. Although they have undoubtedly become far more complex organizationally, as well as far more extensive geographically, production networks are a *generic* form of economic organization.' Global production networks thus involve both business firms and economies in organizationally complex and geographically extensive ways (Henderson *et al.*, 2002: 445–6).

In this perspective, a global production network is defined as one that is coordinated and controlled by a globally significant TNC and involves a vast network of their overseas affiliates, strategic partners, key customers and non-firm institutions. Unlike most domestic firms in the three East Asian economies, global lead firms refer to powerful firms that orchestrate and coordinate complex global production networks in their respective industries, which span different territories and regions. These lead firms are often large TNCs that, in turn, are movers and shapers of the global economy (Harrison, 1997; Peck and Yeung, 2003; Gereffi, 2005; Dunning and Lundan, 2008; Dicken, 2011). They are market leaders in terms of their brand names, technology, products/services and marketing capabilities. Good examples are Hewlett-Packard and Motorola in ICT industries, Sony and Philips in consumer electronics, Toyota and General Motors in automobile, The Gap and Nike in clothing and footwear, Citicorp and HSBC in banking, Hilton and Marriott in hospitality, British Airways and Singapore Airlines in passenger air travel, Wal-Mart and Carrefour in retailing, and UPS and Exel/DHL in logistics. In the manufacturing sector, global lead firms often specialize in the upstream activities of research and development and downstream activities of branding, marketing and post-sale services. While they continue to engage in high-value manufacturing activities, these global lead firms are increasingly compelled to outsource a large portion of their product categories to strategic partners and independent manufacturers (e.g., ICT, clothing and garment, toys and footwear, machinery industries). There is thus a movement of global lead firms towards market control via product and market definitions, rather than leadership in manufacturing processes and technologies.

With the rise of global production networks in the late 1980s and beyond, East Asian firms in global industries are much less determined by domestic industrial policies, unlike the earlier state-market governance model in the 1960s and the 1970s. How do we put this dynamic change into a sound conceptual framework premised on the recent development in theorizing global production networks? This analytical challenge can be met by taking an evolutionary view of the rise of East Asian firms in a globalizing era. Three decades of successful policy interventions by the developmental state have now produced a significant number of leading national firms from these economies, which can compete on their own feet in the global economy. Graduating from their earlier dependence on the developmental state for capital and technologies, these East Asian firms have taken on a more direct role in steering the development of their respective industries and sectors, a role previously occupied exclusively by the developmental state. This evolutionary change in 'role play' between leading firms and the developmental state does not take place naturally or in an institutional vacuum. More importantly, it is firmly grounded in a process of new path creation that entails a shift of strategic partnership from state-firm to firm-firm relations in economic governance. These *inter-firm dynamics*, rather than state-firm relations, have come to the forefront of governing the articulation of these national economies into global production networks.

This process of strategic coupling is defined as a mutually dependent and constitutive process involving shared interests and cooperation between two or more groups of actors who otherwise might not act in tandem for a common strategic objective. In the context of East Asian development, strategic coupling refers to the dynamic processes through which economic actors in these national economies coordinate, mediate and arbitrage strategic interests with their counterparts in the global economy. These trans-local and trans-national processes involve both material flows in transactional terms and non-material flows (e.g., information, intelligence and practices). There are two mutually constitutive dimensions to this dynamic process of strategic coupling. The first dimension refers to the *disembedding* of leading firms from the developmental state over time in response to the changing selection environment. The second dimension points to the *re-embedding* of these firms in global production networks orchestrated by lead firms from advanced industrialized economies. These two dimensions are mirror images of each other – two sides of the same coin. The growing disembedding of firms from home states necessitates the re-embedding of these economic actors in another organizational platform such as global production networks.

Starting with the late 1980s, this disembedding of lead firms from the developmental state began to take shape in all three East Asian economies. In South Korea, perhaps the strongest form of the developmental state among the three economies, leading *chaebol* groups have embarked on a massive globalization drive since the early 1990s, partly facilitated by the financial liberalization implemented by the first civilian government under the Kim Young-Sam administration. This disembedding was a product of both willing *chaebol* groups and the reluctant state, which saw its power and control waning in the context of democratization and liberalization. Kalinowski (2008: 449–50) thus observes that:

> . . . the large business conglomerates (chaebol) emerged as an independent interest group and stopped following the government's economic plans . . . and in the 1990s the *chaebol*'s interest dominated the public discourse and government policies . . . [S]tate interventions in the late 2000s are very different from what they were during the heyday of the developmental state. State interventions are becoming less and less strategic and more and more reactive, mitigating the economic and social costs of market-oriented reforms. Thus, the state is getting bigger, but at the same time weaker. It is less strategic, and less associated with 'midwifery' than with a 'nursing' function – feeding the losers of market reforms and cleaning up the mess when markets get out of control.

In Taiwan, the developmental state was never as powerful and effective in governing the market and growing national champions as in South Korea. This weaker embedding of domestic firms in the Taiwanese state was already acknowledged by Amsden (1989) and Wade (1990). Recent evidence by Wu (2005) and Greene (2008) further shows that even this 'weaker' strength of embedding in the earlier work is exaggerated. The rapid emergence and success of leading firms from Taiwan in the global ICT industry since the 1990s has, therefore, created a favourable condition for them to disembed from the developmental state bureaucracy in search for new strategic partnerships in global production networks. In his recent analysis of Taiwan's developmental state under the influence of globalization, Hsu (2011: 603) notes that:

> By and large, engaging in global production and competition aligns local capitals with the interests of their international partners, and undermines their embeddedness in domestic state policies. Consequently, it puts a ceiling on the state's leadership in intervening in firms' activities, and forces the state to restructure itself to be better positioned to handle global connections.

In Singapore, the developmental state had chosen to work with foreign capital since its inception and, therefore, produced a domestic capitalist class that was not dependent on, if not alienated by, the state's priority. Still, the state deliberately intervened in the domestic economy by establishing a wide range of state-owned enterprises (SOEs), certainly much more so than in South Korea and Taiwan, which have since come to the forefront of global competition today (e.g., Singapore Airlines, Keppel Corp. and Sembcorp Industries). But even this strong state had to reduce its stake in the corporate sector in order to enable these SOEs to thrive in global competition (Yeung, 2005, 2011). Starting in the early 1990s, the developmental state embarked on a difficult process of corporatizing and privatizing major SOEs, which symbolized the first wave of disembedding national firms from the state. The difficulty though rested with the lack of local private entrepreneurs and capitalists who were able to take over these gigantic SOEs. This was also the time when Singapore underwent what Rodan (1989) terms its 'Second Industrial Revolution' in order to upgrade its domestic industries and economic competitiveness through carefully managed wage increase and flexible labour policies.

By the late 1980s, the developmental state in all three East Asian economies had almost completed its task of deliberately governing the market in order to promote industrial transformation. This very success in latecomer industrialization has produced an unintended effect of their leading domestic firms increasingly seeking to disembed themselves from the (neo-)developmental state at home and to re-embed in emerging global production networks in search of new sources of capital, technologies, market and capabilities. This re-embedding process requires national firms to venture beyond their domestic economies and to participate directly in the competitive dynamics of global production networks through which global lead firms adopt organizational and technological innovations to fix their competitive problems. These fixes, in turn, create a new form of industrial organization that provides a window of opportunity for East Asian firms to integrate into global production networks. Since the early 1990s, global lead firms in different global production networks and sectors have moved towards a business model of increasing specialization in value-chain activities. This trend has been much further accelerated since the late 1990s, particularly in the electronics, automobile, and apparel sectors (Gereffi *et al.*, 2005; Dicken, 2011; Sturgeon and Kawagami, 2011; Staritz *et al.*, 2011). What this value-chain specialization entails is a more strategically focused role played by global lead firms in the upstream (research and development) and downstream (marketing, distribution and post-sale services) segments of the value chain, leaving much of the manufacturing portion of the value chain to its international strategic partners and supply-chain managers in these East Asian economies. This 'organizational fix' in global production networks refers to the strategies through which global lead firms reorganize and reconfigure their value activities in order to extract greater value from specialization in core competencies and to increase the market competitiveness of their products manufactured by strategic partners. In certain industries, this organizational fix may entail spatial relocation of productive facilities. In other instances, the fix can come from international outsourcing to manufacturing partners from developing economies who are more attuned to local cost structures and changing policy conditions. As observed by Saxenian (2002: 184–5), 'The deepening social division of labor in the industry creates opportunities for innovation in formerly peripheral regions – opportunities that did not exist in an era of highly integrated producers [before the 1980s].'

The rise of vertical specialization by brand-name firms and/or original equipment manufacturing in many industries is linked to the vertical disintegration of value-chain activity within individual lead firms and the subsequent vertical reintegration of this activity in geographically dispersed locations (see Dunning and Lundan, 2008). By the late 1990s, the world of the electronics industry experienced another 'revolution' with the emergence of *contracting manufacturing* as the key platform to achieve cost efficiency through economies of scale and supply-chain management (Sturgeon, 2002, 2003). In this mode of industrial organization, lead firms in global production networks engage large globalized contract manufacturers as their strategic partners to take care of their manufacturing activities, while they specialize in the higher return premium product markets and higher value-added activities such as research and development, production development, marketing and, sometimes, distribution. Most of the world's leading brand-name computer companies outsource a large proportion of their notebook and desktop computers, peripherals and accessories to contract manufacturers in East Asia. This reorganization of global production networks continues to benefit East Asian firms that are well integrated into the production networks of large contract manufacturers and system integrators. Meanwhile, electronics manufacturers in East Asia are quick to capitalize on their established market positions and production know-how to emerge as manufacturing partners in the global electronics industry (Yeung, 2007; Ernst, 2009).

The case of Taiwan's Hon Hai Precision is particularly instructive here.[8] Founded by Terry Gou in 1974 as a family-owned company making plastic parts such as channel-changing knobs for black-and-white television sets, Hon Hai did not experience exponential growth until the late 1990s. It has grown very rapidly only in the 2000s and has subsequently become Taiwan's largest industrial firm and the world's largest provider of electronics manufacturing services (EMS). During its heyday in the mid-1970s and the 1980s, Taiwan's developmental state was promoting only selective segments of the ICT industry such as semiconductors (and, later, TFT-LCD panels). Hon Hai was thus not a direct recipient of state support. Its success cannot be attributed to the state's industrial policy. Instead, its emergence should be accounted for by its strategic coupling with global lead firms in the electronics industry. As a true latecomer in global competition, Hon Hai has benefited from the increasing demand for strategic partners and supply-chain management from global lead firms that are mostly based in advanced industrialized economies in North America, Western Europe and Japan. It has relentlessly pursued firm-specific competitive strategies that give rise to its greater 'capability to cost' ratios developed on the basis of world-class production capabilities and competitive cost advantages (Hobday, 1995; Yeung, 2007). There is thus a strategic coupling between global lead firms' greater demand for manufacturing partners in East Asia and the growing capability of Hon Hai to fulfil this demand.

During much of its formative years in the 1980s, Hon Hai was a large diversified electronics parts manufacturer, specializing in a range of connectors and cable assemblies for desktop and notebook PCs and PC peripherals. As recently as in 1996, Hon Hai's revenue was only half a billion in US dollars. Measured in annual revenue, it was smaller than top original design manufacturing (ODM) firms such as Quanta and Compal until after 2000.[9] But by 2010, Hon Hai had achieved US$100 billion in sales for the first time and its compound annual growth rate since 1996 has been a whopping 46 per cent. How then did Hon Hai grow from an unknown component maker in the 1980s to become a US$100 billion company with more than a million employees in 2010? The key lies in its adoption of the EMS model of strategic partnership with global lead firms such as Apple, Dell, Hewlett-Packard, Intel, Motorola, Nokia, Sony and Toshiba. Its competitive advantages are predicated on its ability to combine discretion with a solid record of quality control and competitive pricing. Established in China's southern city of Shenzhen in 1988, its Foxconn City is well known for guarding the identities of Hon Hai's key customers and strategic partners. And yet its optimal production operation and in-house manufacturing of many parts for its EMS products have significantly reduced its per unit cost.

Of all these strategic partnerships with global lead firms, Hon Hai's EMS work for Apple Inc. is the most significant. Through its China-based company, Foxconn International, established in 2000, Hon Hai has been serving as Apple's EMS provider for the exclusive production of iPhones (since its launch in 2007) and iPads (since its launch in March 2010) and one of the few manufacturers of Apple's iPods (since its launch in November 2001). Hon Hai's competitive strength in EMS is phenomenal and highly critical to Apple's success since launching its iPhones. When the late Steve Jobs announced the first iPhone on 9 January 2007, the time-to-market was about six months.[10] The first shipment of iPhones came on 29 June 2007. Five years later, the time-to-market of new iPhones was reduced to less than two weeks. The new iPhone 5 was announced on 12 September 2012. Nine days later, on 21 September, it was available in the US, Australia, Canada, France, Germany, Hong Kong, Japan, Singapore and the UK.[11] This very quick time-to-market is a key competitive strength of Apple and accentuates the great success of many of its cool products. Its rivals in smartphones, such as Samsung, Nokia and Motorola, often take one to several months to deliver their newly launched handsets. In the quarter ending in June 2012, the iPhone was synonymous with Apple's success when it accounted for 58 per cent of Apple's US$39.2 billion revenue from all products.[12] As the exclusive manufacturer of more than 250 million units of the iPhone since its launch, Hon Hai's EMS capability has become a critical part of Apple's success. While Hon Hai's profit margin from such EMS provisions may appear to be small relative to the profitability of brand-name lead firms such as Apple,[13] its EMS capabilities in speedy ramping up of production volume, high quality control and competitive pricing should not be underestimated because they play a critical role in the competitive success of Hon Hai's strategic partners.

Unlike many other high-tech firms from Taiwan, Hon Hai's story is perhaps quite unique. Its founder, Terry Gou, is not a transnational technopreneur who has spent time working in world-class high-tech companies. His company is not a 'national champion' on the state's list for favourable incentives and promotion policies. The timing of Hon Hai's rise to global leadership in EMS is also peculiar because it grew rapidly during the 2000s, when the state's developmental efficacy was in decline and its industrial policy was less effective. In short, Hon Hai's emergence as Taiwan's largest industrial firm owes to neither state-led industrialization efforts nor indigenous industrial capabilities derived from the 'brain circulation' of transnational technologists and elites. Its success as the world's leading EMS provider is explained by the changing industrial dynamics of global production networks, which offers a critical window of opportunity for it to serve as a strategic manufacturing partner of global lead firms.

As its economies of scale and scope have increased since the 2000s, Hon Hai's EMS model of industrial production has outdone its North American rivals such as Flextronics, Jabil Circuit, Celestica and Sanmina-SCI. During this period, Hon Hai has developed strong manufacturing capabilities through continuous innovations. It was the most profitable among all top 10 EMS providers throughout the 2000s. In Sturgeon's (2002: 460) original study, all of the world's top five EMS providers in 1995 were based in North America. By 2010, three leading firms from Taiwan (Hon Hai and Foxconn) and Singapore (Venture Corp.) had emerged amongst the top seven EMS providers. Throughout the 2000s, they were also much more profitable than the four US-origin EMS giants in Sturgeon's (2002) study – Flextronics, Solectron, Celestica and Sanmina-SCI. These four American EMS providers suffered from record losses when the three East Asian EMS providers grew their revenues and market share. In 2010, Taiwan's Hon Hai alone had revenue in excess of US$100 billion and eclipsed the combined total of all other EMS providers in the top 10.

CONCLUSION

The dynamic interaction between domestic political economies and global economic change has been one of the core analytical foci in international political economy. In this paper, I have revisited the developmental state approach to the understanding of industrial transformation in three East Asian economies. I have argued that the existing studies of the developmental state in these economies have not paid sufficient attention to the changing state role in a globalizing era. As a contribution to the growing literature on the international political economy of development, the paper has offered a dynamic conception of state-firm relations that takes into account the changing context of economic development in the global economy and the rise of new forms of economic organization and governance beyond the developmental state-firm nexus. In particular, it has demonstrated the usefulness of an evolutionary perspective on state-firm relations that casts new light on economic governance. Instead of placing national firms as the passive outcome of the developmental state governing the domestic market in its quest for rapid industrialization, I have explained how changing selection environments since the late 1980s have reduced the state's embedded autonomy in governing the market and reconfigured this economic governance through inter-firm dynamics in global production networks. In this process of changing economic governance, East Asian firms, such as the case study firm, Hon Hai, have gradually disembedded from their domestic state governance and re-embedded into global production networks. Through the strategic coupling of national firms with lead firms in global production networks, these East Asian economies can possibly charter a new pathway of development in this era of globalization.

This conceptual paper, however, has not fully addressed several critical issues that call for more future theoretical and empirical research. First, the dynamic role of the state in governing economic development has not been adequately dealt with in this paper because of its analytical focus on new inter-firm dynamics in global production networks. Implicitly, the paper does point to the changing role of the state in domestic economic governance. As more domestic firms in these East Asian economies become articulated into diverse global industries through such inter-firm dynamics, the state's 'husbandry' role in such mature industries as ICT and semiconductors will necessarily be reduced. In the wake of domestic firms becoming world-class leaders in these industries, particularly those from South Korea (Samsung, LG and SK Hynix) and Taiwan (Hon Hai, Acer, Quanta and Compal), the state and its economic planning bureaucracy can no longer shoulder a leadership role in steering further domestic development and transformation in such global industries. These world-class domestic firms have all the necessary capital, technology and human resources to advance further their market positions in different global production networks. In doing so, these leading East Asian firms become the primary actor in both the domestic and global arenas of such industries.

Even in these mature global industries, however, the dominance of large domestic firms does not mean the state's role should be reduced to a mere regulator or 'nursing' the losers from market failures. As argued strongly by Mazzucato (2011: 91), the state's role should be about fixing 'network failures' and 'opportunity failures' that might otherwise occur due to the lack of collective action or long-term horizons among private sector actors. In the three East Asian economies, it makes no sense for us to expect the state to wither away in a globalizing world. But the emergence of large domestic firms and their embedded global production networks does entail a shift in the state's focus away from industrial policies targeting specific 'winners', as widely practised during the 1960s–1980s period, to one that *catalyses* public and private interests in ways that promote new technologies, market development and, ultimately, economic development. This reorientation in industrial policy and state involvement towards a 'catalyst' role is particularly important in new high-tech and high-risk industries such as biotechnology and green technologies, where uncertainty is high and private interests remain fairly lukewarm and short-term. In this regard, Wong's (2011) recent study of 'wrong bets' by East Asian developmental states in biotechnology is particularly telling because it demonstrates the failure of the developmental state's application of its risk mitigation strategy, as practised successfully in the earlier phase of state-led industrialization in electronics and automobiles, to this new and uncertain industry where the state should be actively involved in managing this uncertainty in collaboration with private and international interests.

Second, as the three East Asian states are 'trending to the normal' (Wong, 2011: 186) and shedding some of their distinctiveness in state-led capitalist development (Bello, 2009; Yeung, 2009b), other latecomers are curiously more interested in adopting this model of state-led industrialization, such as China (Nee and Opper, 2007) and South Africa (Edigheji, 2010). While a large domestic market in China presents an opportunity for the socialist state to implement some of the policy instruments of the classic developmental state, many recent studies have pointed to the tremendous challenges to such a form of state-led development. For one, the predatory state behaviour and intrastate organizational dynamics in China, described by Pei (2006) as a 'development autocracy', represent an antithesis to Evans' (1995) structural precondition of embedded autonomy. For another, scholars have found the Chinese state 'dysfunctional' (Breslin, 1996), 'polymorphous' (Howell, 2006) or even 'regulatory' (Hsueh, 2011). In fact, China's developmental model has been less directed by central state planning since the mid-1990s because of the emergence of local corporatism. Described by Naughton (1995) as 'growing out of the plan', these locally and regionally specific pathways to economic development can hardly be compared to the national state-led industrial transformation in South Korea, Taiwan and Singapore. To Breznitz and Murphree (2011: 5), this local corporatism in China resembles what they term the 'run of the Red Queen': 'Unlike those countries where governments had specific policies with clearly defined goals and the pathways to get there, China developed its Red Queen run by accident, partly as a result of local experimentation, and the outcome looks quite different from the declared goals of the central government.' Given these various structural constraints within the Chinese socialist state and the deep integration of the Chinese firms and industries in global production networks, it is indeed quite hard to imagine an internally cohesive and bureaucratically rational developmental state emerging from this socialist transitional economy.

Last but not least, this paper has not considered the weaknesses of strategic coupling in global production networks as a development strategy. Just like the earlier studies of the dark sides of the East Asian developmental state (Bello and Rosenfeld, 1990; Hart-Landsberg, 1993), the trend towards tighter integration of domestic industries and political economies into global capitalist dynamics described in this paper does point to possibilities of structural lock-ins at the industrial level and divided loyalties among leading domestic firms.[14] As Chu (2009) has illustrated, Taiwan's strategy of embedding its ICT firms in global production networks has worked very well in terms of the rapid growth of various ICT sectors such as computers and semiconductors. But such a strategic partnership with global lead firms also leads to the structural lock-in of these Taiwanese ICT firms in the lower-value segments of the global value chain. With the exception of Acer, ASUS and HTC, few of these ICT firms have managed to evolve from ODM and EMS providers to become original brand manufacturers (OBMs). Compared to South Korea's techno-nationalist approach to building such giant national champions as Samsung and LG, she argues that Taiwan's strategy has not gone beyond 'second movers', which are always treading behind first movers or OBMs in computers (Hewlett-Packard, Apple and Dell) and semiconductors (Intel and Qualcomm). While Chu's argument contains some validity in terms of her comparison of ICT firms from South Korea and Taiwan, she has underestimated the importance of different pathways to industrial leadership and economic development. The domination of Samsung, LG and Hyundai in the South Korean economy has become a major political issue in the 2010s. The lack of success in reining in these *chaebol* groups in the earlier era of the developmental state in the 1980s and through to the mid-1990s means that their much *greater* concentration and dominance in the 2010s dwarfs any serious state-led effort in restructuring domestic industrial organization and economic governance. Even in Thurbon's (2012) study, she has shown that the *chaebol* were unwilling to follow the state's 'requests' to invest in service robotics that was designated as a strategic industry in 2003. Wong's (2011) study also demonstrates that the state's industrial policy in biotech cannot be implemented without the explicit consent and participation of these leading *chaebol* groups.

In addition, as more East Asian firms have become strategically coupled with lead firms in global production networks, their firm-specific interests may not be entirely consistent with the goals of national development. Their strategic positions in global production networks may compel these national firms to act in the interest of their lead firm customers and/or global market imperatives. Taiwan's Hon Hai, for example, is deeply embroiled in mainland China's electronics industry because of its large employment of cheap migrant workers in its mammoth plants and its role as one of the largest manufacturers and exporters from China. Its strategic posture is often based on its China consideration, rather than its home economy in Taiwan. The same issue of divided loyalties also applies to other high-tech ICT firms from Taiwan and South Korea. Most of them have developed state-of-the-art facilities in mainland China. Greater integration into such global production networks may indeed lead to industrial hollowing out in Taiwan and, to a certain extent, South Korea.

In a globalizing era, where economic activity is increasingly organized on the basis of global production networks spanning different countries and regions, it is beyond the capacity and control of any state, developmental or otherwise, to govern the market without taking into account inter-firm dynamics that articulate domestic firms into these networks. Economic governance of industrial transformation is no longer just about catching-up strategies premised on state-led industrial policy in nurturing specific industries and picking national champions. In this evolutionary and dynamic context of economic development, the state's role has to go well beyond 'getting prices wrong' in the domestic market and must embrace new challenges of governing industrial upgrading and transformations through strategic coupling of national firms in such inter-firm dynamics of global production networks. This repositioning of the state role in a globalizing era entails a better understanding of not just changing state capacities and policies, but also the evolving capacities and strategies of national firms emanating from these economies.

ACKNOWLEDGEMENTS

This is a substantially revised version of an earlier paper presented at the DIME Workshop on 'Globalisation and the Changing Geographies of Production and Innovation' held in Academiegebouw, Utrecht, the Netherlands, 5–7 November 2009, and the Workshop on 'Value Chains, Production Networks, and the Geographies of Development: Emerging Challenges and Future Agenda' held at the National University of Singapore, 1–2 December 2011. I would like to thank Ron Boschma from the University of Utrecht for inviting me and funding my visit to the DIME Workshop in November 2009, and Jeff Nielson and Bill Pritchard, both at the University of Sydney, for co-organizing and co-funding the December 2011 workshop. Funding from the NUS Academic Research Grant (R-109-000-116-112) made this joint workshop possible. I am also very grateful to the participants in both workshops and two anonymous referees of *RIPE* for their constructive comments and suggestions. The generous writing residency at the Rockefeller Foundation's Bellagio Center in Italy between 7 and 29 November 2012 has allowed me to rework and finesse this paper to my satisfaction. I thank my fellow residents for their superb insights during our many meal-time discussions. I take full responsibility for all errors and/or misinterpretations in this paper.

NOTES

1 Company-specific data are from the Bloomberg *Businessweek* online database: <http://investing.businessweek.com> (accessed 7 July 2012).

2 Some recent examples are Lim (2010), Thurbon (2012) and Kim (2012) on South Korea, Hu (2012) on Taiwan, and Pereira (2008) on Singapore.

3 Some receptions to this statist approach are O'Riain (2004) and Breznitz (2007). But even in these studies, the emergence of national firms in global production networks tends to be explained by the political choice of the developmental network state.

4 There are two relatively recent and parallel schools in the field of international political economy: the global value-chain approach (Gereffi, 1994, 1999; Schmitz, 2004; Gereffi *et al.*, 2005; Bair, 2009; Pietrobelli and Rabellotti, 2011) and the global production networks perspective (Dicken *et al.*, 2001; Ernst and Kim, 2002; Henderson *et al.*, 2002; Coe *et al.*, 2004, 2008; Hess and Yeung,

2006; Yeung, 2009a, 2013). See Parrilli *et al.* (2013) for an integration of these two strands of the literature. For some recent empirical studies in the context of East Asian developmental states, see Bowen and Leinbach (2006), Bowen (2007), Yeung (2007, 2010) and the papers in this special issue of *RIPE* (e.g., Gereffi, 2013).

5 My argument for inter-firm dynamics in governing the market does not reduce the state's role to a passive actor in the domestic economy or point to the complete dismantling of the developmental state. Instead, it places the state squarely in the evolutionary dynamics of global competition in which the active role of the state becomes less necessary and effective in industries where domestic firms have 'grown up' and succeeded in their participation in global production networks. Couched in these terms, the state continues to function actively in certain areas such as promoting new industries (e.g., biomedical and environmental technologies sectors) and steering the restructuring of the domestic economy (e.g., the 2008 global financial crisis). But as Wong (2011) has demonstrated clearly in his comparative study of state-led initiatives in biotechnology in all three East Asian economies, the inherent technological, economic and long-term uncertainty in such new industries as biotechnology has obliterated the viability of the state-led model in an era of science-based industries.

6 For a critical view of the developmental state in relation to the 2008 global financial crisis and the rise of the state in economic governance, see Block (2008) and Radice (2008). Block (2008) offers an important argument that the developmental state in the US is much hidden behind Congress' 'competitiveness policy' since the 1980s (cf. Krugman, Tyson, Reich). Drawing upon O'Riain (2004), he distinguishes between the 'developmental network state', such as the US, and the 'developmental bureaucratic state', such as Japan.

7 This tendency towards presenting national firms as pawns of the developmental state is common in the early literature. See examples of Hyundai Heavy Industries and POSCO in Amsden (1989). Writing in the late 1980s, Woo (1991: 15) reflects that 'Daewoo did not even appear until the late 1960s. The others [Hyundai and Samsung] did not grow into anything big until the 1970s; thus, the conglomerates are a very recent phenomenon.'

8 Despite repeated attempts during the entire period of this research, I was unable to secure an interview with Hon Hai, a company well known for its secrecy and avoidance of publicity. *The Wall Street Journal* carried a report on Hon Hai's founder, Terry Gou, on 11 August 2007, entitled 'The Forbidden City of Terry Gou'. The reporter, Jason Dean, was the first from Western media to conduct an interview with Gou since 2002 and the interview was granted after more than five years of requests by the *WSJ*. The spate of worker suicides between 2009 and 2012 has made Hon Hai even more wary of the media and academic researchers. The following case study is thus based on secondary materials (e.g., the *WSJ* article in 2007), company reports and its corporate websites.

9 This size difference explains why Hon Hai was not really featured in Amsden and Chu's (2003) study of the industrial upgrading of leading Taiwanese firms.

10 'Apple Reinvents the Phone with iPhone', 9 January 2007, Apple's press release, <http://www.apple.com/pr/library/2007/01/09Apple-Reinvents-the-Phone-with-iPhone.html> (accessed 7 November 2012).

11 'Apple Introduces iPhone 5', 12 September 2012, Apple's press release, <http://www.apple.com/pr/library/2012/09/12Apple-Introduces-iPhone-5.html> (accessed 13 November 2012).

12 'Apple Reports Third Quarter Results', 24 July 2012, Apple's press release, <http://www.apple.com/pr/library/2012/09/12Apple-Introduces-iPhone-5.html> (accessed 13 November 2012).

13 For detailed studies of such value-chain distribution of profits, see Dedrick *et al.* (2010) and OECD (2011). In the case of Hon Hai, while its profit margins decreased sharply from 17 per cent in 1997 to 6 per cent in 2007 and 3 per cent in 2011, the decrease in its return on shareholders' funds was less drastic, from 35 per cent in 1997 to 29 per cent in 2007 and 17.7 per cent in 2011. In comparison, Apple's profit margins increased dramatically from -15 per cent in 1997 to 20 per cent in 2007 and 32 per cent in 2011, and its return on shareholders' funds grew from −87 per cent in 1997 to 34 per cent in 2007 and 45 per cent in 2011 (all data from OSIRIS online database, http://www.bvdinfo.com/Products/Company-Information/International/OSIRIS.aspx accessed 12 November 2012).

14 An alternative approach to this critical understanding of strategic coupling is Bair and Werner's (2011: 992) 'disarticulations perspective' of global value chains, where they show how disarticulations lend 'dispossession its concrete geographical and social form, reworking the uneven geographies of capitalism'. See also MacKinnon's (2011) evolutionary analysis of strategic coupling and decoupling processes.

NOTES ON CONTRIBUTOR

Professor Yeung is Professor of Economic Geography at the National University of Singapore. His research interests cover broadly theories and the geography of transnational corporations, global production networks, East Asian firms, and the political economy of development in the Asia-Pacific region. Professor Yeung has published 3 single-authored monographs, 7 edited books, over 85 journal articles, and 40 book chapters. Some of his key publications include Transnational Corporations and Business Networks (Routledge, 1998), Entrepreneurship and the Internationalisation of Asian Firms (Edward Elgar, 2002), Chinese Capitalism in a Global Era (Routledge, 2004) and as co-author of Economic Geography: A Contemporary Introduction (Wiley Blackwell, 2007/2013). Professor Yeung is Editor of Environment and Planning A, Economic Geography, and Review of International Political Economy, Asia-Pacific Editor of Global Networks, Contributing Editor of International Journal of Urban and Regional Research, and Business Manager of Singapore Journal of Tropical Geography. He sits on the editorial boards of 14 other international journals in the fields of human geography, management, urban studies, area studies, and general social science, such as Asia Pacific Journal of Management, European Urban and Regional Studies, Journal of Economic Geography, Asia Pacific Viewpoint, and Eurasian Geography and Economics.

REFERENCES

Amsden, Alice H. (1989) *Asia's Next Giant: South Korea and Late Industrialization*, New York: Oxford University Press.

Amsden, Alice H. (2001) *The Rise of 'The Rest': Challenges to the West from Late-Industrializing Economies*, New York: Oxford University Press.

Amsden, Alice H. (2007) *Escape from Empire: The Developing World's Journey through Heaven and Hell*, Cambridge, MA: MIT Press.

Amsden, Alice H. and Chu, Wan-Wen (2003) *Beyond Late Development: Taiwan's Upgrading Policies*, Cambridge, MA: MIT Press.

Bair, Jennifer (ed.) (2009) *Frontiers of Commodity Chain Research*, Stanford, CA: Stanford University Press.

Bair, Jennifer and Werner, Marion (2011) 'Commodity Chains and the Uneven Geographies of Global Capitalism: A Disarticulations Perspective', *Environment and Planning A*, 43(5): 988–97.

Beeson, Mark (2006) 'Politics and Markets in East Asia: Is the Developmental State Compatible with Globalization?', in Richard Stubbs and Geoffrey R.D. Underhill (eds) *Political Economy and the Changing Global Order*, 3rd edn, Oxford: Oxford University Press, pp. 443–53.

Bello, Walden (2009) 'States and Markets, States Versus Markets: The Developmental State Debate as the Distinctive East Asian Contribution to International Political Economy', in Mark Blyth (ed.) *Routledge Handbook of International Political Economy: IPE as a Global Conversation*, New York: Routledge, pp. 180–200.

Bello, Walden and Rosenfeld, Stephanie (1990) *Dragons in Distress: Asia's Miracle Economies in Crisis*, San Francisco, CA: Food First Books.

Berger, Suzanne and Lester, Richard K. (eds) (2005) *Global Taiwan: Building Competitive Strengths in a New International Economy*, Armonk, NY: M.E. Sharpe.

Block, Fred (2008) 'Swimming against the Current: The Rise of a Hidden Developmental State in the United States', *Politics and Society*, 36(2): 169–206.

Bowen, John T., Jr. (2007) 'Global Production Networks, the Developmental State and the Articulation of Asia Pacific Economies in the Commercial Aircraft Industry', *Asia Pacific Viewpoint*, 48(3): 312–29.

Bowen, John T., Jr. and Leinbach, Thomas R. (2006) 'Competitive Advantage in Global Production Networks: Air Freight Services and the Electronics Industry in Southeast Asia', *Economic Geography*, 82(2): 147–66.

Boyd, Richard and Ngo, Tak-Wing (2005) 'Emancipating the Political Economy of Asia from the Growth Paradigm', in Richard Boyd and Tak-Wing Ngo (eds) *Asian States: Beyond the Developmental Perspective*, London: RoutledgeCurzon, pp. 1–18.

Breslin, Shaun G. (1996) 'China: Developmental State or Dysfunctional Development?', *Third World Quarterly*, 17(4): 689–706.

Breznitz, Dan (2007) *Innovation and the State: Political Choice and Strategies for Growth in Israel, Taiwan, and Ireland*, New Haven, CT: Yale University Press.

Breznitz, Dan and Murphree, Michael (2011) *The Run of the Red Queen: Government, Innovation, Globalization, and Economic Growth in China*, New Haven, CT: Yale University Press.

Chibber, Vivek (2002) 'Bureaucratic Rationality and the Developmental State', *American Journal of Sociology*, 107(4): 951–89.

Chu, Wan-wen (2009) 'Can Taiwan's Second Movers Upgrade via Branding?', *Research Policy*, 38(6): 1054–65.

Chu, Yun-han (2007) 'Re-engineering the Developmental State in an Age of Globalization: Taiwan's Quest for High-Tech Industries', in Robert Ash and J. Megan Greene (eds) *Taiwan in the 21st Century: Aspects and Limitations of a Development Model*, London: Routledge, pp. 154–76.

Coe, Neil, Dicken, Peter and Hess, Martin (2008) 'Global Production Networks: Realizing the Potential', *Journal of Economic Geography*, 8(3): 271–95.

Coe, Neil, Hess, Martin, Yeung, Henry Wai-chung, Dicken, Peter and Henderson, Jeffrey (2004) '"Globalizing" Regional Development: A Global Production Networks Perspective', *Transactions of the Institute of British Geographers*, New Series, 29(4): 468–84.

Dedrick, Jason, Kraemer, Kenneth, L. and Linden, Greg (2010) 'Who profits from innovation in global value chains? A study of the iPod and notebook PCs', *Industrial and Corporate Change*, 19(1), 81–116.

Deyo, Frederic C. (ed.) (1987) *The Political Economy of the New Asian Industrialism*, Ithaca, NY: Cornell University Press.

Dicken, Peter (2011) *Global Shift: Mapping the Changing Contours of the World Economy*, 6th edn, London: Sage.

Dicken, Peter, Kelly, Philip, Olds, Kris and Yeung, Henry Wai-chung (2001) 'Chains and Networks, Territories and Scales: Towards an Analytical Framework for the Global Economy', *Global Networks*, 1(2): 89–112.

Dunning, John H. and Lundan, Sarianna M. (2008) *Multinational Enterprises and the Global Economy*, 2nd edn, Cheltenham: Edward Elgar.

Edigheji, Omano (ed.) (2010) *Constructing a Democratic Developmental State in South Africa: Potentials and Challenges*, Cape Town: HSRC Press.

Ernst, Dieter (2009) *A New Geography of Knowledge in the Electronics Industry? Asia's Role in Global Innovation Networks*, Policy Studies No.54, Honolulu: East-West Center.

Ernst, Dieter and Kim, Linsu (2002) 'Global Production Networks, Knowledge Diffusion and Local Capability Formation', *Research Policy*, 31(8–9): 1417–29.

Evans, Peter (1995) *Embedded Autonomy: States and Industrial Transformation*, Princeton, NJ: Princeton University Press.

Gereffi, Gary (1994) 'The Organization of Buyer-Driven Global Commodity Chains: How US Retailers Shape Overseas Production Networks', in Gary Gereffi and Miguel Korzeniewicz (eds) *Commodity Chains and Global Capitalism*, Westport, CT: Praeger, pp. 95–122.

Gereffi, Gary (1999) 'International Trade and Industrial Upgrading in the Apparel Commodity Chain', *Journal of International Economics*, 48(1): 37–70.

Gereffi, Gary (2005) 'The Global Economy: Organization, Governance, and Development', in Neil J. Smelser and Richard Swedberg (eds) *The Handbook of Economic Sociology*, 2nd edn, Princeton, NJ: Princeton University Press, pp. 160–82.

Gereffi, Gary (2013) 'Global Value Chains in a Post-Washington Consensus World: Shifting Governance Structures, Trade Patterns and Development Prospects', *Review of International Political Economy*, 20.

Gereffi, Gary, Humphrey, John and Sturgeon, Timothy (2005) 'The Governance of Global Value Chains', *Review of International Political Economy*, 12(1): 78–104.

Ghoshal, Sumantra and Bartlett, Christopher A. (1990) 'The Multinational Corporation as an Interorganizational Network', *Academy of Management Review*, 15(4): 603–25.

Greene, J. Megan (2008) *The Origins of the Developmental State in Taiwan: Science Policy and the Quest for Modernization*, Cambridge, MA: Harvard University Press.

Gulati, Ranjay (2007) *Managing Network Resources: Alliances, Affiliations, and Other Relational Assets*, Oxford: Oxford University Press.

Haggard, Stephan (1990) *Pathways from the Periphery: The Politics of Growth in the Newly Industrializing Countries*, Ithaca, NY: Cornell University Press.

Hamilton-Hart, Natasha (2000) 'The Singapore State Revisited', *The Pacific Review*, 13(2): 195–216.

Harrison, Bennett (1997) *Lean and Mean: The Changing Landscape of Corporate Power in the Age of Flexibility*, New York: Guilford.

Hart-Landsberg, Martin (1993) *The Rush to Development: Economic Change and Political Struggle in South Korea*, New York: Monthly Review Press.

Hayashi, Shigeko (2010) 'The Developmental State in the Era of Globalization: Beyond the Northeast Asian Model of Political Economy', *The Pacific Review*, 23(1): 45–69.

Henderson, Jeffrey, Dicken, Peter, Hess, Martin, Coe, Neil and Yeung, Henry Wai-chung (2002) 'Global Production Networks and the Analysis of Economic Development', *Review of International Political Economy*, 9(3): 436–64.

Hess, Martin and Yeung, Henry Wai-chung (2006) 'Whither Global Production Networks in Economic Geography? Past, Present and Future', *Environment and Planning A*, 38(7): 1193–204.

Hobday, Michael (1995) *Innovation in East Asia: The Challenge to Japan*, Cheltenham: Edward Elgar.

Hobday, Michael (2001) 'The Electronics Industries of the Asia-Pacific: Exploiting International Production Networks for Economic Development', *Asian-Pacific Economic Literature*, 15(1): 13–29.

Howell, Jude (2006) 'Reflections on the Chinese State', *Development and Change*, 37(2): 273–97.

Hsu, Jinn-Yuh (2011) 'State Transformation and Regional Development in Taiwan: From Developmentalist Strategy to Populist Subsidy', *International Journal of Urban and Regional Research*, 35(3): 600–19.

Hsueh, Roselyn (2011) *China's Regulatory State: A New Strategy for Globalization*, Ithaca, NY: Cornell University Press.

Hu, Mei-Chih (2012) 'Technological Innovation Capabilities in the Thin Film Transistor-Liquid Crystal Display Industries of Japan, Korea, and Taiwan', *Research Policy*, 41(3): 541–55.

Jayasuriya, Kanishka (2005) 'Beyond Institutional Fetishism: From the Developmental to the Regulatory State', *New Political Economy*, 10(3): 381–7.

Johnson, Chalmers (1982) *MITI and the Japanese Economic Miracle: The Growth of Industrial Policy, 1925–1975*, Stanford, CA: Stanford University Press.

Johnson, Chalmers (1995) *Japan: Who Governs? The Rise of the Developmental State*, New York: W.W. Norton.

Kalinowski, Thomas (2008) 'Korea's Recovery since the 1997/98 Financial Crisis: The Last Stage of the Developmental State', *New Political Economy*, 13(4): 447–62.

Kang, David C. (2002) *Crony Capitalism: Corruption and Development in South Korea and the Philippines*, Cambridge: Cambridge University Press.

Kim, Sung-Young (2012) 'Transitioning from Fast-Follower to Innovator: The Institutional Foundations of the Korean Telecommunications Sector', *Review of International Political Economy*, 19(1): 140–68.

Kohli, Atul (2004) *State-Directed Development: Political Power and Industrialization in the Global Periphery*, Cambridge: Cambridge University Press.

Lim, Haeran (2010) 'The Transformation of the Developmental State and Economic Reform in Korea', *Journal of Contemporary Asia*, 40(2): 188–210.

MacKinnon, Danny (2011) 'Beyond Strategic Coupling: Reassessing the Firm-Region Nexus in Global Production Networks', *Journal of Economic Geography*, in press, doi:10.1093/jeg/lbr009.

Mazzucato, Mariana (2011) *The Entrepreneurial State*, London: Demos.

Naughton, Barry (1995) *Growing Out of the Plan: Chinese Economic Reform, 1978–1993*, New York: Cambridge University Press.

Nee, Victor and Opper, Sonja (2007) 'On Politicized Capitalism: Developmental State and the Firm in China', in Victor Nee and Richard Swedberg (eds) *On Capitalism*, Stanford, CA: Stanford University Press, pp. 93–127.

Ngo, Tak-Wing (2005) 'The Political Bases of Episodic Agency in the Taiwan State', in Richard Boyd and Tak-Wing Ngo (eds) *Asian States: Beyond the Developmental Perspective*, London: RoutledgeCurzon, pp. 83–109.

OECD (2011) *Global Value Chains: Preliminary Evidence and Policy Issues*, DSTI/IND(2011)3, Paris: Organisation for Economic Co-operation and Development, <http://www.oecd.org/dataoecd/18/43/47945400.pdf> (accessed 12 November 2012).

O'Riain, Sean (2004) *The Politics of High-Tech Growth: Developmental Network States in the Global Economy*, Cambridge: Cambridge University Press.

Parrilli, Mario Davide, Nadvi, Khalid and Yeung, Henry Wai-chung (2013) 'Local and Regional Development in Global Value Chains, Production Networks and Innovation Networks: A Comparative Review and the Challenges for Future Research', *European Planning Studies*, 21.

Peck, Jamie and Yeung, Henry Wai-chung (eds.) (2003) *Remaking the Global Economy: Economic-Geographical Perspectives*, London: Sage.

Pei, Minxin (2006) *China's Trapped Transition: The Limits of Developmental Autocracy*, Cambridge, MA: Harvard University Press.

Pereira, Alexius A. (2008) 'Whither the Developmental State? Explaining Singapore's Continued Developmentalism', *Third World Quarterly*, 29(6): 1189–203.

Pietrobelli, Carlo and Rabellotti, Roberta (2011) 'Global Value Chains Meet Innovation Systems: Are There Learning Opportunities for Developing Countries?', *World Development*, 39(7): 1261–9.

Piore, Michael J. and Sabel, Charles F. (1984) *The Second Industrial Divide: Possibilities for Prosperity*, New York: Basic Books.

Radice, Hugo (2008) 'The Developmental State under Global Neoliberalism', *Third World Quarterly*, 29(6): 1153–74.

Ravenhill, John (2003) 'From National Champions to Global Partners: Crisis, Globalization, and the Korean Auto Industry', in William W. Keller and Richard J. Samuels (eds) *Crisis and Innovation in Asian Technology*, Cambridge: Cambridge University Press, pp. 108–36.

Rodan, Garry (1989) *The Political Economy of Singapore's Industrialization: National State and International Capital*, London: Macmillan.

Saxenian, AnnaLee (2002) 'Transnational Communities and the Evolution of Global Production Networks: The Cases of Taiwan, China and India', *Industry and Innovation*, 9(3): 183–202.

Schmitz, Hubert (1999) 'Collective Efficiency and Increasing Returns', *Cambridge Journal of Economics*, 23(4): 465–83.

Schmitz, Hubert (ed.) (2004) *Local Enterprises in the Global Economy: Issues of Governance and Upgrading*, Cheltenham: Edward Elgar.

Staritz, Cornelia, Gereffi, Gary and Cattaneo, Olivier (eds) (2011) Special Issue on 'Shifting End Markets and Upgrading Prospects in Global Value Chains', *International Journal of Technological Learning, Innovation and Development*, 4(1–3): 1–259.

Stubbs, Richard (2009) 'Whatever Happened to the East Asian Developmental State? The Unfolding Debate', *The Pacific Review*, 22(1): 1–22.

Sturgeon, Timothy J. (2002) 'Modular Production Networks: A New American Model of Industrial Organization', *Industrial and Corporate Change*, 11(3): 451–96.

Sturgeon, Timothy J. (2003) 'What Really Goes On in Silicon Valley? Spatial Clustering and Dispersal in Modular Production Networks', *Journal of Economic Geography*, 3(2): 199–225.

Sturgeon, Timothy J. and Kawagami, Momoko (eds) (2011) *Local Learning in Global Value Chains: Experiences from East Asia*, Basingstoke: Palgrave Macmillan.

Thurbon, Elizabeth (2012) *Why the Declinists are Wrong: Misconstructing the 1970s Korean State as The Developmental State Model*, unpublished manuscript.

Underhill, Geoffrey R.D. and Zhang, Xiaoke (2005) 'The State-Market Condominium Approach', in Richard Boyd and Tak-Wing Ngo (eds) *Asian States: Beyond the Developmental Perspective*, London: RoutledgeCurzon, pp. 43–66.

Wade, Robert (1990) *Governing the Market: Economic Theory and the Role of Government in East Asian Industrialization*, Princeton, NJ: Princeton University Press.

Wade, Robert (2003) *Governing the Market: Economic Theory and the Role of Government in East Asian Industrialization*, Paperback edition with new Introduction, Princeton, NJ: Princeton University Press.

White, Gordon (ed.) (1988) *Developmental States in East Asia*, New York: St. Martin's Press.

White, Gordon and Wade, Robert (1988) 'Developmental States and Markets in East Asia: An Introduction', in Gordon White (ed.) *Developmental States in East Asia*, New York: St. Martin's Press, pp. 1–29.

Wong, Joseph (2011) *Betting on Biotech: Innovation and the Limits of Asia's Development State*, Ithaca, NY: Cornell University Press.

Woo, Jung-en (1991) *Race to the Swift: State and Finance in Korean Industrialization*, New York: Columbia University Press.

Woo-Cumings, Meredith (1999a) 'Introduction: Chalmers Johnson and the Politics of Nationalism and Development', in Meredith Woo-Cumings (ed.) *The Developmental State*, Ithaca, NY: Cornell University Press, pp. 1–31.

Woo-Cumings, Meredith (ed.) (1999b) *The Developmental State*, Ithaca, NY: Cornell University Press.

Worthington, Ross (2003) *Governance in Singapore*, London: RoutledgeCurzon.

Wu, Yongping (2005) *Political Explanation of Economic Growth: State Survival, Bureaucratic Politics, and Private Enterprises in the Making of Taiwan's Economy, 1950–1985*, Cambridge, MA: Harvard University Asia Center.

Yeung, Henry Wai-chung (2005) 'Institutional Capacity and Singapore's Developmental State: Managing Economic (In)security in the Global Economy', in Helen E.S. Nesadurai (ed.) *Globalisation and Economic Security in East Asia: Governance and Institutions*, London: Routledge, pp. 85–106.

Yeung, Henry Wai-chung (2007) 'From Followers to Market Leaders: Asian Electronics Firms in the Global Economy', *Asia Pacific Viewpoint*, 48(1): 1–25.

Yeung, Henry Wai-chung (2009a) 'Regional Development and the Competitive Dynamics of Global Production Networks: An East Asian Perspective', *Regional Studies*, 43(3): 325–51.

Yeung, Henry Wai-chung (2009b) 'The Rise of East Asia: An Emerging Challenge to the Study of International Political Economy', in Mark Blyth (ed.) *Routledge Handbook of International Political Economy*, London: Routledge, pp. 201–15.

Yeung, Henry Wai-chung (ed.) (2010) *Globalizing Regional Development in East Asia: Production Networks, Clusters, and Entrepreneurship*, London: Routledge.

Yeung, Henry Wai-chung (2011) 'From National Development to Economic Diplomacy? Governing Singapore's Sovereign Wealth Funds', *The Pacific Review*, 24(5): 625–52.

Yeung, Henry Wai-chung (2013) 'Globalizing Competition in Asia: An Evolutionary Perspective', in Michael W. Dowdle, John S. Gillespie and Imelda Maher (eds) *Asian Capitalism and the Regulation of Competition: Towards a Regulatory Geography of Global Competition Law*, Cambridge: Cambridge University Press.

The role of the state as an inter-scalar mediator in globalizing liquid crystal display industry development in South Korea

Yong-Sook Lee,[1] Inhye Heo[2] and Hyungjoo Kim[3]

[1]*Department of Public Administration, Korea University, Seoul, Republic of Korea*

[2]*Department of Political Science, Korea University, Seoul, Republic of Korea*

[3]*Science & Technology Policy Institute, Seoul, Republic of Korea*

ABSTRACT

Deriving insights from the global production network (GPN) framework, we examine the recent development of the liquid crystal display (LCD) industry in South Korea. Using the GPN framework, we focus on the role of the national state as an active inter-scalar mediator in the dynamic strategic coupling process between global leading firms and local actors in globalizing regional development. We argue that the role of the national state as an inter-scalar mediator was crucial in coordinating localized growth factors with globalizing external factors to create and develop the LCD industry. This was achievable because of the legacy of the developmental state and the top-down implementation of policy in South Korea. Using the idea of the inter-scalar mediator, we specify the role of the state as a container of laws and practices and as a constructor of regional innovation systems to globalize regional development in the context of a centripetal society. A multi-strategy approach, which included one month of participatory observation, in-depth interviews and secondary data collection, was adopted in order to enhance the validity and reliability of the data.

1. INTRODUCTION

Within the global trend towards the development of knowledge-based economies, liquid crystal display (LCD) has emerged as the dominant

This article was originally published with errors. This version has been corrected. Please see corrigendum (http://dx.doi.org/10.1080/09692290.2014.881628)

information technology of the twenty-first century, with the industry based predominantly in East Asia, particularly Japan, South Korea, Taiwan and China. Korean big businesses such as Samsung Electronics and LG Electronics have most notably made strategic investments in the LCD sector, which consists of almost 90 per cent of the total display industry. Accordingly, this industry has grown rapidly in South Korea. Samsung Electronics and LG Display, as global LCD panel players, ranked first and second, respectively, in terms of LCD display market share. The market share of the Korean LCD panel producers was 53.8 per cent as of 2011. LCD industry clusters have emerged in the Asan-Tangjeong region and in the Paju region, with a further display mini-cluster of foreign electronic suppliers in Gyeonggi province. In this paper, we analyse the main determinants of South Korean LCD industry development from a multi-scalar perspective.

The global production network (GPN) perspective can provide an extensive alternative view on globalizing regional development in East Asia by serving as a corrective to the new regionalism approach, which places excessive emphasis on local institutional structures (Coe *et al.*, 2004; Henderson *et al.*, 2002; Yeung, 2009a; Yang *et al.*, 2009; Yang, 2009; Wei, Lu and Chen, 2009). The GPN perspective stresses the multi-scalarity of the forces and processes underlying cluster development by considering both economies internal to the cluster and non-cluster economies that are linked through external networks. The GPN perspective, therefore, does not only demonstrate how clusters are economically integrated, but further clarifies the asymmetries of socio-economic development among clusters (Henderson *et al.*, 2002). In exploring the asymmetries of regional development, the GPN perspective pays close attention to the power relations among actors and institutions connected to GPNs (Coe *et al.*, 2004; Coe, Dicken and Hess, 2008). In particular, it focuses on the 'strategic coupling' of GPNs and regional assets (Coe *et al.*, 2004: 469). In other words, the dynamic connections between 'globalizing processes' that are led by transnational corporations, and regional development that involves local actors and the state, are better assessed using the GPN perspective.

However, recent studies on GPNs in the East Asian regional context have focused on how local/regional key actors become strategically coupled with the imperatives of these lead firms in GPNs from the viewpoint of competitiveness (Yeung, 2009b; Yang *et al.*, 2009; Yang, 2009; Wei, Lu and Chen, 2009). As such, they place less emphasis on the role of the national state in regional development due to an analytical disjuncture from state-centric assumptions and analyses. Hence, they may disregard the complex scale politics and the potential role of the national state in coordinating localized growth factors with globalizing external factors under the legacy of the developmental state and its top-down implementation of policy.[1]

In this paper, we focus on analysing the proactive role of the state, based on the legacy of the developmental state period, in the dynamic strategic coupling processes between trans-local actors and regional actors in an increasingly globalizing economy. To achieve this, we posit a more actor-centred framework, which acknowledges the new role of the state and its relations with multiple actors in determining the globalizing of the LCD industry's development. Based on this framework, we articulate the complex multi-scalar processes of strategic coupling between the state and other actors in regional development and investigate how the state's role in the interplay between the GPNs and the local/regional actors shapes the emerging LCD industry map and development. To illustrate our arguments, we examine LCD industry development in South Korea, where the state has strategically supported this industry as a growth engine since the 1990s.

The South Korean LCD case study provides important insights into the changing role of the state in the creation of a knowledge-intensive industry, in the context of a purported global shift toward knowledge-based economies, in which there is ever increasing utilization and production of digital information. In line with this trend, LCD has been identified by industry specialists as the dominant information technology of the twenty-first century. To take advantage of this, the South Korean state has attempted to develop information technology (IT) industries with a particular focus on LCD technology. In this context, we seek to examine and evaluate the South Korean state's role as an inter-scalar mediator in the strategic coupling process between the big Korean electronics companies such as Samsung and LG and LCD-related firms (both foreign and local) such as Sony and Phillips, and other suppliers, both foreign and local.

From the GPN perspective, we also identify the multi-scalar nature of the industry development into clusters, which are associated with the dynamics of external connections, in addition to internal linkages and spill-overs. To identify the multi-scalar nature of a cluster operation, we follow Yeung, Liu and Dicken's (2006: 521) definition of clusters as 'specific territorial entities in which functionally defined groups of firms and institutions within particular industries and sectors engage in transactions along specific production chains'.

We adopt a 'triangulation' of methods (Nightingale, 2003: 79), which is a multiple-strategy approach, to allow for more diverse ways of examining data and to enhance the validity and reflexivity of our research process. In order to provide in-depth insights into the strategic coupling processes between the state, local government and LCD firms, we undertook field research from May 2008 to October 2010 for the South Korean LCD case study. In-depth interviews (n = 32) were conducted with key informants in the Ministry of Commerce, Industry and Energy (MOCIE), the Ministry of Knowledge and Economy (MOKE), the Ministry of Finance and Economy (MOFE), focal firms, local governments, local research institutes, local universities, local LCD firms, a local LCD research and development

(R&D) centre and a venture capital firm.[2] Ethnographic field research was conducted in October 2010 for one month in the Samsung LCD industry agglomerated area, Asan-Tangjung. Secondary data were gathered from official government annual reports, from foreign and local LCD firms, and from newspaper articles and speeches by key industry players.[3]

In the following section, we critically review the existing literature, which explores regional development in Asia through the GPN perspective, and present a multi-scalar framework that acknowledges the role of the state as an inter-scalar mediator and highlights its relations with other multiple actors in determining the globalizing of LCD industry development. In section three, we provide profiles of both South Korean LCD industry development and of the emerging LCD agglomerated areas, Paju, Asan-Tangjung and the LCD supplier cluster in Gyeonggi. In section four, we examine the complex multi-scalar processes of strategic coupling between the state and other actors in regional development and the role of the state in coordinating localized growth factors with globalizing external factors in the South Korean LCD cluster development. We then conclude by suggesting the theoretical and policy implications that arise from South Korean LCD industry development.

2. GPNS AND THE ROLE OF THE STATE IN STRATEGIC COUPLING

The GPN multi-scalar approach seeks to understand the connections between 'globalizing' processes as they are embodied in the production networks of transnational corporations and regional development in specific territorial formations (Henderson *et al.*, 2002; Coe *et al.*, 2004).[4] Deriving insights from the GPN perspective (Henderson *et al.*, 2002), Coe *et al.* (2004) devised a new term, strategic coupling, to determine regional development in the era of globalization.[5] They argue that 'the dynamic strategic coupling of global production networks and regional assets, an interface mediated by a range of institutional activities across different geographical and organizational scales' (Coe *et al.*, 2004: 469), is critical in determining regional development.[6] Hence, success or failure in regional development depends on the ability of this coupling to stimulate the processes of value creation, enhancement and capture.

They stress that power and control are critical in coupling processes, but also acknowledge the very strong bargaining positions of focal firms in GPNs and their asymmetrical power relations with regional institutions. Despite these reflections on asymmetrical power relations in the coupling processes, they normatively highlight the cooperative bargaining process between focal firms in *global* production networks and *regional* institutions. Here, "'regional" institutions include not only regionally-specific institutions, but also local arms of national/supranational bodies (e.g., a trade union's "local" chapters), and extra-local institutions that affect activities within the region without necessarily having a presence (e.g., a national tax authority)' (Coe et *al.*, 2004: 474).

This theory is further developed to note that '[r]egional assets can become an advantage for regional development only if they fit the strategic needs of global production networks. The process of "fitting" regional assets with strategic needs of global production networks requires the presence of appropriate institutional structures that simultaneously promote regional advantages and enhance the region's articulation into global production networks. The likelihood of value capture in specific regions is, therefore, greatly enhanced by a cooperative set of state, labor, and business institutions that offer region-specific assets to focal firms in global production networks' (Coe *et al.*, 2004: 474, 476).

Drawing upon Coe *et al.*'s work (2004), Asian scholars have examined the ways in which local and regional firms in some Asian regions are articulated into GPNs through the process of strategic coupling (Yeung, 2009b; Yang *et al.*, 2009; Yang, 2009; Wei, Lu and Chen, 2009). They use the concept of strategic coupling to indicate a key trans-regional process to account for globalizing regional development in Asia. Drawing on empirical evidence from Taiwan, Singapore and China, they clearly explain how regions become incorporated into their GPNs through the process of strategic coupling. Among these studies, Yeung defines 'strategic coupling as a mutually dependent and constitutive process involving shared interests and cooperation between two or more groups of actors who otherwise might not act in tandem for a common strategic objective' (Yeung, 2009a: 332). Based on this definition, it is argued that the strategic coupling process is strategic because the process does not happen without active intervention and intentional action on the part of participants (Yang *et al.*, 2009; Yang, 2009; Wei, Lu and Chen, 2009). From this perspective, the coupling process, which transcends territorial boundaries, is subject to change and is neither automatic nor invariably successful. To achieve successful coupling for growth, research has placed greater emphasis on shared interests and cooperation between two or more groups. Moreover, there has been focus on how local actors in selected East Asian regions have risen and played an important role in GPNs, while breaking with state-centric assumptions and analyses. Based on East Asian empirical evidence, it has been shown how the East Asian developmental state[7] can play a necessary, but not sufficient, role in engendering regional development (Yeung, 2009b; Yang *et al.*, 2009; Yang, 2009; Wei, Lu and Chen, 2009).

Consequently, given their normative stance on growth, recent studies on GPNs have overly highlighted strategic coupling between focal firms in *global* production networks and *regional* institutions, while underestimating the potential role of the national state in coordinating localized growth factors with globalizing external factors under the legacy of the developmental state and its top-down implementation of policy. Recent studies on GPNs are, therefore, limited in their ability to fully analyse the role of the state as an inter-scalar mediator in the dynamic strategic coupling between local firms/institutions and lead firms and among lead firms in GPNs in the Asian context.

We (re)define strategic coupling[8] as a behavioural and/or relational complementarity among actors. In other words, it consists of intentional attempts to coordinate the action of different actors and organizations so as to produce specific results in relation to growth and stabilization, which is the strategic aspect of the relational interplay between and among actors (Jessop, 1990: 328). This nexus focuses on the complex interrelations, habits, political practices and cultural forms that allow a highly dynamic, and consequently unstable, capitalist system to acquire a sufficient semblance of order to function coherently, at least for a certain period of time (Harvey, 1989: 122; Tickell and Peck, 1992: 193).

The precise form of this strategic coupling is historically and geographically contingent, being conditioned by balance and power relations among multiple actors at a particular time and place. The precise nature of any coupling will still vary from country to country, and the nation-state remains an important arena of class struggle (Lambert, 1991; Tickell and Peck, 1992: 209). When a state currently has a developmental state legacy,[9] one that disciplines capital (Amsden, 1989), it has a tendency to engage in strategic coupling with certain social groups through its accumulation strategies. As a result, some groups are favoured as a matter of strategic policy for developmental purposes, while others are excluded. The strategic coupling process thus embodies a power relation in which one party exercises power by controlling resources and rewards.

In a more globalizing economy, a state that has the legacy of a developmental state[10] tends to play a crucial role as an inter-scalar mediator, as an enabler of strategic coupling between trans-local actors and regional/local actors and among trans-local actors for developmental purposes. As 'globalization is a supercomplex series of multicentric, multiscalar, multi-temporal, multiform and multicausal processes' (Dicken, 2011: 7), diverse actors, functioning on different geographical scales, are intertwined, intersecting and interacting in the globalizing economy. In this context, the new role of the national state as an inter-scalar mediator is becoming increasingly important as it can reflect both local and global intermeshing and interplay. The inter-scalar mediator is thus an enabler, the role of which is to act as a go-between the different interests that exist among different actors working on multiple geographical scales in ways that promote economic development. In the context of the state with a developmental legacy, the role of the national state as an inter-scalar mediator is more crucial because it can help its national firms to become global leading firms and also make its local firms more competitive globally so

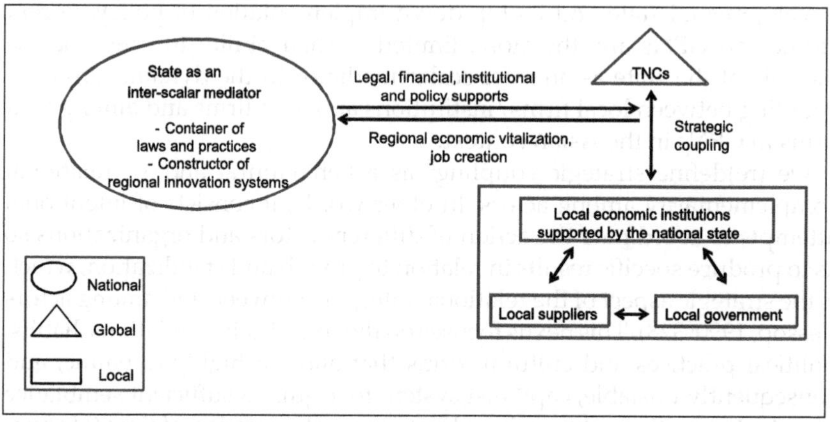

Figure 1 The role of the national state as an inter-scalar mediator in strategic coupling.

that they can achieve integration into GPNs. Thus, the inter-scalar mediator can play an important role as an enabler, facilitating strategic coupling between trans-local actors and regional/local actors and among trans-local actors (Figure 1).

In the strategic coupling process, the inter-scalar mediator can also serve as the container of laws and practices in a way that privileges national firms in order to create a supportive environment to transform national firms into global focal firms. That is, by enacting and modifying laws and practices, the inter-scalar mediator can provide various incentives such as (de)regulatory policies, physical infrastructure, tax incentives, and grants and subsidies to national firms. Global firms, which have been transformed from national firms, can then begin to create extensive GPNs. Based on these networks, they also possess key information and expertise, which can help to increase their bargaining power when seeking resources to meet their needs in the coupling process. As a result of this strategic coupling, global focal firms flourish and expand their businesses at the global level by utilizing their GPNs, while local supplier firms, which have limited access to strategic coupling, lag behind. As global focal firms grow, the traditional role of the state in disciplining capital is cut back.

Although the role of the state in disciplining focal firms is less prominent, the state can play a significant role as a inter-scalar mediator in coordinating localized growth factors with globalizing external factors by constructing regional innovation systems (i.e., establishing and financing local institutions and technical centres, public–private R&D consortiums) under the legacy of the developmental state. This role of the inter-scalar mediator is intended to improve the backwardness of local supplier firms, which impedes both national and regional development and lowers the degree of value capture. This role is crucial for facilitating the growth of the capitalist social order (capitalist reproduction). The promotion efforts to construct regional innovation systems set important preconditions for local firms to become high-tech firms and enable them to engage in strategic coupling with global leading firms. However, such efforts at promotion do not necessarily iron out the unequal relationships between focal global firms and local suppliers.

3. THE EMERGENCE OF LCD INDUSTRY CLUSTERS IN SOUTH KOREA

The South Korean state has promoted the IT industry as a growth engine in the knowledge-based economy era since the late 1990s. Due to enormous state support, Korean big businesses such as Samsung Electronics and LG Electronics have strategically invested in the LCD sector, almost 90 per cent of which consists of the display industry. As a result, this industry has grown rapidly. There were only two LCD-related firms and very few employees in 1991. However, the number of firms and employees began to grow rapidly from 1992, and had increased to 438 firms in 2008 and more than 76,000 employees in 2006 (Table 1). Samsung Electronics and LG Display have rapidly grown as global LCD panel players. They were ranked first and second in the LCD world market in terms of market share, respectively (Table 2). As a result, three LCD clusters have successfully emerged in South Korea: the Asan-Tangjeong LCD cluster in Chungcheong

Table 1 Profile of the South Korean LCD sector (1991–2008)

Year	Number of companies	Number of employees	Value of shipment (million won)	Value added (million won)
1991	2	-	-	-
1992	4	101	1,064	1,047
1999	36	7,519	3.862,504	2,439,008
2000	65	11,610	5,133,215	2,973,458
2001	120	17,843	6,490,175	1,900,811
2002	163	28,879	13,202,244	6,670,748
2003	202	43,372	21,286,177	9,277,149
2004	234	51,451	31,585,065	14,933,606
2005	277	63,125	35,189,712	15,422,710
2006	310	76,718	40,143,289	14,973,338
2007	369	n.a.	n.a.	n.a.
2008	438	n.a.	n.a.	n.a.

Source: Korea National Statistical Office, www.kostat.go.kr (accessed 12 January 2012).

Table 2 TFT-LCD panel manufacturers' market share (%) (2000–11)

Year	2000		2004		2005		2006*		2007*		2008*		*Q4 2009		*Q4 2010		**2011	
Ranking	Manufacturer	Market share	Manufacturer	Market share	Manufacturer	Market share	Manufacturer	Market share	Manufacturer	Market share	Manufacturer	Market share	Manufacturer	Market share	Manufacturer	Market share	Manufacturer	Market share
1	Samsung	21	Samsung	22	LG Philips	21	Samsung	24	Samsung	23	LG Display	25	LG Display	24.7	LG Display	27.9	Samsung	27.6
2	LG Philips	14	LG Philips	21	Samsung	22	LG Philips	21	LG Philips	21	Samsung	21	Samsung	21.5	Samsung	23.9	LG Display	26.2
3	Hitachi	10	AUO	13	AUO	14	AUO	16	AUO	19	AUO	17	CMO	19.8	CMI	16.9	AUO	15.7
4	Sharp	8	CMO	9	CMP	13	CMO	12	CMO	13	CMP	14	AUO	16.1	AUO	15.8	CMI	15.3
5	Toshiba	7	CPT	8	CPT	6	CPT	7	Sharp	6	CPT	8			Sharp	3.9	Sharp	7.4
6	NET	7	Sharp	7	Sharp	6	Sharp	6	CPT	6	Sharp	4						
Korean companies' market share		35		43		43		45		45		46		46.2		51.8		53.8

Source: Bok *et al.* (2007); *Displaybank (2011); **etnews (2 February 2012).

province, the Paju LCD cluster in Gyeonggi province and an LCD mini-cluster of foreign electronic suppliers, also in Gyeonggi province.

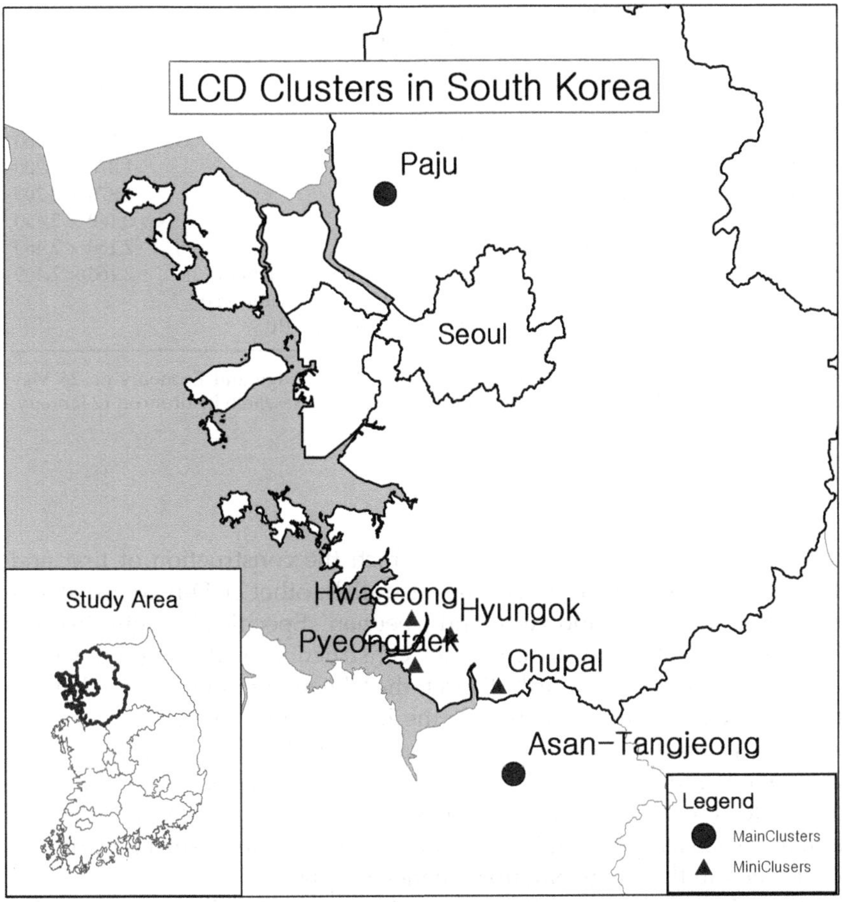

3.1. The Asan-Tangjeong LCD cluster

The Asan-Tangjeong LCD cluster emerged around 1995 in the Tangjeong area, which is located in Asan in Chungcheong province, in the central part of South Korea. Samsung Electronics (SE) is a focal firm, and 153 display related firms were located in this cluster as of February 2009.[11]

This cluster is called the Crystal Valley and includes the two cities of Asan and Cheonan. According to a manager at the Display Center, which supports firms' activities in this cluster, '[T]he Crystal valley covers not

Table 3 LCD lines from Samsung Electronics (1995–2011)

Line (generation)	Location	Beginning of operation/current status	Panel size (mm x mm)
1(2)	Giheung	March 1995	370 × 470
2(3)	Giheung	September 1996	550 × 650
3(3.5)	Cheonan	February 1998	600 × 720
4(4)	Cheonan	August 2000	730 × 920
5(5)	Cheonan	August 2002	1,100 × 1,250
6(5)	Cheonan	October 2003	1,100 × 1,300
7-1(7)	Tangjeong	April 2005	1,870 × 2,200
7-2(7)	Tangjeong	March 2006	1,870 × 2,200
8-1(8)	Tangjeong	Q3 2007	2,160 × 2,460
8-2(8)	Tangjeong	February 2009	2,160 × 2,460
8-2-2(8)	Tangjeong	Decided on establishment of additional eighth generation of LCD line, January 2010	2,160 × 2,460

Source: Interview with a staff from the Ministry of Knowledge and Economy on 26 May 2008; *Interview with staff members of Samsung Economic Research Institute on 12 January; **Moneytoday, 14 January 2010.

only the Tangjeong LCD district in which the construction of first and second LCD lines was completed but also all the other LCD-related districts that are scattered around Asan and Cheonan'. Specifically, eight districts have been constructed or are under construction in the Crystal Valley. Of these, the Cheonan fourth district, the Cheonan foreign firms' district, the Hongseong-Eunha first district, the Tanjeong first techno-complex, the Asan-Inju first district and the Cheonan third district have already been completed, and the Asan Technovalley and the Tangjeong second district are under construction. Among these districts, SE's LCD lines and its affiliates such as Samsung Corning Precision Glass and Samsung Corning are located in the Tangjeong first techno-complex.

SE, which entered into the LCD industry in 1994, has also played a crucial role in growing the LCD sector by lowering the prime costs of the larger LCD panels through massive investments. SE made a decisive decision to construct third to sixth generation LCD lines and to produce large-sized panels in Asan and Cheonan in the mid-1990s (Table 3).[12] Moreover, SE established S-LCD (the 7–1, 7–2 and 8–1 generation of LCD lines) in Tangjeong on 8 March 2004 through a joint venture with Sony in order to produce large-sized LCD TV panels (Table 3). Its total investment touched 2,100 billion won (about 1,858 million US dollars). S-LCD was registered as a foreign investment firm on 28 April 2004 and invested $923 million in the first investment project and $900 million in the second

(Ministry of Finance and Economy, 2006). It is a representative case of the successful attraction of FDI in the Korean context.

The Asan-Tanjeong cluster contributes to regional development: after its creation, the local population grew up to 16 per cent within five years and 31 per cent within 10 years;[13] tax revenues increased from 147 billion won in 2007 to 246 billion won in 2010.[14] The LCD products from this cluster accounted for 44.6 per cent of the domestic market and 27.6 per cent of the world market in 2011.[15] To develop this cluster further, the Asan local government has also made concerted efforts through its investment plans. Specifically, it has made a plan to invest 30 trillion won in the Tangjeong first techno-complex up to 2015, expecting to produce 20 trillion won of yearly manufacturing output and to create 50,000 new jobs. The local government started to construct the Tangjeong second techno-complex in October 2006 and anticipates its completion by 2015.[16] The government has attempted to induce the display-related firms, which are scattered in the Asan and Cheonan areas, to move into this second district.

3.2. The Paju LCD cluster

The Paju LCD cluster is located in the northern part of Gyeonggi province, only 10 km away from the Demilitarized Zone within the Seoul metropolitan region (SMR). Its focal firm is LG Display, formerly LG Philips LCD.

The Paju LCD cluster was designed to produce seventh generation LCD lines for LG Philips LCD (LPL) Corporation. LPL was established in September 1999 and produced generation 3.5 and sixth generation LCD lines in Kumi. When LPL, whilst looking for a new factory site, sought information from the Gyeonggi provincial government about eligible sites, the provincial government took proactive action to induce LPL to move into the Paju area. Not only the provincial government, but the central and local governments, too, provided financial and institutional support to enable the creation of the Paju cluster, and construction began in 2002. At present, it is the site of the eighth generation LCD factory, which produces 2200 mm×2250 mm panels; the ninth generation LCD line (2500 mm×2900 mm) is under investment in this cluster (Table 4).

This cluster consists of three districts: the main district, Moonsan district, and Pajuwollong district. LG Display and its three partner firms are located in the main district. Moonsan district, which is divided into Dangdong and Sunyoo, is an industrial district for LCD suppliers and related firms. Specifically, Dangdong is a district exclusively for foreign firms, while Sunyoo houses domestic firms. Four LG affiliates, including LG Electronics, LG Chemical, LG Innotek and LG Micron, are located in Pajuwollong district.

Table 4 LCD lines from LG Display (1995–2011)

Line (generation)	Location	Beginning of operation/current status	Panel size (mm x mm)
1(2)	Kumi	August 1995	370 × 470
2(3)	Kumi	February 1998	590 × 670
3(4)	Kumi	June 2000	680 × 880
4(5)	Kumi	March 2002	1,000 × 1,200
5(5)	Kumi	May 2003	1,100 × 1,250
6(6)	Kumi	August 2004	1,370 × 1,670
7(7)	Paju	November 2006	1,950 × 2,250
8(8)	Paju	May 2010	2,200 × 2,500
8(8)	Paju	Decided to establish additional eighth generation LCD line, March 2010	2,200 × 2,500
8(8)	Paju	Decided to establish additional eighth generation LCD line, January 2011	2,200 × 2,500
9(9)	Paju	9th generation LCD line, under investment	2,500 × 2,900

Source: The Ministry of Commerce Industry and Energy. 27 April 2006. Paju is in the advance guard of LCD Industry. Press Release.

LG Display, as the focal firm in this cluster, has led to the development of the global LCD market. LPL ranked first in 2005, and LG Display ranked first in 2008, 2009 and 2010 and second in 2011 in terms of LCD panel market share (Table 2). In addition, once the Paju cluster began to operate, the population of Paju grew very rapidly due to job creation by LPL. The population grew by more than 12 per cent from 240,000 in 2003 to 387,273 in early 2008.[17] Moreover, the Gross Regional Domestic Product (GRDP) of Paju increased from 3,696,538 million won in 2004 to 7,366,733 million won in 2009.[18]

3.3. Mini-cluster for foreign electronics suppliers

As a result of the formation and operation of the above two LCD clusters, display-related foreign suppliers, especially those from Japan, began to build operations in Gyeonggi province. Foreign firms preferred to locate in Hyungok, Pyeongtaek, Hwaseong and Chupal, which lie within Gyeonggi province in the middle of the two LCD clusters, in order to supply their parts and materials to both S-LCD (SE) and LPL (LG Display). To reflect the foreign firms' needs, the Gyeonggi provincial government specifically designated Hyungok as an industrial district for foreign firms (Table 5). Therefore, a mini-cluster for foreign electronics suppliers has been created near Hyungok district.

Table 5 LCD-related foreign direct investments in South Korea

	Company	Type of investment	Investing company	Domestic joint company	Location/time of investment
Glass	Asahi Glass Fine Techno Korea (AFK)	Full	Asahi Glass (Japan)		Kumi, April 2005 Supply LPL's manufacturing line under 6th generation
	Paju Electric Glass (PEG)	Joint	NEG (Japan)	LPL	Paju, June 2006
	Schott-kuramoto Processing Korea	Joint (Germany, Japan)	Schott (Germany, 75%) Kuramoto (Japan, 25%)		Ohchang, November 2005
	NH Techno Glass Korea	Joint	NSG (Japan, 50%), Hoya (Japan, 50%)		Pyeongtaek, November 2005
Polarizing plate/polarizing film	Dongwoo Fine Chem	Full	Sumitomo Chem (Japan)		Pyeongtaek Started as a joint venture between Dongyang Chem. and Sumitomo, Itochu, in 1991 → Sumitomo acquired 100% stake in 2002 (color filter, diffusion plate used for BLU, polarizing film)
	Korea Nitto Optical	Joint	Nitto Denko (Japan, 75%)		Pyeongtaek, Hyungok, Q1 of 2005 (polarizing film)
	3M Korea	Full	3M (US)		Hwaseong, May 2006 (polarizing film, dual brightness enhancement film)

	ASE		ASE (US)		Hyungok (thin film vapour deposition)
	Nissan Chemical		Nissan (Japan)		Chupal (chemicals used for LCD)
Colour filter	Dongwoo STI	Full	Sumitomo Chem (Japan)		Pyeongtaek Merger with Dongwoo fine chem. in 2005
Back light unit	Delagras Korea	Joint	Delaglas (US)	Raygen	Chupal, December 2004
	Toraysaehan	Joint	Toray (Japan)	Saehan	Kumi, December 1999 (films used in optics, diffusion plate, prism sheets)
	Harison Toshiba Lighting Korea	Full	Harison Toshiba Lighting (Japan)		Ohchang Producer of cold cathode fluorescent lamps (CCFL) Since March 2004
Liquid crystal	Merck Advanced Technology	Full	Merck (Germany)		Poseung, August 2002
Other materials	Chisso Korea	Full	Chisso (Japan)		Pyeongtaek, November 2005 (chemicals used to coat films)
	Hoya Electronics Korea	Joint	Hoya (Japan)		Pyeongtaek, June 2004 (photo mask)
	Nano Techmikuni	Joint	Mikuni (Japan)		Pyeongtaek, December 2005 (inks used for colour filters)
	Graphion Technologies Korea		Graphion (US)		Hyungok. (thin film technology)

(Continued on next page)

Table 5 LCD-related foreign direct investments in South Korea *(Continued)*

	Company	Type of investment	Investing company	Domestic joint company	Location/time of investment
Equipment	Ulvac Korea	Full	Ulvac (Japan)		Pyeongtaek/ Huyngok, June 2005 (LCD thin film facilities)
	Ulvac Korea Precision	Full	Ulvac (Japan)		Pyeongtaek, June 2005 (vacuum changer)
	PS Technology	Full	Ulvac (Japan)		Pyeongtaek, June 2005 (equipment and parts cleaning)
	AI	Full	AI (US)		Ansan, 2004 (chemical vapour deposition facilities)
	Carys	Full	Nakan (Japan)		Pyeongtaek, June 2006 (apparatus applying LCD alignment layer)
	Daihen	Full	Daihen (Japan)		Pyeongtaek, June 2006 (robots used in LCD industry)
	Nikko Materials Korea	Full	Nikko Materials (Japan)		Pyeongtaek, May 2005 LCD sputtering target
	HMF Technology Korea		Hitachi (Japan)		Pyeongtaek, July 2005 LCD sputtering target
	M&S Fine Tech	Full	M&S Fine Tech (Japan)		Pyeongtaek. (LCD glass grinder)

Source: Bok *et al.* (2007); The Seoul Shinmun (14 November 2005); Newsis (1 February 2007), Etnews (30 December 2002), EBNnews (9 July 2008); Digital Times (2 November 2005).

4. THE ROLE OF THE NATIONAL STATE AS AN INTER-SCALAR MEDIATOR IN STRATEGIC COUPLING PROCESSES

The creation of LCD clusters in South Korea resulted from strategic coupling between South Korean transnational corporations (TNCs) such as Samsung and LG, foreign TNCs such as Sony and Phillips, and various regional actors/and institutions such as the provincial and local governments and local suppliers. Samsung and LG's strategic needs were to expand their businesses and to find suitable production sites for this purpose.[19] The provincial and local governments in South Korea wanted to keep Samsung's and LG's investments within their jurisdictions and thus competed against one another to attract those investments. The national state's interest was in strengthening national competitiveness by boosting new industry growth.[20] Under the developmental state legacy, relatively large industrial establishments can be approved only by the national state in South Korea. In this context, the state has played a crucial role as the inter-scalar mediator in the strategic coupling between global TNCs and regional actors and institutions. This role was shaped and facilitated through not only the state's containment of laws and practices, but also through the construction of regional innovation systems.

4.1. The state as the container of laws and practices in strategic coupling

The national state played a crucial role as the container of laws and practices in the creation of the Paju and Asan-Tangjung clusters. LG and Samsung initially wanted to use the Seoul metropolitan region (SMR) for their production sites, but this was strictly prohibited by law under the developmental state legacy. On the basis of the 1982 Capital Region Management Act and its 1994 amendment, the national state has restricted relatively large industrial establishments, as any plans for construction can be approved only by the Capital Region Growth Management Deliberation Committee. This regulation measure is aimed to prevent the overconcentration of factories, schools and other population-concentrating facilities as prescribed by Presidential Decree in the SMR. Despite this strong regulation measure, there was room to ease the regulation because any exceptional cases could also be prescribed by Presidential Decree.

In this context, Samsung chose a new location in Asan-Tangjung, the closest region to the SMR. In response, the national state provided huge funding to facilitate cluster creation. The state subsidized 1,430 million won for the construction of the Tangjeong first techno-complex out of the total funding requirement of 9,472 million won, while the provincial government provided 93 million won (Asan Local Government, 2009).

In the construction of the Tangjeong second techno-complex, the state provided 2,422 million won (Asan Local Government, 2009). This took place in 2004, when Samsung was seeking permission for a company town project with the aim of constructing an industrial district as well as a new town. This was despite the fact that private companies were not allowed to construct industrial districts or towns by law in South Korea.[21] However, the MOFE approved the building of a Samsung company town as an exceptional circumstance. As huge development gains were expected from the creation of the new town, the speculation that the state had granted favours to Samsung provoked strong opposition from the public against the company town project. The state cancelled the company town project as such, but permitted Samsung to build LCD industry plants and apartments only for the Samsung LCD employees, relaxing regulations against the construction of houses and factories based on a presidential ordinance.[22] This example indicates the national state's role as the container of laws and practices, which could foster strategic coupling between Samsung and the Asan-Tangjung region.

In the LG case, the state demonstrated its distinctive role as the inter-scalar mediator by approving the location site within the SMR and arranging strategic coupling between LG and Philips. When LG was also looking for a new location site, the Gyeonggi provincial government was eager to attract the firm's investment within its jurisdiction and initiated negotiations with LG.[23] However, under the legacy of the centralized developmental state, the provincial government did not have substantial policy tools to create an industrial cluster within the SMR, where new constructions of manufacturing plants and plant extensions of large businesses were strictly restricted based on a balanced national development strategy. The creation of the Paju cluster would not have been possible without the crucial role played by the national state, which had the policy tools to relax planning control in the SMR.

At that time, large domestic firms were prohibited from building factories, and only joint-venture companies with foreign firms, whose share was more than 51 per cent, in 24 high-tech sectors were temporarily allowed to establish new factories within the SMR.[24] This indicates the way in which the national state, as the inter-scalar mediator, could orchestrate strategic coupling between big Korean companies and foreign TNCs in order to induce foreign direct investment. However, the LCD industry was not included in the 24 high-tech sectors, and Phillips' share in LPL was not more than 51 per cent. Moreover, the Ministry of Defense (MOD) put forward strong dissenting opinion about the creation of an LCD cluster, as the Paju region has many military installations and the expected location for the cluster was very close to where army troops were based. The MOD argued against the creation of a large industrial cluster in Paju because it would be liable to cause significant difficulties in conducting military operations. The Ministry of Construction and Transportation (MOCT) also expressed its concern about the possibility of the cluster overcrowding the SMR. Both the MOD and the MOCT were opposed to amending the planning control ordinances, while the MOCIE wanted to create the cluster in order to boost the economy. The Gyeonggi provincial and the Paju local governments also continued to make pleas to the state for the relaxation of planning control.[25]

The national state responded positively to these requests for deregulation since it recognized that the creation of the LCD cluster in Paju could contribute to promoting LCD industry development, improving Korea's national image by attracting a foreign TNC near the Demilitarized Zone, and thus boosting the national economy. In this context, the planning control ordinances were amended.[26] In March 2003, based on presidential ordinances, the MOFE permitted construction and extension of LCD factories in the SMR by temporarily (by December 2003) lowering the mandated foreign firms' share from 51 per cent to 50 per cent. The MOFE also, as an exception, lowered foreign firms' share up to 30 per cent within the Paju LCD cluster, and joint ventures with foreign firms whose shares were above 30 per cent were thus able to build new factories and make extensions (Ministry of Finance and Economy, 2003; Ministry of Commerce, Industry and Energy, 2006). Alongside this deregulatory policy, the state provided 223 million won in 2004 and 1,265 million won in 2005 for the construction of industry water facilities. It also provided 37 million won in 2003 and 377 million won in 2005 for the building of a waste water disposal plant. The MOCT helped further by subsidizing 250 million won in 2004 and 169 million won in 2005 when the local government faced a fund shortage in constructing main roads (Lee, 2008).

Both the Asan-Tangjung and the Paju cases show the new role of the national state as the container of laws and practices, which could foster strategic coupling between the focal firms and the region. In the Asan-Tangjung cluster case, the state gave Samsung the right to construct the industrial cluster for growth, but regulated the location of the cluster to the non-Seoul metropolitan area for balanced regional development. In the Paju cluster case, the state relaxed planning control and lowed foreign firms' share in joint ventures in order to construct the cluster. These cases show that the traditional role of the national state in disciplining capital was cut back.

4.2. The state as constructor of regional innovation systems

As shown in the above examples, the national state, as the container of laws and practices, privileged focal firms with GPNs, such as Samsung and LG, in order to enhance national competitiveness. This targeting strategy for focal firms, however, placed limits upon the further growth of the

LCD industry because it relied on expensive imported materials and components and did not nurture local suppliers.[27] In this context, the national state began to play a crucial role as the constructor of regional innovation systems by establishing and financing local institutions and technical centres and public–private R&D consortiums for the further growth of the LCD industry in the non-SMR areas.

In Asan-Tangjung, the state established regional/local institutions and technology centres such as the Chungnam Techno Park Display Center and the Display R&D Cluster Center.[28] These centres played a supporting role for firms (in particular small firms) by providing technological assistance, stimulating cooperative interaction among small firms and inter-firm linkages, and helping to commercialize R&D results. They thus contributed to promoting the growth of LCD-related suppliers and advancing technology. The state provided 345 million won from 2002 to 2006 in order to establish the Chungnam Techno Park Display Center (Table 6). The state also provided funding for setting up the Display R&D Cluster Center. This centre was set up at a local university (Sun Moon University). According to the director of the centre, the state has provided 2 billion won every year since 2004, and this level of funding will be continued until 2013.[29] The main aim of this centre is to establish a regional innovation system to support local firms, nurture local talent, and strengthen industry–academic cooperation. In particular, this centre provides support to local firms, which produce display parts and equipment, through its 'Generic technology development for display parts and equipment' project.[30]

This project has resulted in positive outcomes in terms of patents, academic papers and commercialization (Table 7). From this three-stage project (2004–11), a total of 145 patents related to display industries were registered domestically and internationally, and 146 academic papers focusing on display technologies were published in Science Citation Index (SCI) journals. The efforts to commercialize the project results brought 56 cases of technology transfer along with engineering fees of 911 million won. Current projects for individual companies involved in display parts and equipment include developing complex input devices

Table 6 Funds for the establishment of the Display Center (unit: million won)

	2002	2003	2004	2005	2006	Total
Total funds	8.885.0	5,549.4	7,061.5	13,161.4	11,461.4	46,118.7
National	5,600.0	3,700.0	4,900.0	11,000.0	9,300.0	34,500.0
Provincial	3,285.0	1,849.4	648.5	648.4	648.4	7,079.7
Private	0	0	1,513.0	1,513.0	1,513.0	4,539.0

Source: Ministry of Commerce, Industry and Energy (24 September 2008).

Table 7 Outcomes of the Display R&D Center

Outcome	Patent				Academic papers and presentations (number)				Commercialization			
	Domestic patent		Foreign patent									
Project name	Application (case)	Registration (case)	Application (case)	Registration (case)	Papers in SCI journals	Papers in other journals	Presentations at international conferences	Presentations at domestic conferences	Technology transfer (case)	Technology consulting (case)	Company visit (case)	Engineering fee(million won)
Record of first stage (October 2004–June 2007)	89	28	15		62	27			25	89		232
Record of second stage (July 2007–June 2009)	58	98	13	9	46	45			21	101		309
Record of third stage (July 2009–June 2011)	46	2	5	8	38	30	29	31	10	71	99	370

Source: Display R&D Center, 2012.

with touch and tablet functions, low-power and high-efficiency LED backlight component technology, high-power LED packages applying colour uniformity, enhancement and high heat-proof technologies, next generation equipment for LCD surface inspection and repairing, and rollers and carriers for LCD using CNT nanocomposites. The total budget for the project from October 2004 to June 2013 was 26 billion won. Of this, the majority – 18 billion won – came from the MOCIE (2004–08) and the MOKE (2008–present), while 2.25 billion won came from the local government and 5.75 billion won came from local universities and companies (Ministry of Knowledge and Economy, 2007). A number of international conferences and seminars hosting leading international scholars were also held successfully by the Display R&D Cluster Center.

The creation and operation of the Chungnam Techno Park Display Center and Display R&D Cluster Center shows the role of the national state in constructing regional innovation systems. At a wider level, this example also shows the inter-scalar mediator role of the national state in coordinating localized growth factors with globalizing exogenous factors.

5. CONCLUSION

By providing an analysis of South Korean LCD industry development, we have examined how the state can play a crucial role in coordinating localized growth factors with globalizing external factors through the creation of newly-emerging clusters. In the South Korean context, it would have been almost impossible to create the LCD industry clusters without state amendment of planning control ordinances, coordination of the contrasting views held by different ministries, and the construction of regional innovation systems. The role of the state as an inter-scalar mediator, coordinating contrasting opinions and views among related actors and facilitating strategic coupling between and among these related actors, was distinctive because of the way in which the state amended and enacted related regulations and laws and constructed regional innovations. This example demonstrates the new role of the South Korean state, which held the legacy of a developmental state, as the inter-scalar mediator in the dynamic strategic coupling processes between trans-local actors and regional actors in an increasingly globalizing economy.

This theoretically grounded empirical study may improve on early GPN work, which highlighted only the strategic coupling between trans-local actors (global) and regional/local actors in globalizing regional development, by specifying the role of the state as an inter-scalar mediator, which can facilitate strategic coupling among related actors and coordinate localized growth factors with globalizing external factors in the creation of the newly-emerging clusters. Early GPN work has tended to highlight inter-firm dynamics, rather than state–firm relations and has confined the role of the state to a facilitator in helping firms to innovate and integrate with GPNs. However, the current study, which highlights the inter-scalar mediator role, presents the idea of a more active role for the state as a container of laws and practices and as a constructor of regional innovation systems. In particular, the role of the state as a constructor of regional innovation implies the possibility of direct protection and support of local firms as well as state intervention in inter-firm relations.

This case study can provide theoretical and policy implications for other countries which have developmental states or the legacy of a developmental state and which also aim to create and develop new knowledge-intensive industries. Particularly, this study can give theoretical insights to Japan, Taiwan and China, nations in which the LCD industry has emerged successfully. In these countries, the state has played a significant role in promoting the LCD industry, but the way in which the state facilitates strategic coupling with related other actors may be different, depending on the power relations between the state and these related actors. However, we cannot recommend that the state should assume a role as an inter-scalar mediator in promoting the LCD industry to non-former developmental states, as the LCD industry is not favourable to newcomers.[31]

In this paper, we focus on specifying the role of the state as a successful inter-scalar mediator in the strategic coupling processes between trans-local actors and regional/local actors in creating the LCD clusters, rather than analysing the changing power relations between the state and related actors such as focal firms. The role of the South Korean state as an inter-scalar mediator was, however, rather limited in terms of coordinating and mitigating the severe competition between Samsung and LG. To reduce the competition between these two Korean focal firms in global markets and to achieve the international competitiveness of the Korean LCD industry, the state attempted to promote the cross-purchase of panels between the two in the late 2000s, but this was unsuccessful.[32] This example demonstrates that the traditional role of the state in disciplining capital has been cut back. Further, it indicates that the relations between the state and the focal firms are much more complex than might be expected. Future research should take into account the changing power relations between the state and diverse related actors, such as focal firms (both domestic and foreign) and local suppliers, as well as the inter-firm dynamics. Civil society is well developed in South Korea, which has raised the possibility for voices to be heard that are critical of the dominant global lead firms such as Samsung and LG. The strong role of civil society may drive the state's actions. In our future research, we will examine the politics that drives the state's action and shapes its various (de)regulatory policies.

NOTES

1 However, as Coe, Dicken and Hess (2008) argue, the national state remains a key actor in GPNs.
2 We were unable to officially interview the LCD focal firms, but interviewed informally former managers in Samsung and LG-Philips and research fellows at the Samsung Economy Research Institute. In addition, we were able to meet with and listen to managers in the focal firms in formal local meetings in the ethnographic field research process. Through these interviews, we were able to collect information and data on the views of the LCD focal firms.
3 Although we adopted a multi-strategy approach to enhance the validity and reliability of the data, our research has some methodological limitations. Since the emergence and development of the LCD industry is a recent phenomenon, the impact cannot be fully assessed by snapshot analysis.
4 Since the GPN approach highlights extra-local links, not all GPN-related literature used the term, cluster, and, in some cases, this term is even deliberately avoided.
5 Despite the importance of the concept of strategic coupling in their account of regional development, they 'acknowledge the term is imperfect and may be perceived as a rather crude structural interpretation of regional development' in their notes (Coe *et al.*, 2004: 482). The current paper will as such provide a redefinition in a subsequent section.
6 They highlight three sets of conditions for regional development: first, 'the existence of economies of scale and scope within specific regions'; second, 'the possibility of localization economies within global production networks'; and last, 'the appropriate configurations of "regional" institutions to "hold down" global production networks and unleash regional potential' (Coe *et al.*, 2004: 470).
7 The East Asian developmental states have more independent, or autonomous, political power as well as more control over the economy. They are characterized by strong state intervention as well as extensive regulation and planning. However, there is a typological difference between the developmental bureaucratic state (DBS) in Japan and South Korea and the developmental network state (DNS) in Taiwan. The former is characterized by industrial policy, that is, the deliberate choice to develop certain strategic industries (Johnson, 1982) as well as to govern the market (Wade, 1990), while the latter plays a role as a catalyst in helping firms develop product and process innovations so as to promote economic development (Ó Riain, 2004; Block, 2008).
8 This term, strategic coupling, is deeply influenced by Jessop's work (1990) and Tickell and Peck's study (1992). These use the concept of 'structural coupling' to explain the co-evolution of autonomous structures. In that sense, 'the development of one structure affects the evolution of the other, but it neither controls it in a hierarchical relation of command nor subordinates it through a functionalist logic which requires one system to act for and on behalf of the other system' (Jessop, 1990: 359). They, therefore, focus primarily on the structural aspect of the coupling process of two or more systems and structures (i.e., structural coupling between accumulation and regulation), while we focus on the strategic aspect of the coupling process among/between actors in the multi-scalar setting.
9 The developmental state provided cheap credit and other subsidies and incentives to firms if they met the performance criteria that the state imposed on the recipient firms (Amsden, 1989). In this paper, we do not attempt to elaborate the typological difference of developmental states between the DBS and

the DNS and the evolution of both. To attempt this, we would need to scrutinize the evolutionary relations between the state and firms as well as inter-firm dynamics, an attempt that is beyond the scope of this paper. We, thus, leave a certain scope for future investigation into the evolution of both the DBS and the DNS. Broadly, it can be suggested that both the DBS and the DNS evolve over time, and the DBS may shift toward the DNS.

10 After experiencing the Asian financial crisis since 1997, there have been ongoing debates on the characteristics of the South Korean state. Chang (1998) and Chang, Park and Yoo (1998) argued that the traditional mechanism of the industrial policy and financial regulation were dismantled after the Asian financial crisis. Pirie (2005, 2007) argued for the new Korean state as a neoliberal state. Yet, Wong (2004) and Jo, Jung and Lee (2007) argued for the democratic developmental state. Evans (2010) and Chang (2010) normatively urged the need for the democratic development state.

11 There were just 66 firms in 1999 and 126 firms in 2007 (Interview with a staff member at the Asan Display Firms Association on 19 October 2009).

12 SE's main LCD plants are now in the Crystal Valley, but its earlier main LCD plants, which produced small-sized panels for mobile instruments, were located in Giheung in Gyeonggi province (Table 3).

13 Interview with staff members of Asan City Government on 5 February 2009.

14 Asia Business Daily, 18 October 2010. Asan stands high as a new industrial center. Retrieved from http://view.asiae.co.kr/news/view.htm?idxno=2010101807330187147&nvr=Y

15 Etnews, 2 February 2012. Samsung and LG occupied 58.3% of the world LCD market. Retrieved from http://www.etnews.com/news/device/device/2554081_1479.html

16 Asia Business Daily, 18 October 2010. Asan stands high as a new industrial center. Retrieved from http://view.asiae.co.kr/news/view.htm?idxno=2010101807330187147&nvr=Y

17 Gyeonggi provincial government website, www.gg.go.kr (accessed 2 April 2012).

18 Gyeonggi Provincial Government. 2010. An Estimation of the Gross Regional Domestic Products of Cities and Counties in Gyeonggi Province. Retrieved from http://stat.gg.go.kr/publication/publication01_01.jsp?pub_sosok=005&htxt_code=125369690800028424172917544O7235 (accessed on 2 April 2012).

19 Interview with a former manager in both Samsung and LG on 22 January 2010 and with two research fellows at the Samsung Economic Research Institute on 12 January 2009.

20 Interview with an MOKE official on 26 May 2008.

21 Interview with two officials in both MOFE and MOKE on 26 May 2008.

22 Interview with a former MOFE official on 25 July 2008.

23 Interview with a research fellow in the Gyeonggi Development Institute on 25 July 2008.

24 Interview with an MOFE official on 26 May 2008.

25 Interview with an official in the Paju local government on 24 September 2008.

26 Interview with a former MOFE official on 25 July 2008.

27 Interview with two research fellows in the Chungnam Techno Park Display Center on 5 February 2009.

28 The MOCIE, now known as the MOKE, pursued a regional R&D project in order to construct a regional innovation system from the mid-2000s. In 2005, the Regional Research & Development Centre Business Leaders' Council was

established. As of 2010, nine regional R&D centres have been established in nine regions, excluding the SMR.

29 Interview with a director in the Display R&D Center on 5 February 2009.

30 Interview with a director and a research professor in the Display R&D Center on 19 October 2009.

31 That is, newcomers without huge government support would face considerable difficulty in entering the industry and competing with incumbents because the industry requires large-scale investments for the economy, given the scale of production (Lee, Lim and Song, 2005). A firm's success in the display industry also requires aggressive and fast investments for next-generation panels, and newcomers are thus disadvantaged. In addition, they would be unlikely to survive in the global market without government support as the display industry experiences cyclical fluctuations.

32 The MOKE and the Korea Display Industry Association held a meeting to pursue policy that could promote the cross-purchase of panels between Samsung and LG in May 2007. According to this policy, Samsung and LG had to agree to the cross–purchase of panels. More specifically, the TV sector of Samsung Electronics would buy 37-inch modules from LG Display, while LG Electronics would buy 52-inch modules from Samsung's LCD sector. This policy, which showed direct government intervention even in purchase, however, fizzled out due to a change of government from the Roh to the Lee government in the late 2000s.

FUNDING STATEMENT

The research upon which this paper is based was supported by Korea University.

REFERENCES

Amsden, A. (1989). *Asia's Next Giant: South Korea and Late Industrialization*, New York: Oxford University Press.

Asan Local Government (2009) Internal Data, February 2009.

Block, F. (2008) 'Swimming Against the Current: The Rise of a Hidden Developmental State in the United States', *Politics & Society*, 36(2): 169–206.

Bok, D.K., Koo, B.K., Chang, S.W., Lim, T.Y., Jung, D.Y., Lim, Y.M. and Choi, B.S. (2007) *Network Structure and the Way of Cooperation of East Asian LCD Clusters*, Seoul: Samsung Economy Research Institute & Japan Research Institute.

Breschi, S. and Lissoni, F. (2001) 'Knowledge Spillovers and Local Innovation Systems: A Critical Survey', *Industrial & Corporate Change*, 10(4): 975–1005.

Chang, H.J. (1998). 'Korea: The Misunderstood Crisis', *World Development*, 26(8): 1555–1561.

Chang, H.J. (2010) 'How to "Do" a Developmental State', in O. Edigheji (ed.) *Constructing a Democratic Developmental State in South Africa*, Cape Town: HSRC Press, pp. 82–96.

Chang, H.J., Park, H.J. and Yoo, C.G. (1998) 'Interpreting the Korean Crisis: Financial Liberalization, Industrial Policy, and Corporate Governance', *Cambridge Journal of Economics*, 22(6): 735–46.

Coe, N., Dicken, P. and Hess, M. (2008) 'Global Production Networks: Realizing the Potential', *Journal of Economic Geography*, 8(3): 271–95.

Coe, N., Hess, M., Yeung, H.W.C., Dicken, P. and Henderson, J. (2004) "'Globalizing" Regional Development: A Global Production Networks Perspective', *Transactions Institute of British Geography*, 29: 468–84.

Dicken, P. (2011) *Global Shift: Mapping the Changing Contours of the World Economy*, 6th edn, New York and London: The Guilford Press.

Digital Times (2005) Japanese semiconductor and LCD related firms head to Pyeongtake, Hyungok. Accessed at: http://news.naver.com/main/read.nhn?mode=LSD&mid=sec&sid1=105&oid=029&aid=0000119024.

Display R&D Cluster (2012) Internal Report.

EBNnews (9 July 2008) Merke started construction of a hightechnology center in Korea. Accessed at: http://www.ebn.co.kr/news/n_view.html?id=339900.

Etnews (30 December 2002) Sunmitomo plans to construct color filter plant in Korea. Retrieved from http://www.etnews.com/news/device/public/1743382_2566.html.

Etnews (2 .2012) Samsung and LG occupy 58.3% of the world LCD market. Retrieved from http://www.etnews.com/news/device/device/2554081_1479.html.

Evans, P.B. (2010) [PDF] 'Constructing the 21st Century Developmental State: Potentialities and Pitfalls', in O. Edigheji (ed.) *Constructing a Democratic Developmental State in South Africa*, Cape Town: HSRC Press, pp. 37–58.

Harvey, D. (1989) *The Condition of* Postmodernity, Oxford: Basil Blackwell.

Henderson, J., Dicken, P., Hess, M., Coe, N. and Yeung, H.W.C. (2002) 'Global Production Networks and the Analysis of Economic Development', *Review of International Political Economy*, 9(3): 436–64.

Jessop, B. (1990) *State Theory: Putting the Capitalist State in Its Place*, Cambridge: Polity Press.

Jo, H.J., Jung, G.N. and Lee, J.H. (2007) 'A Way for a New Progressive Developmental Model', in I.Y. Lee (ed.) *Korean Peninsula Economy*, Seoul: Changbi Publishers (in Korean), pp. 24–47.

Johnson, C. (1982) *MITI and the Japanese Miracle: The Growth of Industrial Policy, 1925–1975*, Stanford, CA: Stanford University Press.

Korea National Statistical Office (2012), www.kostat.go.kr (accessed 12 January 2012).

Lambert, J. (1991) 'Europe: The Nation State Dies Hard', *Capital and Class*, 43(1): 3–17.

Lee, K., Lim, C. and Song, W. (2005) 'Emerging Digital Technology as a Window of Opportunity and Technological Leapfrogging Catch-up in Digital TV by the Korean Firms', *International Journal of Technology Management*, 29(1): 40–63.

Lee, S.H. (2008) *Fostering Wide-range LCD Clusters in the Metropolitan Area*, Suwon: Gyeonggi Research Institute.

Ministry of Commerce, Industry and Energy (2006) 'A Report on the Completion of LG Philips LCD's Paju Plant', 'Press Release,' 27 April 2006. Retrieved from www.kdi.re.kr.

Ministry of Knowledge and Economy (2007) 'Local Technology Innovation Industry Plan'. Internal Report.

Moneytoday (14 January 2010) Samsung plans to establish additional 8th generation of LCD line in Tangjeong. [Accessed at: http://www.mt.co.kr/view/mtview.php?type=1&no=2010011315472096685&outlink=1]

Newsis (1 February. 2007) Schott-Kuramoto Processing Korea competed plant in Ohchnag. Accessed at: http://news.naver.com/main/read.nhn?mode=LSD&mid=sec&sid1=101&oid=003&aid=0000304122

The Ministry of Commerce, Industry and Energy (13 September 2006) The Opening of the 3rd Foreign Investment Committee, 'Press Release' Retrieved from http://www.mocie.go.kr (accessed on 20 May 2011).

The Seoul Shinmun (14 November 2005) Asahi Glass completed LCD glass plant. Accessed at: http://newswire.seoul.co.kr/newsRead.php?no=97376

Wong, J. (2004) 'The Adaptive Developmental State in East Asia', *Journal of East Asian Studies*, 4(3): 345–62.

Yang, C. (2009) 'Strategic Coupling of Regional Development in Global Production Networks: Redistribution of Taiwanese Personal Computer Investment from the Pearl River Delta to the Yangtze River Delta, China', *Regional Studies*, 43(4): 385–407.

Yang, D. and Coe, N. (2009) 'The Governance of Global Production Networks and Regional Development', *Growth and Change*, 41(1): 30–5.

Yang, Y.R., Hsu, J.Y. and Ching, C.H. (2009) 'Revisiting the Silicon Island? The Geographically Varied 'Strategic Coupling' in the Development of High-technology Parks in Taiwan', *Regional Studies*, 43(4): 369–384.

Yeung, H.W.-C. (2009a) 'Regional Development and the Competitive Dynamics of Global Production Networks: An East Asian Perspective', *Regional Studies*, 43(3): 325–51.

Yeung., H.W.-C. (2009b) 'Transnational Corporations, Global Production Networks, and Urban and Regional Development: A Geographer's Perspective on Multinational Enterprises and the Global Economy', *Growth and Change*, 40(2): 197–226.

Yeung, H.W.C., Liu, W. and Dicken, P. (2006) 'Transnational Corporations and Network Effects of a Local Manufacturing Cluster in Mobile Telecommunications Equipment in China', *World Development*, 34(3): 520–40.

Market rebalancing of global production networks in the Post-Washington Consensus globalizing era: Transformation of export-oriented development in China

Chun Yang

Department of Geography, Hong Kong Baptist University, Hong Kong

ABSTRACT

The current global financial crisis has prompted researchers to revisit the export-oriented development models, known as the 'Washington Consensus' paradigm, that have prevailed in East Asia during the past few decades. Host domestic markets have been generally neglected in the conceptual construct and empirical analysis of export-oriented development. Drawing upon the global production networks (GPNs) perspective, the study advances an evolutionary framework to shed light on the rising domestic market in China as emerging dynamics of regional transformation in contemporary economic globalization. The study is conducted based on updated investigations of the market rebalancing of transnational corporations (TNCs) in China, and particularly the Pearl River Delta (PRD), in response to the post-crisis global–local interaction. It argues that the institutional and network embeddedness of TNCs in the processing trade regime have hampered their 'recoupling' with the domestic market and 'decoupling' from external markets. Instead, a domestic market oriented production network is emerging, driven by strategic contract manufacturers through relocation to inland China. As a pilot attempt to articulate the domestic market in the GPN framework, this study urges more research to reflect the implications of the restructuring of GPNs and market reorientation of TNCs for reshaping regional trajectories in the post-Washington Consensus global economy.

1. INTRODUCTION

The 'East Asian Miracle' (World Bank, 1993), based on the rapid economic growth in Japan and the East Asian 'tigers' (South Korea, Taiwan, Hong Kong and Singapore) since the 1960s, has highlighted a distinctive development model: export-oriented industrialization (EOI), known as the 'Washington Consensus'[1] paradigm in the literature (Williamson, 2008). Since 2000, particularly after the 2008 global financial crisis and economic downturn, contemporary globalization has been marked by significant transformation in the organization and governance of production, consumption and distribution (Gereffi, 2013). The 'Washington Consensus' as a paradigm for developing countries has been discredited (Gore, 2000). The past decade has witnessed dramatic shifts of production from North to South in the global economy, with the prominent roles of producers/exporters and new markets played by the emerging economies (Staritz *et al.*, 2011). With the global shift of end markets from North to South, emerging economies such as China and India have looked inward toward redirecting production for their domestic markets and regional neighbours in order to secure alternatives to the EOI model. One of the implications of this post-Washington Consensus global economy is that the extreme asymmetries of power in favour of lead firms are shifting in many cases toward the strategic contract suppliers in emerging economies (Gereffi, 2013). Increasing attention has been paid to the post-crisis reorganization of global production and demand primarily from the perspective of developed economies (Cattaneo *et al.*, 2010). However, relatively little is known about the role of the emerging economies as new powers in the global economy, as, for example, China, and their implications for restructuring the EOI models in the shift to the post-Washington Consensus paradigm (Babb, 2013).

Since the early 2000s, the global value chain (GVC) and global production networks (GPNs) perspectives have gained popularity as ways to analyse the international expansion and geographical fragmentation of production and consumption (Coe *et al.*, 2004, 2008; Gereffi *et al.*, 2005; Henderson *et al.*, 2002). Since 2000, particularly following the 2008 global financial crisis, the organization of the global economy has entered a new era (Gereffi, 2013), namely the end of the 'Washington Consensus' and the rise of contending centres of economic and political power. A consolidation is emerging of the global supply base among developing countries and local firms, which, in some cases, is shifting the bargaining power from lead firms in GVCs/GPNs to key contract suppliers. In the dynamic transformation of the global economy, national and regional development models have come under increasing scrutiny and countries/regions are trying to determine what kinds of policies and institutions provide the best opportunities for long-term growth and prosperity (Gereffi, 2009; Yeung, 2009).

The spectacular performance of the EOI in East Asia's newly industrialized economies (NIEs) was initially designated as a model for China in the late 1970s, and particularly the Pearl River Delta (PRD) region, when it took 'one step ahead' in China's 'Opening and Reform'. For more than three decades, the rise of the PRD as a 'workshop of the world' has been conceptualized as externally driven development induced by transnational corporations (TNCs), primarily from Hong Kong and Taiwan (Sit and Yang, 1997). From the GPN perspective, the EOI model in the PRD could be conceptualized as a 'strategic coupling' process of regional assets, such as cheap labour and land, geographical proximity and the strategic needs of GPNs, such as cost-down and time-to-market, through conducive institutions, as, for example, pro-export policies and the processing trade regime (Yang, 2012). Recently, attention has been paid to regional transformation with increasing local sourcing of components and parts, that is, localization of the backward 'end' of the cross-border production networks of TNCs (He *et al.*, 2009; Yang, 2007). Relatively little has been written to reflect the emerging localization of the forward 'end', that is, the procurement and distribution of intermediate components and finished products in China's domestic market. Recoupling with the immense and fragmented domestic market is a new lesson for both TNCs and cities/regions in China. However, the understanding of these issues remains a 'black box'. The extent to which these changes impact on the established strategic coupling of regional assets and global lead firms is unclear.

Taking the export-oriented electronics production networks in the PRD as a case, this study offers an updated and systematic investigation into the post-crisis regional restructuring in global change and institutional evolution. The paper argues that the prevailing nature of TNCs' institutional and network embeddedness has hampered their attempt to 'recouple'[2] with the domestic market and 'decouple' from external markets in the post-Washington Consensus global economy. Further, this paper sheds light on the emergence of domestic market driven production networks resulting from the strategic supplier-initiated relocation to inland China. The remainder of the paper is organized as follows. After the introduction, the paper critically reviews the theoretical perspectives of GPNs/GVCs in conceptualizing regional development in contemporary economic globalization. An analytical framework with an evolutionary lens of strategic coupling is developed to examine regional transformation in China. The paper further examines the difficulties in recoupling with the domestic market and decoupling from external markets during the transformation of export-oriented development. The paper concludes with a summary of the main findings and policy implications for export-oriented regions in the post-Washington Consensus global economy.

2. CHANGING DYNAMICS OF GPNS, INSTITUTIONAL EVOLUTION AND REGIONAL TRANSFORMATION IN THE CONTEMPORARY GLOBAL ECONOMY

2.1. Conceptualizing regional development in GPNs: Beyond strategic coupling

Over the past decade, both the GVC and the GPN perspectives have been widely adopted to examine the organization of economic globalization. Unlike the GVC approach, with its emphasis on national development and the international context (Gereffi, 2013; Sturgeon and Kawakami, 2011), the GPN framework attempts to 'hold down' globalization to regional/subnational development, that is, 'globalizing regional development' (Coe and Hess, 2011; Coe *et al.*, 2004, 2008; Hess and Yeung, 2006). GVC/GCC analysis 'has surprisingly little to say about regional and subnational processes, because of the focus on the international dimensions of commodity chains and global divisions of labour' (Smith *et al.*, 2002: 49). Recent explorations in East Asia have focussed increasing attention on the local and subnational impacts of the global economy (Yeung, 2007, 2009). The major contribution of the GPN approach is the conceptualization of regional development in relational terms (Coe *et al.*, 2004), which successfully overcomes the neglect of exogenous processes that characterized new regionalist research in the 1990s (Yeung, 2013). The GPN approach, which aims to 'incorporate all kinds of networks relationships' and to 'encompass all relevant sets of actors and relationships' (Coe *et al.*, 2008: 272), provides a broad relational framework for investigating the uneven impacts of economic globalization (Bathelt, 2006; Yeung, 2005). It offers an open and context-sensitive perspective beyond the linear framework offered by the related concepts of GCC/GVC.

In contemporary economic globalization, urban and regional development is a complex process in which GPNs and regions interact through a 'strategic coupling' process mediated by appropriate configurations of regional institutions that 'glue' GPNs to regional assets (Coe *et al.*, 2004). Strategic coupling is defined as 'a time-space contingent convergence of interests and cooperation between two or more groups of actors who might not act in tandem for a common strategic objective' in regional development (Yeung, 2009: 332). The central concept of strategic coupling highlights the dynamic processes by which relational assets are matched to the strategic needs of lead firms in GPNs, with regional institutions playing a key role in the process. Such coupling is characterized by its reliance on intentional action, time and space contingency and transcendence of territorial boundaries (Yeung, 2009). While achieving increasing theoretical elaboration and empirical application in East Asia (Yeung, 2009), Taiwan (Yang *et al.*, 2009; Yang and Coe, 2009) and China (Yang, 2009), recent studies have tended to question GPNs' overemphasis on global lead firms and the applicability of the 'strategic coupling' notion in China, particularly the Yangtze River Delta (YRD), as, for example, Suzhou and Wenzhou (Wei, 2010, 2011).

The transformation of GPNs and regional assets over time and space and the subsequent effects on strategic coupling processes have been understudied thus far (Coe and Hess, 2011; Henderson and Navdi, 2011; Levy, 2008). Taking into account the variable and contingent *spatio-temporality* of GPNs (Coe *et al.*, 2008: 272, italics in original), an evolutionary perspective on strategic coupling is an imperative for conceptualizing regional transformation in contemporary economic globalization. The past decade has witnessed the convergence between two key literatures in contemporary economic geography, that is, GPNs and evolutionary economic geography (EEG) (Boschma and Martin, 2007, 2010; Gertler, 2010; MacKinnon *et al.*, 2009). As Boschma and Martin (2007: 538) put it, '(T)he "evolutionary turn" in economic geography has gained sufficient momentum to merit recognition as a distinct perspective no less promising in scope than the other approaches to economic geography that have been proposed in recent years (such as the cultural, institutional and relational "turns".' Coe (2011) identifies three main branches of EEG: work on path dependence and lock-in in different geographic contexts; research on clusters, localized learning and related variety; and examinations of the spatial evolution of industries across the economic landscape. The economic landscape inherits the legacy of its own past industrial and institutional development, and this history can exert a major influence on conditioning its future development and evolution (Martin and Sunley, 2006). The conventional analysis of the evolution of the economic landscape based on the 'new regionalist' literature in the 1990s, particularly path dependence and lock-ins, has primarily focused on endogenous regional assets and institutions, while neglecting exogenous linkages and regional evolution under the impact of globalization. In recent efforts to link GPNs and EEG, MacKinnon (2012) attempts to develop a broader conception of the range of coupling, recoupling and decoupling processes that take place between regions and GPNs, moving beyond strategic coupling *per se*. Regions have the capacity to enhance their position within a GPN through processes of upgrading and value enhancement, based on a recoupling process of regional assets and lead firms in the GPN (MacKinnon, 2012). Such recoupling may, however, occur at the expense of other regions, which lose out on new rounds of investment through processes of intra-corporate competition (Dawley, 2011; Phelps and Fuller, 2000). Despite growing theoretical consideration of these issues, to date, little empirical examination has been conducted of the evolutionary process of strategic coupling and its implications for regional restructuring (Yang, 2013). Notably, the rise of the domestic market for intermediate and finished goods as the final demand in host countries/regions, as, for example, China, has been largely neglected in the conceptual construct and empirical analysis of regional development from the GPN/GVC perspectives.

According to the GPN approach, the process of 'fitting' regional assets with the strategic needs of GPNs requires appropriate institutional structures that simultaneously promote regional advantages and enhance the region's articulation into wider networks. As argued by Coe and Hess (2011: 134), 'the embedding of GPNs into regional economies is of course no guarantee of positive developmental outcomes, even if it results in new or enhanced opportunities for value capture at the local level'. Unlike the GVC/GCC perspectives, which focus on the role of internal factors in the governance of the global value chain, '*regardless* of the institutional context within which they are situated' (Gereffi *et al.*, 2005: 99, emphasis added), GPNs regard institutions, including state and non-governmental organizations, as important actors and integral parts of global production (Hess and Yeung, 2006). As shown in their empirical analysis in India, Neilson and Pritchard (2009) postulate that local institutional formations are integral to regional transformation. 'Regional assets can become an advantage for regional development only if they fit the strategic needs of global production networks' (Coe and Hess, 2011: 132). Nevertheless, relatively little has been written on institutional transition and its impacts on the strategic coupling of regional development and GPNs.

2.2. Market rebalancing of GPNs: An evolutionary analytical framework

The 2000s have witnessed the extension of industrial restructuring from regions in North America, Western Europe and Japan in the 1970s and 1980s to the Asian NIEs in the mid-1990s and, most recently, to China and particularly the two regional powerhouses of the PRD and the YRD. The development of prominent regional hotspots in the economic geography literature, including Silicon Valley, the Boston region, Cambridge (UK), the so-called 'Third Italy' and Baden-Wurttemberg, has primarily emphasized their endogenous dynamism, rather than exogenous linkages, which can be regarded as 'generator regions' for GPNs, spawning a variety of lead firms that tend to retain their headquarters there (MacKinnon, 2012). The rise of contract manufacturers has resulted in a power shift from lead firms and the subsequent impacts on the developing host regions in which they are embedded warrant systematic investigation. For instance, Taiwan-based subcontractor firm Foxconn, which moved its manufacturing to Shenzhen in the 1980s, became the topmost contract manufacturer in the world in 2008 (Table 1). As the surveys conducted by the Boston Consulting Group (2006) indicate, 67 per cent of the surveyed companies declared that they would significantly increase their investment in sales in rapidly developing economies (RDEs), including China and

Table 1 Top 10 contract manufacturers in the world, 2008

Rank	Name	Headquarters	Turnover (USD billion)
1	Hon Hai (Foxconn)	Taiwan	55.0
2	Flextronics	Singapore	33.0
3	Jabli	USA	13.0
4	Celestica	Canada	8.0
5	Sanmina	USA	7.0
6	Elcoteq	Luxembourg	5.0
7	Venture	Singapore	2.7
8	Benchmark	USA	2.6
9	Universal Scientific	Taiwan	2.0
10	Plexus	USA	2.0

Source: iSuppli, revenue estimates (2008).

India, compared with 49 per cent in sourcing, 51 per cent in manufacturing and just 26 per cent in research and development (R&D). Notably, China has become one of the most attractive RDEs for the global shifts of sales and sourcing activities by Western-based TNCs, in addition to manufacturing (Boston Consulting Group, 2006). Furthermore, accompanying the rapid income increase, the market demand in Asia, particularly China, for electronics products has significant room to grow. It is predicted by the Economic Intelligence Unit (EIU) (2011) that the demand for telecom and information technology (IT) equipment in Asia (excluding Japan) will increase from US$700 billion, or 14 per cent of the world market, in 2000 to US$4.1 trillion, or 36.8 per cent of the global demand, in 2014. The global market shift from North to South will significantly change the governance of GPNs, which is an emerging phenomenon that has been far from sufficiently explored in the literature, with few exceptions (Kaplinsky *et al.*, 2011; Liu *et al.*, 2009).

The changing roles of China in the global economy have led to the reorganization of production networks in Asia as a triangular trade pattern: firms in advanced Asian economies, particularly the Asian NIEs and Japan, use China as an export base and, instead of exporting finished goods to the US and Europe, now export intermediate goods to their affiliates in China. Since the mid-1990s, China has become the global centre of the final assembly in electronics and electrical goods and a number of other related global industries based on parts and components imported from other countries in East Asia. An asymmetry has emerged in China's trade links with the other Asian countries: parts and components dominate China's trade with the other Asian countries, whereas the bulk of Chinese exports are destined for extra-regional markets, particularly the US and Europe. Since the early 2000s, particularly during the onset of the global financial crisis, the 'decoupling' thesis has become a popular theme in Asian policy circles (Pula and Peltonen, 2009); it postulates that East Asia has become a self-contained economic entity with the potential for maintaining its own growth dynamism independent of the economic outlook for the traditional developed market economies. The controversial thesis of 'decoupling', or the world economy delinking from the American economy and *recoupling* with emerging economies, is finding growing confirmation. However, some scholars argue that contrary to popular belief, the dependence of the export dynamism of these countries on the global economy has not lessened (Athukorala, 2010). It is argued that due to China's heavy reliance on imported inputs from the East Asian region, China's economy is actually less export-dependent than was traditionally thought (Ma *et al.*, 2009). Since the early 2000s, increasingly dissatisfied with its low-end position in the GPNs, the Chinese government has proactively initiated quests for more balanced development between export and domestic markets. Engaging in the domestic market in China has been recognized as a viable strategy and pursued by export-oriented TNCs. Despite such a consensus, selling the products previously targeted at Western markets in China has turned into a daunting task, the process of which has rarely been discussed in the literature.

With the above theoretical and empirical backdrops, this paper draws on the theoretical construct of regional development from the GPN perspective and develops an analytical framework with an evolutionary lens on strategic coupling to understand the on-going regional restructuring process in China. The evolutionary framework incorporates dynamic GPNs, multiscalar institutional change and the transformation of regional assets, paying particular attention to the articulation of the domestic market and consumers in the host countries/regions (Figure 1). In response to the changing regional assets and institutional environment, TNCs have attempted to rebalance the export and domestic markets of products manufactured in China through recoupling and decoupling initiatives. On the one hand, the TNCs in the coastal areas have attempted to leverage between the external and domestic markets, though achieving a balance between them has turned out to be difficult owing to the established institutional and territorial embeddedness. On the other hand, spatial relocation/expansion of TNCs to inland China is emerging as a viable strategy for market reorientation. The transformation of the export-led development in China and the PRD has been conducted based on years of on-site field investigation with renewed funding sources since 2005, and updated in-depth interviews with four groups of relevant actors/institutions, including senior executives of export-oriented TNCs, government officials, business associations, research institutions and other NGOs during the period from 2008 to 2011. The firm surveys in relation to the market rebalancing of TNCs were implemented in collaboration with various business associations, such as the Federation of Hong Kong Industries (FHKI)

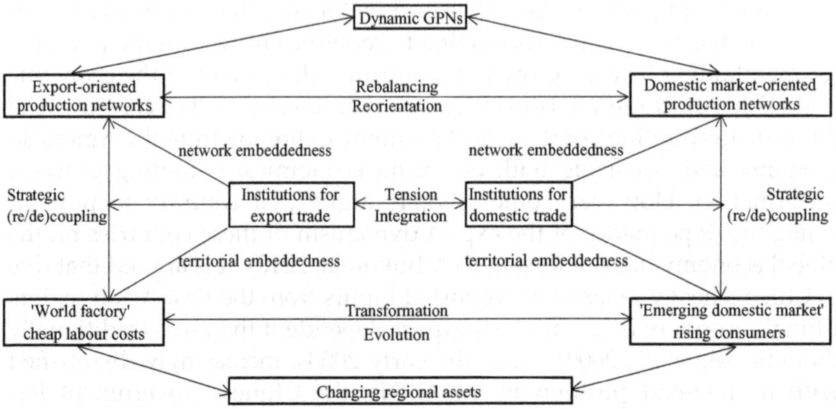

Figure 1 Strategic coupling of regional evolution and dynamic GPN: An evolutionary framework. *Source*: Compiled by the author.

and the Hong Kong Chinese Manufacturing Association (HKCMA), with which the author has established long-term collaboration as an individual member. More than 45 open-ended interviews with senior managers were conducted through the 'snowball' introduction of various entrepreneurs, mainly in the PRD, and their inland branches, among them Chengdu, Chongqing, Wuhan and Zhengzhou. It is not an intention of the study to conduct exhaustive firm interviews; instead, it aims to identify crucial issues common to export-oriented TNCs, which are undergoing dramatic restructuring and market rebalancing in particular.

3. TRANSFORMATION OF THE EXPORT-ORIENTED REGIONAL DEVELOPMENT IN CHINA: THE CASE OF THE PRD

Over the past decade, massive relocation of the global electronics production has turned China into a world electronics factory, producing 25.7 per cent of the world's total output in value terms. China is the world's major producer of end-consumer products, including audio-visual equipment, computers and mobile phones. The rise of China and particularly the PRD as 'a workshop of the world' has been attributed to the flexible business environment, including relaxed inspection of import materials and export products in customs; half-hearted implementation of environmental and labour regulations; and more flexible tax policies (Hsing, 1998). However, this favourable environment conducive to export-oriented industrialization has encountered unprecedented challenges since the early 2000s. The most dramatic transformation resulted from the increasing production

Table 2 Changing business environment in the PRD, 2008–11

	2008	2009	2010	2011
Rising labour costs	3.52	3.04	3.61	3.31
RMB appreciation	3.49	2.89	3.20	3.03
Upsurge of raw materials	3.52	2.73	3.45	3.28
New Labour Contract Law	3.46	3.22	3.44	3.08
Labour shortage	3.05	–	3.09	2.73
Decrease of/unstable order	–	3.08	2.39	2.32
Limited supply of water/electricity	3.27	–	–	2.46
Keen market competition	–	–	3.03	2.60
Strict environment protection	2.68	–	2.69	2.40

Notes: 4 indicates the most severe impact, 1 represents no impact, 2 and 3 are in between.
Source: Compiled based on HKCMA figures (2011).

costs related to the rise of labour costs, appreciation of the RMB, inflation and upsurge of raw materials and shortage of labour, which indicates that the era of low-cost production in the PRD is at an end (Table 2). After enjoying a low wage level of migrant labour for almost 15 years, export-oriented processing firms have encountered an upsurge of labour costs since 2000, with several rounds of wage rises in major cities of the PRD. In Dongguan and Shenzhen, the average minimum wage doubled during 2002 and 2010, after stagnating at a minimal increase for a decade. Foxconn, the largest contract supplier for global lead firms such as Apple, Sony and HP, increased its wages by 67 per cent in 2010, following high-profile labour disputes in Shenzhen. Moreover, the export-led model became more volatile upon the outbreak of the global financial crisis. The changing regional assets before the global downturn, coupled with the decrease in orders, tight bank credit, price drops required by customers and loan delays by customers in the wake of the global financial crisis (Table 2), have exerted unprecedented pressure on the EOI in China.

In practice, the EOI in China, and the PRD in particular, has been undertaken through a processing trade (*jiagongmaoyi*) regime beginning in the early 1980s, which grants firms duty exemptions on imported raw materials and other inputs as long as they are used solely for export purposes. The share of processing exports, that is, exports conducted under the processing regime, in China's total exports rose from 30 per cent in 1988 to 55 per cent in 2005 and 47 per cent in 2010. The figures are much higher in the PRD, particularly Dongguan and Shenzhen, which recorded higher proportions of 88 per cent and 58 per cent, respectively, in 2009 (Yang, 2012). However, since 2006, the central government has made several rounds of changes to its processing trade regime, including the removal and reduction of export VAT rebates[3] and the expansion of the prohibited and restricted categories of the processing trade. Moreover, the 2000s have witnessed top-down government intervention in restructuring the model. The prevailing EOI model in the PRD was criticized for the first time in the regional plan outline of the PRD (2008–20), endorsed by the State Council in December 2008 at the onset of the global financial crisis (NDRC, 2008). The PRD model has been regarded as unsustainable development, which is low value-adding, low technology, labour-intensive, resource-intensive, overly dependent on exports and foreign companies, and environmentally and socially unsound. The then Party Secretary of Guangdong province, Wang Yang, appreciated the financial crisis as a good opportunity, as '(d)uring the economic downturn, we've reached consensus on the need to transform our development model' (Yang, 2012), which was further assured in the national 12th Five-Year Plan (2011–15).

Ever since the early 2000s, especially after China's accession to the World Trade Organization (WTO) in 2001, the rising domestic market has gradually replaced cheap labour as the emerging dynamics of China's regional development (Yang, 2007). According to a series of surveys on domestic sales by the member firms of the HKCMA, the proportion of firms engaged in domestic sales increased from 44 per cent in 2001 to 56.6 per cent in 2011 (HKCMA, 2011). However, the market share of China among the surveyed firms stagnated at 29 per cent in 2009, 27 per cent in 2010 and 30 per cent in 2011, while the market shares of the US fluctuated between 38.7 per cent, 44.8 per cent and 39.3 per cent during the same period (Table 3). The HKPC's survey (2010) indicates that among the firms that have engaged in domestic sales in China, 52 per cent declared that domestic sales accounted for less than 20 per cent of their total sales (Table 3). Worse still, 43 per cent of the surveyed firms have not yet reached a payment balance in domestic sales business (HKPC, 2010). The field investigation found that some firms managed to hold onto their major export business even when the external market suffered a crisis. It is claimed by an interviewed entrepreneur that 'embarking on the domestic market is a new challenge, rather than a solution' (Interview in Shenzhen, April 2011). Taking the electronics industry as an example, while foreign-invested firms (FIEs) contributed three-quarters of the total output value, they accounted for less than 30 per cent of the domestic sales in China, in contrast to the ratio of exports/domestic sales of 20:80 by domestic firms in 2009 (HKTDC, 2011).

To capture the robust growth of the domestic market for electronics products, export-oriented NCs have actually complied with the well-known 'smiling curve' in which TNCs can move either upstream by designing and building the components, such as computer chips, and intellectual property that are used in maufacturing products, or downstream into brands and manage the relationship with end-customers. Both ends offer much bigger opportunities for adding value than being stuck in the middle as a mere product assembler. Many Asian manufacturers have

Table 3 Progress of domestic sales engaged by export-oriented TNCs in the PRD

A. Market distribution, 2008–11 (mean% of sales value)

	China	HK	USA	Europe	Other Asian countries	Others
2009	29	35.7	38.7	30.5	22.9	18.0
2010	27	32.2	44.8	29.7	18.0	16.4
2011	30.3	31.7	39.3	28.4	21	16.7

Source: HKCMA (2009 and 2011).

B. Proportion of domestic sales in total turnover

Firms engaging in domestic sales as% of surveyed firms	Domestic sales as% of total sales turnover
14%	81–100
6%	61–80
12%	41–60
16%	21–40
52%	1–20

Source: HKPC (2010).

C. The initial year for engaging in domestic sales in China

Year	Of total surveyed firms
2010 and afterwards	10%
2005–09	31.3%
2000–04	16.3%
1995–99	17.5%
1990–94	15%
1989 and before	10%

Source: HKCMA (2011).

D. The initial year for engaging in domestic sales in China

Sector	% of companies engaged in domestic sales in China	Mean % of annual sales turnover
Machinery and equipment	64	58
Building materials	60	49
Clothing/textiles	53	39
Chemical products	53	46
Electronic products	50	41

Source: HSBC (2010).

already ventured deep into the upstream part of the value chain, but few have ventured into the downstream, branded end (EIU, 2011). In the context of China, increasing attention has been paid to the spatial relocation (Yang, 2009) and technological upgrading of electronics TNCs (Lin *et al.*, 2011; Wei *et al.*, 2012; Zhou *et al.*, 2011), but relatively little research has been undertaken on the dynamic interaction of market reorientation with spatial relocation and technological upgrading strategies. The stagnating progress of domestic sales has usually been explained by China's controversial market environment, which is 'plagued by lack of transparency, onerous burden of opaque levies and sub-charges, rampant violations of intellectual property rights, and insufficiency in financial services' (Li & Fung, 2010). While concurring with these observations, this study aims to extend the evolutionary investigation into the strategic coupling of the changing regional assets and dynamic GPNs in response to the market reorientation (Figure 1).

4. RESTRUCTURING OF THE EXPORT-ORIENTED PRODUCTION NETWORKS IN CHINA

4.1. Institutional embeddedness and recoupling with the domestic market

To embark on domestic market sales, ownership transformation of TNCs is required in practice. There are two major forms of processing trade in China. One is 'processing with imported materials' (*jinliaojiagong*), usually engaged in by FIEs (*sanzi qiye*), which include equity joint ventures (EJVs), cooperative joint ventures (CJVs) and wholly foreign-owned enterprises (WFEs). The other is processing with supplied materials (*lailiaojiagong*), which involves processing supplied materials, samples and parts. These 'three supplies', together with 'compensation trade', are collectively entitled 'three supplies and one compensation' (*sanlaiyibu*), which have been labelled 'other forms of foreign investment' in China's official statistics of foreign investment to differentiate them from the '*sanzi*' enterprises. The prerequisite for changing from exports to domestic sales is a transition from *sanlaiyibu* to *sanzi* enterprises, which is not easy. The major differences between *sanlaiyibu* and *sanzi* enterprises lie in the fact that *sanlaiyibu* firms are signed as cooperative contracts with town or village level foreign economic and trade offices (*waijingban*) in the form of business entities and are registered in the name of the Chinese partners. *Sanlaiyibu* factories are neither foreign investment enterprises nor domestic investment corporate enterprises, they are domestic investment non-corporate enterprises. The *sanlaiyibu* firm is generally operated and managed directly by the foreign enterprise, with the Chinese partner only providing assistance; both parties will finally collect the processing fee as agreed. More than

80 per cent of Hong Kong firms took the form of *sanlaiyibu* with informal contracts with the local authorities primarily at the town and village levels in oral arrangements with open-ended agreements and loose enforcement of contracts (Interview in Dongguan, 9 July 2008).

The explicit 'recoupling' of export-oriented TNCs in the regional restructuring designated by the upper-level governments has changed the prevailing asymmetrical power relations over the past three decades. With the top-down intervention of industrial restructuring, the bargaining power of both TNCs and lower-level authorities has been on the decline, which could be reflected in the increase in ownership transition of the TNCs in the PRD in recent years. According to the survey conducted by the HKCMA, the share of *sanlaiyibu* firms in the surveyed firms decreased from 46.6 per cent to 36.2 per cent during the period from 2008 to 2011, while that of wholly foreign-owned firms increased from 55.2 per cent to 71.8 per cent (HKCMA, 2011). It is predicted by a local official in Dongguan that the salient *sanlaiyibu* mode will disappear in the next 10–20 years because of the termination of issuing and/or renewing *sanlaiyibu* licences for TNCs (Interview in Dongguan, April 2010). Nevertheless, most of the interviewed firms that have transformed their ownership predict that the share of domestic sales will increase at a very slow growth rate and will not surpass 15–20 per cent in the coming five years (interview in Dongguan, April 2011). The reasons are related to export-oriented processing firms being embedded territorially in the town- and village-level economy in the PRD and in Dongguan in particular. The territorial embeddedness of the export-oriented processing activities can be demonstrated by over half (for example, 53 per cent in 2008) of the industrial output at the village level (Yang, 2012). A large number of local villagers from the agricultural population have diversified their occupations and shifted into more profitable non-agricultural activities, such as profiting from various sources of rent for factory plants and dormitories for migrant labour. The processing companies are required to pay processing fees to the local authorities. The regulation regarding processing fees is very flexible and differs in each town and village, which leaves a large amount of room for negotiation. Export-oriented processing firms regard the negotiation of processing fees as a potential means of cutting production costs and increasing profit margins. From the perspective of the local authorities, any changes of *sanlaiyibu*, or transformation into *sanzi* enterprises, which are required to pay taxes to the central and provincial government, would lead to the loss of processing fees and other relevant income.

4.2. Network embeddedness and decoupling from external markets

The operation of export-oriented production networks has been attributed to the home-based inter-firm supply linkages (Yang, 2007). This paper

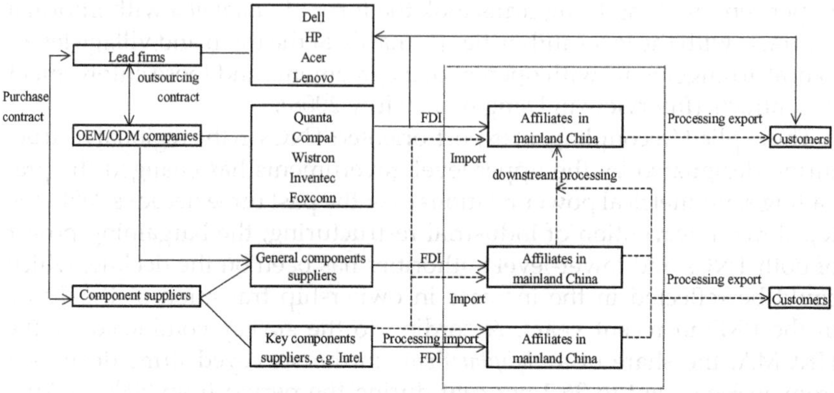

Figure 2 Lead firms-dominated sourcing and sales controlling power in export-oriented production networks. *Source*: Compiled by the author.

argues that the embeddedness of the network trade has turned into obstacles in market reorientation in the segregated institutional context for exports and domestic sales. For the past three decades, the home-based supply linkages between the second and lower tiers of suppliers and their customers, usually the first-tier downstream suppliers, such as Foxconn, have established close collaborations with the local customs in charge of processing trade, so as to leverage at most in the pro-export institutions (Figure 2). Selling to foreign markets often grants enterprises more stable returns and involves fewer risks. Many manufacturers thus blame the little incentive to engage in selling domestically, when compared to preferential policies for exports. At present, enterprises engaging in China's domestic and foreign trade sectors are governed by differential policies. The latter is often said to enjoy more favourable government-approved treatment, such as export tax rebates. For processing trade operations, imported parts, raw materials, semi-manufactured products, machinery and equipment are generally tax-bonded. The made-to-export products are also exempted from value-added tax. However, the tax policy for domestic sales enterprises is less favourable. Enterprises engaging in domestic sales have to incur taxes ranging from import duty to value-added tax as well as consumption tax. In such a pro-export institutional context, the downstream firms as customers of the lower-tier suppliers, usually the contract manufacturers in the GPNs, tend to source parts and components from the upstream supplier firms via either indirect exports, such as inter-plant transfers, or reimports after exports by upstream firms (Figure 3). The differences among these sales channels could be reflected by the taxation duties involved. In practice, if a business enterprise wishes to transfer its processed bonded goods to another processing trade enterprise for deep

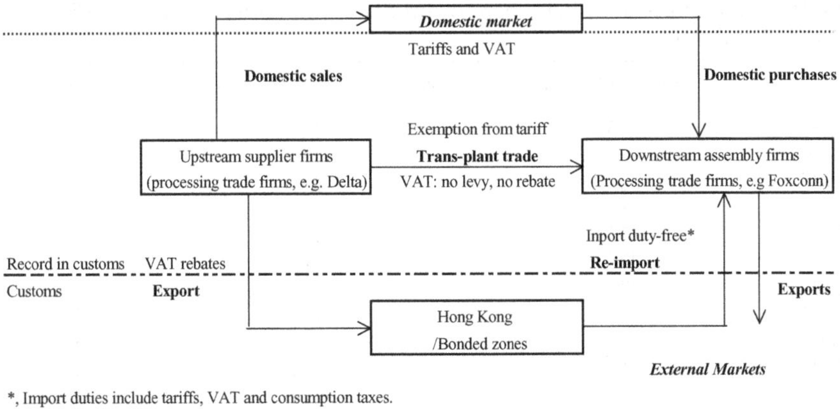

Figure 3 Network embeddedness of export-oriented production and trade. *Source*: Compiled by the author.

processing and re-exporting, it must seek approval from the commerce authorities and complete the necessary customs formalities before making the actual transfer.

In order to leverage the preferential policies on exports better, another salient practice of domestic sales (entitled 'reimports') has been widely adopted by the supplier firms in the relevant GPNs, particularly in the electronics sector. The 'reimports' are a type of round trip trade originating from a country and shipped back to the same country.[4] China has become the fourth largest such importer in the world since 2005, importing more from itself than from the US. Reimports from China have accounted for more than 20 per cent of the total processing imports since 2005, which surged from 3.9 per cent in 1995 to 25.6 per cent in 2010 (Table 4). In terms of sector composition, electronics represented 88.1 per cent of the total reimports in 2007. In particular, Guangdong is the leading province engaging in reimport trade, owing to its outstanding processing activities. As for Dongguan, China ranked top among all the sources of import markets, with more than a quarter of the total imports during the period from 2007 to 2009 (Interview with Dongguan official, May 2010). The process of reimporting involves at least two traders: an initial exporter (supply side) and a subsequent reimporter (demand side) (Figure 3). This motive should be strongest when an initial exporter and a subsequent reimporter both belong to processing trade firms. The upstream firms may prefer to export their products first to obtain VAT rebates and then downstream firms can reimport them back to China under the processing trade regime (Figure 3). When these goods are reimported back into China, the subsequent reimporters, if they belong to the processing trade, are exempt

Table 4 Re-imports and their share of processing imports in China, 1995–2010 (US$100 million)

	Processing imports	Re-imports after exports	Share (%)
1995	583.7	22.6	3.9
1996	622.7	24.2	3.9
1997	702.1	29.2	4.2
1998	686	30.2	4.4
1999	735.8	41.4	5.6
2000	925.6	71.7	7.7
2001	939.7	87.7	9.3
2002	1222	149.8	12.3
2003	1629	250.9	15.4
2004	2216.9	386.7	17.4
2005	2740.1	551.6	20.1
2006	3214.7	733.6	22.8
2007	3684.8	857.4	23.3
2008	3784	924.5	24.4
2009	3223.4	864.2	26.8
2010	4174.3	1068.2	25.6

Source: Compiled according to China's *Customs Statistical Yearbook*, various issues.

from import duties (including tariffs, VAT and consumption taxes). This lowers the costs of the round trip to processing firms. Hence, processing firms with supplied materials would prefer to reimport even if they could buy domestically. Processing firms with imported materials, in order to delay VAT payment on inputs and avoid export taxes (that is, the unrefunded part of the VAT), may also prefer to buy domestically made products through reimports that are duty-free because purchasing them domestically requires immediate VAT payment with only partial rebates later.

As pointed out by an official at Delta, a Taiwanese initial exporter firm in Dongguan, which provides power switches for downstream subsequent reimporting firms, such as Foxconn, in Shenzhen, 'After comparison between time and logistic costs, there is a greater incentive for us to participate in reimports as an alternative strategy in selling our products in China' (Interview, June 2010). The preferential policies on processing trade, particularly the export rebate and the exemption from import duties, have resulted in the institutional embeddedness of export-oriented firms in the pro-export institutions. Despite efforts to launch domestic sales, the sales in the domestic market accounted for less than 15 per cent of Delta's total sales in 2010. Accordingly, the lower tiers of suppliers have been 'requested' by their customers as downstream suppliers to engage in 'inter-plant transfer' or 'reimports', as 'pseudo exports, de facto domestic sale'. As a result, domestic sales have been generally regarded as an ad hoc alternative strategy when encountering difficulties in exports. A wait-and-see strategy could better reflect the aspiration of the TNCs, as expressed by a marketing manager: 'Once the external markets revive, it is likely that many firms will seek growth through exports again' (Interview in Hong Kong, May 2011). It has recently been reported that integrated planning for exports and domestic trade is currently being worked on by China's Ministry of Commerce, after implementing the export promotion policies for three decades.

5. EMERGING DOMESTIC MARKET-ORIENTED PRODUCTION NETWORKS: RELOCATION TO INLAND CHINA

The transformation from exports to the domestic market means that manufacturers should expand their positions and roles in GPNs beyond manufacturing to sourcing, sales and distribution, which have been controlled by the respective upper tiers of firms, especially the lead firms in the GPNs. As argued by an official at a third-tier supplier firm, which provides power switches for the second- and first-tier supplier firms for final products such as home electronic appliances, 'we are "manufacturers" (*Changlao*) who just know how to manage factories and production and have no idea how to do retailing. As a supplier firm, we produce components for customers as downstream firms; we usually do not know where final products have been sold. Sometimes, we can guess the final market of the products according to the distinctive configurations requested by customers' (Interview, March 2011). Such difficulties have been self-described by lower supplier entrepreneurs as 'experts in export trade while laments in domestic trade' (*waixiao neihang, neixiao waihang*) which means that they are good at exports while in lack of knowledge of domestic sales (Interview in Shenzhen, May 2011). According to both the GPN and the GVC perspective, market power has been highly concentrated in the leading global firms and unevenly distributed among the various tiers of firms in the networks/chains. The institutional dynamics may change the power relations and governance structure of GPNs/GVCs. As analysed in the above section, upstream suppliers have been involved passively in 'domestic sales' through indirect exports or reimports, as requested by their downstream customers, usually first-tier suppliers in GPNs. While going ahead in engaging in domestic sales, lower-tier supplier firms have relied on first-tier contract manufacturers to foster the market reorientation of the production network. Together with the government policy changes, the penetration into the domestic market has been promoted through the spatial relocation of manufacturing from the coast to the inland cities and provinces. Different from the spatial relocation of the Taiwanese PC industry from the PRD to the YRD, which was primarily requested by the lead firms, such as HP and Dell, since the early 2000s (Yang, 2009), the relocation of export-oriented firms from coastal to inland provinces has been led by key contract suppliers, such as Foxconn. Despite the gradually declining bargaining power with local governments in the host regions, such as the Guangdong provincial government, the export-led TNCs were welcomed by the inland cities and provinces, such as Chengdu in Sichuan and Chongqing in West China, which are eager for inflows of TNCs, including those transplanted from the coastal regions. Foxconn announced its ambitious plan for relocation to the inland provinces after the spate of suicides in Shenzhen in 2010. The Henan provincial government was the first province to attract such investment from Foxconn after the '13th jump' in 2010. The production capacity for the iPhone at the Foxconn factory in Zhengzhou soared to 200,000 per day at the end of 2011. Apart from upward pressure on industrial wages, Guangdong Province's stricter enforcement of the New Labour Contract Law and selective outbreaks of labour unrest, the recent relocation to inland China is related to the TNCs' growing interest in strengthening the development of the domestic supply chain/network in order to reduce the need to ship goods through the key foreign trade ports and placing more emphasis on the domestic supply chain, which is targeted specifically at satisfying local consumption needs. Previous studies (Yang, 2012) and a series of surveys conducted by the HKTDC (Hong Kong Trade Development Council), FHKI and HKCMA in 2007 prior to the crisis reflected the lukewarm attitudes of supplier TNCs towards the relocation to the inland provinces expected by the central government. Instead, they preferred the less developed areas in the PRD or Guangdong, near Hong Kong (HKTDC, 2011). However, the situation has been changing since early 2011, when Foxconn, the largest contract manufacturer located in Shenzhen, initiated its ambitious relocation of manufacturing with 20,000 employees to inland provinces, near the hometowns of the majority of the migrant labour. Foxconn's plan is to eventually move all of the mass manufacturing to sites outside Shenzhen in inland provinces, such as Hubei, Henan, Sichuan and Chongqing (Figure 4).

It is reported that Apple was hesitant and even reluctant when Foxconn announced its 'relocation plan' to inland China with lower labour costs (Sutherland, 2010). However, 'what surprised the inspection crew of Apple was that they did not expect the iPad to become popular in the southwest area in China, i.e. Sichuan province. The government officials who accompanied them were proficient in using iPad 1, and some local banks conducted promotions with free iPads. The Apple inspection team has realized that the people living in Chengdu are following the world trend. Finally, Apple approved Chengdu's factory to produce iPads' (Fieldwork in Sichuan, December 2011). The relocation of Foxconn has fundamentally changed power relations between lead firms (such as Apple) and

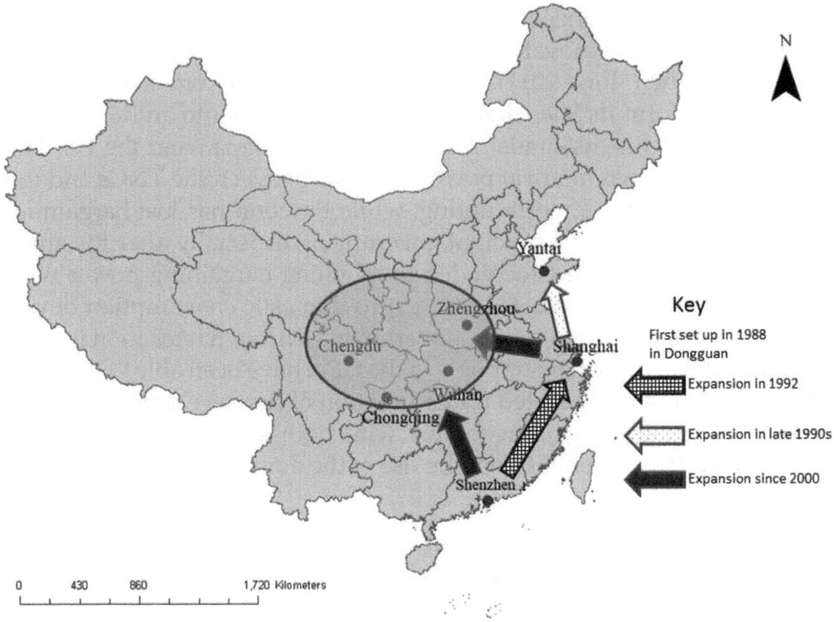

Figure 4 Spatial relocation of Foxconn in mainland China. *Source*: Compiled by the author.

key contract suppliers (such as Foxconn) in the GPNs. Despite the reluctance, even challenge, from Apple, the relocation to inland China was initiated by Foxconn, with the emergence of the domestic market-oriented production network, which has evolved in parallel to the export-oriented production network orchestrated by the lead firms. With the emerging shift in the asymmetries of power in favour of lead firms towards key contract suppliers, the governance of the GPNs/GVCs has undergone a dramatic transformation, which warrants comprehensive investigation in future research.

As a result of the relocation to inland provinces, first-tier supplier-led domestic market-oriented production networks have emerged in China. Taking Hubei Province in central China as an example, with the establishment of branch plants by Foxconn in Wuhan, the capital city of Hubei, the electronics industry sales indicated a clear domestic sales-driven pattern, with 77 per cent of the total sales in the domestic market. A similar domestic market orientation has been found in Hunan (domestic sales accounting for 91 per cent of the total sales value), Sichuan (82 per cent), Shanxi (89 per cent) and Chongqing (97 per cent) (HKTDC, 2011). Meanwhile, Foxconn's relocation to the inland cities and provinces, while keeping the R&D activities active in the Shenzhen factory campus, has been appreciated by Shenzhen's municipal government, which seeks to turn the city into an innovative city from a low-end 'world factory' (Interview in Shenzhen, June 2011). According to company officials, Foxconn began to transform its Shenzhen manufacturing base into an R&D centre as early as 2003, like its similar centres in Taiwan, Japan and the US. The evolution of the asymmetrical power relations between the TNCs and the various host regions is worth noting: while Foxconn has lost bargaining power with Shenzhen's municipal government, especially after the spate of suicides in 2010, it has succeeded in retaining bargaining power with the inland provinces, mediated by the pro-domestic consumption development designated by the central government. Through relocation inland, Foxconn and its lower-tier suppliers in the GPN have been able to leverage with the top-down designated transformation of the development model, in order to regain bargaining power with both sending and receiving regions, as well as to benefit from the rise of the domestic market in China.

6. CONCLUSIONS

The 2000s, particularly the aftermath of the 2008 global financial crisis and subsequent world economic recession, have prompted researchers to revisit the export-oriented development models known as the Washington Consensus paradigm in the literature. This paper sheds light on the unprecedented challenges of export-oriented regional development in China, and the PRD in particular, in the post-Washington Consensus global economy, particularly the changing dynamics of GPNs. Through an evolutionary conceptual framework of strategic coupling from the GPN perspective, which incorporates the dynamic changes of the GPNs, the transformation of regional assets and institutional evolution, this paper has advanced the literature on the GPN/GVC framework for the transformation of regional development trajectories in contemporary globalization. The study has enriched the recent debates on the changing roles of emerging Asian economies, such as China, as rising markets in the changing global economy. The evolution of the export-led development model in China has echoed the recent plea for exploring 'underdeveloped' areas, such as consumption and the so-called 'dark side' of the strategic coupling process in contemporary globalization (Coe and Hess, 2011). It argues that while having made a significant contribution to the phenomenal growth of exports over the past three decades, export-oriented TNCs have become locked into the processing trade regime and embedded in the 'network trade' of the supply chain in the pro-export institutional contexts, which have hampered their attempts at reorientation towards China's domestic market as post-crisis restructuring strategies designated by the upper levels of governments.

Domestic markets and local consumers in host countries/regions have so far been neglected in the theoretical construct and empirical analysis of the export-oriented regional development. This paper sheds light on the domestic market and consumers in host countries, such as China, as emerging dynamics in the evolution of strategic coupling between regional transformation and dynamic GPNs, mediated by institutional transition and changing government policies. It argues that the shifting power from lead firms in the GPNs to strategic contract manufacturers, such as Foxconn, in the emerging domestic market-oriented production networks in China has challenged the inherent assumption that 'global' drives 'local' in the existing literature. The on-going relocation from coastal areas to inland China, led by the contract suppliers, while faced with reluctance from the lead firms (such as Apple), elucidates that global lead firms may unnecessarily lead market reorientation from exports to the domestic market in regional transformation in emerging economies, such as China. Moreover, through relocation to inland China, the TNCs have regained their bargaining power with the inland governments and remained consistent with the central government's restructuring initiatives, while decreasing their bargaining power in the coastal export-led regions, the PRD, for example. The new evidence in China thus echoes the shift in powers from lead firms to developing country suppliers, which are actively renegotiating their relationship with the lead firms (Gereffi, 2013). In doing so, the TNCs have been leveraging between exports and domestic markets through multi-regional distribution in various regions in the host countries, such as China. As a matter of fact, the study demonstrated two parallel processes: on the one hand, the TNCs in the coastal areas have made efforts to maintain exports and explore the opportunities in the domestic market. On the other hand, there emerges spatial relocation/expansion to inland destinations, which has been regarded as a viable strategy for TNCs to rebalance between exports and domestic sales. While having relatively small market shares when compared with the Western markets for the TNCs, the rising domestic market in emerging countries has been exerting fundamental influences on the reorganization/restructuring of the GPNs, which needs further investigation in future research.

As a pilot attempt to articulate the domestic market in the analytical framework and empirical applications of the GPN approach, the study elucidates the fundamental implications of the evolving interactions among the changing dynamics of GPNs, institutional transition and market reorientation of the TNCs for reshaping regional trajectories and landscapes in the dynamic global–local interactions. Numerous avenues are opened and proposed for future research agenda, such as regional transformation in the global South in response to dramatic shifts in global production and demand in the context of the post-Washington Consensus world order; emerging domestic market oriented production networks in different sectors and sources of origin; the impacts of the rising domestic market in host countries on the global networks of production and trade; the market shifts of TNCs and competition with indigenous firms for domestic markets and consumers; and the transformation of national/regional development models in the changing era of globalization. Furthermore, this study has significant policy implications for export-oriented TNCs and regions in the junction in which the world, national and local economies are in flux due to dramatic restructuring. The study also highlights the urgent need for institutional building and reform with balanced policies on exports and domestic markets in response to the market reorientation of TNCs and the reorganization of GPNs in contemporary globalization.

ACKNOWLEDGEMENTS

An earlier version of the paper was presented at the international workshop on "Value Chains, Production Networks, and the Geographies of Development: Emerging Challenges and Future Agenda" held at the National University of Singapore (NUS), December 1–2, 2011. I would like to thank Henry Yeung at NUS, Jeff Nielson and Bill Pritchard both at the University of Sydney for inviting and funding me to present my paper at the workshop. I am very grateful to the participants of the workshop and three anonymous referees of *RIPE* for their constructive comments and suggestions. Financial supports of the General Research Grant (HKBU 457210 and HKBU 251712) from Hong Kong Research Grant Council for conducting the research are gratefully acknowledged.

NOTES

1 The 'Washington Consensus' was first presented in 1989 by John Williamson, an economist from the Institute for International Economics in Washington DC. It was a paradigm that focused on economic growth and advocated the market as a universally efficient mechanism to allocate resources and foster economic growth. Since 2000, especially following the 2008 global financial crisis, it has been replaced by a contrasting paradigm, termed the 'post-Washington Consensus', which emphasizes the need of different institutions for different economies and recognizes cases in which governments' market interventions play a positive role.

2 While 'exploring the domestic market in China' was listed among the top five driving forces by TNCs for cross-border investment, domestic sales have been constrained by the pro-export institutional environment, a particularly stringent restriction designated by the Chinese government, even though TNCs have practised 'domestic sales' in other ways, such as reimporting, as discussed in this paper. The notion of 'recoupling' is, therefore, used to reflect the on-going market reorientation of TNCs, which has been encouraged by the Chinese states as one of the measures of 'transformation of the export-oriented development to

domestic consumption-driven development' in the recently released 12th Five-Year Plan.

3 Export tax rebate refers to the money the tax authority returns to exporting enterprises for the indirect tax they pay in the production and distribution process. Value-added tax (17 per cent for most products in China) applies to all activities of value formation, including the production and distribution of goods and the provision of services. Five major adjustments to export VAT refund policies have taken place over the past 20 years due to various reasons, such as increasing fiscal revenue, adjusting to international market fluctuations, commitment to the WTO and the 2008 global financial crisis.

4 Although most of the reimports travelled through Hong Kong (the so-called 'Hong Kong one-day round trip trade', *xianggang yiriyou*), they are recorded as 'China–China' trade and should not be confused with 'China–Hong Kong' trade or China's indirect trade with other countries via Hong Kong. The top five reimporters during 2000–08 were China, the UK, Canada, Thailand and Malaysia. The share of reimports in China's total imports increased from 0.12 per cent in 1980 to 9.35 per cent in 2006 and dropped to 8.2 per cent in 2008 and 7.7 per cent in 2010 (China Customs Administration, 2011). For other countries with large reimport values, such as France, the UK, Canada, Australia and Thailand, reimports made up only 0.5–1.2 per cent of the total imports.

NOTES ON CONTRIBUTOR

Chun Yang is Associate Professor in the Department of Geography, Hong Kong Baptist University. Her research interests cover urbanization and regional development in China, cross-border production networks of transnational corporations, industrial clusters of Hong Kong and Taiwanese investment in the Pearl River Delta and Yangtze River Delta, regional innovation systems and indigenous innovation, and cross-border city-region governance of the Hong Kong- Pearl River Delta region. Dr Yang is currently studying restructuring of global production networks and urban/regional transformation in China.

REFERENCES

Athukorala, P. (2010) *Production Networks and Trade Patterns in East Asia: Regionalization or Globalization?* ADB Working Paper Series on Regional Economic Integration, No. 56, Asian Development Bank. Manila, Philippines: Asian Development Bank.

Babb, S. (2013) 'Washington Consensus as Transnational Policy Paradigm: Its Origins, Trajectory and Likely Successors', *Review of International Political Economy*, 20.

Bathelt, H. (2006) 'Geographies of Production: Growth Regimes in Spatial Perspective 3 – Towards a Relational View of Economic Action and Policy', *Progress in Human Geography*, 30(2): 223–36.

Boschma, R. and Martin, R. (2007) 'Constructing an Evolutionary Economic Geography', *Journal of Economic Geography*, 7(5): 537–48.

Boschma, R. and Martin, R. (2010) *A Handbook of Evolutionary Economic Geography*, Cheltenham: Edward Elgar.

Boston Consulting Group (2006) *Organizing Global Advantage in China, India and Other Rapidly Developing Economies*, BCG Report. Boston, MA: Boston Consulting Group.

Cattaneo, O., Gereffi, G. and Staritz, C. (2010) *Global Value Chains in a Postcrisis World: A Development Perspective*, Washington, DC: The World Bank.

China Customs Administration (2011) *China Customs Monthly Statistics*, various issues.

Coe, N. M. (2011) 'Geographies of Production I: An Evolutionary Revolution?', *Progress in Human Geography*, 35(1): 81–9.

Coe, N. M., Dicken, P. and Hess, M. (2008) 'Global Production Networks: Realizing the Potential', *Journal of Economic Geography*, 8(3): 271–95.

Coe, N. M. and Hess, M. (2011) 'Local and Regional Development: A Global Production Networks Approach', in A. Pike, A. Rodríguez-Pose and J. J. Tomaney (eds) *Handbook of Local and Regional Development*, Milton Park, Abingdon, Oxon and New York: Routledge, pp. 128–38.

Coe, N. M., Hess, M., Yeung, H., Dicken, P. and Henderson, J. (2004) '"Globalizing" Regional Development: A Global Production Networks Perspective', *Transactions of the Institute of British Geographers*, New Series, 29(4): 468–84.

Dawley, S. (2011) 'Transnational Corporations and Local and Regional Development', in A. Pike, A. Rodriguez-Pose and J. J. Tomaney (eds) *Handbook of Local and Regional Development*, London: Routledge, pp. 394–412.

EIU (Economic Intelligence Unit) (2011) *Rising Consumption, Rising Influence: How Asian Consumerism Will Reshape the Global Electronics Industry*, London: EIU.

FHKI (Federation of Hong Kong Industries) (2007) *Made in PRD: Challenges and Opportunities for Hong Kong Industry*, Hong Kong: FHKI.

Gereffi, G. (2013) 'Global Value Chains in a Post-Washington Consensus World', *Review of International Political Economy*, 20.

Gereffi, G. (2009) 'Development Models and Industrial Upgrading in China and Mexico', *European Sociological Review*, 25(1): 37–51.

Gereffi, G., Humphrey, J. and Sturgeon, T. J. (2005) 'The Governance of Global Value Chains', *Review of International Political Economy*, 12(1): 78–104.

Gertler, M. (2010) 'Rules of the Game: The Place of Institutions in Regional Economic Change', *Regional Studies*, 44(1): 1–15.

Gore, C. (2000) 'The Rise and Fall of the Washington Consensus as a Paradigm for Developing Countries', *World Development*, 28(5): 789–804.

He, C. F., Wei, Y. H. D. and Xie, X. (2009) 'Globalization, Institutional Change, and Industrial Location: Economic Transition and Changing Industrial Concentration in China', *Regional Studies*, 42(7): 923–45.

Henderson, J., Dicken, P., Hess, M., Coe, N. and Yeung, H. W.-C. (2002) 'Global Production Networks and Economic Development', *Review of International Political Economy*, 9(3): 436–64.

Henderson, J. and Nadvi, K. (2011) 'Greater China, the Challenges of Global Production Networks and Dynamics of Transformation', *Global Networks*, 11(3): 285–97.

Hess, M. (2004) '"Spatial" Relationships? Towards a Reconceptialization of Embeddedness', *Progress in Human Geography*, 28(1): 165–86.

Hess, M. and Yeung, H. W.-C. (2006) 'Whither Global Production Networks in Economic Geography? Past, Present and Future', *Environment and Planning A*, 38(7): 1193–204.

HKCMA (Hong Kong Chinese Manufacturing Association) (2011) *Member Survey of Business Environment in the Pearl River Delta*, Hong Kong: HKCMA.

HKPC (Hong Kong Productivity Council) (2010) *The Practical Guidebook for Smart Domestic Sales in China* (in Chinese), Hong Kong: HKPC.

HKTDC (Hong Kong Trade Development Council) (2011) *China's New, Improved World Electronics Factory: Moving Up the Value Chain in the 12th Five-year Program*, 5 May. Hong Kong: HKTDC Research Department.

Hsing, Y. (1998) Making Capitalism in China: The Taiwan Connectionn, New York: Oxford University Press.

Kaplinsky, R., Terbeggen, A. and Tijaja, J. (2011) 'China as a Final Market: The Gabon Timber and Thai Cassava Value Chains', *World Development*, 39(7): 1177–90.

Levy, D. L. (2008) 'Political Contestation in Global Production Networks', *Academy of Management Review*, 33(4): 943–63.

Li & Fung Research Centre and China Chain Store & Franchise Association (2010) *Distribution in China: Perspective from a Leading Retailer*, No.70, August. Hong Kong: Li & Fung Research Centre.

Lin, G. C. S., Wang, C. C., Zhou, Y., Sun, Y. and Wei, Y. D. (2011) 'Placing Technological Innovation in Globalizing China: Production Linkage, Knowledge Exchange, and Innovative Performance of the ICT Industry in a Developing Economy', *Urban Studies*, 48(14): 3019–42.

Liu, W., Pannell, C. W. and Liu, H. (2009) 'The Global Economic Crisis and China's Foreign Trade', *Eurasian Geography and Economics*, 50(5): 497–512.

Ma, A., Van Assche, A. and Hong, C. (2009) 'Global Production Networks and China's Processing Trade', *Journal of Asian Economics*, 20(6): 640–54.

MacKinnon, D. (2012) 'Beyond Strategic Coupling: Reassessing the Firm-region Nexus in Global Production Networks', *Journal of Economic Geography*, 12(1): 227–45.

MacKinnon, D., Cumbers, A., Birth, K., Pike, A. and McMaster, R. (2009) 'Evolution in Economic Geography: Institutions, Political Economy and Regional Adaptation', *Economic Geography*, 85(2): 129–50.

Martin, R. (2010) 'Rethinking Path Dependence: Beyond Lock-in to Evolution', *Economic Geography*, 86(4): 395–437.

Martin, R. and Sunley, P. (2006) 'Path Dependence and Regional Economic Evolution', *Journal of Economic Geography*, 6(4): 395–437.

NDRC (National Development and Reform Commission) (2008) *The Outline of the Plan for the Reform and Development of the Pearl River Delta (2008–20)*, Beijing: NDRC.

Neilson, J. and Pritchard, B. (2009) *Value Chain Struggles: Institutions and Governance in the Plantation Districts of South India*, Chichester: Wiley-Blackwell.

Phelps, N. A. and Fuller, C. (2000) 'Multinationals, Intracorporate Competition and Regional Development', *Economic Geography*, 76(3): 224–43.

Pula, G. and Peltonen, T. A. (2009) *Has Emerging Asia Decoupled? An Analysis of Production and Trade Linkages Using the Asian International Input-Output Table*, Asian Development Bank.

Sit, V. F. S. and Yang, C. (1997) 'Foreign Investment-induced Exo-urbanization in the Pearl River Delta, China', *Urban Studies*, 34(4): 647–77.

Smith, A., Rainnie, A., Dunford, M., Hardy, J., Hudson, R. and Sadler, D. (2002) 'Networks of Value, Commodities and Regions: Networking Divisions of Labour in Macro-regional Economies', *Progress in Human Geography*, 26(1): 41–63.

Staritz, C., Gereffi, G. and Cattaneo, O. (eds) (2011) 'Editorial', Special Issue on 'Shifting End Markets and Upgrading Prospects in Global Value Chains', *International Journal of Technological Learning, Innovation and Development*, 4(1): 1–3.

Sturgeon, T. J. and Kawakami, M. (eds) (2011) *The Dynamics of Local Learning in Global Value Chains: Experiences from East Asia*, Basingstoke: Palgrave Macmillan.

Sutherland, E. (2010) 'Apple "Reluctant" about Foxconn Relocation Plans', *Financial Times*, 28 June, 2010.

Wei, Y. H. D. (2010) 'Beyond New Regionalism, Beyond Global Production Networks: Remaking the Sunan Model, China', *Environment and Planning C: Government and Policy*, 28(1): 72–96.

Wei, Y. H. D. (2011) 'Beyond the GPN–New Regionalism Divide in China: Restructuring the Clothing Industry, Remaking the Wenzhou Model', *Geografiska Annaler: Series B*, 93(3): 237–51.

Wei, Y. H. D., Zhou, Y., Sun, Y. and Lin, G. C. S. (2012) 'Production and R&D Networks of Foreign Ventures in China: Implications for Technological Dynamism and Regional Development', *Applied Geography*, 32(1): 106–18.

Williamson, J. (2008) 'A Short History of the Washington Consensus', in N. Serra and J. E. Stigliz (eds) *The Washington Consensus Reconsidered: Towards a New Global Governance*, Oxford: Oxford University Press, pp. 14–30.

World Bank (1993) *The East Asian Miracle*, Oxford: Oxford University Press.

Yang, C. (2007) 'Divergent Hybrid Capitalisms in China: Hong Kong and Taiwanese Electronics Clusters in Dongguan', *Economic Geography*, 83(4): 395–420.

Yang, C. (2009) 'Strategic Coupling of Regional Development in Global Production Networks: Redistribution of Taiwanese Personal Computer Investment from the Pearl River Delta to the Yangtze River Delta', *Regional Studies*, 43(3): 385–407.

Yang, C. (2012) 'Restructuring the Export-oriented Industrialization in the Pearl River Delta, China: Institutional Evolution and Emerging Tension', *Applied Geography*, 32(1): 143–57.

Yang, C. (2013) 'From Strategic Coupling to Recoupling and Decoupling: Restructuring Global Production Networks and Regional Evolution in China', *European Planning Studies*, 13, doi: 10.1080/09654313.2013.733852.

Yang, D. Y. and Coe, N. (2009) 'The Governance of Global Production Networks and Regional Development: A Case Study of Taiwanese PC Production Networks', *Growth and Change*, 40(1): 30–53.

Yang, D. Y., Hsu, J.-Y. and Ching, C. H. (2009) 'Revisiting the Silicon Island: The Geographically Varied 'Strategic Coupling' in the Development of High-technology Parks, Taiwan', *Regional Studies*, 43(3): 369–84.

Yeung, H. W.-C. (2005) 'Rethinking Relational Economic Geography', *Transactions of the Institute of British Geographers*, 30(1): 37–51.

Yeung, H. W.-C. (2007) 'From Followers to Market Leaders: Asian Electronics Firms in the Global Economy', *Asia Pacific Viewpoint*, 48(1): 1–30.

Yeung, H. W.-C. (2009) 'Regional Development and the Competitive Dynamics of Global Production Networks: An East Asian Perspective', *Regional Studies*, 43(3): 325–52.

Yeung, H. W.-C. (2013) 'Governing the Market in a Globalizing Era: Development States, Global Production Networks and Inter-firm Dynamics in East Asia', *Review of International Political Economy*, 20.

Zhou, Y., Sun, Y., Wei, Y. H. D. and Lin, G. C. S. (2011) 'De-centering "Spatial Fix" – Patterns of Territorialization and Regional Technological Dynamism of ICT Hubs in China', *Journal of Economic Geography*, 11(1): 119–50.

Global models of networked organization, the positional power of nations and economic development

Matthew C. Mahutga

Department of Sociology, University of California, Riverside, USA

ABSTRACT

Interdisciplinary literature on global commodity chains (GCCs)/global value chains (GVCs) and global production networks (GPNs) contends that inter-firm power differentials within globally networked forms of economic organization have implications for the developmental trajectories of nation-states. In this article, I advance these literatures in three ways. First, I bridge the two approaches by elaborating an exchange-theoretic conceptualization of inter-firm power that is latent in the two literatures. This conceptualization focuses narrowly on the determinants of inter-firm power asymmetries and is useful for explaining why actual production networks vary in terms of the relative power of buyers and producers. Second, I develop an empirical framework to advance basic research on the link between globally networked forms of economic organization and national economic development. In particular, I derive cross-nationally and temporally comparable country-level measurements of the average bargaining power of a country's resident firms using industry-specific international exchange (trade) networks. I demonstrate the validity of these indices through a historical analysis of trade networks in the transport equipment and garment industries and by analysing cross-national variations in wages in the two industries. Finally, I conclude by charting a parallel path for GCC/GVC and GPN research that implicates global models of network organization in macro-comparative analyses of economic development.

INTRODUCTION

Much has already been written comparing the global commodity chain (GCC)/global value chain (GVC) and global production network (GPN) approaches to global models of networked organization (for example, Bair, 2005; Coe, Dicken and Hess, 2008a; Henderson *et al.*, 2002). The approaches differ in that GPN analysts argue that the discourse of networks provides a broader lexicon with which to consider the dynamics of the globalization of production than does the linear imagery of the chain metaphor (for example, Henderson *et al.*, 2002). For example, while the GCC/GVC literature is more narrowly focused on inter-firm relations, the GPN literature is more sensitive to the impact of additional forces, such as national, regional and global institutions, labour groups and other stakeholders, and thereby draws from the Polanyian tradition of 'embeddedness' that informs the literature on comparative business systems and political economy (for example, Hall and Soskice, 2001; Whitley, 1998).[1] The network imagery in GPN discourse is thus not only more capable of providing a broader language with which to describe issues of power in inter-firm networks, it also allows for the inclusion of non-firm actors in the dynamics of production globalization.

However, these differences in language and scope obscure crucial points of convergence. First, both argue that production globalization has not only increased the extent to which economic behaviour is organized between, rather than within, firms and societies, but also that the modes of coordination through which this organization is achieved are qualitatively new. Second, both literatures tend to suggest that power differentials have implications for economic development insofar as certain actors have a disproportionate ability to set the terms under which other actors gain entry into production networks. Third, both approaches use detailed and sophisticated qualitative case studies of the linkages among firms in globally organized industry in order to understand how such linkages facilitate or impede economic development. Crucially, however, power asymmetries in globalized production networks play a central role in both approaches, but the analytical scope in which power operates and the precise determinants of power are underspecified in each.[2] And, the centrality of power portends ambiguous implications for development in theory, and the detailed qualitative case studies yield contradictory empirical findings with respect to the developmental consequences of globally networked models of economic organization.

This article thus bridges and expands the two approaches by explicating the conceptualization of inter-firm power that is latent in the two literatures, and by sketching an empirical framework to advance basic research on the link between globally networked forms of economic organization and national economic development. I begin by outlining an exchange theoretic approach to power in production networks that adopts the network language of the GPN approach and then synthesize it with insights from power-dependence theory in order to revisit the different power asymmetries that reside in buyer- and producer-driven networks.

I then logically extend this exchange theoretic conceptualization to the level of nation-states in order to derive cross-nationally and temporally comparable country-level measurements of the average bargaining power of a country's resident firms. I apply these measurement strategies to two international exchange (trade) networks known for their archetypical governance – the buyer-driven garment and producer-driven transportation equipment industries. I validate these empirics by examining the network structure of these industries in 2000, discussing the rise/fall of national industries within these structures over time and assessing the extent to which national wages in the two industries are distributed unequally across levels of positional power. I conclude by charting a *complementary* and *parallel* path of chains research that implicates globally networked models of economic organization in quantitative macro-comparative studies of economic development.

POSITIONAL POWER IN GLOBAL PRODUCTION NETWORKS: AN EXCHANGE THEORETIC CONCEPTUALIZATION OF INTER-FIRM POWER DIFFERENTIALS

Power in globalized production processes is central to both the GCC/GVC and GPN literatures, but the determinants to power and the domains in which power is exercised vary between them. The GCC/GVC articulation of inter-firm 'governance', for example, has evolved over time in terms of providing a theory for what power is and why it matters. In the original distinction between buyer and producer-driven commodity chains, leading firms varied across the two types in not only the *kind* of power they possessed, but also in the *direction in which that power was exercised* in the chain. In producer-driven chains, power derived from a unique combination of resources and capabilities internal to the lead firms, which exercised this power both 'backward' towards raw material and supplier markets and 'forward' into final consumer markets. In buyer-driven chains, power derived from less tangible resources, which included branding and supply chain management, and was directed principally 'backward' from the leading firms to the diffuse suppliers in their supply chains (for example, Gereffi, 1994; Gibbon and Ponte, 2005). The more recent formulation of GVC governance thus created a five-fold governance typology using combinations of the values (high and low) of three variables describing the production process – complexity, codifiability and supplier capability. Crucially for the present discussion, the five-fold governance types were compared in terms of the relative power of the lead firm over its (first-tier) supplier, which was conceptualized both as the 'degree of explicit coordination' achieved by a leading firm and as the level of 'power asymmetry' between a leading and subordinate firm (Gereffi, Humphrey and Sturgeon, 2005).[3]

For GPN analysts, the independent role of power is more central to the dynamics of production globalization relative to the treatment of GCCs/GVCs, and characterizes not only the relations between firms within a given production process, but also the relations between additional stakeholders in the global economy. Thus, whereas GCC/GVC analysts would suggest that the salience of power asymmetry varies according to the governance of the chain, the broader focus of the GPN construct argues instead that all the processes involved in production globalization are 'heavily laden within asymmetries of power' (Coe, Dicken and Hess, 2008b: 273). At the same time, however, GPN discussions of power that do limit themselves to the domain of inter-firm relations provide a useful point of departure to talk about inter-firm power asymmetries in general. In one of the seminal programmatic statements of the literature, for example, Henderson *et al.* (2002) state that what they term 'corporate' power is 'the extent to which the lead firm in the GPN has the capacity to influence decisions and resource allocations – vis-à-vis other firms in the network – decisively and consistently in its own interests' (450). And, a more recent programmatic statement highlights the additional analytical leverage made possible by the adoption of network imagery. While the authors did not intend to develop a systematic treatment of inter-firm power, they clearly recognize that power is relational insofar as the power of any firm depends on (1) its relationships to other firms; (2) the resource differentials between it and the firms to which it is related; and (3) its position in the network of possible ties between firms. Thus, the authors invite a dialogue with more classical treatments of positional power in networks by arguing that 'the *position* a firm develops within a GPN may well, in itself, confer significant bargaining power . . . ' (Coe, Dicken and Hess, 2008b, emphasis in original; also see Dicken *et al.*, 2001).

This interjection of a distinctly network language and attendant relational view of power by GPN analysts makes possible a conceptualization of inter-firm power that makes sense of some of the empirical descriptions of industries in the GCC/GVC literatures. Take, for example, the original GCC distinction between buyer- and producer-driven governance. Here, the crucial distinction between the two types resolves to the asymmetric power between retailers and other branded buyers on one hand, and manufacturers on the other. In buyer-driven chains, retailers and/or distributers do not engage in manufacturing, but rather in the 'intangible' phases of the production process, where profits and value capture are purportedly highest. And, while the precise mechanisms by which these big buyers achieve a degree of power over manufacturers is under-theorized, the case study literature is clear that they do possess a strong degree of power over manufacturers, both in terms of their ability to set the parameters of the production process and to dictate the price of outputs (for example, Kaplinsky, 2005; Gereffi, 1994). In producer-driven chains, the exact opposite holds – leading manufacturing firms possess a high degree of power *vis-à-vis* retailers, or might even do the retailing and distribution themselves.[4]

The most prominent explanation for why buyers have more power in buyer-driven networks and producers have more power in producer-driven networks makes reference to differences in the height of entry barriers to manufacturing across the two types. Entry barriers can include factors that are endogenous to the production process – such as capital, skill and technological intensity – as well as external factors such as government protectionism (OECD, 2007), but the key point is that they limit the entry of firms into a given economic activity and thereby lower competition for the activities they protect. Thus, buyers have more power in buyer-driven chains and producers have more power in producer-driven chains because entry barriers to manufacturing are higher in producer-driven chains than in buyer-driven ones (for example, Gereffi, 1994; Gibbon and Ponte, 2005; Mahutga, 2012). Ultimately, this explication of entry barriers is a resource view of power – 'what distinguishes lead firms from their followers or subordinates is that they control access to major resources that generate the most profitable returns in the industry' (Gereffi, 2002: 4).

However, entry barriers should also determine differences in bargaining power between chain participants along the lines suggested by the GPN literature. Compared to resource power, bargaining power is a relational concept that is a function of the autonomy and dependency that accrue to actors in different types of network positions. In power dependence theory, for example, actors in positions with high bargaining power have both (1) a large number of partners with whom it would be possible to exchange; and (2) partners who are limited in their ability to exchange with alternative partners (for example, Emerson, 1962). Resources do play a critical role in power dependency theory insofar as a firm that possesses a scarce resource is an attractive exchange partner, so that power differentials are a 'joint function of the value of the resource desired and the availability of that resource (or its equivalent) from alternative sources' (Yamagashi, Gillmore and Cook, 1988: 837). What is crucial to the operation of power in exchange networks, however, is that power differentials allow powerful firms to bargain their potential exchange partners against each other and thereby extract economic concessions.

To see how entry barriers can impact the bargaining position of firms, consider the hypothetical networks in Figure 1, which depicts the network of possible ties under three conditions. Assume that the desirability of the resources owned by the actors in Networks A–C is an inverse function of their number, and that asset specificity is such that buyers source from

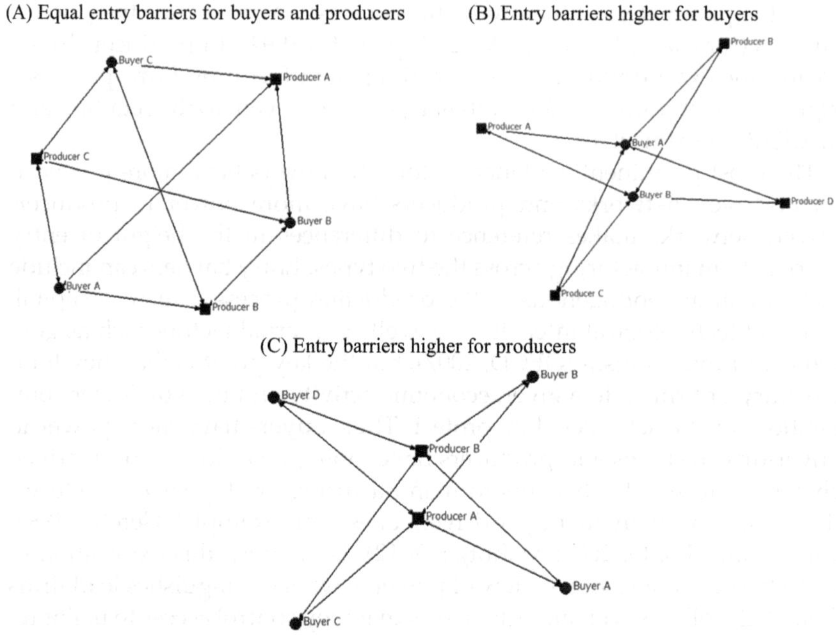

Figure 1 Network structure as a function of entry barriers. *Note:* Buyers are circles; producers are squares.

only one producer. Thus, the probability of a loss of economic output is equal to the number of redundant partners as a proportion of the total. Network A represents the situation in which buyers and producers are equal in number and all producers are equally capable of filling the orders of buyers – that is, a situation in which the entry barriers to buying and producing are equal. In Network A, neither buyers nor suppliers have any more bargaining power than the other and the two groups are perfectly interdependent. Neither buyers nor producers have a viable exit threat when negotiating the terms of the exchange with their partners.

Network B represents the situation that prevails in buyer-driven networks, where entry barriers are higher for buyers. In Network B, buyers have four possible partners, while producers have only two, which induces competition among producers to meet the demands of buyers. The network structure yields a probability of losing economic output for producers equal to .5 (2/4), and will reduce the economic output to producers most unwilling to meet the demands of buyers. Thus, buyers are in a better position to determine the price of the goods sold by producers. Network C represents the situation that prevails in producer-driven networks, in which entry barriers are higher for producers than buyers. In Network C, producers have a more favourable bargaining position than do buyers – each producer has four possible partners while buyers have only two. Failing to meet the demands of producers will result in a loss of economic output for two buyers, who have the same probability of economic loss as producers in Network B (.5). Thus, producers are in a better position to determine the price at which they sell their manufactures in Network C. In short, firms whose resources are protected by the highest entry barriers will, *ceteris paribus*, possess greater bargaining power *vis-à-vis* their exchange partners.[5]

While Figure 1 represents a hypothetical set of ideal-typical networks, both case study and theoretic research suggest that the link between barriers to entry and bargaining power hypothesized above manifests in the relations among buyers and producers in industries that embody archetypically buyer- or producer-driven governance. For example, a theoretic model that explains the returns to buying in the garment industry finds that the limited 'scope for subcontractors to raise production costs without triggering a substantial loss of output' is critical to the returns to buying because big buyers can use the exit threat to extract gains from their suppliers (Heintz, 2006: 509; also see Schrank, 2004). Similarly, case study research on the relationships between US auto manufacturers and their dealers paints the opposite picture. Manufacturers have 'more applicants who would like to be dealers than [there are] dealerships available. [Manufacturers] can either replace a particular dealer with another or even afford to lose representation in one dealer's market area without suffering a serious loss . . . ' (Macaulay, 1966: 11; also see Forehand and Forehand, 2002).

There is also a good deal of evidence that the number of manufacturing firms worldwide – a key indicator of the height of entry barriers to manufacturing in each industry – is much higher in archetypically buyer-driven industries than in producer-driven ones. Figure 2 plots the estimated number of manufacturing firms over time in the buyer-driven garment industry and producer-driven transportation equipment industries. These data come from UNIDO (2006).[6] There were already many more garment establishments in 1980 than there were transport equipment establishments. Moreover, the number of garment establishments exploded almost exponentially after 1990, while the number of transport equipment firms increased much more modestly. Indeed, there were roughly three times as many of the former by 2003. Thus, if a firm's bargaining power is an inverse function of the availability of alternatives, then transport equipment producers should have more power in their respective production networks than garment producers, and *vice versa* for buyers. In other words, the network of possible inter-firm relations among buyers and producers in the global garment industry must approximate the hypothetical Network B in Figure 1, while the network of possible inter-firm relations among

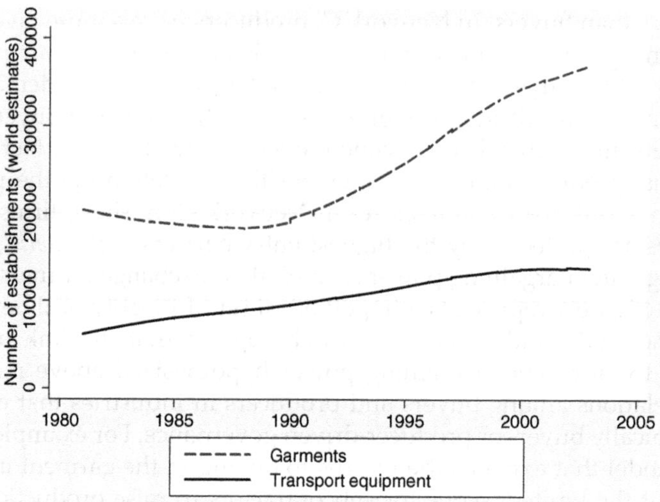

Figure 2 World estimate of the number of garment and transport equipment establishments. *Notes:* Data for garment and transport equipment firms come from UNIDO (2006). Garment firms reflect Category 322 (Wearing Apparel, except Footwear) and transport firms reflect Category 384 (Transportation Equipment).

buyers and producers in the global transport equipment industry must approximate the hypothetical Network C.

FROM FIRMS TO STATES: PRODUCTION NETWORKS, ECONOMIC DEVELOPMENT AND THE POSITIONAL POWER OF NATIONS

To recapitulate, a central theme in both the GCC/GVC and GPN literatures is that the power relations observed in production networks matter for the viability of participating firms and, by extension, the economic development of the states in which they reside (for example, Coe, Dicken and Hess, 2008a, 2008b; Gibbon and Ponte, 2005; Kaplinsky, 2005; Mahutga, 2012). Yet, the units of analysis that predominate in both GPN and GCC/GVC research – firms and the transnational networks in which they are embedded – pose a bit of a methodological challenge in drawing conclusive links between networked production and economic development, particularly when statistics on both development and economic behaviour are compiled cross-nationally, and 'development' is by definition a concept that must go beyond the performance of any single firm (for example, Bair, 2005).

Indeed, both literatures begin with the premise that the nation-state is a 'level of aggregation [that] is becoming less useful in light of the changes occurring in the organization of economic activities which increasingly tend to slice through, while still being unevenly contained within, state boundaries' (Henderson *et al.*, 2002: 437; also see Bair, 2005; Gereffi, 1996). The predominant solution to this problem is the case study, where authors provide detailed accounts of the way in which particular firms or geographical sub-regions are integrated into a larger production network. This methodology has produced a wealth of information on the organizational processes at work in the global economy. But cases of successful firm-level upgrading can be read alongside cases of failure, and even cases of successful upgrading at the level of the firm can have ambivalent implications for development in a particular location if, for example, upgrading occurs at the expense of wages and working conditions for workers or negatively impacts the viability of other domestic firms that compete for access to a given network (Bair and Gereffi, 2003; Schrank, 2004). Thus, scholars within the tradition recognize that conclusions regarding the link between production networks and economic development based on 'extrapolations from specific case studies and instances must be treated with caution . . . ' (Dicken *et al.*, 2001: 89).

As a point of departure, I pursue the GPN/GCC/GVC argument that production network dynamics matter for economic development by extending and measuring the latent exchange theoretic conceptualization of power discussed above at the level of the nation-state and proposing a parallel path of chains research that would implicate such measurements in cross-national models of development outcomes. Extending the exchange theoretic conceptualization of power in production networks up to its implications for national development requires the measurement of the aggregate positional power of resident firms according to the exchange theoretic determinants of power. Because industries vary in how they are governed, such an exercise must begin with the recognition that valid national indicators of average firm power must also vary by industry. In order to measure the positional power of resident firms across countries, then, one could measure the pattern of their exchanges with firms in other countries. Here, one could focus on buyers in the garment industry and producers in the transport equipment industry, where Nation X would have powerful firms in the garment industry if buying was concentrated among a handful of large buyers, who, in turn, sourced from a diffuse network of small producers that were dependent upon these concentrated buyers. Conversely, Nation X would have powerful firms in the transport equipment industry if production was concentrated among a handful of large producers, who, in turn, inculcated many dependent buyers (for example, Bonacich, 1987). However, 'publicly available and detailed information at the level of firms is generally lacking' (Gereffi, 2005: 169).

Given the lack of cross-nationally comparable firm-level data, I instead derive relational measures of bargaining power using the trade relations that firms forge between national economies. Indeed, despite widespread recognition that states are imperfect containers of production network activity, there is no shortage of empirical work in the GCC/GVC/GPN tradition making use of national-level statistics on industry- and sector-specific trade (for example, Bair and Gereffi, 2003; Hamilton and Gereffi, 2009; Kaplinsky, 2005; Sturgeon, Van Biesebroeck and Gereffi, 2008). The utilization of these data underscores the intuition that they reflect the way in which 'lead firms go about setting up and maintaining production and trade networks' as a given industry becomes organized via production networks over time (Gibbon and Ponte, 2005: 93). That is, because manufacturing industries are increasingly organized via production networks, national-level industrial statistics tend to reflect the way in which firms within these countries are positioned within them. I limit the measurement of national power to two industries – garment and transportation equipment manufacturing. I select these two industries because they are widely regarded as exemplifying buyer- and producer-driven governance (for example, Gibbon and Ponte, 2005; Mahutga, 2012) and, therefore, allow for a clear derivation of theoretically meaningful power relations among countries in the industry.[7]

In buyer-driven networks, the firms who capture the most value in their respective networks are buyers, rather than producers. And, consistent with empirical literature on the industry and resource dependence theory, this disproportionate value capture is a function of the scarcity of the requisite resources to buying – 'the lavish advertising budgets and promotional campaigns required to create and sustain global brands' – and the ability of big buyers to use their bargaining power to induce competition among potential suppliers and thereby reduce the unit price of manufactured inputs (Gereffi, 2002: 4; Heintz, 2006). If powerful firms in the garment industry are recognizable by their buying behaviour and have more bargaining power when they inculcate dependent producers, then the countries in which they reside occupy favourable bargaining positions in buyer-driven networks when they import from a diverse set suppliers, particularly when suppliers are dependent on them for export outlets.

In producer-driven networks, the firms that capture the most value in their respective networks are producers, rather than buyers. Value capture in producer-driven industries is also a function of the scarcity of both requisite resources and bargaining power, but the type of resources and bargaining power varies from those in buyer-driven networks. The resources that are critical to powerful firms in producer-driven networks are highly capitalized and technologically advanced production facilities as well as knowledge and technology intensive research and development operations (Gibbon and Ponte, 2005). Moreover, manufacturers – both the leading firms and many of their suppliers – have more bargaining power than their counterparts in buyer-driven networks because there are fewer alternative sources for both finished and intermediate goods. Thus, if powerful firms in the transport equipment industry are recognizable by their producing behaviour and their ability to increase the unit price of their manufactured goods by inculcating dependent buyers, then countries occupy favourable bargaining positions in producer-driven networks when they export to many countries that are dependent on them for imports.

With this logic in mind, I estimate the average network position of resident firms on a large sample of countries in both the garment and transportation equipment industries with a modified version of Wallace, Griffin and Rubin's 'logarithmic method' (Wallace, Griffin and Rubin, 1989: 212; also see Jorgenson (2006) for a comparable analysis of economic networks and deforestation).[8] Because positional power varies by the driven-ness of the network, two versions of the logarithmic method are applied to trade networks for the buyer-driven garment and producer-driven transportation equipment industries, respectively.

In the case of buyer-driven networks, where bargaining power accrues to concentrated buyers rather than diffuse producers, I measure the positional power of countries in the garment industry with *Buyer-driven power* (P_j^B), which is defined in equation (1).

$$P_j^B = \sum_{i=1}^{n} \log(Y_{ij}/X_i \cdot +1) \tag{1}$$

In (1), Y_{ij} is the import received by country j from country i in the garment industry, $X_i\cdot$ is the total garment exports of the sending country i and *log* is the base 10 logarithm. This measure takes the value in every cell on the import columns of receiving country j, divides it by the total exports of each sending country, adds one to define empty cells, and then transforms these ratios with the base 10 logarithm. These transformed values are then summed down the import vector to create the *Buyer-driven power* of country j in the global garment industry. Countries rank high when they have many dependent import partners – that is, when they have many partners from which they import a large proportion of their total garment exports – and low when they have few, with scores increasing with the absolute dependency of each import partner thereafter.

The case of producer-driven power is the reverse. Countries are powerful in producer-driven networks when they inculcate many dependent buyers and capture a large share of their markets. Thus, I measure country j's

Producer-driven power (P_j^P) with

$$P_j^P = \sum_{i=1}^{n} \log(X_{ji}/Y_i \cdot +1) \tag{2}$$

where X_{ji} is the exports from country j to country i in a producer-driven industry, $Y_i \cdot$ is the total imports of receiving country i and *log* is the base 10 logarithm. This measure operates across the rows (export vector), rather than down the columns, and normalizes by the total imports of the receiving country, rather than the sending one. Countries rank high when they have many dependent export partners – that is, when the focal country has many partners to which they export a large proportion of their partner's total transport equipment imports – and low when they have few, and increase in power with the absolute dependency of each export partner thereafter.

Trade data

The trade networks used to estimate buyer- and producer-driven power come from UNCOMTRADE and are categorized according to the Standard Industrial Trade Classification (SITC) Rev. 1 (United Nations, 2006, 1963). The data for buyer-driven power are Category 84 (Clothing) and those for producer-driven power are Category 71 (Transportation equipment). In both cases, I build the network with reported imports collected at five points in time over the 35-year period from 1965 to 2000.[9] The networks track the same sample of countries in each period in order to preclude biases owing to partner attrition/addition. The year-on-year variation in which countries report restricted the sample to the 96 listed in Table 3, which account for between 95.5 per cent and 98.6 per cent of world trade and between 92.5 per cent and 96.8 per cent of world gross domestic product (GDP) over the period.

VALIDATING BUYER- AND PRODUCER-DRIVEN POWER

While buyer- and producer-driven power as defined in Equations 1 and 2 above are logically consistent with the exchange theoretic conceptualization of positional power developed throughout, I conduct a series of validating exercises to assess the extent to which these measurements correspond with what we know of the role countries play in the two industries from case studies. The first validation exercise considers information that is internal to the measurements – the pattern of relations in the two industrial networks and in the waxing and waning of the positional power of individual nations within these industries over time.

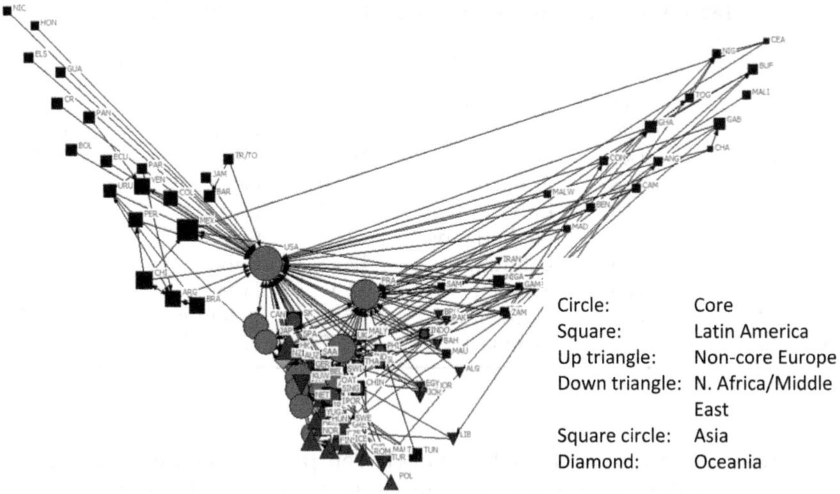

Figure 3 Correspondence analysis of garment trade network, 2000. *Notes:* Node size is a function of buyer-driven power, with a size ratio of 1:5 for the minimum to maximum value in 2000. Color and shape is geographical region. Core countries are those identified by Mahutga and Smith (2011). Directed ties indicate an import of greater than or equal to 10 per cent of an exporter's total garment exports.

Internal validity: Network structure and the rise and fall of national industries and firms

Figure 3 displays a graph of the garment trade network in 2000. The placement of countries in the graph is based on a correspondence analysis, which is a scaling technique that represents the countries in the trade network in a two-dimensional space, so that those with similar trading patterns are placed close together and those with dissimilar trade patterns are placed far apart.[10] For example, regional similarity is reflected in the clustering of countries in the same region close together – Latin America and Africa reside in the leftmost and rightmost 'periphery' of the network, respectively. 'Core' countries are clustered towards the centre, with countries from Asia, non-core Europe and Oceania clustered around them.

The size of the nodes in Figure 3 is determined by their measured level of buyer-driven power, with larger nodes connoting higher buyer-driven power. The presence of a tie in Figure 3 indicates a garment import representing at least 10 per cent or more of the *focal exporter's total garment exports*. What is particularly informative in Figure 3 from the perspective of both the GPN and GCC/GVC approaches is that the countries with the highest measures of buyer-driven power are clustered towards the 'core' of the graph. Moreover, export dependencies tend to flow from countries at the periphery of the graph with low buyer-driven power to countries at

Table 1 Top 10 countries on buyer-driven power, 1965–2000

1965		1980		2000	
USA	13.11	Germany	17.55	USA	23.18
UK	10.96	USA	17.42	France	19.87
Germany	9.41	UK	16.9	UK	19.15
Sweden	7.88	France	15.89	Germany	18.3
Canada	7.56	Italy	14.12	Canada	16.36
Switzerland	7.48	Netherlands	13.93	Spain	15.89
Netherlands	6.96	Belgium	12.45	Italy	15.7
France	6.86	Sweden	12.4	Japan	15.41
Denmark	6.4	Switzerland	12.24	Belgium	15.09
Australia	6.32	Denmark	11.62	Netherlands	14.97

the core of the graph with high buyer-driven power. The only exception to this rule is the small number of dependent and interdependent (two-way flows of exports greater or equal to 10 per cent of the exporters' total garment exports) ties that flow within regions in Figure 3. In short, there is a clear pattern of power and dependency depicted in Figure 3, where countries with powerful firms in the garment industry reside in the core of the network and inculcate dependent import relations with countries out in the periphery that contain subordinate firms.

Table 1 lists the top 10 countries from my sample according to their score on buyer-driven power in 1965, 1980 and 2000. Consistent with the literature on buyer-driven networks, the top 10 countries reside in the 'core' of the world economy. Germany is the top country in 1980, which corresponds precisely to the seminal work of Frobel, Heinrichs and Kreye (1980), who were the first to recognize the new international division of labour resulting from the outsourcing endeavours developed by Western countries, with a particular emphasis on Germany's formation of production networks in the garment industry. The placement of countries over time also corresponds closely to country case studies of the garment industry, which 'has undergone several migrations of production since the 1950s' (Gereffi, 1999: 49; also see Amsden, 2001; Gereffi and Wyman, 1990).

The first migration flowed from North America and Western Europe to Japan in the 1950s and early 1960s. Thus, Japan starts out in the middle tier of the distribution in 1965, but moves up monotonically over time to the 14th and eighth positions in 1980 and 2000, respectively, as it transitions from a container of producing firms to one of leading firms in buyer-driven production networks. According to Gereffi, the second supply shift was from Japan to Hong Kong, Taiwan and South Korea, which dominated global clothing exports in the 1970s and 1980s. Thus, one would expect these countries to ascend in the network much later than Japan and fail to achieve a central position because of their continued role in garment manufacturing. South Korea appears in the bottom quintile of the distribution in 1965, but moves into middle-range positions over time as it moves out of the initial stage of labour-intensive manufacturing to increased outsourcing, or 'triangle manufacturing' (Korea is in Position 61 in 1980 and Position 25 in 2000), while Hong Kong remains fairly stable over time in the middle tier (see also Amsden, 2001; Gereffi, 1999; Gereffi and Wyman, 1990; Mahutga, 2006).[11] This migration is also reflected in country studies of late industrializers such as Turkey, India and China (Amsden, 2001; Gereffi and Wyman, 1990). Each started their labour-intensive manufacturing later than South Korea and Hong Kong. Turkey, India and China remain in the bottom quintile through 1980, but begin their assent to the middle tier by 2000 (by 2000, China is in Position 44, India in Position 62 and Turkey in Position 34).

Figure 4 displays the results of a correspondence analysis of international trade in transportation equipment for 2000. The placement of countries is in many ways similar to that in the garment trade network – Latin America and Africa reside in the leftmost and rightmost 'periphery' of the network;

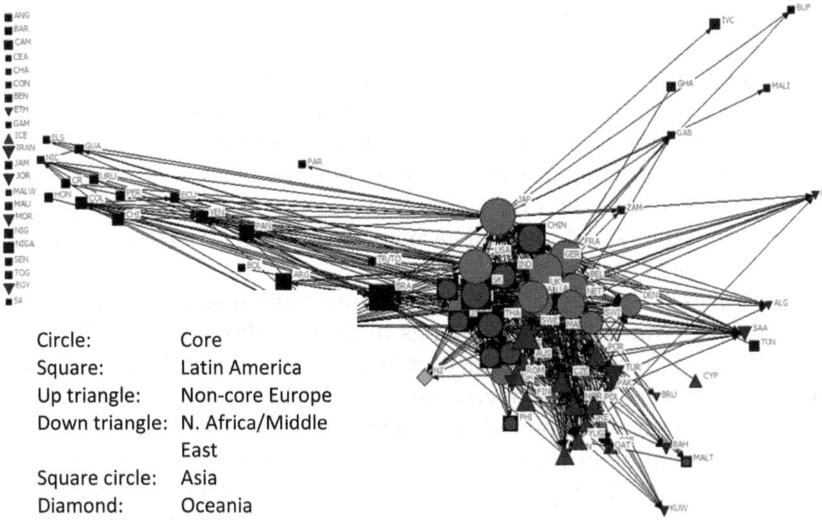

Figure 4 Correspondence analysis of transportation equipment trade, 2000. *Notes:* Node size is a function of producer-driven power, with a size ratio of 1:5 for the minimum to maximum value in 2000. Color and shape is geographical region. Core countries are those identified by Mahutga and Smith (2011). Directed ties indicate an export of greater than or equal to 10 per cent of an importer's total transport equipment imports. Isolated countries do not export at least 10 per cent of any partner's imports or receive at least 10 per cent of their imports from any one partner.

Table 2 Top 10 countries on producer-driven power, 1965–2000

1965		1980		2000	
UK	23.89	Japan	24.81	Japan	25.90
Germany	23.53	Germany	23.91	Germany	24.55
USA	22.99	USA	23.86	USA	24.10
France	21.39	UK	23.01	France	23.38
Italy	19.79	France	22.84	UK	21.78
Japan	18.02	Italy	20.99	South Korea	21.16
Netherlands	14.09	Sweden	18.70	Italy	20.83
Sweden	13.88	Netherlands	16.95	Spain	20.04
Belgium	12.83	Spain	16.49	Belgium	19.85
Canada	11.97	Belgium	16.43	China	19.44

Note: Values reflect equation 2 applied to transport equipment trade data defined above.

'core' countries are in the centre, and countries from Asia, non-core Europe and Oceania are clustered around them. The size of the nodes in Figure 4 is a function of the measured level of producer-driven power. However, the presence of a tie in Figure 4 indicates a transport equipment export representing at least 10 per cent or more of the *focal importer's total transport equipment imports*. Thus, the substantive implication in terms of the direction of dependency depicted in Figure 4 is similar to that in Figure 3, even though the arrows flow in the opposite direction. Countries with low producer-driven power at the periphery of the graph are dependent on those with high producer-driven power at the core of the graph. There are a smaller number of dependent ties within peripheral regions and a larger number of interdependent (two-way flows of exports greater or equal to 10 per cent of the exporters' total garment exports) ties between countries in the centre of Figure 4.

Table 2 lists the top 10 countries according to their score on producer-driven power. Much like the rankings in Table 1, those in Table 2 correspond to global trends in the transportation industry. In 1965 and 1980, the top 10 countries are all developed Western countries. The early global dominance of the transportation industry of the UK auto firms is also reflected in their top standing in 1965, as is their subsequent decline through 2000. The UK remains in the top five in 2000 because it is a preferred destination for Japanese transplants (Maxton and Wormald, 2004; Todd, Simpson and Humble, 1985). Furthermore, the rising prominence of Japanese transport firms is apparent in Japan's ascent to the top position by 1980, which reflects not only the status of Japanese auto firms, but also shipbuilding firms (Maxton and Wormald, 2004; Todd, 1985, 1991). The top four positions also correspond precisely to expert analyses of the automotive industry, which suggest that Japan, Germany, the US and France are 'the core countries of the world automotive industry' (Maxton and Wormald, 2004: 99).[12]

The rank ordering of producer-driven power also reflects some remarkable developments in less developed countries. By 1980, Brazil (12) and Spain (9) move from the middle up to the top quintile, reflecting the development of their auto industries (Evans, 1979, 1995; Shapiro, 1994; Biggart and Guillen, 1999). The ascendance of South Korean firms is remarkable, as Korea occupies the sixth position in 2000, corresponding to the boom of Hyundai, Kia and Daewoo (Green, 1992; Maxton and Wormald, 2004) as well as its dominant ship-building firms (Amsden, 1989; Todd, 1985, 1991). Likewise, the high placement by 2000 of China (10), India (14) and Thailand (15) is also exceptional and reflects the rapid growth of these countries' own auto industries (Abbot, 2003), their ability to capture a large share of the intermediate component market for lead auto firms, and shipbuilding prowess in the case of China (Maxton and Wormald, 2004; Todd, 1991; Yang, 1995).

External validity: Positional power and wages in the garment and transport equipment manufacturing industries

The information communicated in Figures 3 and 4 and Tables 1 and 2 suggests that buyer- and producer-driven power capture important characteristics of the distribution of national power in two industries that are known for distinct kinds of network governance. First, countries ranking high on buyer-/producer-driven power are known containers of the leading firms in the two industries. Second, the observed pattern of dependent trade ties is in keeping with what we know about the organization of the two industries, where countries that contain the lead firms inculcate dependent relations with those that do not. Finally, they also capture the changes that these archetypical industries underwent over the past 35 years. On one hand, they tend to reflect the continued dominance of firms in developed, Western countries. On the other, there has been a small, but important, degree of change over time, wherein certain countries – such as South Korea and Japan – ascended the ranks of buyer-/producer-driven power because they became containers of globally prominent leading firms in the two industries. Thus, Figures 3 and 4 and Tables 1 and 2 provide some internal validity to buyer and producer power as measures of the extent to which a country's firms occupy powerful positions in globally organized production networks.

However, these exercises in internal validity make no attempt to assess the nature of the link between positional power and development outcomes of interest to GCC/GVC/GPN scholars. Thus, as a first step toward charting a parallel path of empirical research on the production network–economic development link, I examine the distribution of a key developmental outcome across levels of positional power. To reiterate the crux of the argument in GPN/GCC/GVC literatures, the emergence and consolidation of production networks means that the viability of national economies is increasingly a function of the bargaining position of the firms located within them. And, if inter-firm power differentials impact the distribution of the gains in globally organized production networks, we should expect these gains to accrue disproportionately to the countries in which leading firms locate, or, in other words, the countries with high positional power. While there are an infinite number of developmental outcomes amenable to this line of inquiry, in what follows, I consider the distribution of industry-specific wage rates.

First, wages are a key indicator of economic development insofar as they capture not only the gains to an individual firm or industry, but also the workers who engage in productive activity in these firms/industries. Moreover, rising wages increase demand for goods and services produced domestically and, therefore, have tremendous implications for economic development economy-wide. Indeed, wages are of keen interest to GCC/GVC and GPN analysts who explore the implications of chain/network dynamics for economic development (Schrank, 2004). Second, an analysis of wages provides for a theoretic dialogue with world-system analysis, which was a key theoretic antecedent to the commodity chain concept, out of which evolved theories of value chains (Bair, 2005). In particular, an underlying premise of the world-systems perspective is that the boundary between 'core', 'semiperipheral' and 'peripheral' positions in the world-system is a function of the extent to which a given country contains the powerful nodes in commodity chains (for example, Chase-Dunn and Grimes, 1995; O'Hearn, 1994; Smith and Mahutga, 2009; Wallerstein, 2009). And this spatial concentration of powerful commodity chain nodes in core countries is one of several explanations for wage inequality across world-system zones, which includes differential processes of class formation, unequal exchange in and declining terms of trade between core and non-core zones, and the greater institutional power of core working classes *vis-à-vis* those in the periphery (Arrighi and Drangel, 1986; Prebisch, 1949; Chase-Dunn, 1998). Thus, I control for the world-system position a country occupies by assessing the association between positional power and wages, which allows for an assessment of how much any observed wage differentials between world-system zones can be accounted for by positional power in commodity chains.

DATA AND STATISTICAL PROCEDURES

Dependent variables

Wages. The dependent variables in the models that follow are wages in the garment and transport equipment industries, which I obtained from UNIDO (2006). In order to measure the average hourly wage for each country, I take variable 05 (Wages and salaries paid to employees) for industries 322 (Clothing) and 384 (Transportation equipment), and divide it by variable 04 (Number of employees) for the same industries, for each country. I then divide this yearly wage per worker by a constant 40-hour work week to arrive at the hourly wage. To the extent that work weeks vary systematically in length by positional power, this probably provides a rather conservative estimate of wage differentials because work weeks are probably longer in countries with less powerful firms. These dependent variables were measured in 1966, 1971, 1981, 1991 and 2001 and logged for skewness.

Explanatory variables

Positional power. The key explanatory variables in the regressions that follow are buyer- and producer-driven power, as defined in Equations 1 and 2, using the trade data for the garment and transport equipment industries described above. Both variables were logged for skewness.

World-system zone. Each country was assigned to the core, semi-periphery or periphery using the categories detailed in Mahutga and Smith (2011), which derive from a longitudinal analysis of multiple trade networks. In the regressions that follow, the core is the excluded category for world-system position. Table 3 shows which countries are in which world-system zones.

Control variables.

Human capital. Standard economic explanations for wage differentials evoke differences in human capital. Workers with higher levels of education possess greater stocks of knowledge, which increases productivity (Becker, 1993). Thus, I control for secondary education enrolment rates, which are standard in cross-national models of economic development (Barro, 1997; data from World Bank, 2002). This variable was logged for skewness.

Index of Industrial Production. I also control for growth in industrial output with the Index of Industrial Production in the garment and transport equipment industries (UNIDO, 2006). UNIDO's Index of Industrial Production measures output growth by indexing output in a base year. Wages should be correlated cross-nationally with rising industrial output, which reflects increases in labour productivity, international competitiveness, or both. This variable was logged for skewness.

Table 3 Countries by world-system zone

	World-system zone				World-system zone		
	1965–70	1980–90	2000		1965–70	1980–90	2000
Algeria #%	3	3	3	Jamaica	3	3	3
Angola	3	3	3	Japan #%	1	1	1
Argentina #%	2	2	2	Jordan #%	3	3	3
Australia #%	2	2	2	Kuwait #%	3	3	3
Austria #%	2	2	2	Libya	3	3	3
Bahrain	3	3	3	Madagascar #%	3	3	3
Barbados #%	3	3	3	Malawi #	3	3	3
Belgium #%	1	1	1	Malaysia #%	2	2	2
Benin	3	3	3	Mali	3	3	3
Bolivia #%	3	3	3	Malta #%	3	3	3
Brazil #%	2	2	2	Mauritius #%	3	3	3
Brunei Darussalam	3	3	3	Mexico #%	2	2	2
Burkina Faso	3	3	3	Morocco #%	2	2	3
Cameroon #%	3	3	3	Netherlands #%	1	1	1
Canada #%	1	1	1	New Zealand #%	2	2	2
Central African Republic%	3	3	3	Nicaragua	3	3	3
Chad	3	3	3	Niger	3	3	3
Chile #%	3	2	2	Nigeria #%	2	3	3
China #%	2	2	2	Norway #%	2	2	2
Colombia #%	3	2	3	Pakistan #%	2	3	3
Congo, Dem. Rep.%	3	3	3	Panama #%	3	2	3
Costa Rica #%	3	3	3	Paraguay	3	3	3
Cote d'Ivoire #%	3	3	3	Peru #%	3	3	3
Cyprus #%	3	3	3	Philippines #%	2	2	2
Czechoslovakia #	2	2	2	Poland #%	2	2	2
Denmark #%	2	2	2	Portugal #%	2	2	2
Ecuador #%	3	3	3	Qatar #	3	3	3

Egypt #%	2	3	3	Romania #%	2	2	2
El Salvador #%	3	3	3	Samoa	3	3	3
Ethiopia	3	3	3	Saudi Arabia #%	3	3	2
Finland #%	2	2	2	Senegal #%	3	3	3
France #%	1	1	1	Singapore #%	2	2	2
Gabon #	3	3	3	South Korea #%	2	2	2
Gambia	3	3	3	Spain #%	2	2	1
Germany #%	1	1	1	Sri Lanka #%	3	3	3
Ghana #%	3	3	3	Sweden #%	1	1	2
Greece #%	2	2	2	Switzerland	1	2	2
Guatemala #%	3	3	3	Thailand #%	2	2	2
Honduras #%	3	3	3	Togo	3	3	3
Hong Kong #%	2	2	2	Trinidad/Tobago #%	3	3	3
Hungary #%	2	2	2	Tunisia #%	3	3	3
Iceland	3	3	3	Turkey #%	2	3	2
India #%	2	2	2	UK #%	1	1	1
Indonesia #%	2	2	2	Uruguay #%	3	3	3
Iran #%	3	3	3	USA #%	1	1	1
Ireland #%	2	2	2	Venezuela #%	3	3	3
Israel #%	2	2	2	Yugoslavia	2	2	2
Italy #%	1	1	1	Zambia #%	3	3	3

Notes: Group 1 = Core; Group 2 = Semi-periphery; Group 3 = Periphery. # appears in garment wage model; % appears in transport wage model.

Periodization of the network form. The emergence of global models of network organization was an historical phenomenon that got consolidated in the latter part of the twentieth century. For example, Sturgeon, Van Biesebroeck and Gereffi (2008) suggest that the 1980s were a crucial decade for the auto industry, in which it truly 'went global'. Mahutga (2012) finds similarly that offshoring skyrocketed after 1980 for the garment, electronics and auto industries. Thus, I control for the period when these two network forms became the predominant organizational logics in the industries with a dummy variable that = 1 in 1990 and 2000, and zero otherwise. In addition, I interact positional power with this dummy variable to test the hypothesis that the link between positional power and wages gets stronger during the network period.

Panel regression models. In order to gauge the distribution of industry-specific wage rates across levels of buyer- and producer-driven power, I regress average hourly wages in the garment and transport equipment industries on buyer- and producer-driven power. The data are pooled across the five time periods in which the independent variables were observed: 1965, 1970, 1980, 1990 and 2000. Pooling these data allows me to account for omitted variables that vary across units, but not over time (unit effects). Because world-system position is nearly time invariant, I employ the fixed effects vector decomposition model (FEVDM). In practice, the FEVDM model proceeds in three stages. In the first stage, a baseline model is estimated including the fixed effects. The first stage excludes the time invariant or nearly invariant variables and ends when the fixed unit effects are estimated and saved for the second stage. In the second stage, the fixed unit effects are regressed on the time invariant or nearly invariant variables and the residual values are saved for the third stage. In the third stage, the dependent variable is regressed on all independent variables along with the residual decomposed vector of fixed effects from the second stage. Substantively, this decomposed vector of fixed effects is interpreted as a part of the fixed unit effects that are uncorrelated with the time invariant or nearly invariant predictors.[13]

Because of missing data on wages, secondary educational enrolment rates and industrial production, fewer than the 96 countries that appear in the trade networks also appear in the regression models. The panels are also unbalanced, with countries yielding a varying number of observations across time. The maximum number of observations is 480 for each model, but missing data reduced this to 288 and 271 country-year observations in the garment and transport equipment industry models, respectively. Table 3 identifies the countries that appear in either model. All regressions were carried out with Stata 11.0.

RESULTS

Table 4 reports the coefficients from the FEVDM of wages in the garment industry. Model 1 includes world-system position and a dummy variable for the years, 1990 and 2000, when the two network forms of organization became the predominant organizational logic in the industry. Controlling for variation in wages across world-system zones, the average wage in the garment industry increased by roughly \$3.18 (10^.502) an hour. The coefficients on the semi-periphery and periphery dummy variables indicate that semi-peripheral and peripheral garment wages are, on average, \$2.72 and \$5.57 dollars less, respectively, than wages in the core. Model 2 introduces secondary education enrolment, which has a positive and significant impact on wages in the garment industry. The substantive impact of secondary education appears fairly large when judged by its t statistic and the change in BIC′ relative to Model 1.[14] Moreover, the average wage differential *vis-à-vis* the core falls by 22.7 and 63.9 per cent, respectively, for the semi-periphery and periphery. Model 3 includes the Index of Industrial Production, which also has a strong positive effect on wages in the garment industry when judged by its BIC′ and t statistics. The wage differential *vis-à-vis* the core falls by about 8.5 and 26.4 per cent, respectively, for the two zones.

Model 4 introduces buyer-driven power, which yields an effect that is larger than both education and industrial production in the industry when judged by the change in the BIC′ and its t statistic. Moreover, the wage differentials between the core and both zones are no longer significant, suggesting that these inter-zonal wage differentials are explained almost entirely by positional power. Model 5 includes all three covariates simultaneously. The size of each coefficient attenuates slightly controlling for the others, which suggests some redundancy among them. Still, both buyer-driven power and secondary education enrolments remain positive and highly significant and the BIC′ statistic prefers this model over the previous four by a good margin. The core/non-core wage differentials remain insignificant. Finally, Model 6 introduces the interaction term between buyer-driven power and the network period, which tests the hypothesis that the link between wage rates and buyer-driven power becomes more important as the buyer-driven model becomes the predominant organizational logic in the industry. The interaction term is positive and highly significant, and the BIC′ statistic indicates a significantly improved fit relative to Model 5.

Table 5 reports coefficients for models of wages in the transport equipment industry. Similar to what we observed in Table 4, there are significant wage gaps between core and non-core zones equal to roughly \$2.72 and \$5.07, respectively, for the semi-periphery and periphery. The coefficients in Model 2 also corroborate with the same coefficients in Table 4, where

Table 4 Unstandardized coefficients from regression of hourly wages in the garment industry in select independent variables

	(1)	(2)	(3)	(4)	(5)	(6)
Buyer-driven power				1.104***	0.926***	0.607***
				(7.732)	(6.305)	(3.435)
Buyer-driven power* Network period						0.567***
						(3.901)
Industrial production in garments			0.311***		0.112	0.204*
			(3.551)		(1.320)	(2.328)
Secondary education		0.848***			0.517**	0.607***
		(4.843)			(2.940)	(3.531)
Semi-periphery	−0.436***	−0.322**	−0.396***	−0.019	−0.001	−0.013
	(−4.243)	(−3.179)	(−4.071)	(−0.199)	(−0.016)	(−0.145)
Periphery	−0.660***	−0.304*	−0.613***	−0.035	0.097	0.119
	(−6.463)	(−2.504)	(−6.409)	(−0.325)	(0.853)	(1.066)
Network period	0.502***	0.315***	0.459***	0.274***	0.181***	−0.274*
	(12.797)	(5.871)	(11.539)	(6.429)	(3.851)	(−2.363)
Constant	0.308***	−1.250***	−0.304	−0.845***	−1.829***	−1.939***
	(3.365)	(−3.775)	(−1.585)	(−5.219)	(−6.775)	(−7.422)
N	288	288	288	288	288	288
R^2	0.794	0.833	0.817	0.858	0.880	0.895
BIC′	−190.228	−214.020	−202.577	−234.303	−250.439	−264.682

Notes: 2–5 observations on 74 countries account for the sample size. VDFE is not reported. T statistics in parentheses. *p < .05; **P < .01; ***P < .001. Core is the excluded category for world-system zone.

Table 5 Unstandardized coefficients from regression of hourly wages in the transport equipment industry on select independent variables

	(1)	(2)	(3)	(4)	(5)	(6)
Producer-driven power				1.056***	0.559*	0.576*
				(6.948)	(2.544)	(2.579)
Producer-driven power* Network period						0.453***
						(3.675)
Industrial production in transport			0.422***		0.193†	0.118
			(4.941)		(1.886)	(1.121)
Secondary education		0.983***			0.547**	0.672**
		(5.666)			(2.649)	(3.161)
Semi-periphery	−0.434***	−0.281**	−0.405***	0.069	−0.069	0.020
	(−4.417)	(−2.862)	(−4.246)	(0.588)	(−0.556)	(0.156)
Periphery	−0.705***	−0.314**	−0.726***	0.252	0.010	0.250
	(−7.169)	(−2.745)	(−7.633)	(1.513)	(0.050)	(1.253)
Network period	0.552***	0.335***	0.434***	0.305***	0.247***	−0.175
	(13.329)	(6.396)	(9.934)	(6.057)	(5.129)	(−1.517)
Constant	0.563***	−1.243***	−0.181	−0.716***	−1.460***	−1.663***
	(6.386)	(−3.822)	(−1.033)	(−3.532)	(−5.194)	(−5.926)
N	271	271	271	271	271	271
R^2	0.796	0.846	0.844	0.861	0.880	0.897
BIC′	−179.791	−210.450	−208.931	−222.511	−234.944	−250.490

Notes: 2–5 observations on 73 countries account for the sample size. VDFE is not reported. †p < .10; *p < .05; **P < .01; ***P < .001. T statistics in parentheses. Core is the excluded category for world-system zone.

secondary education has a large, positive impact on wage rates, and explains 35.2 and 55.4 per cent wage gap between the core and the semi-periphery and periphery, respectively. Industrial production also has a large, positive impact on wages in the transportation equipment industry, but does not have an appreciable impact on inter-zonal wage gaps. Model 4 introduces producer-driven power, which has a large positive impact on average wages in the industry and, much like the results in Table 5, renders insignificant the inter-zonal wage gaps.

Model 5 includes each of the three covariates and, much like the same results in Table 4, indicates some redundancy among them. However, all three covariates remain positive and at least marginally significant. The BIC′ statistic prefers this model over the previous four, and the core/non-core wage differentials remain insignificant. Finally, Model 6 introduces the interaction term between producer-driven power and the network period to test the hypothesis that network power matters more after the producer-driven model became predominant in the industry, and suggests that the wage premium to residing in countries with high producer-driven power increases considerably during the network period.

The results in Tables 4 and 5 imply that positional power matters for wage differentials in these two industries, and increasingly so as the two network forms become the predominant organizational logics in the industries. But just how much does positional power matter relative to the standard explanans of human capital and output growth? In order to answer this question, Table 6 reports the results of a counterfactual analysis that assesses how semi-peripheral and peripheral wages would differ from what we observe if they had the average level of secondary education, industrial output and positional power as the core. The first two columns provide the starting point for the analysis by reporting the observed average wage for each zone in each industry decomposed across the two periods, as well as the observed gap between each non-core zone and the core in each period. The observed average wage gaps are substantial, varying from \$1.08 between core and semi-peripheral garment wages in the earlier period to \$13.45 between the core and peripheral transport equipment wages in the more recent period.

The third and fourth columns report what wages in each industry would have been in the semi-periphery and periphery if each zone had the average rate of secondary education enrolment as the core, controlling for all other factors in Model 6 of Tables 4 and 5. Under this hypothetical scenario, garment wages in the semi-periphery would increase by roughly 23 per cent and 9 per cent and the garment wage gap with the core would decrease by roughly 19 per cent and 5 per cent, respectively, in the two periods. Similarly, average transportation equipment wages would increase by roughly 29 per cent and 23 per cent, respectively, in the two periods and the gap in average wages with the core would fall by roughly 36 per

Table 6 Counterfactual analysis of average wages in the global garment and transport equipment industry

	Observed wage/gap		If core education		If core output growth		If core positional power	
	1965–80	1990–2000	1965–80	1990–2000	1965–80	1990–2000	1965–80	1990–2000
Garments								
Core	$1.76	$7.79	—	—	—	—	—	—
Semi-periphery	$0.68	$2.63	$0.89	$2.89	$0.80	$2.46	$1.25	$6.36
% increase over observed	—	—	23.01%	8.83%	14.90%	−7.27%	45.29%	58.61%
wage gap with core	($1.08)	($5.15)	($0.87)	($4.90)	($0.96)	($5.33)	($0.51)	($1.42)
% reduction in gap	—	—	18.98%	4.95%	11.13%	−3.46%	52.59%	72.39%
Periphery	$0.53	$1.15	$0.97	$1.98	$0.57	$1.22	$1.03	$6.44
% increase over observed	—	—	45.54%	42.24%	6.23%	6.12%	48.25%	82.22%
wage gap with core	($1.23)	($6.64)	($0.78)	($5.80)	($1.19)	($6.57)	($0.73)	($1.35)
% reduction in gap	—	—	36.11%	12.61%	2.87%	1.12%	40.28%	79.74%
Transport equipment								
Core	$3.20	$15.51	—	—	—	—	—	—
Semi-periphery	$1.25	$5.30	$1.77	$6.92	$1.34	$5.95	$2.82	$13.14
% increase over observed	—	—	29.28%	23.32%	6.83%	10.78%	55.61%	59.63%
wage gap with core	($1.95)	($10.21)	($1.43)	($8.59)	($1.85)	($9.57)	($0.38)	($2.37)
% reduction in gap	—	—	26.64%	15.81%	4.72%	6.28%	80.57%	76.78%
Periphery	$0.89	$2.06	$1.91	$3.71	$0.94	$2.19	$3.49	$15.31
% increase over observed	—	—	53.26%	44.58%	4.68%	6.02%	74.39%	86.56%
wage gap with core	($2.30)	($13.45)	($1.28)	($11.80)	($2.26)	($13.32)	$0.30	($0.20)
% reduction in gap	—	—	44.25%	12.30%	1.91%	0.98%	112.82%	98.48%

Notes: The counterfactual wage estimates are estimated by two equations (one for each period) for each world-system zone using the coefficients in Model 6 of Tables 4 and 5 under three scenarios. In columns 3–4, I replace the observed peripheral and semi-peripheral average education level with that of the core; in columns 5–6, I replace the observed peripheral and semi-peripheral average output growth with that of the core; in columns 7–8, I replace the observed peripheral and semi-peripheral average positional power level with that of the core. I otherwise use the observed zonal averages.

cent and 13 per cent. A similar story holds for the periphery: garment wages would rise by roughly 46 per cent and 42 per cent and the wage gap with the core would fall by roughly 36 per cent and 13 per cent, respectively, in the two periods. Transport equipment wages would rise by 53 per cent and 45 per cent and the transport equipment wage gap with the core would fall by 44 per cent and 12 per cent, respectively, in the two periods.

The fifth and sixth columns engage the same thought experiment by changing semi-peripheral and peripheral industrial output to that observed in the core. Somewhat surprisingly, such a change would increase garment wages in the semi-periphery (by 15 per cent) and decrease its average wage gap with the core (by 11 per cent) only in the first period, which is because output growth in garments was (unsurprisingly) higher in the semi-periphery than the core in the second period. On the other hand, if the semi-periphery had the same industrial output growth in transport equipment as the core, its wages would rise by 6.8 per cent and 10.8 per cent, respectively, in each period and its average transport equipment wage gap with the core would fall by 4.7 per cent and 6.3 per cent. The story is largely the same for the periphery. Average garment wages would increase roughly by 6 per cent in each period, and the average garment wage gap with the core would fall by only 2.9 per cent and 1 per cent, respectively, in each period. Average transport equipment wages would increase by roughly 4.7 per cent and 6 per cent, respectively, in each period, while the transport wage gap with the core would decrease by only 1.9 per cent and 1 per cent, respectively, in each period.

Finally, Columns 6 and 7 engage the same thought experiment with respect to positional power. The wage gain that would occur if the semi-periphery and periphery had the average level of positional power as the core is striking. Semi-peripheral garment wages would rise by roughly 45 per cent and 59 per cent and the wage gap with the core would fall by 53 per cent and 72 per cent, respectively, in each period. Semi-peripheral transport wages would rise by roughly 56 per cent and 60 per cent and its average wage gap with the core would decline by roughly 81 per cent and 77 per cent in each respective period. Similarly, peripheral garment wages would increase by 48 per cent and 82 per cent and the peripheral wage gap with the core would decline by 40 per cent and 80 per cent, respectively, in the two periods. The impact of increased positional power on peripheral transport equipment wages is even more striking – the average wage would rise by 74 per cent and 87 per cent, respectively, and the peripheral wage gap with the core would close entirely in the first period (average peripheral wages would be roughly 13 per cent higher than the core) and nearly close in the second with a roughly 98 per cent reduction. In short, positional power is *much* more important for cross-national variation in industry-specific wage rates than are human capital and output growth, and it accounts for the vast majority of wage inequality between world-system zones in both industries.

CONCLUDING DISCUSSION

Both the GCC/GVC and GPN approaches to production globalization argue that global models of networked organization are integrating firms into production networks characterized by power asymmetry between participating firms, and that these power asymmetries have implications for economic development in the countries where these firms are located. This article contributes to this project in three ways. First, I articulate an exchange theoretical conceptualization of positional power in global production networks that is latent in the two sets of literatures. Here, inter-firm power differentials are a function of the scarcity of resources possessed by lead firms and, more importantly, by the ability of leading firms to exercise bargaining power in negotiations with other firms in their networks. This inter-firm differential in bargaining power should matter for economic development because it allows leading firms to extract economic concessions from their network partners.

Second, in order to bring new evidence to bear on the link between production networks and economic development, I extend this exchange theoretical conceptualization to the nation-state by developing cross-nationally comparable indices of buyer- and producer-driven power in the garment and transport equipment industries, respectively. I validate these indices internally through a historical analysis of the network structure of these industries and the rise/fall of nations within them. I validate these indices externally by showing that (1) industry-specific wage rates are distributed unequally across levels of positional power and increasingly so over time; (2) cross-national variation in positional power explains nearly all of the observed differences in wage levels between core and non-core zones of the world-system; and (3) semi-peripheral and peripheral wages in the two industries would increase dramatically if these countries had just the average positional power of the core.

Third, the model of cross-national wage inequality illustrates the promise of forging a parallel path of basic research on the implications of globally networked forms of economic organization for the foundational explanandum driving the literature – economic development. As I've argued throughout, the extant literature is ambivalent about the link between production network formation and economic development. While part of this ambivalence is based on divergent empirical findings, the more fundamental source is theoretic. On one hand, scholars of global production networks agree that '[i]n order for countries to succeed in today's international economy, they need to position themselves strategically within ... global networks and develop strategies for gaining access to the lead firms... '

(Gereffi, 2001: 32). That is, because an increasing proportion of manufacturing activity is coordinated within global production networks, countries need to develop ways of encouraging their firms to become embedded within these networks or risk exclusion from the global manufacturing economy altogether. At the same time, we also assume what the analysis in Tables 4–6 suggest empirically – production networks tend to operate in such a way that the returns to network participation vary by the position in which a firm (and, by extension, a country) is located (for example, Bair, 2005; Gereffi, 1994; Dicken *et al.*, 2001). If a country's only hope for development is to encourage its firms to integrate into global production networks as subordinate producers, and the returns to these networks accrue unequally among firms, then new entrants really are stuck between a 'rock and a hard place' (Kaplinsky, 2005).

Thus, the key kinds of empirical questions confronting the literature involve determining exactly how hard the hard place is, for which there are at least two possibilities. First, countries with firms in subordinate positions may develop more quickly by integrating into production networks than they would if their firms remained outside these networks even though they might gain less than the countries containing the leading firms. Indeed, while subordination might be a clear consequence of integrating into production networks, there is well documented evidence that leading firms transfer a significant amount of knowledge and technology to subordinate firms, either through direct interaction with subordinate firms, rigorous certification programmes, or indirectly through intermediate sub-assembly producers (Humphrey and Memedovic, 2003; Gereffi and Memedovic, 2003; Memedovic, 2004; Kessler, 1999; Gibbon, 2001). Thus, subordinate integration may put 'firms and economies on potentially dynamic learning curves' (Gereffi, 1999: 39). That is, even though leading firms extract concessions from other firms in their networks, subordinate firms benefit from dynamic 'learning by doing' so that the returns to networked production are positive for both lead and subordinate positions and the returns may become more equally distributed over time. However, a second possibility emerges if (1) the productivity gains to learning by doing are small; (2) lead firms resist the encroachment of subordinate firms into higher value capturing activities. Under this scenario, subordinate firms become 'stuck' in network positions 'associated with declining terms of trade, and hence with worsening of relative and/or real incomes' (Kaplinsky, 2000: 132). That is, not only might subordinate firms gain less than their leading firm counterparts, but their returns might approach zero or less than zero and the differential may increase over time. Adjudicating between these two possibilities is relatively straightforward – one need simply compare the developmental returns to network participation across countries whose firms occupy different network positions, and make these comparisons over time.

The GCC/GVC discussion of governance also suggests a third theoretic possibility: the developmental disparities between countries with dominant and subordinate firms may depend on the way in which a particular network is governed. That is, if the level of power asymmetry among lead and subordinate firms varies by governance type (Gereffi, Humphrey and Sturgeon, 2005), then the differentials in the returns to these firms – and the countries in which they are embedded – should vary accordingly. Such variance seems to operate across the buyer- and producer-driven networks in focus here, insofar as the linkages between lead and subordinate firms appear 'thicker' and suppliers less expendable in producer-driven networks than in buyer-driven ones (for example, Bair and Gereffi, 2001; Humphrey, 2000; Kimura, 2007; Rothstein, 2005; Schrank, 2004). In short, the GCC/GVC/GPN approach to economic globalization not only calls for the comparison of economic gains across countries with firms in powerful and subordinate network positions, but also comparisons of the magnitude of these differences across networks with different forms of governance (for example, Bair and Mahutga, 2011).

Efforts to answer questions about developmental differentials across positions *within* production networks or in the size of the differentials *between* differentially governed production networks, along the lines developed here, require measurements of subordinate network positions at the level of the nation-state.[15] Figures 3 and 4 provide insights insofar as subordination at the firm level implies import/export dependency at the national level. Such measurements would allow for direct comparisons of the developmental returns to network participation across countries with firms in different network positions, as well as comparisons of the returns to countries with firms in similar positions across networks with varying governance. Moreover, I have bracketed entirely the role of local, national and supra-national institutions in theorizing the link between network integration and development in order to emphasize what I see as the most powerful and unique contribution of both the GCC/GVC and GPN approaches – *positional power matters* for the developmental consequences of globalized production. However, the kinds of quantitative macro comparative assessments I advocate above are entirely capable of introducing institutional variations to better understand how institutions can mediate the link between production networks and development (for example, Bair and Mahutga, 2012). The sky is indeed the limit.

Let me conclude by reiterating that the vision for scholarly examinations of production networks cast here should be seen as a *parallel path* to the extant literature. It provides a *new type* of evidence with which to advance basic research on the link between production network dynamics and economic development. While this parallel path holds promise for providing new kinds of evidence, it cannot supplant the qualitative case studies that allow for the quantification of production network dynamics in the first place. Nor does it anywhere near exhaust the range of industries and governance structures amenable to this kind of inquiry. As one of the earliest scholars of production networks admonishes, our community is 'measuring indirectly and imperfectly a total phenomenon that we cannot see directly no matter what we do... it [therefore] requires imagination and audacity along with rigor and patience. The only thing we have to fear is looking too narrowly' (Wallerstein, 2009: 89).

ACKNOWLEDGEMENTS

This research was funded by a grant from the University of California Institute for Global Conflict and Cooperation. I would like to thank the participants of the Workshop on the Future of Global Value Chain and Production Networks at the National University of Singapore in December 2011 for insightful feedback and a great time in Singapore. I am also grateful to Scott V. Savage and the anonymous *RIPE* reviewers for exceptionally thorough and helpful commentary.

NOTES

1 Another difference rarely commented upon is that the GCC/GVC approach is more nomothetic than the GPN approach. This epistemological variance is most evident in the discussion of GVC governance, where different forms of governance are a function of the combination of the three variables characterizing a production process – complexity, codifiability and supplier capability – that allow not only for an understanding of the differentiation of governance across value chains, but also for the evolution from one form of governance to another within a given value chain. In contrast, GPN analysts treat production network dynamics as the result of a broader set of place-bound processes and actors, where 'the precise nature and articulation of GPNs are deeply influenced by the concrete socio-political, institutional and cultural "places" within which they are embedded' (Coe, Dicken and Hess, 2008b: 279). Thus, the GCC/GVC scheme is a variable based and probabilistic theory of chain governance that would allow for predictions of chain governance that transcend space, whereas the GPN scheme is a place-bound ideographic theory that envisions infinite variations across geographic space.

2 In GCC/GVC treatments, for example, power tends to operate primarily at the dyadic level of the link between a lead and a subordinate firm (for example, Gereffi, Humphrey and Sturgeon, 2005; c.f. Sturgeon, Van Biesebroeck and Gereffi, 2008). On the other hand, power operates on multiple levels in GPN discussions, including firms, states, interest groups and supra-national institutions (for example, Coe, Dicken and Hess, 2008b; Henderson *et al.*, 2002; Smith *et al.*, 2002).

3 While this conceptualizion of power is clearly relational insofar as it reflects the power of a leading firm *vis-à-vis* its supplier, it also breaks down a bit (for example, Gibbon and Ponte, 2005: Ch. 1). For example, 'hierarchy' is the governance type in which 'the degree of explicit coordination and power asymmetry' was highest. While it is clearly the case that a single firm has complete control over

a production process when it is entirely internal to the firm, it is not entirely clear what 'power asymmetry' means in the context of a single firm – who has power over whom? The five-fold governance scheme also creates something of a problem for those who would like to draw a clear boundary between what is and is not a value chain or production network insofar as it appears to include everything from a vertically integrated firm to spot market transactions between firms, and thereby represents a serious point of departure from the conceptualization of network forms of organization in management studies and economic sociology (for example, Granovetter, 1985; Powell, 1990).

4 Much of the GVC literature now focuses on the link between lead firms in producer-driven industries such as automobiles and their suppliers, rather than retailers, but the point nevertheless remains.

5 This exchange theoretical conceptualization problematizes Gereffi, Humphrey and Sturgeon's (2005) characterization of 'markets' as low in terms of the level of power asymmetry alluded to above. What was crucial to Gereffi, Humphrey and Sturgeon's claim that power asymmetries are low in 'markets' was the claim 'that the costs of switching to new partners are low for both parties' (83). Yet, the conditions that prevail in the production processes that should be governed by 'markets' – low transaction complexity, high transaction codifiability and a large number of capable suppliers – should also prevail in any production process with low barriers to entry (for example, Bair and Mahutga, 2012; Mahutga, 2012; Schrank, 2004). And, since this situation is most closely approximated by Network B in Figure 1, it would seem that the costs of switching are decidedly higher for producers than buyers – there is a significant degree of power operating in 'markets'.

6 These are estimates because they are based on an unbalanced panel of countries over time. I first estimate the trend in the average number of firms per country in a given year using all available countries in each year. I then multiply this average by a constant panel of 116 countries in each year to yield a world estimate of the total number of firms.

7 To be sure, I make no claim that these two ideal-typical governance types exhaust the full range of governance types observed empirically, nor that all industries fit neatly into the buyer/producer-driven dichotomy. However, these industries are convenient because there is an adequate amount of empirical evidence that the garment and transport equipment industries are governed in ways that conform to the buyer- and producer-driven archetypes, respectively (for example, Gereffi, 1994; Gibbon and Ponte, 2005; Kimura, 2007; Mahutga, 2012; Schrank, 2004).

8 Buyer- and producer-driven power are modifications of Wallace, Griffin and Rubin's logarithmic method because they employ slightly different normalizing procedures. Buyer-driven power is analogous to Wallace, Griffin and Rubin's (1989) 'receive vector', or 'upstream power', except that each entry in country j's receiving vector is divided by the total exports of the sending country i, rather than an attribute of country j. Similarly, producer-driven power is analogous to Wallace, Griffin and Rubin's (1989) 'supply vector', or 'downstream power', except that each entry in country j's export vector is divided by the total imports of the receiving country i, rather than an attribute of country j. In both cases, this reflects the power-dependency principal that the power of actor j over i is a function of the dependency of i on j (for example, Cook, 1977; Thompson, 1967).

9 Given an N by N matrix, where cell *ij* represents the export from actor *i* to *j*, one can use either actor *i*'s reported exports, or actor *j*'s reported imports to

measure the flow. It has been shown that reported imports tend to be slightly more accurate because of the care taken by state agencies to record imports for the purpose of tariffs (Durand, 1953).

10 The correspondence analysis used here is standard, except that the diagonal entries were transformed with the approach of Boyd *et al.* (2010). I refer the interested reader to Weller and Romney (1990) for the technical details.

11 Data for Taiwan are unavailable because the United Nations does not recognize that country's sovereignty.

12 France's high position also reflects the global dominance of its national firm, Airbus.

13 The most conservative approach for addressing unmeasured unit effects is the fixed effects model (FEM), which is equivalent to OLS estimates that include a series of dummy variables for N-1 countries. However, the FEM estimator cannot identify coefficients on world-system position, which is almost perfectly collinear with the fixed effects. The alternative random effects model (REM) is capable of producing estimates for world-system position, but the consistency of REM estimates hinges crucially on the validity of the assumption that the country-specific error term is uncorrelated with the right-hand covariates. Diagnostic (Hausman) tests show that this assumption is violated by these data (Halaby, 2004; Wooldridge, 2002). Monte Carlo simulations suggest the FEVDM is preferable to the REM model when the assumption of uncorrelated unit effects is not met, and to FE models when the between case variation is sufficiently large relative to the within variance, as is the case here (Plumper and Troeger, 2007).

14 BIC′ measures the improvement in model fit of additional covariates for 'nested' models. Smaller BIC′ scores are better. Thus, BIC′ reductions of 0–2 indicate weak evidence; 2–6 indicate positive evidence; 6–10 indicate strong evidence and >10 indicates very strong evidence (Raftery, 1995).

15 These questions could also be pursued on smaller scales with firm-level studies. At minimum, a researcher maps out the relations between lead firms and their entire network of subordinates and then compares firm-level outcomes across lead and subordinate positions. Ideally, we would want to make these comparisons across networks with different types of governance and over time.

REFERENCES

Abbot, Jason P. (2003) *Developmentalism and Dependency in Southeast Asia*, London: Routledge Curzon.

Amsden, Alice (1989) *Asia's Next Giant: South Korea and Late Industrialization*, Oxford: Oxford University Press.

Amsden, Alice (2001) *The Rise of 'The Rest': Challenges to the West from Late-Industrializing Economies*, Oxford: Oxford University Press.

Arrighi, Giovanni and Drangel, J. (1986) 'The Stratification of the World Economy', *Review*, 10, (1): 9–74.

Bair, Jennifer (2005) 'Global Capitalism and Commodity Chains: Looking Back, Going Forward', *Competition and Change*, 9(2): 153–80.

Bair, Jennifer and Gereffi, Gary (2003) 'Upgrading, Uneven Development, and Jobs in the North American Apparel Industry', *Global Networks*, 3(2): 143–69.

Bair, Jennifer and Gereffi, Gary (2001) 'Local Clusters in Global Chains: The Causes and Consequences of Export Dynamism in Torreon's Blue Jeans Industry', *World Development*, 29(11): 1885–903.

Bair, Jennifer L. and Mahutga, Matthew C. (2012) 'Varieties of Offshoring? Spatial Fragmentation and the Organization of Production in 21st Century Capitalism', in Richard Whitely and Glen Morgan (eds) *Capitalisms and Capitalism in the 21st Century*, Oxford: Oxford University Press, pp. 270–97.

Bair, Jennifer and Mahutga, Matthew C. (2011) 'Beyond the Relational Network: Fragmentation and the Organization of Production in the Global Economy.', Paper presented at teh annual meeting of the American Sociological Association, Caesar's Palace, Las Vegas, Aug 19th. http://www.allacademic.com/meta/p507919_index.html.

Barro, Robert J. (1997) *Determinants of Economic Growth: A Cross-country Empirical Study*, Cambridge, MA: MIT Press.

Becker, Gary S. (1993) *Human Capital: A Theoretical and Empirical Analysis, with Special Reference to Education*, Chicago, IL: University of Chicago Press.

Biggart, Nicole Woolsey and Guillen, Mauro F. (1999) 'Developing Difference: Social Organization and the Rise of the Auto Industries of South Korea, Taiwan, Spain, and Argentina', *American Sociological Review*, 64(5): 722–47.

Bonacich, Phillip (1987) 'Power and Centrality: A Family of Measures', *American Journal of Sociology*, 92(5): 1170–82.

Boyd, John, Fitzgerald, William, Mahutga, Matthew C. and Smith, David A. (2010) 'Computing Continuous Core/Periphery Structures for Social Relations Data Using MINRES SVD', *Social Networks*, 32(2): 125–37.

Chase-Dunn, Christopher and Grimes, Peter (1995) 'World-Systems Analysis', *Annual Review of Sociology*, 21: 387–417.

Coe, Neil M., Dicken, Peter and Hess, Martin (2008a) 'Introduction: Global Production Networks – Debates and Challenges', *Economic Geography*, 8(3): 267–9.

Coe, Neil M., Dicken, Peter and Hess, Martin (2008b) 'Global Production Networks: Realizing the Potential', *Economic Geography*, 8(3): 271–95.

Cook, Karen S. (1977) 'Exchange and Power in Networks of Interorganizational Relations', *The Sociological Quarterly*, 18(Winter): 62–82.

Dicken, Peter, Kelly, Philip F., Olds, Kris and Yeung, Henry Wai-Chung (2001) 'Chains and Networks, Territories and Scales: Toward a Relational Framework for Analyzing the Global Economy', *Global Networks*, 1(2): 1470–2266.

Durand, Edward D. (1953) 'Country Classification', in Roy George, Douglas Allen and J. E. Ely (eds) *International Trade Statistics*, New York, John Wiley, pp. 117–29.

Emerson, R. M. (1962) 'Power-Dependence Relations', *American Sociological Review*, 27(1): 31–40.

Evans, Peter (1979) *Dependent Development: The Alliance of State, Multinational and Local Capital in Brazil*, Princeton, NJ: Princeton University Press.

Evans, Peter (1995) *Embedded Autonomy: States and Industrial Transformation*, Princeton, NJ: Princeton University Press.

Forehand, Walter E. and Forehand, John W. (2002) 'Motor Vehicle Dealers and Motor Vehicle Manufacturers: Florida Reacts to Pressures in the Marketplace', *Florida State Law Review*, 29(3): 1057–107.

Frobel, Folker, Heinrichs, Jurgen and Kreye, Otto (1980) *The New International Division of Labor*, Cambridge: Cambridge University Press.

Gereffi, Gary (1994) 'The Organization of Buyer-Driven Global Commodity Chains: How US Retailers Shape Overseas Production Networks', in Gary Gereffi and Korczenewics, Miguel (eds) *Commodity Chains and Global Capitalism*, Westport, CT: Praeger Press, pp. 95–122.

Gereffi, Gary (1996) 'Global Commodity Chains: New Forms of Coordination and Control among Nations and Firms in International Industries', *Competition and Change*, 1(1): 427–39.

Gereffi, Gary (1999) 'International Trade and Industrial Upgrading in the Apparel Commodity Chain', *Journal of International Economics*, 48(1): 37–70.

Gereffi, Gary (2001) 'Beyond the Producer-driven/Buyer-driven Dichotomy: The Evolution of Global Value Chains in the Internet Era', *IDS Bulletin*, 32(3): 30–40.

Gereffi, Gary (2002) 'The International Competitiveness of Asian Economies in the Apparel Commodity Chain', ERD Working Paper No. 5, Asian Development Bank.

Gereffi, Gary (2005) 'The Global Economy: Organization, Governance and Development.'', in Neal Smelser and Richard Swedberg (eds) *The Handbook of Economic Sociology*, 2nd Edition, Princeton: Princeton University Press, pp. 75–122.

Gereffi, Gary, Humphrey, John and Sturgeon, Timothy (2005) 'The Governance of Global Value Chains', *Review of International Political Economy*, 12(1): 78–104.

Gereffi, Gary and Memedovic, Olga (2003) *The Global Apparel Value Chain: What Prospects for Upgrading by Developing Countries?*, Vienna: UNIDO.

Gereffi, Gary and Wyman, Donald L. (eds) (1990) *Manufacturing Miracles: Paths of Industrialization in Latin America and East Asia*, Princeton, NJ: Princeton University Press.

Gibbon, Peter (2001) 'Upgrading Primary Production: A Global Commodity Chain Approach', *World Development*, 29(2): 345–63.

Gibbon, Peter and Ponte, Stefano (2005) *Trading Down: Africa, Value Chains, and the Global Economy*, Philadelphia, PA: Temple University Press.

Granovetter, Mark (1985) 'Economic Action and Social Structure: The Problem of Embeddedness', *American Journal of Sociology*, 91(3): 481–510.

Green, Andrew E. (1992) 'South Korea's Automobile Industry: Development and Prospects', *Asian Survey*, 32(5): 411–28.

Halaby, Charles (2004) 'Panel Models in Sociological Research: Theory into Practice', *Annual Review of Sociology*, 30: 507–44.

Hall, Peter and Soskice, David (2001) 'An Introduction to Varieties of Capitalism', in Peter Hall and David Soskice (eds) *Varieties of Capitalism: The Institutional Foundations of Comparative Advantage*, Oxford: Oxford University Press, pp. 1–69.

Hamilton, Gary and Gereffi, Gary (2009) 'Global Commodity Chains, Market-makers, and the Rise of Demand-responsive Economies', in Jennifer Bair (ed.) *Frontiers of Commodity Chain Research*, Palo Alto, CA: Stanford University Press, pp. 136–61.

Heintz, James (2006) 'Low-wage Manufacturing and Global Commodity Chains: A Model in the Unequal Exchange Tradition', *Cambridge Journal of Economics*, 30(4): 507–20.

Henderson, Jeff, Dicken, Peter, Hess, Martin, Coe, Neil and Yeung, Henry Wai-Chung (2002) 'Global Production Networks and the Analysis of Economic Development', *Review of International Political Economy*, 9(3): 436–64.

Humphrey, John (2000) 'Assembler-Supplier Relations in the Auto Industry: Globalization and National Development', *Competition and Change*, 4(2): 245–71.

Humphrey, John and Memedovic, Olga (2003) *The Global Automotive Industry Value Chain: What Prospects for Upgrading by Developing Countries?* Vienna: UNIDO.

Jorgenson, Andrew K. (2006) 'Unequal Ecological Exchange and Environmental Degradation: A Theoretical Proposition and Cross-national Study of Deforestation, 1990–2000', *Rural Sociology*, 71(4): 685–17.

Kaplinsky, Raphael (2000) 'Globalization and Unequalization: What Can Be Learned from Value Chain Analysis?', *Journal of Development Studies*, 37(2): 117–46.

Kaplinsky, Raphael (2005) *Globalization, Poverty and Inequality*, Cambridge: Polity Press.

Kessler, Judi (1999) 'The North American Free Trade Agreement, Emerging Apparel Production Networks, and Industrial Upgrading: The Southern California/Mexico Connection', *Review of International Political Economy*, 6(4): 565–608.

Kimura, Seishi (2007) *The Challenges of Late Industrialization: The Global Economy and the Japanese Commercial Aircraft Industry*, Hampshire: Palgrave Macmillan.

Macaulay, Stewart (1966) *Law and the Balance of Power: The Automobile Manufacturers and Their Dealers*, New York: Russell Sage Foundation.

Mahutga, Matthew C. (2006) 'The Persistence of Structural Inequality? A Network Analysis of International Trade, 1965–2000', *Social Forces*, 84(4): 1863–89.

Mahutga, Matthew C. (2012) 'When Do Value Chains Go Global? A Theory of the Spatialization of Global Value Chains', *Global Networks*, 12(1): 1–24.

Mahutga, Matthew C. and Smith, David A. (2011) 'Globalization, The Structure of the World Economy and Economic Development', *Social Science Research*, 40(1): 257–72.

Maxton, Graeme P. and Wormwald, John (2004) *Time for a Model Change*, Cambridge: Cambridge University Press.

Memedovic, Olga (2004) *Inserting Local Industries in Global Value Chains and Global Production Networks*, Vienna: UNIDO.

OECD (Organisation for Economic Co-operation and Development) (2007) 'Competition and Barriers to Entry', OECD Competition Division Policy Brief, OECD Observer, Paris: OECD.

O'Hearn, Dennis (1994) 'Innovation and the World-system Hierarchy: British Subjugation of the Irish Cotton Industry, 1780–1830', *American Journal of Sociology*, 100(3): 587–621.

Plumper, Thomas and Troeger, Vera E. (2007) 'Efficient Estimation of Time-Invariant and Rarely Changing Variables in Finite Sample Panel Analyses with Unit Fixed Effects', *Political Analysis*, 15(2): 124–39.

Powell, Walter (1990) 'Neither Market Nor Hierarchy: Network Forms of Organization', *Research in Organizational Behavior*, 12: 295–336.

Raftery, Adrian E. (1995) 'Bayesian Model Selection in Social Research', *Sociological Methodology*, 25: 111–63.

Rothstein, Jeffery (2005) 'Economic Development Policymaking Down the Global Commodity Chain: Attracting an Auto Industry to Silao, Mexico', *Social Forces*, 84(1): 49–69.

Schrank, Andrew (2004) 'Ready-to-Wear Development? Foreign Investment, Technology Transfer, and Learning by Watching in the Apparel Trade', *Social Forces*, 83(1): 123–56.

Shapiro, Helen (1994) *Engines of Growth: The State and Transnational Auto Companies in Brazil*, Cambridge: Cambridge University Press.

Smith, Adrian, Rainnie, Al, Dunford, Mick, Hardy, Jane, Hudson, Ray and Sadler, David (2002) 'Networks of Value, Commodities and Regions: Reworking Divisions of Labour in Macro-Regional Economies', *Progress in Human Geography*, 26(1): 46–63.

Sturgeon, Timothy, Van Biesebroeck, Johannes and Gereffi, Gary (2008) 'Value Chains, Networks and Clusters: Reframing the Global Automotive Industry', *Journal of Economic Geography*, 8(3): 297–321.

Thompson, James D. (1967) *Organizations in Action*, New York: McGraw-Hill.

Todd, Daniel (1985) *The World Shipbuilding Industry*, London: Croom Helm.

Todd, Daniel (1991) *Industrial Dislocation: The Case of Global Shipbuilding*, London: Routledge.

Todd, Daniel, Simpson, Jamie and Humble, Ronald (1985) *Aerospace and Development: A Survey*, Winnipeg, Canada: Department of Geography, The University of Manitoba.

UNIDO (United Nations Industrial Development Organization) (2006) *Industrial Statistics Database: 3-digit Level of the ISIC Code, Revision 2*, Vienna: Statistics Unit, UNIDO.

United Nations (1963) 'Commodity Indexes for the Standard International Trade Classification, Revision 1', Statistical Papers M: 38(II), New York: United Nations.

United Nations (2006) *COMTRADE*, New York: United Nations.

Wallace, Michael, Griffin, Larry J., and Rubin, Beth A. (1989) 'The Positional Power of American Labor, 1963–1977', *American Sociological Review*, 54(2): 197–214.

Wallerstein, Immanuel (2009) 'Protection Networks and Commodity Chains in the Capitalist World Economy', in Jennifer Bair (ed.) *Frontiers of Commodity Chains Research*, Stanford, CA: Stanford University Press, pp. 83–9.

Weller, Susan C. and Romney, A. Kimball (1990) *Metric Scaling: Correspondence Analysis*, Volume 75 of Quantitative Applications in the Social Sciences Series, Newbury Park, CA: Sage.

Whitley, Richard (1998) 'Internationalization and Varieties of Capitalism: The Limited Effects of Cross-national Coordination of Economic Activities on the Nature of Business Systems', *Review of International Political Economy*, 5(3): 445–81.

Wooldridge, Jeffrey M. (2002) *Econometric Analysis of Cross Section and Panel Data*, Cambridge, MA: MIT Press.

World Bank (2002) *EdStats*, Washington, DC: World Bank.

Yamagashi, Toshio, Gillmore, Mary R. and Cook, Karen S. (1988) 'Network Connections and the Distribution of Power in Exchange Networks', *The American Journal of Sociology*, 93(4): 833–51.

Yang, Xiaohua (1995) *Globalization of the Automobile Industry: The United States, Japan and the People's Republic of China*, London: Praeger.

Explaining governance in global value chains: A modular theory-building effort

Stefano Ponte[1] *and Timothy Sturgeon*[2]

[1]*Department of Business and Politics, Copenhagen Business School, Frederiksberg, Denmark*
[2]*Industrial Performance Center, Massachusetts Institute of Technology, Cambridge, USA*

ABSTRACT

In this article, we review the evolution and current status of global value chain (GVC) governance theory and take some initial steps toward a broader theory of governance through an exercise in 'modular theory-building'. We focus on two GVC governance theories to which we previously contributed: a theory of linking and a theory of conventions. The modular framework we propose is built on three scalar dimensions: (1) a micro level – determinants and dynamics of exchange at individual value chain nodes; (2) a meso level – how and to what extent these linkage characteristics 'travel' upstream and downstream in the value chain; and (3) a macro level – looking at 'overall' GVC governance. Given space limitations, we focus only on the issue of 'polarity' in governance at the macro level, distinguishing between unipolar, bipolar and multipolar governance forms. While we leave a more ambitious analysis of how overall GVC governance is mutually constituted by micro/meso factors and broader institutional, regulatory and societal processes to future work, we provide an initial framework to which this work could be linked. Our ultimate purpose is to spur future efforts that seek to use and refine additional theories, to connect theories together better or in different modular configurations, and to incorporate elements at the macro level that reflect the changing constellation of key actors in GVC governance – the increasing influence of, for example, NGOs, taste and standard makers, and social movements in GVC governance.

1. INTRODUCTION

The rise of industrial capabilities in emerging economies has rendered static notions of *permanent* dependency and underdevelopment obsolete. Regions, countries and individual localities *can* improve (and have improved) their relative position in the global economy. Still, others have been excluded, marginalized or expelled from this process, or have experienced increased inequality and social polarization. A main difference from past development dynamics has been the geographic fragmentation of the value chain and functional integration of various fragments in spatially extensive systems that have been characterized as 'global value chains' (GVCs) (Gereffi *et al.*, 2001; Dicken, 2007). GVCs can lower barriers to entry for developing countries by opening up specialized, yet large-scale, industry segments as possible drivers of export-oriented economic development and technological learning. GVC governance theory can provide important contributions in understanding the specifics of how and why inclusion and exclusion take place at the industry level, and with what outcomes.

In this article, we review the evolution and current status of various strands of the GVC governance literature. The modular theory-building approach draws out and links compatible elements across otherwise distinct, and often interdisciplinary, theoretical realms. Points of contact and compatibility across theoretical 'modules' are used to build broader, flexible, multi-scalar theoretical frameworks that can be used for explanation in areas of high complexity, dynamism and variation. The goal is to seek out, accommodate and link key theoretical insights from various literatures and disciplinary fields, rather than ignore or dismiss these insights because they are inadequate, partial or obfuscating. Because we believe in multi-causality, we view endless substitution of one partial theory with another as a self-limiting exercise.

In building a modular theory of GVC governance, we are not seeking a single comprehensive theory or a static menu of existing and relevant theories. Our goal is at once more ambitious and more modest: to refine and link highly compatible existing theories in a framework that is incrementally broader than what has come before. In order to keep the modular theory-building process within the limitations of an article-length piece, we focus on two GVC governance theories to which we previously contributed: a theory of linking in GVCs, based on an elaboration of Gereffi, Humphrey and Sturgeon (2005), and a theory of conventions in GVCs, based on an elaboration of Ponte and Gibbon (2005).

The GVC governance framework we propose has three scalar dimensions: (1) the micro level – seeking to explain the determinants and dynamics of bilateral exchange as embodied in individual value chain links; (2) the meso level – examining how and to what extent micro-level aspects 'travel' up and down the value chain; and (3) the macro level – focusing on the issue of 'polarity' in the 'overall' governance of GVCs. This aspect of GVC governance is of particular importance because much of the existing literature implicitly characterizes governance as unipolar, where power-in-the-chain resides mainly in one functional position in the value chain (for exceptions, see Fold, 2002; Islam, 2009). We propose an explicit distinction between unipolar, bipolar and multipolar governance forms.

Given space limitations, we cannot take on a more ambitious analysis of how, overall, GVC governance is mutually constituted by broader institutional, regulatory and societal processes. We do, however, acknowledge that this is an important area for future work and hope that the incremental improvements we make here can provide an impetus and initial structure for such efforts. We recognize that the current effort takes a narrow approach to the role of agency by focusing mostly on inter-firm dynamics, thus controlling for the agency of workers, social movements, non-governmental organizations (NGOs), local communities, gendered/domestic household labour and states in shaping GVC governance. While our previous work has focused on issues of inclusion, exclusion and marginalization (see, for example, Gibbon and Ponte, 2005 and Sturgeon, 2009: 118), we are aware that a focus on how actors participate in GVCs gives an 'inclusivist' bias to our framework, which places alternative outcomes and perspectives to one side (temporarily we hope), such as the disarticulation approach proposed by Bair and Werner (2011).[1] The additive, inclusive impulse behind modular theory-building invites future efforts to build out and refine GVC governance theory by developing links to additional theoretical elements and realms at the micro, meso and macro levels of analysis.[2] Ideally, the end result will be a broad and flexible framework of GVC governance that can help guide research and analysis of overlapping and shifting constellations of key GVC actors, reveal the complex roles they play in shaping chain governance, and inspire effective responses to the dynamic forces of economic globalization.

Why is a theory of GVC governance needed? We split this question into two elements: (1) why GVC analysis as opposed (or in addition) to other approaches? and (2) why a *modular* approach to theory building?

Why global value chain governance?

Dicken (2007) argues that it is the *functional integration* of internationally dispersed activities that differentiates the current era of 'globalization' from the earlier era of 'internationalization', characterized by the simple geographic spread of economic activities across national boundaries. The GVC governance literature has provided important insights into functional integration, not least by describing the various ways that spatially dispersed economic activity can come with tighter coordination (a seeming paradox), both within an expanding set of multinational firms (Zanfei, 2000) and between firms (Borrus, Ernst and Haggard, 2000; Sturgeon and Lester, 2004). It has also highlighted the expanding global sourcing networks serving retailers and branded merchandisers (Gereffi, 1994, among many others; see also Feenstra and Hamilton, 2006), as well as 'manufacturers' and agro-food processors that have shed internal capacity as they rely more heavily on an emergent set of global and regional contract manufacturers, contract farming schemes, intermediaries and franchise operators (Sturgeon, 2002; Gibbon and Ponte, 2005; UNCTAD, 2011).

Beyond highlighting these changes, the GVC governance literature has chronicled and sought to explain why and how new opportunities have opened up for firms, localities and countries to engage in the global economy – as suppliers, processors, value-added resellers, distributors, contractors, intermediaries and service providers. These roles are venerable, of course, but what GVC scholars have documented as novel is the ease with which companies can establish and manage long-distance business linkages, a dynamic that is both enabled by, and helps to drive, vertical specialization in the global economy (Sturgeon and Lee, 2005; Kawakami, 2011). GVCs have created new challenges, risks and value distributions, as well as opportunities, in both developed and developing countries. Because cross-border activities are being integrated in at an increasingly granular level, pressure has increased for firms and individual workers that may have been insulated from global competition in the past. The result is accelerating change and an increased sense of economic insecurity, even among the 'winners' in the global economy.

Policy-makers responsible for responding to the pressures of global integration are eager for more open, inclusive and flexible conceptual frameworks and theoretical constructs to guide their work, which often includes making difficult trade-offs in the context of extremely complex and rapidly changing situations. The so-called 'Washington Consensus' view that countries simply need to get their macroeconomic house in order and be open to international trade and investment to advance in the global economy provides little guidance to policy-makers and non-governmental activists dealing with the concerns of workers, communities and industries that are in the midst of wrenching change or which remain completely severed from the global economy. The rising power of emerging economies and the recent economic crisis have opened a period of questioning and experimentation for policy-makers. One tendency has been to look back to industrial policy, to revive the selective sectoral approaches that many argued have been behind the success of recently industrialized countries such as South Korea, Singapore and Taiwan (Amsden, 1989; Wade, 1990). But at the same time, there is growing recognition that the world has changed since the 1980s, that the very meaning of 'industry' has morphed from a localized, cluster-based concept to value chain forms that exhibit greater spatial dispersion and more detailed and immediate operational integration. For the places with the most deeply integrated GVCs, the process of development has become 'compressed' to the point where many of the old rules and assumptions of economic development – for example, that the gains from trade and domestic innovation accrue within national industries and labour forces – are being set aside (Whittaker *et al.*, 2010). While there has always been a need to break open the black box of firms and industries, understanding how and by whom GVCs are governed, and what the consequences of various governance patterns are, has become essential.

Why a modular approach to theory building?

Sound macroeconomic policy, sector-specific industrial development policies, technological borrowing and firm-level responses to the demands of overseas buyers have all been put forward as explanations and prescriptions for rapid upgrading and economic development in East Asia and elsewhere (Amsden, 1989; World Bank, 1993; Wade, 1990; Feenstra and Hamilton, 2006). Proponents of these different views have debated each other to a standstill, or have simply chosen to talk past each other. The specificities of technology, industry, society and historical moment all have the potential of being decisive in shaping individual, aggregate and distributive outcomes for places, firms, farmers and workers. As a result, the variety that can be observed in the global economy can hamper the process of theory building. Given the complexity of economic systems, any theory aiming to comprehensively explain and predict outcomes for entire industries, countries, regions or the global economy as a whole should be treated as highly suspect, at best. Because multiple forces of change are always at play, theory, if used in a totalizing manner, can obscure as much as it reveals. But complexity and contingency should not lead to the abandonment of theory. It is better to develop discrete theoretical areas that can help answer specific questions and then search for points of complementarity and contact between them.

Theories with a modest and clearly defined explanatory scope that identify one or a few important mechanisms that can be used to *partially* explain and perhaps even predict outcomes – in the absence of other, more powerful determining factors – can have great utility. What is important is to recognize the limits inherent in partial theories and to actively seek compatibility and linkages with complementary frameworks. Not least, this modular approach to theory building is useful because it directs us to a manageable set of questions that can be tested in the field or applied to specific policy problems. But because of the variety of explanatory factors at work in the global economy, it is important to be cautious and actively consider alternative explanations and approaches. In this article, we approach two specific theories in this pragmatic way.

In the next section, we provide a brief review of the existing debate on GVC governance and then focus on two specific theoretical areas: linkages and conventions. In section three, we build a modular framework at three scalar levels: micro, meso and macro. At the macro level, we focus on 'polarity' of governance as an analytical lens, but also provide a broader framework within which other theories and factors shaping 'whole chain' governance might be added. In the last section, we reflect upon what our framework can be used for and provide indications for further research.

2. THE GOVERNANCE OF GLOBAL VALUE CHAINS

GVC scholars approach the question of governance in the global economy differently from most other literatures. For mainstream international political economy and law, global economic governance is embedded in institutions (the World Trade Organization, International Monetary Fund, World Bank, Group of 20). This literature mainly asks how effective these institutions are in comparison to regional and national governance systems (for example, Kirton, Larionova and Savona, 2010). Radical political economy looks at the relation between global capital (mainly multinational corporations) and these same institutions and other actors such as the World Economic Forum, which are understood to represent the interests of corporations as well as of some governments (Cammack, 2003; Held, 2010). Both political economy perspectives are internally divided on how effective global economic governance is, in whose interest, by what means governance is exercised, and with what implications for whom.

The GVC governance literature underscores the role played by particularly powerful companies, especially those that exert 'buyer power' by placing large orders in their value chains, but instead of focusing on how they influence governments or international organizations to obtain favourable rules, 'lead firms' are mainly of interest as core actors in cross-border business networks. These networks are both internal to the (multinational) firm, and linked to independent suppliers and customers in increasingly elaborate and spatially extensive systems of sourcing, production, distribution and consumption. The idea of 'governance' in GVCs rests on the assumption that, while both disintegration of production and its re-integration through inter-firm trade have recognizable dynamics, they do not occur spontaneously, automatically or even systematically (Gibbon, Bair and Ponte, 2008). Instead, these processes are 'driven' by the strategies and decisions of specific actors. The relevance of GVC governance is that it examines the concrete practices, power dynamics and organizational forms that give character and structure to cross-border business networks.

In the rest of this section, we unpack the three approaches to GVC governance by adopting and adapting some of the categories illustrated in Gibbon, Bair and Ponte (2008):[3] 'governance as driving', 'governance as linking' and 'governance as normalizing'.

2.1. Governance as driving

The early approach to governance developed by Gereffi (1994) framed governance of what he then called global commodity chains (GCCs) as the process of organizing activities along a value-adding chain. The end result is an observable functional division of labour with a specific geography. Because some activities have higher entry barriers and are more profitable than others, this division of labour influences the allocation of resources and distribution of gains among chain actors (firms and workers). As for who does the organizing, a group of 'lead firms' play a critical role by defining the terms of supply-chain membership, incorporating or excluding other actors, and allocating where, when and by whom value is added (Gereffi, 1994; Gibbon and Ponte, 2005; Kaplinsky, 2005).

In Gereffi's GCC framework, there are two types of lead firms: buyers and producers. The producer-driven variant is akin to the internal and external networks emanating from large multinational manufacturing firms, such as General Motors and IBM. Multinational firms have long been a focus of research and debate among scholars of the global economy (for example, Hymer, 1976; Caves, 1996; Zanfei, 2000; Doz, Santos and Williamson, 2001). This work examined and debated the methods, timing and motivations of multinational firms' engagement with the global economy, with some scholars focusing on the degree to which they acted as conduits for the transfer of capabilities from developed to developing countries (Lall, 2000). The novel aspect of the GCC framework was the attention it paid to a set of firms that had been largely ignored in previous research: 'global buyers'. Global buyers include large retailers, such as JC Penny, Sears and, later, Wal-Mart, Tesco and Carrefour, as well as highly successful branded merchandisers and agro-food processors, such as Nike, Liz Claiborne, Nestlé and Kraft. The research of Gereffi and others (Gereffi, Korzeniewicz and Korzeniewicz, 1994) initially focused on the apparel industry and found that global buyers often do more than place orders: they actively help to create, shape and coordinate their supply chains, sometimes directly from headquarters or 'overseas buying offices' and sometimes through intermediaries, which include a wide range of actors, most notably international trading companies such as Hong Kong's Li & Fung. While global buyers typically own few, if any, of their own factories and processing plants, the volume of their purchases affords them great power over suppliers. Global buyers and their intermediaries sometimes specify in great detail what, how, when, where and by whom the goods they sell are produced. But even when explicit coordination is not present, extreme market power has allowed global buyers to extract price concessions from their main suppliers. Suppliers have responded by locating more of their operations in low-cost locations and working hard to extract price reductions from their own workers and upstream suppliers.[4]

Why are commodity chains buyer or producer driven? Gereffi did not explore this question in detail, but instead let the empirical evidence speak for itself: capital- and technology-intensive industries such as electronics and autos tend to be governed by producers (multinational manufacturers), while labour-intensive industries such as apparel and consumer goods tend to be governed by buyers (retailers and branded merchandisers). But how are capital and technological intensity related to an industry's governance characteristics? Because innovation in buyer-driven GCCs lies more in product design and marketing than in manufacturing know-how, it is relatively easy for lead firms to outsource the manufacturing of labour-intensive products. In the more technology- and capital-intensive items made in producer -driven chains, technology and production expertise are core competencies that need to be developed and deployed in-house, or in closely affiliated 'captive' suppliers that can be blocked from sharing them with competitors.

The buyer- and producer-driven GCC typology was thus based on a historical depiction of technology and barriers to entry that was appropriate for a specific set of industries in a specific time period, mainly the 1970s and 1980s. While the buyer- and producer-driven lead firm categories are still useful, technological change, firm- and industry-level learning, and the emergence of new norms and standards are on-going processes. The chain governance shifts of the 1990s, when technology-intensive firms engaged in extensive outsourcing, and thus became more buyer-like, highlighted the need for a more nuanced and dynamic theory to help explain the changes in the organization of global industries over time. This led Gereffi, Humphrey and Sturgeon (2005) and a group of close collaborators to develop a dynamic model that could help to explain shifts between buyer-driven and producer-driven governance forms and highlight new ways in which firms were linking activities in value adding chains.[5]

At the same time, many researchers in the field were motivated to replace the term 'commodity' with 'value' because of popular connotations of the word 'commodity' with undifferentiated products, especially primary products such as crude oil and bulk agricultural goods (*not* the stuff of 'driven' chains), and because the term 'value' captured the concept of 'value added', which fit well with the chain metaphor, and also focused attention on the main source of economic development – the application of human effort, often amplified by machinery, to generate returns on invested capital. Hence, the theory-building focus partially shifted from chain 'drivers' to the characteristics of inter-firm linkages as the term 'global value chain' began to replace 'global commodity chain' in published work.

2.2. Governance as linking

In moving beyond the historically-situated typology of chain governance developed in the GCC stream, Gereffi, Humphrey and Sturgeon (2005) constructed an operational theory that could, in the absence of other factors, account for observed changes and anticipate future developments in how inter-firm linkages are governed in GVCs. The first step was to review the research on a range of global industries to identify: (1) what activities tend to be bundled in one node of the chain or split among various nodes; (2) how knowledge, information and materials are passed from one node to the next; and (3) where like nodes tend to be located.

From this comparison, Gereffi, Humphrey and Sturgeon identified five generic ways in which firms set up and govern linkages in value chains: (1) simple *market* linkages, governed by price; (2) *modular* linkages, where complex information regarding the transaction is codified and often digitized before being passed to highly competent suppliers, governed by standards; (3) *relational* linkages, where tacit information is exchanged between buyers and suppliers with unique or at least difficult-to-replicate capabilities, governed by trust and reputation; (4) *captive* linkages, where less competent suppliers are provided with detailed instructions by very dominant buyers, governed by buyer power; and (5) linkages within the same firm, governed by management *hierarchy*. Gereffi, Humphrey and Sturgeon (2005) posited that these five linkage types would be associated with predictable combinations of three variables: the *complexity* of information exchanged between value chain tasks; the *codifiability* of that information; and the *capabilities* resident in the supply base relative to the requirements of the transaction (Figure 1).

As the top half of Figure 1 shows, this framework yielded three network forms (based on linkage characteristics) situated between the market and hierarchy poles established in the transaction costs literature (Coase, 1937; Williamson, 1985). The first, and most 'hierarchy like', of the network forms was for lead firms to dominate their supplier's business to the point where they were unlikely to act in opportunistic ways (the captive form). The second was for buyers and suppliers to maintain relationships in the face of asset specificity, either by building up mutual trust, or by simply tolerating it out of necessity because of the barriers to easy internalization created by learning or scale (the relational form). The third was for buyers and suppliers to reduce asset specificity by passing very complex information in codified form, according to standard protocols, while keeping tacit knowledge contained within each firm or node of the value chain (the

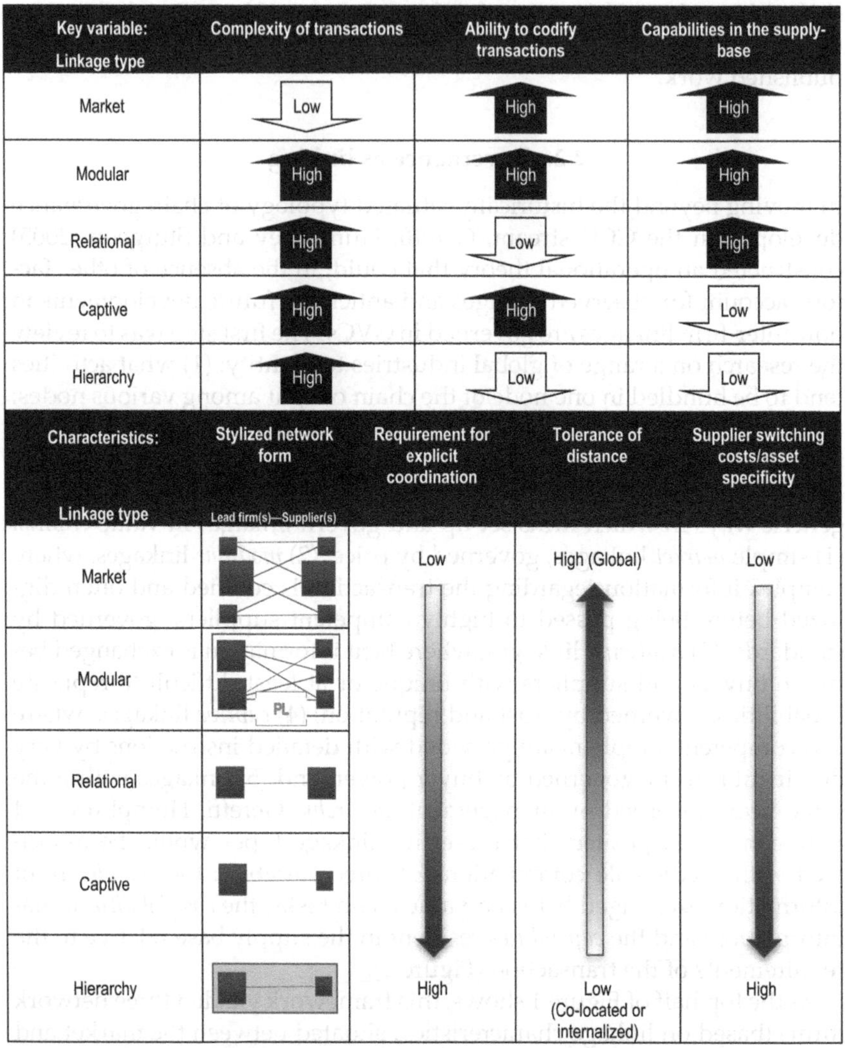

Figure 1 Global value chain linkage mechanisms and stylized network characteristics. *Notes:* 1) There are eight possible combinations of the three variables. Five of them generate global value chain types. The combination of low complexity of transactions and low ability to codify is unlikely to occur. This excludes two combinations. If the complexity of the transaction is low and the ability to codify is high, then low supplier capability would lead to exclusion from the value chain. While this is an important outcome, it does not generate a linkage and, therefore, no governance type is assigned. 2) PL = Platform Leader. In some products and industries (e.g., personal computers and bicycles), key component or sub-system suppliers (e.g., Intel and Shimano) set *de facto* standards that frame and partially constrain the actions of lead firms. 3) The shaded box denotes corporate ownership and control. *Source:* Modified from Gereffi, Humphrey and Sturgeon (2005), as adapted by Dicken (2007: 158).

modular form). The bottom half of Figure 1 further elaborates the 2005 framework by showing the stylized network forms related to each linkage type, the possible role of very powerful component suppliers, or 'platform leaders' (PL), in the modular type, and the encapsulating function of hierarchy, with the shaded area in the figure denoting the ownership boundary. As mentioned earlier, the GVC governance framework added a focus on variations in the character of dyadic transactions characterized by linkages to the GCC framework's focus on the role that powerful lead firms play in shaping the character of geographically-extensive business networks.[6]

The role of power, a key concept in organization theory, was not ignored, but nuanced and linked into an operational theory of GVC governance based on linkage characteristics. The 2005 theory posited a range of lead firm–supplier power asymmetry from high (lead firm dominance) in the case of hierarchy and captive network forms, to low in the context of arm's length spot markets. However, subsequent empirical research in a range of industries suggests that the ease of supplier switching can keep supplier power low, certainly in market arrangements and even in modular GVC arrangements, where suppliers are highly capable and concentrated (see Sturgeon and Kawakami, 2011). The need to access high and even unique supplier competences across relational linkages might motivate lead firms to tolerate relatively high supplier power, but even in industries where suppliers are highly competent and engaged in relational linkages, supplier power can be truncated when lead firms are also highly concentrated, as they are in the automotive industry (see Herrigel and Wittke, 2008; Sturgeon and Van Biesebroeck, 2011). In sum, except for rare cases of platform leadership, supplier power appears to be a rare commodity in GVCs and does not vary systematically between markets and hierarchies.

Because of this, the dimension of power asymmetry has been omitted from Figure 1 and replaced by three dimensions that can be more effectively mapped along the spectrum of linkage types developed in the 2005 theory. First, the tendency and need for lead firms to explicitly coordinate the GVC – for example, by setting precise requirements for quality and delivery, production processes, and component and material sources – runs along a clear spectrum from high in the case of hierarchy and captive network forms, to low in the context of arm's length spot markets. Running counter to this are different levels of tolerance of geographic distance: from low in the relational form, where the exchange of tacit knowledge favours co-location, to high in the market form, where simple transactions and transparent, price-based information exchanges diminish the need for proximity. In the captive form and within corporate hierarchies, stark power differences can sometimes ensure compliance, even at great distance. Hence, internalization or near-internalization can stand in for co-location in the captive and hierarchical forms. Finally, the codification and standardization prevalent in market and modular linkages reduces supplier switching costs and asset specificity, whereas the proprietary and idiosyncratic nature of products and technologies in captive and hierarchical governance can be associated with a tendency toward internalization, following the classic logic of transaction costs theory (see the lower section of Figure 1).

To sum up, 'governance' in Gereffi's (1994) GCC formulation refers to the role played by powerful firm-level actors, or chain 'drivers' (buyers or producers), while Gereffi, Humphrey and Sturgeon (2005) focus on the determinants of 'make-versus-buy' decisions in transactions and the characteristics of linkages between value chain activities. While these perspectives differ, they share, among other things, a firm-level frame of reference. The Gereffi, Humphrey and Sturgeon (2005) framework is therefore not a grand theory of globalization or economic development, but a more circumscribed theory of linkages. While the character of linkages present in key nodes of a value chain may have great influence on how a value chain in its entirety is governed, it is clear that most value chains (and industries) contain a range of linkage types. Network forms are rarely if ever pervasive. Firms may form different types of linkages with different business partners. Linkages typically differ between different segments of the value chain. Hence, it is risky to characterize the macro-level governance of a GVC, much less entire industries, from research on inter-firm linkages alone. Certain types of linkages do seem to be more common in certain industries and between certain business functions and the link between lead firms and their most important suppliers can go a long way in characterizing a GVC, but other factors can easily overwhelm the influence of the three variables identified by Gereffi, Humphrey and Sturgeon (2005), as, for example, institutional effects (see Sturgeon, 2007). This suggests a need to parse the concept of governance into several levels, from micro to macro, something that we will return to in Section 3.

2.3. Governance as normalizing

The approach to 'governance as normalizing' moves a step away from Gereffi, Humphrey and Sturgeon's parsimonious approach and explores the discursive dimension that frames buyer–supplier relations. The term 'normalizing' does not mean 'making things normal' but re-aligning a given practice to be compatible with a standard or norm (Gibbon, Bair and Ponte, 2008). While the focus on standards resonates with the governance as linking approach just discussed (especially the modular form), much of the work on GVC governance as normalizing has drawn on convention theory (Ponte, 2002, 2009; Ponte and Gibbon, 2005; Ouma, 2010).[7] Convention theory builds upon the seminal work of Boltanski and Thévenot (1991), who argue that establishing equivalence between different people, firms or objects is often based on a form of judgement drawn from some 'higher principle'. They identify six ideal-type 'orders of worth', drawn from philosophical texts, and illustrate how they are used to frame the justification of human interaction and economic practice, including the organization of firms (see also Boltanski and Chiapello, 1999). To illustrate how these orders of worth are used as justificatory devices in practice, they examine a set of action-oriented manuals for business managers, showing that multiple and competing orders of worth may coexist within organizations. Even when one is dominant at one particular time, it may be challenged, thus leading to clarification, adaptation, compromise and/or demise over time.

Convention theory has been used not only to explain internal firm organization (see review in Jagd, 2011), but also how coordination takes place among firms via the establishment of quality conventions (Eymard-Duvernay, 1989, 2006a, 2006b; Wilkinson, 1997; Thévenot, 1995; Ponte and Gibbon, 2005; Ponte, 2009). Table 1 provides an elaboration of how each of these six orders of worth[8] and their related organizational principles can lead to different foci of justification once they are challenged; how these challenges are based on different sets of testing questions and measures of product quality; and, most importantly, how they have different transmission potential along value chains, a feature that we will draw on to construct a modular connection with the governance as linking approach in Section 3.

Price is the main measure of quality only if there is no uncertainty about the quality of the product or service that is being exchanged (Eymard-Duvernay, 1989). If this is the case, differences in price are equal to differences in quality. Such *market* quality conventions are easily transmitted along a value chain because, once established, exchange does not require co-location or multiple interactions to be maintained (see Table 1). This convention underpins what Gereffi, Humphrey and Sturgeon characterize as a 'market linkage'. When price alone cannot evaluate product quality, and quality is difficult to measure, buyers and sellers adopt more detailed and specific conventions to resolve uncertainty. Under an *industrial* quality convention, quality is verified via instrument-based testing and inspection, and sometimes assured by external parties via certification against a set of *a priori* norms or standards. When these standards are universally accepted, or once an objective measure has been agreed between the parties of exchange, industrial conventions can operate in ways that are quite similar to market conventions. Industrial quality conventions are easily adopted and thus transmittable along the value chain, as long as there is common agreement on the objectivity of indicators and measurement devices. Industrial conventions often underpin modular GVC linkages. In relational linkages, also referred to as 'incomplete contracts' in contract law, outcomes and requirements cannot be specified in advance. Nevertheless, agreement over

Table 1 Key features of orders of worth and quality conventions

	Orders of worth and quality conventions					
	Market	Industrial	Domestic	Civic	Inspirational	Opinion
Organizational principle	Competitiveness	Productivity	Loyalty	Representation	Creativity	Reputation
Focus of justification	Product units	Plans, systems, controls, forecasts	Specific assets	Negotiation, consultation, distributional arrangements	Innovation, creation	Public relations, media coverage, brand reputation
Key testing questions	Is it economic?	Is it technically efficient, scaleable, functional?	Does it follow tradition? Can it be trusted?	What is the impact on society? Is it safe, healthy, environmentally sound?	Is it new? Is it a breakthrough?	Is it accepted by the public?
Measure of product quality	Price	Objective technical measurement	Trust, repetition, history	Social, labour, environmental, collective impact	Spirit, personality, osmotic processes	Opinion poll, social media coverage, subjective judgement by expert
Ease of transmission along value chains	High	High	Low	Medium	Low	Medium

Source: Authors' elaboration; the six orders of worth (as in Boltanski and Thévenot, 1991) in relation to five main elements: entries in organizational principle, measure of product quality and ease of transmission are adapted from Ponte (2009); entries in focus of justification and key testing questions are adapted from Gibbon and Riisgaard (2012).

outcomes can often be measured according to industrial conventions, so they can play an *ex-post* role in governing relational GVC linkages. Under a *domestic* quality convention, quality is determined through trust, repetition and history. This makes them difficult to transmit along the value chain, although systemic approaches to solve place-based quality uncertainty (such as appellations or indications of geographic origin) can partially ease this barrier. Domestic quality conventions often characterize relational and captive GVC linkages.

While these three quality conventions (market, industrial, domestic) can be often associated with the specific types of inter-firm GVC linkages developed by Gereffi, Humphrey and Sturgeon (market, modular/relational, relational/captive), the other three quality conventions (civic, inspirational and optional) cannot be linked unequivocally to a specific form of GVC linkage. Under a *civic* quality convention, collective commitment to welfare is explicit and the quality of a product is judged by its impact upon society, specific groups or the environment. When the measurement of impact is embedded in widely agreed upon third-party certification systems, civic conventions are similar to industrial conventions, but in cases where the definition of welfare and its operationalization are contested, equivocal and/or locally-embedded, conventions can be less than clear, shifting, or geographically variegated (see Ponte and Gibbon, 2005; Ponte, 2009, for empirical examples). Because civic conventions are part of an embedded political dynamics, we characterize their ease of transmission along value chains as 'medium' in Table 1.

Under an *inspirational* quality convention, quality is judged on the newness of products or the personality of one of the actors in the exchange, that is, the perception of their genius, intuition, creativity or vision. Alternatively, one of the parties in the exchange can invite the other to absorb a particular 'spirit' of doing things or the 'feeling' that is created, for example, in retail spaces (see Gibbon and Ponte, 2005). While the technological and artistic developments underpinning inspirational conventions can easily transcend specific locations, they cannot be easily separated from the artisans and other individuals that inspire them. Because of this need to establish personal connections (not necessarily repetitive, though) and to understand the specificities and experiences that inhabit a particular space, these conventions tend to be difficult to transmit along the value chain over the short term. However, when personality becomes (or is embedded in) celebrity or products are consumed widely enough to influence cultural norms, inspirational conventions can take the traits of opinion conventions and thus travel more easily.

Finally, in an *opinion* quality convention, uncertainty about quality is resolved through two main mechanisms: the subjective judgement (rather than objective measurement) of an expert that is external to the exchange (for example, Robert Parker's score for a specific wine), and/or the reception by the 'public' through measuring media coverage, social media response (for example, how many Facebook 'likes' a product attracts) and opinion polls. While these conventions tend to be more easily portable along a value chain than domestic or inspirational conventions because they underpin perceptions (that is, public image), they are typically more contested and localized than market or industrial conventions. French retailers, for example, are less likely to base their wine quality assessment on Robert Parker's scores than US or UK retailers; hence, the 'medium' classification on ease of transmission in Table 1.

While quality conventions typically overlap, one or a specific combination (for example, market and industrial, or domestic and opinion) often forms a dominant underpinning for linkages in a value chain node at a particular time. However, conventions and their combinations also evolve, are subjected to testing, and are adjusted or give way to different conventions or combinations over time. Convention theory allows researchers to ask questions about the normative nature of coordination that go beyond the three GVC linkage variables of complexity, codifiability and supplier competence. At the same time, examination of the conventions underpinning GVC linkages can contribute to a deeper understanding of how commonly agreed notions of 'quality' in a transaction actually take shape – and, thus, how transactions can become more or less 'codified' as products, business practices and technologies change (an issue addressed by Gereffi, Humphrey and Sturgeon, 2005). Repeating the exercise of examining GVC linkages across several nodes of a value chain (see an empirical application in Ponte, 2009) can highlight whether dominant conventions 'travel' along a chain, what makes them travel, and what actors have the normative power to impose one convention over another beyond a single value chain node. This provides the meso-level bridge between the micro-level explanations of linkages and the macro-level governance of value chains.

3. A MODULAR APPROACH TO GVC GOVERNANCE THEORY

In this section, we use a modular theory-building approach to develop a GVC governance framework with three scalar levels: (1) the micro level – how linkages and conventions are forged at individual nodes of the value chain; (2) the meso level – how readily linking mechanisms and conventions regulating exchange at one node 'travel' up and down the value chain to other nodes; and (3) the macro level – how governance is shaped at the level of the 'whole chain'. Again, we are not proposing a grand theory, only further elaborating and linking previous theoretical work to create a broader frame of reference with the hope of encouraging further theoretical work along these lines.

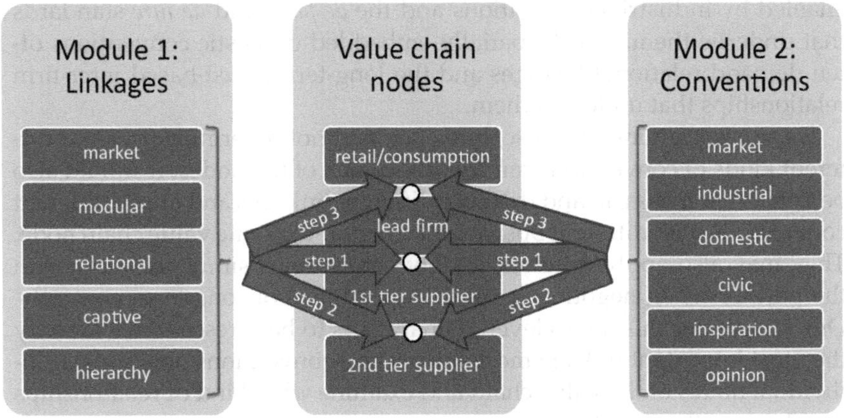

Figure 2 Micro-level analysis of governance with two modules (linkages and conventions).

3.1. The micro level

Figure 2 illustrates how different GVC linkage mechanisms and conventions can help to explain the characteristics of exchange at individual nodes of the chain (the micro level). We begin modestly with just two modules. Module 1 lists the five GVC linkage mechanisms developed by Gereffi, Humphrey and Sturgeon (2005) (Figure 1). Module 2 lists the typology of conventions (Table 1). These modules can be applied, sequentially or in combination, to an overall framework (the middle box in Figure 2) that represents a simplified succession of stylized value chain nodes (represented by circles) where exchange takes place – either internally in a firm or externally between independent firms.[9] Figure 2 shows how these two modules can be applied to different value chain nodes. In Step 1, they are applied to the node between the lead firm and their first-tier supplier. But the same exercise can be carried out successively to other value chain nodes – for example, in Step 2, between first-tier and second-tier suppliers, and in Step 3, between lead firms and retailers, or between retailers and consumers.[10] This means that: linkage mechanisms and types of conventions can differ at different nodes of the chain and need not apply to the whole chain; and that different kinds of conventions can overlap, creating layers at any given point in the chain. As explained earlier, there can be parallels between the linkage categories on the left and the upper three convention categories on the right in Figure 2. First, market linkages are fully enabled by market conventions in simple transactions where the association of product characteristics (including, but not limited to, quality) with price is straightforward. Second, modular linkages are typically enabled by industrial conventions and the *de facto* and *de jure* standards that underlie them. Third, spatially-embedded domestic conventions often demand relational linkages and the long-term, trust-based inter-firm relationships that underpin them.

These associations are loose, however, and not deterministic, since different kinds of conventions can coexist in each of the nodes. It should also be noted that firms can and do forge different linkages and apply different conventions with different business partners at the same value chain node. They may also apply different quality conventions simultaneously with the partner when negotiating product portfolios or long-term contracts. Our purpose at this micro level of analysis is to help researchers identify the most important linkage mechanisms and conventions operating at individual nodes of the value chain and examine what kind of relationships they have with each other.

For the sake of clarity, we restricted ourselves to two modules in our current construction, but other modules could well be used together with, or instead of, these two. For example, an additional or alternative module could focus on the influence of regulation in shaping exchange dynamics at individual value chain nodes. Another one could examine embedded institutional factors and/or the nature of national and regional business systems. It is not our aim here to provide an exhaustive list or elaboration of possible theoretical modules, only to provide a framework for future theory-building efforts related to governance of GVCs.

3.2. The meso level

Not all nodes in a value chain have the same analytical importance. Again, a micro-level explanation of the linkage mechanisms and conventions applied between 'lead firms' and 'first-tier suppliers' can go a long way in explaining the nature of overall governance of the chain. However, there is no automatic correlation between the type of linkage or convention observed at one node in the chain and overall chain governance. For this reason, meso-level transmission mechanisms need to be examined before tracing a macro-picture of overall value chain governance. To do this, researchers can explore how linkage mechanisms and/or conventions operating at one node of the chain 'travel' to other nodes along the chain, represented by the vertical arrows between nodes in the central part of Figure 3. While at the micro level, analytical attention is on the linkages and conventions that operate at individual nodes, at the meso level the focus is on comparison between nodes, with the goal of establishing what factors operate exclusively at the level of individual nodes and what factors are transmitted between nodes in the chain.

The analytical categories used in the two modules in Figure 3 to explain transmission mechanisms arise from our previous analysis, included in

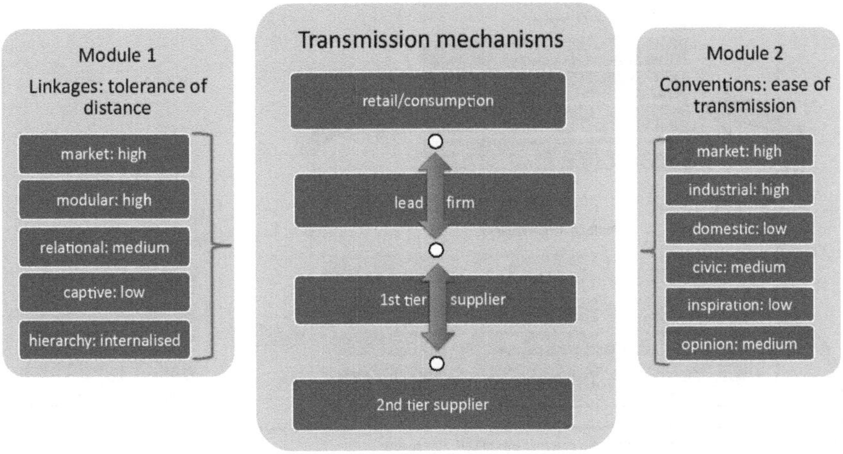

Figure 3 Meso-level analysis of governance with two modules.

Figure 1 (for the linkage mechanisms) and Table 1 (for conventions). Again, there are clear instances of relation between categories in the two modules. For example, the linkage mechanisms that tolerate distance (market and modular) are often tied to market and industrial quality conventions, while relational linkages based on exchange of proprietary, non-standard, tacit, uncodified information and knowledge are often tied to less portable quality conventions, such as domestic or inspirational conventions. But these parallels need to be assessed empirically and cannot be assumed *ex-ante*.

In this particular framework, we select factors that shape transmission mechanisms from the two theoretical modules we have employed, but other transmission factors linked to regulation, or to local, national and regional institutional features could have an imprint as well. What is important to underline here is that the nature of exchange at one value chain node is not enough to explain overall chain governance, but can provide some important clues. Looking at transmission mechanisms is a way of linking the two dimensions (micro and macro) explicitly.

3.3. The macro level

Our next step is to embed the micro and meso foundations illustrated so far into a macro-level framework of governance applicable to the whole chain – represented in stylized form in Figure 4. Here, the analysis of individual linkages and conventions at key nodes, and their inter-relationship, and the transmission mechanisms that allow them to travel upstream and downstream (illustrated in simplified form in the micro and meso boxes at the bottom of Figure 4) are brought together with other relevant macro

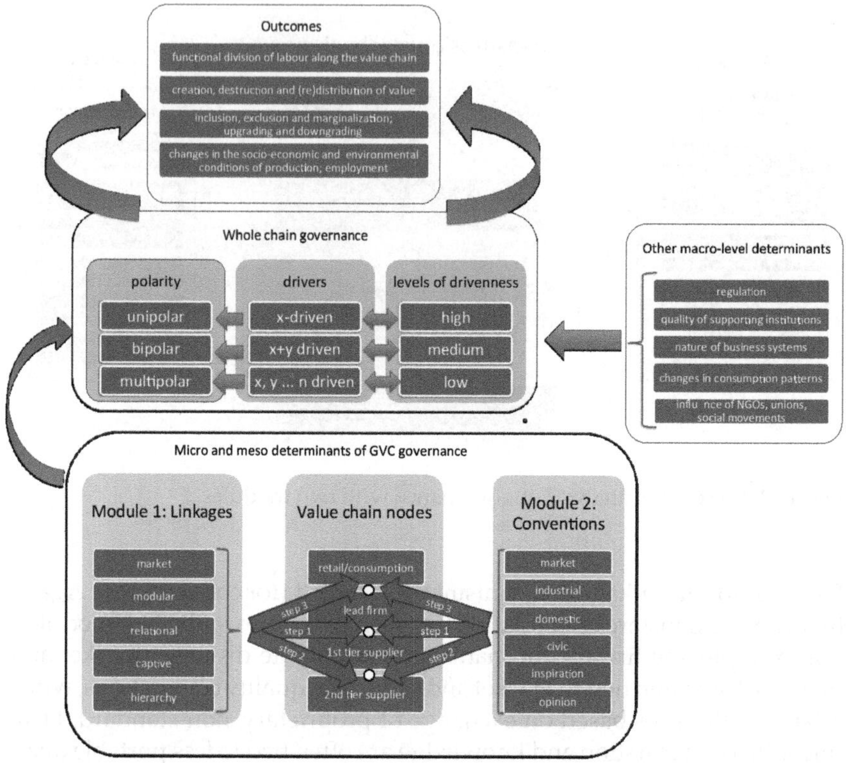

Figure 4 Macro-level framework for the analysis of 'whole chain' governance.

factors (see box on the right). The main purpose is to help build a 'whole-chain' framework for GVC governance to help explain observed outcomes in terms of: the functional division of labour; the creation, destruction, allocation and distribution of value; the processes of inclusion, exclusion and marginalization; upgrading and downgrading trajectories; and the effects of socio-economic and environmental conditions on production and on employment (see top box). Our approach clearly harks back to the original GCC approach of 'governance as driving'. However, we argue that a strong bottom-up (micro- and meso-level) approach is a prerequisite for making sense of macro-level determinants. This combined approach is meant address one of the problems arising in the broad literature on economic governance, where the identification and characterization of governance is often over-simplified and has weak empirical bearing.

We will not discuss all of the macro-level factors governing GVCs in this article. We approach macro-level governance through the very specific and intentionally narrow analytical lenses of 'polarity', in part because we feel that the source of power in GVCs is critically important, and in part because polarity is an area of GVC theory ripe for further development. Much of the existing GVC literature has focused on 'unipolar' value chains – be they buyer-driven or producer-driven (Gereffi, 1994) – where 'lead firms' play a dominant role in shaping the chain. Some scholars have explored the dynamics of governance in GVCs characterized as 'bipolar' or 'twin-driven', where two sets of actors in different functional positions both drive the chain, albeit in different ways (Fold, 2002; Islam, 2009). Research on the notebook PC and mobile phone handset industries by Kawakami (2011) and Imai and Shiu (2011) show the important roles 'platform leaders' can play. We expand this direction further to suggest examining governance across a unipolar to multipolar continuum.

'Multipolar' chains are different from 'markets' as they are strongly shaped by the explicit strategic actions of powerful actors (both inside and outside the chain), even if they exhibit multiple foci of power and various kinds of linkages. This has implications for how the micro and meso elements of GVC governance are embedded into the macro level. In unipolar chains, for example, overall governance is more easily explained on the basis of the dominant linkage mechanisms and conventions that operate in the key node between lead firms and first-tier suppliers. In chains that are bipolar or multipolar, chain dynamics are more complex and the nature of linkage mechanisms and conventions in other nodes (and their transmission dynamics) have to be examined and compared (preferably over time) to develop a clear picture of overall chain governance. For example, Kawakami (2011) shows how the strategies of Intel, a powerful platform leader in the personal computer industry, has shaped both linkage mechanisms at key nodes in the chain and also the distribution of power between lead firms (such as Dell) and first-tier suppliers (for example, the Taiwan-based contract design and manufacturing firm, Quanta). Ponte (2013) shows how governance in the biofuel value chain went from unipolar (and government-driven) to multipolar in the second half of the 2000s – with the increased influence of some groups of actors (large agro-chemical and biotech firms, global agro-food traders and oil majors and fuel distributors) and of standard makers and environmental and social NGOs. As indicated in Figure 4 (the middle box), we expect the level of drivenness to be higher for unipolar chains, where power is concentrated, than for multipolar chains, where power is more dispersed.

A focus on polarity, ranging from unipolar to multipolar governance, allows the construction of a plurality of drivers and of driving mechanisms that go beyond the well-established dichotomy between buyer- and producer-driven governance. This plurality acknowledges that not only firms, but also other actors such as standard-setting bodies, international NGOs, social movements, certification agencies, labour unions and consumer associations can have a bearing on GVC governance. Allowance for a plurality of driving mechanisms enables not only an analysis of power relations between firms (see Sturgeon, 2009), but also of how, at the macro level, regulation, institutions and business cultures, for example, shape GVC governance. Given the complexity of the possible combinations that may be at play at the macro level, our framework in Figure 4 is necessarily simplified. What we want to highlight, however, is that the micro and meso mechanisms are embedded into a macro-level picture that takes a possible plurality of polarity forms as a point of departure.

4. CONCLUSION

Because the stakes are so high, we must take global integration seriously and develop conceptual models that place novel and emergent features of the global economy in the foreground. In simpler times, it made sense to focus on the roles of comparative advantage and the market- and capability-seeking activities of multinational corporations in motivating and structuring international trade and investment. While these concepts have proved to be extremely robust and are still valuable, they do not emphasize the fragmentation of GVCs or the fluid, real-time integration of capabilities in advanced economies with the rapidly rising capabilities in places that were all but outside of the capitalist global economy only two decades ago, such as China, India, Russia and Vietnam. While the rise of GVCs does not render this earlier view of global competition completely anachronistic, it is safe to say that the picture has grown more complex and dynamic.

In an attempt to bring some order to this complexity, the GVC framework developed by Gereffi, Humphrey and Sturgeon (2005) revisited the terrain between markets and hierarchies, expanding the network form into three distinct modes of inter-firm coordination: modular, relational and captive. The framework identified the problem of asset specificity as an important, but not sole or unidirectional, driver of firm-level decision-making and indicated three important variables that dynamically shape the content and character of inter-firm linkages: complexity, codifiability and supplier competence. The focus was not only on the organizational patterns and power dynamics that are generated by different variable combinations, but also on the geographic possibilities (for example, clustering vs. dispersal of industries, rapid vs. gradual relocation of work) that are enabled by each linkage form. At the same time, other branches of GVC theorizing criticized the Gereffi, Humphrey and Sturgeon (2005) framework on the basis that it operated at the level of individual transactions, value chain nodes and bilateral relationships, not at the level of overall chain governance (see Lee, 2010, for a review). Other authors provided complementary ways of understanding governance by unpacking the normative, not just material, elements of GVCs – including quality conventions and broader expectations on corporate organization and strategy (Ponte and Gibbon, 2005).

At the same time, it is evident that powerful factors and actors external to the chain can shape governance through the impact of regulation, lobbying, civil-society campaigns and third-party standard making. Institutional actors, including states and multilateral institutions, shape GVCs by providing a mechanism for signatories to enforce, or not enforce, regulations and a platform for negotiating the terms of international trade agreements. Consumers shape GVCs through the purchasing choices they make, as when they turn the products and services they buy to unintended purposes, and even more so when their wishes are amplified by boycotts, class action litigation or the programmatic efforts of NGOs. Workers can also influence governance, especially when they are represented by labour unions with the ability to call work stoppages at the level of the enterprise, industry or broader economy. Key struggles and contestations take place constantly along value chains and governance is indeed shaped by the specificities of place and path dependency.

The aim of this article is not to provide a simple menu of important topics for researchers. Rather, we have sought to sketch a few of the main features in a framework that can be useful as a starting point for making sense of the complexity and variation observed in GVC governance. It is a partial answer to Sturgeon's (2009) call for 'modular' theory building, where multiple theories can be improved individually, but can also be brought into play jointly to help explain variations in GVC governance. Each theoretical 'module' might have its own internal logic and realm of explanation, yet fall short when forces external to that logic impinge. Additive theorizing is one solution (system A is important, system B is also important, and so on), but if theoretical 'modules' have shared elements, progress can be made towards a theoretical ecosystem that illuminates not only how specific variables influence GVC governance in isolation, but also how key variables and coordination forms themselves co-evolve in larger systems, setting the stage for analysis of historical shifts and trajectories. In this way, the multiple streams of GVC governance theory can eventually be built into a broad, cohesive, but flexible, framework for understanding global industries and for responding to the risks and opportunities they pose. We have tried to take a few steps in this direction by embedding some of the micro, meso and macro foundations of GVC governance into a modular framework.

Scholars of global industries have now had several decades to present, publish and debate their research results. A broad view of these findings reveals that the process of global integration is expressed differently in different industries and places. The precise patterns and effects of global integration depend in some part on the technical and business characteristics that prevail in specific industries, the relative power of firm and non-firm actors in the chain, and the social and institutional characteristics of the places where the tendrils of GVCs are rooted and projected. While field research on industry-specific GVCs remains as important as ever, the accumulation of case studies has created the conditions needed for the development of generic, industry-neutral analytical frameworks that seek to explain observed patterns and predict the outcomes associated with them. More effort is shifting to the construction of classification schemes and conceptual models that can stand in for the mechanisms that work to create the variety observed in the field. Yet, we remain very close to the starting line. The field of GVC-related theory building is still quite young and open to revision, testing and elaboration.

ACKNOWLEDGEMENTS

Useful feedback on earlier versions of this article was received at the the workshop on 'Value Chains, Production Networks, and the Geographies of Development: Emerging Challenges and Future Agenda', National University of Singapore (1–2 December, 2011) and at the convention of the Association of American Geographers (AAG), New York (25–29 February, 2012). The authors would also like to thank Gary Gereffi, John Humphrey and two anonymous referees for insightful and constructive comments.

NOTES

1 Bair and Werner (2011) offer a 'disarticulation' perspective on GVCs that looks at the dynamics of exclusion and expulsion in GVCs (see also other contributions in the same special issue). Building on earlier work by Bair (2009), this perspective calls for a return to the long-range, macro historical roots of GVC analysis, with a focus on historical change, disjunctions, fragmentations and disarticulations. Disarticulation scholars argue that the GVC literature has developed a bias on inclusion dynamics and that attention should be paid to *how* links in the chain are forged, not only in material terms, but also ideologically and in relation to the creation of subjectivities. They examine the set of social relations that secure commodity production and related processes of exclusion (Bair and Werner, 2011) and highlight the social and spatial contours of production through everyday practices and struggles over the creation and appropriation of value (see also Neilson and Pritchard, 2009; Bair, 2011).

2 This does not mean that any theory can be simply 'plugged into' our framework. GVC perspectives are generally 'activity-oriented', thus, for example, an accumulation perspective to understanding the global economy is less likely to fit in our framework of GVC governance.

3 The original classification in Gibbon, Bair and Ponte (2008) mentioned governance as 'driving', as 'coordination' and as 'normalization'. Here, we adopt the term 'linking', instead of coordination, to avoid confusion in Figure 2, where we will use both linkages and conventions to explain the nature of coordination at individual nodes of the value chain. We also use the term

'normalizing', instead of 'normalization', to use the same grammatical form for all three.

4 Feenstra and Hamilton (2006) describe in detail the ways in which retailers gained power relative to manufacturers, beginning in the United States in the 1960s, a trend that continues to the present day. This 'retail revolution' has been a major factor in de-industrialization within the United States, as retailers increased overseas sourcing of apparel, electronics and consumer goods, in turn forcing manufacturers to move their own facilities offshore and increase sourcing in low-cost locations in East Asia. At the same time, it spurred 'late' industrialization and industrial upgrading, first in Japan, and later in Korea and Taiwan (Amsden, 1989; Wade, 1990; Evans, 1995).

5 Global production network (GPN) scholars (Dicken *et al.*, 2001; Henderson *et al.*, 2002; Hess and Yeung, 2006; Coe, Dicken and Hess, 2008; Yeung, 2009) have been similarly motivated to respond to the perceived limitations of the GCC approach: that it was too structuralist and long-range historical in nature, 'linearist' (using the value-added chain for specific commodities as the unit of analysis), and focused on a narrow binomial approach to governance (buyer-driven vs. producer-driven) (Gereffi, 1994). Much has been made in the literature of the differences between the GVC and GPN approaches. The GPN perspective, rooted in the field of economic geography, is less concerned with the hierarchy of power in specific cross-border industries and more concerned with how business networks are embedded in, and intertwine with, institutions and the social and cultural contexts extant in specific locations. Because of this, the GPN literature tends to highlight complexity, messiness and variety in production networks (Dicken *et al.*, 2001; Henderson *et al.*, 2002; Hess and Yeung, 2006). However, many similarities are also apparent. Both sets of literature approach the 'global' in 'bottom-up' fashion, through generalization from field research on product- and even firm-specific experiences. They provide macro representations extrapolated from case studies highlighting the ideal–typical dynamics of inter-firm exchange in specific industries, rather than by examining anonymous trade and investment flows at the level of nation-states. The GVC and GPN literatures have a similar interest in mapping the spatial and organizational division of labour and understanding the qualitative aspects of how value is created, allocated and captured in specific industries and locations. They share a normative interest in the upgrading trajectories of less developed places and how value-creation processes and learning dynamics can benefit or exclude disadvantaged regions and actors. Finally, the more recent GVC literature has in a way been more GPN-like by paying increased attention to institutional, regulatory and standard-making processes (Neilson and Pritchard, 2009; Cattaneo, Gereffi and Staritz, 2010; Ponte, Gibbon and Vestergaard, 2011). It has strived to include in its analysis some of the insights of cultural political economy, it has reflected upon differences in business culture or normative expectations of how a 'good business' is organized (Gibbon and Ponte, 2005; Ponte, 2009; Bair and Werner, 2011), and it has been fine-tuning the territorial and contested dimensions of restructuring in global value chains (Neilson and Pritchard, 2009; Mahutga, 2012).

6 It also drew in key concepts from a range of 'outside' literatures: the asset-specificity problem and the markets versus hierarchy frame from institutional economics, the social embeddedness of economic life from industrial sociology, the relationship between tacit knowledge sharing and spatial agglomeration from economic geography, the enabling role of technology and standards from technology management, and the pragmatic approach to firm-level learning

from management and evolutionary economics. As such, the original GVC governance framework can be seen as a prior exercise in modular theory building.

7 Other work on governance as normalization has been carried out through the lenses of governmentality (Gibbon and Ponte, 2008).

8 This list is not meant to be exhaustive. Other contributions have examined a 'connectivist' convention (Boltanski and Chiapello, 1999) and a 'green' convention (Latour, 1998). However, much of the literature engaging with conventions actually uses only three typologies (market, industrial and domestic), sometimes four (including civic). Ponte (2009), however, has found it helpful to engage with all six conventions that parallel the six orders of worth in Boltanski and Thévenot (1991).

9 These nodes are only meant to illustrate the analytic process; they are not meant to be exhaustive.

10 Of course, the analysis does not need to start with the linkages between lead firms and first-tier suppliers. While these do tend to be important, the analysis can start at any node. The key element of GVC methods, however, is that research and analysis is not confined to a single node. Depending on the nature of the GVC, there may be more or fewer nodes than illustrated in Figure 2.

REFERENCES

Amsden, A. (1989) *Asia's Next Giant: South Korea and Late Industrialization*, Oxford and New York: Oxford University Press.

Bair, J. (ed.) (2009) *Frontiers of Commodity Chain Research*, Stanford, CA: Stanford University Press.

Bair, J. (2011) 'Constructing Scarcity, Creating Value: Marketing the Mundo Maya', in N. Bandelj and F. Wherry (eds) *The Cultural Wealth of Nations*, Palo Alto, CA: Stanford University Press, pp. 177–196.

Bair, J. and Werner, M. (2011) 'Commodity Chains and the Uneven Geographies of Global Capitalism: A Disarticulations Perspective', *Environment and Planning A*, 43: 988–97.

Boltanski, L. and Chiapello, E. (1999) *Le nouvel esprit du capitalisme*, Paris: Gallimard.

Boltanski, L. and Thévenot, L. (1991) *De la justification: Les économies de la grandeur*, Paris: Gallimard.

Borrus, M., Ernst, D. and Haggard, S. (eds) (2000) *International Production Networks in Asia*, London and New York: Routledge.

Cammack, P. (2003) 'The Governance of Global Capitalism: A New Materialist Perspective', *Historical Materialism*, 11(2): 37–59.

Cattaneo, O., Gereffi, G. and Staritz, C. (eds) (2010) *Global Value Chains in a Postcrisis World: A Development Perspective*, Washington, DC: World Bank.

Caves, R. (1996) *Multinational Enterprise and Economic Analysis, 2nd edn*, Cambridge: Cambridge University Press.

Coase, R. (1937) 'The Nature of the Firm', *Economica*, 4: 386–405.

Coe, N., Dicken, P. and Hess, M. (2008) 'Global Production Networks: Realizing the Potential', *Journal of Economic Geography*, 8(3): 271–95.

Dicken, P. (1992) *Global Shift: The Internationalisation of Economic Activity* (6th Ed.), London: Paul Chapman Publishing.

Dicken, P. (2007) *Global Shift: Mapping the Changing Contours of the World Economy* (5th ed.), London: Sage Publications.

Dicken, P., Kelly, P.F., Olds, K. and Yeung, H.W.-C. (2001) 'Chains and Networks, Territories and Scales: Towards a Relational Framework for Analyzing the Global Economy', *Global Networks*, 1(2): 89–112.

Doz, Y., Santos, J.F.P. and Williamson, P. (2001) *From Global to Metanational: How Companies Win in the Knowledge Economy*, Boston, MA: Harvard Business School Press.

Evans, P. (1995) *Embedded Autonomy: States and Industrial Transformation*, Princeton, NJ: Princeton University Press.

Eymard-Duvernay, F. (1989) 'Conventions de qualité et formes de coordination', *Revue Economique*, 40(2): 329–59.

Eymard-Duvernay, F. (ed.) (2006a) *L'économie des conventions, methodes et resultats. Tome 1: Debats*, Paris: La Découverte.

Eymard-Duvernay, F. (ed.) (2006b) *L'économie des conventions, methodes et resultats. Tome 2: Développements*, Paris: La Découverte.

Feenstra, R. and Hamilton, G. (2006) *Emergent Economies, Divergent Paths: Economic Organization and International Trade in South Korea and Taiwan*, Cambridge: Cambridge University Press.

Fold, N. (2002) 'Lead Firms and Competition in "Bi-polar" Commodity Chains: Grinders and Branders in the Global Cocoa-Chocolate Industry', *Journal of Agrarian Change*, 2(2): 228–47.

Gereffi, G. (1994) 'The Organization of Buyer-driven Global Commodity Chains: How US Retailers Shape Overseas Production Networks', in G. Gereffi and M. Korzeniewicz (eds) *Commodity Chains and Global Capitalism*, Westport, CT: Greenwood Press, pp. 95–133.

Gereffi, G., Humphrey, J., Kaplinsky, R. and Sturgeon, T. (2001) 'Introduction: Globalisation, Value Chains and Development', *IDS Bulletin*, 32(3): 1–8.

Gereffi, G., Humphrey, J. and Sturgeon, T. (2005) 'The Governance of Global Value Chains', *Review of International Political Economy*, 12(1): 78–104.

Gereffi G., Korzeniewicz, M. and Korzeniewicz, R. (1994) 'Introduction: Global Commodity Chains', in G. Gereffi and M. Korzeniewicz (eds) *Commodity Chains and Global Capitalism*, Westport, CT: Greenwood Press, pp. 1–14.

Gibbon, P., Bair, J. and Ponte, S. (2008) 'Governing Global Value Chains: An Introduction', *Economy and Society*, 37(3): 315–38.

Gibbon, P. and Ponte, S. (2005) *Trading Down: Africa, Value Chains and the Global Economy*, Philadelphia, PA: Temple University Press.

Gibbon, P. and Ponte, S. (2008) 'Global Value Chains: From Governance to Governmentality?', *Economy and Society*, 37(3): 365–92.

Gibbon, P. and Riisgaard, L. (2012) *'A New System of Labour Management in African Large-scale Agriculture?', mimeo*, Copenhagen: Danish Institute for International Studies.

Held, D. (2010) *Cosmopolitanism: Ideals and Realities*, London: Polity.

Henderson J., Dicken, P., Hess, M., Coe, N. and Yeung, H.W.-C. (2002) 'Global Production Networks and the Analysis of Economic Development', *Review of International Political Economy*, 9(3): 436–64.

Herrigel, G. and Wittke, V. (2008) 'Varieties of Vertical Disintegration: The Global Trend towards Heterogeneous Supply Relations and the Reproduction of Differences in US and German Manufacturing', in G. Morgan, E. Moen and R. Whitley (eds) *Changing Capitalisms: Internationalization, Institutional Change and Systems of Economic Organization*, Oxford: Oxford University Press, pp. 312–351.

Hess, M. and Yeung, H. W.-C. (2006) 'Whither Global Production Networks in Economic Geography? Past, Present and Future', *Environment and Planning A*, 38: 1193–204.

Hymer, S. (1976) *The International Operations of National Firms: A Study of Direct Foreign Investment*, Cambridge, MA: MIT Press.

Imai, K. and Shiu, J.M. (2011) 'Value Chain Creation and Reorganization: The Growth Path of China's Mobile Phone Handset Industry', in M. Kawakami and T. Sturgeon (eds) *The Dynamics of Local Learning in Global Value Chains: Experiences from East Asia*, Basingstoke, UK: Palgrave Macmillan.

Islam, M.S. (2009) 'From Pond to Plate: Towards a Twin-driven Commodity Chain in Bangladesh Shrimp Aquaculture', *Food Policy*, 33: 209–23.

Kaplinsky, R. (2005) *Globalization, Poverty and Inequality*, London: Polity.

Kawakami, M. (2011) 'Inter-firm Dynamics of Notebook PC Value Chains and the Rise of Taiwanese Original Design Manufacturing Firms', in M. Kawakami and T. Sturgeon (eds) *The Dynamics of Local Learning in Global Value Chains: Experiences from East Asia*, Basingstoke, UK: Palgrave Macmillan.

Kirton, J., Larionova, M. and Savona, P. (2010) *Making Global Economic Governance Effective: Hard and Soft Law Institutions in a Crowded World*, Aldershot and Burlington, VT: Ashgate.

Jagd, S. (2011) 'Pragmatic Sociology and Competing Orders of Worth in Organizations', *European Journal of Social Theory*, 14(3): 434–459.

Lall, S. (2000) 'The Technological Structure and Performance of Developing Country Manufactured Exports, 1985–98', *Oxford Development Studies*, 28(3): 337–69.

Latour, B. (1998) 'To Modernise or Ecologise? That is the Question', in B. Braun and N. Castree (eds) *Remaking Reality: Nature at the Millennium*, London and New York: Routledge, pp. 249–272.

Lee, J. (2010) 'Global Commodity Chains and Global Value Chains', in R.A. Denemark (ed.) *The International Studies Encyclopedia*, Oxford: Wiley-Blackwell.

Mahutga, M.C. (2012) 'When Do Value Chains Go Global? A Theory of the Spatialization of Global Value Chains', *Global Networks*, 12(1): 1–21.

Neilson, J. and Pritchard, B. (2009) *Value Chain Struggles: Institutions and Governance in the Plantation Districts of South India*, Malden, MA, and Oxford: Wiley-Blackwell.

Ouma, S. (2010) 'Global Standards, Local Realities: Private Agrifood Governance and the Restructuring of the Kenyan Horticulture Industry', *Economic Geography*, 86(2): 197–222.

Ponte, S. (2002) 'The "Latte Revolution"? Regulation, Markets and Consumption in the Global Coffee Chain', *World Development*, 30(7): 1099–122.

Ponte, S. (2009) 'Governing through Quality: Conventions and Supply Relations in the Value Chain for South African Wine', *Sociologia Ruralis*, 39(3): 236–57.

Ponte, S. (2013) 'The Evolutionary Dynamics of Biofuel Value Chains: From Unipolar and Government-driven to Multipolar Governance', Environment and Planning A, forthcoming.

Ponte, S. and Gibbon, P. (2005) 'Quality Standards, Conventions and the Governance of Global Value Chains', *Economy and Society*, 34(1): 1–31.

Ponte, S., Gibbon, P. and Vestergaard, J. (eds) (2011) *Governing through Standards: Origins, Drivers and Limitations*, Basingstoke: Palgrave Macmillan.

Sturgeon, T. (2002) 'Modular Production Networks. A New American Model of Industrial Organization', *Industrial and Corporate Change*, 11(3): 451–96.

Sturgeon, T. (2007) 'How Globalization Drives Institutional Diversity: The Japanese Electronics Industry's Response to Value Chain Modularity', *Journal of East Asian Studies*, 7(1): 1–34.

Sturgeon, T. (2009) 'From Commodity Chains to Value Chains: Interdisciplinary Theory Building in an Age of Globalization', in J. Bair (ed.) *Frontiers of Commodity Chain Research*, Stanford, CA: Stanford University Press, pp. 110–35.

Sturgeon, T. and Kawakami, M. (2011) 'Global Value Chains in the Electronics Industry: Characteristics, Crisis, and Upgrading Opportunities for Firms from Developing Countries', *International Journal of Technological Learning, Innovation and Development*, 4(1/2/3): 120–47.

Sturgeon, T. and Lee, J.R. (2005) 'Industry Co-evolution: A Comparison of Taiwan and North American Electronics Contract Manufacturers', in S. Berger and R.K. Lester (eds) *Global Taiwan: Building Competitive Strengths in a New International Economy*, Armonk, NY: M.E. Sharpe.

Sturgeon, T. and Lester, R. (2004) 'The New Global Supply-base: New Challenges for Local Suppliers in East Asia', in S. Yusuf, A. Altaf and K. Nabeshima (eds) *Global Production Networking and Technological Change in East Asia*, Oxford: Oxford University Press.

Sturgeon, T. and Van Biesebroeck, J. (2011) 'Global Value Chains in the Automotive Industry: An Enhanced Role for Developing Countries?', *International Journal of Technological Learning, Innovation and Development*, 4 (1/2/3): 181–205.

Thévenot, L. (1995) 'Des marchés aux normes', in G. Allaire and R. Boyer (eds) *La grande transformation de l'agriculture: Lectures conventionnalistes et regulationnistes*, Paris: INRA-Economica, pp. 33–51.

UNCTAD (2011) *World Investment Report 2011: Non-equity Modes of International Production and Development*, Geneva: UNCTAD, www.unctad-docs.org/files/UNCTAD-WIR2011-Full-en.pdf *(accessed)*.

Wade, R. (1990) *Governing the Market: Economic Theory and the Role of Government in East Asian Industrialization*, Princeton, NJ: Princeton University Press.

Whittaker, D.H., Zhu, T., Sturgeon, T., Tsai, M.H. and Okita, T. (2010) 'Compressed Development', *Studies in Comparative International Development*, 45: 439–467.

Wilkinson, J. (1997) 'A New Paradigm for Economic Analysis?', *Economy and Society*, 26(3): 305–39.

Williamson, O. (1985) *The Economic Institutions of Capitalism: Firms, Markets, Relational Contracting*, London: Macmillan.

World Bank (1993) *The East Asian Miracle: Economic Growth and Public Policy*, New York: Oxford University Press.

Yeung, H.W.-C. (2009) 'Regional Development and the Competitive Dynamics of Global Production Networks: An East Asian Perspective', *Regional Studies*, 43(3): 325–51.

Zanfei, A. (2000) 'Transnational Firms and the Changing Organization of Innovative Activities', *Cambridge Journal of Economics*, 24: 515–42.

Missing links: Logistics, governance and upgrading in a shifting global economy

Neil M. Coe

Department of Geography, National University of Singapore, Singapore

ABSTRACT

This article seeks to argue that logistics services, and the independent logistics industry in particular, should be afforded much more attention within political economy approaches to the global economy. Widespread outsourcing processes and the increased sophistication of logistics provisions mean that the industry has arguably evolved beyond being a mere service input to occupying an integral and strategic role within many global industries. It is, therefore, intimately connected to debates about shifting governance regimes and upgrading dynamics within those industries. Conceptualising logistics from a global production network (GPN) perspective offers the potential for revealing both (1) the contribution of logistics providers to value and upgrading dynamics in client sectors and (2) the ways in which the logistics industry itself can be thought of as a multi-actor value-generation network with its own strategic and upgrading dynamics. The article distils the key contributions and limitations of prevailing business studies approaches to logistics, before charting a four-pronged research agenda that foregrounds the political economy of logistics provisions within the global economy. The analysis concludes by thinking about the implications of on-going post-crisis restructuring within the world economy for the proposed research agenda on logistics and GPNs.

1. LOGISTICS AND GLOBAL PRODUCTION NETWORKS: DEVELOPING A DUAL PERSPECTIVE

As economic globalisation has deepened, the ways in which the global economy is organised have also changed substantially. Considerable shifts in the geographical patterns of production and consumption have been accompanied by successive waves of outsourcing and offshoring, resulting in ever more complicated and changeable intra- and inter-firm global divisions of labour. It is increasingly recognised that logistics – referring to the process of planning, implementing and managing the movement and storage of raw materials, components, finished goods and associated knowledge from the point of origin to the point of consumption – have become an ever more important component of these contemporary production systems. The factors driving the growing strategic importance of logistics encompass the rise of new production methods involving increased flexibility, the increased use of just-in-time procurement and delivery systems, the increased geographical extent and complexity of production networks, the changing nature of relationships between customers and suppliers, the growing significance of commercial capital and retailer power, and the growing complexity of consumer tastes and preferences (Dicken, 2011). Indeed, Bonacich and Wilson (2008: 3) diagnose an ongoing *logistics revolution*, characterised by the expansion of the term, logistics, to 'refer to the management of the entire supply chain, encompassing design and ordering, production, transportation and warehousing, sales, redesign and reordering. This entire cycle of production and distribution is now viewed as a single integrated unit that requires its own specialists for analysis and implementation.'[1]

While recent research has shed light on many aspects of the restructuring of transnational production systems by analysing the development and transformation of global production networks (GPNs)[2] (for an overview, see Coe *et al.*, 2008; Coe, 2012), many aspects of the role of logistics activities in organising the spaces of material and informational flows that constitute the global economy remain poorly understood (Hesse and Rodrigue, 2006; Rodrigue, 2006). That logistics represents an important component of the global economy in its own right is widely recognised. As an area of economic activity, logistics were worth an estimated US$3.6 trillion in 2009 – and predicted to reach US$3.9 trillion by 2013 – a global market split fairly evenly between the Asia-Pacific (42 per cent), Europe, the Middle East and Africa (30 per cent) and the Americas (28 per cent) (Rushton and Walker, 2007). Logistics costs account, on average, for 10–15 per cent of the final cost of finished products in the developed world, including transport costs (7–9 per cent), warehousing costs (1–2 per cent) and inventory holdings (3–5 per cent). In the developing world, various forms of inefficiency mean that that figure is more often in the range of 15–25 per cent (Ojala *et al.*, 2008: 443). However, logistics predominantly tends to be understood simply as a service *input* to client industries, rather than as a sector in its own right. A central contention of this paper is that such a view is severely limiting and hampers appreciation of the increasingly strategic role played by *independent* logistics providers within the global economy.

More broadly, this paper seeks to make the argument that logistics need to figure far more prominently in GPN analyses and, conversely, that such analyses can contribute significantly to understandings of logistics in the global economy. GPN research focuses on the complex global webs of intra-, inter- and extra-firm network relations that underpin global production systems, the power and value relationships therein, and how these network relations emanate from and are embedded in different institutional contexts (for more, see Henderson *et al.*, 2002; Coe *et al.*, 2004). GPN analyses are thus well-placed to reveal how logistics functions and firms may be playing increasingly important roles within the value creation, enhancement and capture dynamics of different global industries. There are two separate dimensions to this argument, however:

1. There is much to be learned from exploring the logistics sector as a globally-organised industry in its own right, with its own economic upgrading dynamics. The sector can itself be conceptualised and analysed as a GPN with its own webs of intra-, inter- and extra-firm relations and value processes. Such work will also allow us to move beyond the limits of the existing literature on logistics to develop an integrative perspective that takes both the firms and their institutional environments into account (for example, Bowen and Leinbach, 2006; Leinbach and Bowen, 2004); and
2. There is also great potential in using a GPN framework to explore the contribution of the logistics sector to processes of economic upgrading in client sectors. As logistics providers expand the remit and strategic importance of the services they offer, they rework the governance and value relations of other GPNs. While there are many studies on the evolving nature of logistics activities within a range of sectors, they tend not to explore the power and value transformations that result from the growing sophistication of such provisions. In other words, very little is currently known about the wider governance and upgrading[3] implications of the logistics revolution.

The GPN framework offers a number of specific advantages for pursuing this dual agenda. First, through the explicit consideration of *extra-firm networks*, it necessarily brings into view the broad range of non-firm organisations – for example, supranational organisations, government agencies, trade unions, employer associations, NGOs and consumer groups – that may shape logistics activities. Second, GPN analysis is innately *multi-scalar* and considers the interactions and mutual constitution of all spatial scales from the local to the global. As we will see, this is vital for understanding the intersections of multi-scalar states and corporate formations that heavily shape logistics activities. Third, it takes an explicitly *network* approach, which seeks to move beyond linear notions of value chains, with production systems instead seen as networked 'meshes' of vertical and horizontal connections. This is a highly productive way of framing the intersections of logistics firms and client sectors. Fourth, the GPN framework is attuned to the complexity and fluidity of *governance* regimes within the contemporary global system, moving beyond simple representations of big producers or big buyers being the key drivers of production networks. This opens an important analytical space for consideration of the role of intermediaries – such as logistics providers – as significant shapers of the global economic system. Finally, a central concern of GPN analysis is to reveal the dynamic *developmental impacts* that result for the territories that they interconnect. More specifically, regional development is seen to be driven by the *strategic coupling* of GPN structures with the institutional fabric and economies actors in particular territories. Given the importance of logistics employment and clusters across the global system, these are vitally important dimensions to consider further (*cf.* Sheffi, 2012).

In sum, this paper contends that a GPN perspective offers the potential for a productive political–economy approach to logistics that can move beyond the firm-centric nature of much of the existing literature and foreground issues of power, value, labour, state policy and development. The remainder of the paper develops these arguments in three main stages. First, the existing literature on logistics – hitherto dominated by business/management approaches – is reviewed in more detail and five key contributions pertaining to the evolving nature of logistics provision are distilled. Second, and building directly upon the blind spots of the existing research base, four important research priorities are identified. These both mobilise the above dual approach to logistics and GPNs and utilise the GPN approach's attentiveness to the regulatory/institutional context and shifting power/value configurations. Third, and in conclusion, the wider implications of these arguments are considered in the context of profound on-going shifts in the structures of the global economy.

2. WHAT DO WE KNOW? CHARACTERISING THE EXISTING RESEARCH BASE

How has the role of logistics within global production been studied hitherto? The vast majority of the existing literature on logistics follows the business/management studies tradition and is to be found in supply chain management and the heavily policy-oriented field of transportation studies.[4]

Logistics research of a more critical social science bent is, in turn, much thinner on the ground. Scholars in economic geography and development studies, for example, have thus far paid little attention to the kinds of issues introduced above. This lacuna can be explained by both intellectual and real world trends. In terms of the former, Hall *et al.* (2006) contrast the strong empirical and positivist tradition of transport geography (for overviews, see Knowles *et al.*, 2008; O'Connor, 2009) with an economic geography that is arguably much more theoretical, abstract and interpretative. In empirical terms, the falling relative cost of transport in recent decades has led many economic geographers – and indeed social scientists, more generally – to take transportation and mobility as a given in the contemporary global economy: 'logistics functions have often been viewed as tangential, auxiliary support services to production processes, providing rather simple and labor-intensive transportation and warehousing services' and thereby contributing little value-added to GPNs (Aoyama *et al.*, 2006: 331). Hence, a situation has developed whereby 'few studies exist to date that analyze the logistics industry using the knowledge, tools, and expertise that have been developed in economic geography' (Aoyama *et al.*, 2006: 331). The relatively recent emergence of an independent logistics industry may be another factor explaining the paucity of critical social science research, with the otherwise burgeoning literature on economic globalisation only lately beginning to pay due attention to this industry (for example, Dicken, 2007; Hesse and Rodrigue, 2004).

That being said, the existing literature has made a number of important contributions to our understanding of contemporary logistics provisions. Here I highlight five areas where significant progress has been made. First, there is a clear understanding of the importance of *outsourcing* in driving the growth of the independent logistics industry. In abstract terms, client firms may choose to position themselves at any point on an outsourcing continuum. At one extreme is the situation of *total internal asset management*, whereby a company keeps the entire logistics operation in-house – encompassing management, workers, systems, buildings and transport – and does not outsource anything. At the opposite end, a firm may pursue *total external asset management*, wherein the company outsources all of its logistics operations and undertakes no capital investment, asset management or workforce management (Rushton and Walker, 2007). In reality, the two extreme positions are quite rare, with most large firms seeking to strike a balance between internal and external provisions for strategic reasons. Importantly, however, the dominant trend by far is for increased outsourcing. Although data is patchy, it was estimated in the mid-2000s that only 5 per cent of the global logistics industry was outsourced (Ojala *et al.*, 2008). This figure, however, varies significantly from market to market, ranging from 2 per cent in China to 40 per cent in the UK in the mid-2000s, with the figures for France, Germany, the US and Europe as a whole being 22, 28, 19 and 25 per cent, respectively. In dynamic terms, however, the so-called third-party logistics market is growing rapidly in most territories: in China, for example, the outsourced logistics market was estimated to be growing at 30 per cent per year in the late 2000s (Rushton and Walker, 2007). Industry estimates put the scale of the global third-party logistics market in 2009 at US$507.1 billion (Capgemini, 2010).

These outsourcing trends have driven the growth of a cadre of massive transnational logistics providers. Table 1 details the top 20 global third-party logistics ('3PL') providers in 2009. As with many business service sectors, these firms are predominantly headquartered in the US and the leading economies of Western Europe. While there are already four Asian companies on the list – two from Japan, one from Kuwait and one from China – it is widely expected that more will soon appear on the list as indigenous capacity in the region, and particularly China, continues to develop. The revenues column indicates the scale of these corporations, with the top 15 all accruing more than US$5 billion in revenue in 2009. In terms of scope, these leading providers straddle both developed and developing markets and coordinate huge and complex global operations (Table 1). For instance, Deutsche Post DHL, the world's largest logistics provider, operates in more than 170 countries, generates sales of US$53 billion and employs around 477,000 people – 60 per cent of them outside its home market of Germany. As we will see shortly, a crucial trend accompanying widespread outsourcing has been for independent logistics providers to expand their operations from basic logistics services into the broader domain of supply chain management.[5]

Second, the literature has been highly effective in capturing how the inherent *nature* of logistics systems has changed dramatically in recent decades. One shorthand way of describing this broad shift is from inventory-based or 'push' logistics to replenishment-based or 'pull' logistics (Rodrigue *et al.*, 2006). In 'traditional' arrangements of goods flows within GPNs, there was a storage function acting as a buffer between raw materials suppliers and manufacturers, with a similar inventory-based warehouse on the customer side. Delays were common at all stages, leading to inventory accumulation at the various storage points. In contemporary 'demand-pull' logistics systems, by contrast, many of these costly storage facilities are eliminated. Reverse flows – associated with product returns and recycling – are part of the system and warehousing is kept to a minimum, usually in the form of a distribution centre which is throughput-oriented (see Fernie and Sparks (2004) for an excellent overview of the role of retail capital in driving many of these changes). While these reduced inventory systems are generally characterised as being *lean*, some commentators have contrasted lean supply networks – with an emphasis on efficiency and predictability of supply of relatively standardised commodities – with the emergence of *agile* networks wherein the imperative is rapid response to shifts in market demand for fashion goods (Harrison *et al.*, 1999).

Concomitant with the shift in physical flows have been profound changes in the nature of knowledge flows within supply networks. The traditional system was characterised by limited flow of information from the consumer to the supply network, creating time lags before producers

Table 1 The top 20 global logistics firms, 2009

Rank 2009	Firm	Origin	Total revenue 2009 ($m)	Number of operational countries*				
				Total	Africa	Americas	Asia-Pacific	Europe
1	Deutsche Post DHL[1]	Germany	53039.08	170	53	27	50	40
2	UPS	USA	45297.00	157	45	26	46	40
3	FedEx[2]	USA	34734.00	147	45	17	46	39
4	DB Schenker Transport & Logistics	Germany	21560.83	118	19	23	39	37
5	NYK Line[3]	Japan	18160.59	32	1	6	14	11
6	Kuehne + Nagel	Switzerland	16812.51	111	18	20	35	38
7	Nippon Express[3]	Japan	16794.59	39	2	7	15	15
8	SNCF Geodis	France	10575.42	53	16	4	14	19
9	DSV A/S	Denmark	8123.92	65	6	9	17	33
10	CEVA	Netherlands	7876.01	133	33	15	44	41
11	CH Robinson Worldwide Inc	USA	7577.19	21	0	8	4	9
12	Panalpina Group	Switzerland	7090.05	88	13	16	28	31
13	Agility	Kuwait	5941.89	71	7	14	27	23
14	Toll Holdings Ltd[4]	Australia	5888.11	28	1	2	19	6
15	Bolloré Group Transport & Logistics	France	5780.14	110	46	12	29	23
16	Dachser GmbH & Co KG	Germany	4644.75	89	5	11	34	39
17	GEFCO SA	France	4140.14	31	3	3	2	23
18	Expeditors International	USA	4092.28	69	7	15	26	21
19	Sinotrans Limited	China	4047.31	15	0	3	4	8
20	Norbert Dentressangle	France	3897.87	14	0	0	0	14

Notes:
*Operational countries are those with either fully-owned subsidiaries or part-owned joint ventures/partnerships. Data is for countries with a population of more than 500,000 only.
[1] Excluding revenues for Deutsche Post.
[2] Financial year ended 31 May 2010.
[3] Financial year ended 31 March 2010.
[4] Financial year ended 30 June 2010.
Source: Company annual reports and websites.

were able to respond to shifting consumption patterns. Information flowed through orders passed sequentially from customers to suppliers, and there was limited, if any, visibility or transparency about either downstream or upstream processes within the supply network. The shift to what Skjøtt-Larsen *et al.* (2007) characterise as 'information-based supply chain flows' has seen the advent of integrated and coordinated knowledge transmission along the supply network allowing for far more responsive distribution systems. Interestingly, these changes have also altered the nature of relationships between supply network participants and their leading logistics providers, with contracts getting longer and trust-based relations remaining important despite the use of new technologies (Aoyama and Ratick, 2007). As with any simple periodisation, this narrative grossly simplifies highly variegated and uneven patterns of logistics development across different firms, sectors and geographies. Nonetheless, it does helpfully distil the broad direction of change in logistics systems as supply chain management processes have become ever more integrated and sophisticated.

A third important line of argument is concerned with how the nature of logistical requirements varies *along* GPNs in important ways. Rodrigue *et al.* (2006: 202–3), for example, compare and contrast the logistics requirements at three stages of a notional production network:

1. Parts and raw materials: cost structures for parts and raw materials often lead to global sourcing, supported by international transportation either by bulk cargo (commodities) or containers (parts) in a system characterised by high volumes and low frequencies of delivery;
2. Manufacturing and assembly: this stage usually concerns intermediate goods, with flows being either containerised or on pallets, with smaller volumes and high frequency of deliveries, particularly in GPNs characterised by just-in-time production systems; and
3. Distribution: a much more complex network of flows coordinated by distribution centres with particular territorial responsibilities and characterised by low volume (less than truckload: LTL) and high frequency deliveries.

Building upon the distinction between lean and agile networks introduced above, it is also possible to think of *hybrid* supply network forms combining the characteristics of both types on either side of key decoupling points (for example, a paint manufacturer using lean methods in producing base paints, and agile processes in distributing myriad different colours to retailers/consumers). Clearly, these are highly simplified representations of production networks – many real-world GPNs are far more complex and have many more actors and stages involved – but the huge variation in the kinds of services required through the system is evident. As a result, the challenges facing a logistics provider that seeks to service an entire GPN are profound: in reality, there are complex *functional divisions of labour* between firms that undertake different activities at different points along the GPN.

A fourth strong current in literature has been characterising and categorising the wide range of providers involved in logistics provisions. As Dicken (2011) notes, the various types of organisations involved in logistics include transportation companies, logistics service providers, wholesalers, trading companies (such as Li & Fung and the Japanese *sogo shosha*), retailers and e-tailers and, of course, it should be remembered that in global terms, the majority of logistics activity is still handled *in-house*. While transportation companies (road, rail, shipping, air freight), wholesalers and retailers play reasonably clearly delimited roles in production circuits, the categories of logistics service providers and trading companies, for example, are far more blurred and are becoming increasingly so as such firms expand their range of activities. In short, as Aoyama and Ratick (2007: 193) describe, '. . . the industry is characterized by a high degree of heterogeneity in terms of the types of firms and services'. It is therefore necessary to develop typologies that provide some purchase on this variety. One often used distinction is between first, second, third and fourth party logistics providers:

1. First party (1PL): a fully in-house logistics function;
2. Second party (2PL): whereby a customer contracts a logistics service provider to take care of a logistics function such as transportation or warehousing;
3. Third party (3PL): whereby two (or more) supply network participants agree to outsource their integrated logistics requirements to a logistics service provider. This is the category of firms most commentators are referring to when talking about the 'logistics industry' and the one that has seen the most dramatic growth in recent years; and
4. Fourth party (4PL): in which special logistics integrators serve as market mediators and build value-adding networks connecting together supply network partners with logistics service providers. 4PL entails hybrid organisations, usually a form of joint venture or long-term contract with responsibility for the entire supply network (such as the limited life Vector SCM created by GM and Menlo Logistics).[6]

It is worth noting that this *functional* typology means that an individual firm can straddle several of these categories. The largest transnational logistics operators, for example, will serve different elements of their client base in a 2PL, 3PL or 4PL capacity.

Another distinction can be made between firms that are *asset-based* – such as those providing transportation services over land, air or water or warehousing services – and *non-asset-based* operators that specialise in activities such as supply chain management consulting and software development, freight forwarding, selling space on ocean carriers/consolidating shipments, customs brokerage, and online exchanges and brokerage. In terms of the previous typology, while most 2PL providers tend to be predominantly asset-based, 3PL providers offer varying combinations of asset-based and non-asset-based services, while the competitive advantage of a 4PL provider lies primarily in non-asset-based services.

Fifth, and finally, the literature is replete with studies of the technological innovations that have transformed logistics provisions in recent decades. While logistics have been profoundly changed by the great advances in the time–space shrinking transport and communication technologies that have underpinned economic globalisation more broadly, they have also been transformed, however, by shifts in process technologies towards more flexible and customised production systems, which place demands for different requirements on logistics providers. In particular, the logistics industry is shaped by the need for *speed*, *flexibility* and *reliability* of the services it provides (Dicken, 2011). The broad shift towards lean distribution systems noted above have been underpinned by technological advances in six interrelated areas (typology taken from Rodrigue *et al.*, 2006: 208–9; with inputs from Dicken, 2007: 415–6). First, with respect to *transportation modes*, although there has been limited technological change in transport modes in recent decades, the advent of a standardised system of containerisation and transhipment by the 1970s underpins the global web of intra- and inter-firm trade (Levinson, 2006). There have been more recent developments in the field, including the 'doublestacking' of containers by rail and the development of ever-larger container ships in the pursuit of economies of scale.[7] Second, significant technological changes have seen new *transportation terminals* constructed that can operate at extremely high levels of turnover. Better handling facilities have led to significant improvements in throughput, and container ports have become absolutely critical nodes in the global logistics system. Port facilities are also increasingly supported by inland terminals connected by high-capacity corridors.[8] Third, contemporary *distribution centres* do not hold inventory for long and are characterised by very rapid turnover of goods. They are designed for throughput and have specialised loading and unloading bays and sorting equipment. The aggressive use of cross-docking by leading retailers, for example, allows goods to be brought in, selected, repacked and dispatched to stores with limited, if any, time in inventory (Higginson and Bookbinder, 2005). Fourth, *load units* are the basic units of freight distribution and can take different forms, including pallets, swap bodies, semi-trailers and containers (Rodrigue *et al.*, 2006). While containers are the dominant load unit for long distance transport, the ever-increasing complexity of logistics ensures that a range of units is required, and tight control is maintained through the use of bar codes and RFID (radio frequency identification devices) (Sparks and Wagner, 2004).

Fifth, *integrated IT systems* and common software platforms across the supply network – known as Electronic Data Interchange (EDI) – allow the instantaneous and secure transmission of large quantities of data concerning sales, product specifications, orders, invoices, shipment tracking and the like (Mei and Dinwoodie, 2005). Sixth, and relatedly, the advent of the Internet has brought about a wider series of changes to logistics and supply network configurations that go under the broad rubric of *e-commerce* (Fernie and McKinnon, 2004; Gereffi, 2001; Kenney and Curry, 2001; Leinbach, 2001). Both business–business and business–consumer relationships have been reworked through new forms of electronic marketplace. The once predicted wholesale disappearance of many supply chain intermediaries has not occurred; instead, many existing intermediaries, including logistics providers, have sought new value-adding strategies and, in addition, new forms of intermediaries have emerged. As Aoyama *et al.* (2006) recount, we have seen simultaneous processes of both *disintermediation* through the elimination of some middlemen in global networks and *re-intermediation* through the rise of new types of service providers, such as, for instance, e-commerce brokers, online auction firms and the like. Likewise, the notion that physical logistics infrastructures will become less important has proved unfounded. Instead, a wide range of different approaches to fulfilling e-commerce orders has developed. What is apparent is that contemporary logistics providers need to establish a presence in both *real* and *virtual* space (see also Aoyama and Ratick, 2007; Li *et al.*, 2001).

3. LOGISTICS AND GPNS: FOUR KEY RESEARCH PRIORITIES

This literature has contributed a great deal to our understanding of the logistics industries and their increasingly strategic contributions to processes of supply chain management, and several of these insights inform the remainder of this paper. However, reflecting its disciplinary roots, such work has tended to focus on firm and inter-firm issues concerning efficiency, profitability and competitiveness. General arguments about the nature and growing significance of logistics need to be accompanied by the recognition that logistics services are hugely variable across time, space and GPNs, are provided by a rich array of inter-linked corporate actors, and have a wide range of potential implications for upgrading dynamics across a broad swath of industries. This involves taking the political–economy – for example, involvement in relations of power and value, state policies and labour issues – inherent to logistics seriously. In what follows, and mobilising the dual perspective on logistics provisions identified earlier, I distil four key research priorities that need tackling in order to develop a fuller understanding of the strategic role of logistics within the global economy.

Corporate strategies and intra-industry upgrading in the logistics sector

Perhaps the most glaring gap in the existing literature is the lack of studies that focus upon the logistics *industry*, that is, as a complex of profit-seeking, strategic actors, rather than as simple providers of an important production function. Some logistics firms have sought to become comprehensive logistics providers by upgrading strategies, while others have remained focused on a narrower range of functions. Some have kept a relatively tight geographical focus, while others have sought to expand their geographical remit either within a country, within a given macro-region (for example, the EU, North America) or at a more avowedly global scale. A key mechanism for both functional and geographical expansion has been merger and acquisition activity, resulting in consolidation among the higher echelons of the global industry.[9] Overall, it is clear that the three overlapping processes of upgrading, globalisation and consolidation are pivotal among the leading 3PL providers, although detailed studies of the organisational and growth dynamics of these firms are scarce (however, see Erker, 2008). The net result of these processes at the global level has been the emergence of a cadre of large, transnational players that were profiled in the previous section.

The firms within this top cadre are not homogenous, however, but, rather, have emerged through different developmental trajectories. Berglund *et al.* (1999) identify three types of players in the third-party logistics market in addition to the traditional transport and forwarding companies. First, since the 1980s, *asset-based logistics providers* have developed out of operators of service assets such as trucks, airplanes and warehouses. For example, a transport company may offer distribution centres and information services to clients, or a distribution centre may offer inventory management and order administration services in addition to basic warehousing. Firms that have developed through this route include Geodis, DB Schenker and Penske. Second, and dating to the early 1990s, *network logistics providers* such as DHL, FedEx, UPS and TNT have developed from courier and express parcel companies. They have built up global transportation and communication networks in order to be able to deliver express shipments quickly and reliably and have developed supplementary services such as electronic proof of delivery and track-and-trace options. These firms are increasingly moving into high-margin electronics, spare parts and fashion segments in direct competition with asset-based providers. Third, *skills-based logistics providers* (or 4PL firms) started to emerge in the late 1990s and seek to provide consultancy and financial services, IT and management skills to their clients. They may emerge from the other categories of firms and/or use them as subcontractors. An example would be Agility, now based in Kuwait after a series of acquisitions in recent years.

These different growth trajectories also serve to reveal the different *upgrading* strategies in operation within the global logistics industry as firms have sought to move into higher value-added areas of activity (see Table 2, which shows recent increases in 3PL as opposed to mail, express and freight revenues among the top providers). However, the categorisation of upgrading received from manufacturing analyses – namely product, process, functional and chain upgrading – does not transfer unproblematically to this industry. The notions of product and chain upgrading in particular have no clear analogue in terms of logistics services, with upgrading in the sector seemingly best interpreted through differing combinations of process and functional upgrading. A wide variety of firm-level strategies are apparent. First, and most simply, companies may seek to enhance the quality of traditional transport and forwarding services by, for example, developing a warehouse into a distribution centre or offering refrigerated trucks. Second, providers may endeavour to expand their activity across the GPN by undertaking more of the links between raw material procurement and final consumption. This usually involves upgrading from single-mode transport service providers, like trucking companies or rail freight services, to multi-modal transport firms combining various transport methods to effectively serve more than one link in the supply chain. As such, it often entails a concomitant expansion in the geographical coverage of the logistics service provider (Wang and Cheng, 2010). US-based freight forwarder UPS, for instance, is able to deliver door-to-door services from the manufacturer to the retailer or final consumer through its own fleet of more than 96,000 road vehicles and more than 200 aircraft. The company is also a significant Non-Vessel Operating Common Carrier (that is, it offers and manages shipping services without direct ownership of vessels), allowing it to integrate its service to include shipping as well.[10]

Third, firms may look to increase the proportion of non-asset-based management services that they offer in terms of supply chain management and integration of services across different elements of production networks. Increasingly important areas of activity in this regard include (Rushton and Walker, 2007: 8–9):

1. Transnational supply chain coordination: the integration of contract logistics activities at both source and destination into end-to-end supply chain solutions;
2. Inbound to manufacturing (I2M): the supply chain management of the inbound flow of materials from suppliers to the point of production;
3. Freight management: managing and coordinating global freight movements across all major modes of transport;

Table 2 Business segment data for the 20 leading global logistics firms, 2009

		Revenue distribution for key business segments (%)							
		Mail and express		Freight and transportation		3PL & warehousing		Other/ unspecified	
Rank 2009	Firm	2004	2009	2004	2009	2004	2009	2004	2009
1	Deutsche Post DHL[1]	71	49	0	24	16	24	13	3
2	UPS	92	84	0	0	8	16	0	0
3	FedEx	82	83	11	12	7	5	0	0
4	DB Schenker Transport & Logistics	0	0	31	26	69	74	0	0
5	NYK Line	0	0	69	71	20	19	11	10
6	Kuehne + Nagel	0	0	89	74	11	25	0	1
7	Nippon Express[2]	0	0	57	43	4	6	12	11
8	SNCF Geodis[2]	–	20	–	31	–	19	–	0
9	DSV A/S	0	0	97	90	3	10	0	0
10	CEVA	–	0	–	43	–	57	–	0
11	CH Robinson Worldwide Inc	0	0	83	79	17	21	0	0
12	Panalpina Group	0	0	85	85	15	15	0	0
13	Agility	–	0	–	0	–	95	–	5
14	Toll Holdings Ltd	–	0	–	72	–	28	–	0
15	Bolloré Group Transport & Logistics	–	0	–	44	–	56	–	0
16	Dachser GmbH & Co KG	–	0	–	0	–	99	–	1
17	GEFCO SA	0	–	51	–	49	–	0	–
18	Expeditors International	0	0	82	76	18	24	0	0
19	Sinotrans Limited	10	1	85	93	5	7	0	0
20	Norbert Dentressangle	0	0	62	55	38	45	0	0

Notes:
Where figures were not available, the symbol '–' is used.
[1] From 2007 onwards, Deutsche Post DHL restructured the way they announced segment data, which resulted in some 'Mail/Express' and 'Other' functions being broadly reclassified under the Freight/Transportation category.
[2] The figures for Nippon Express and SNCF Geodis account for only around 60–70 per cent of gross revenues because the company does not publish comprehensive revenue breakdown by business segment.
Source: Company annual reports and websites.

4. Destination management: managing downstream operations, port to distribution centre (DC) delivery, deconsolidation, customs brokerage and quality checking;
5. Contract distribution: storage and delivery, inventory management, DC management, pre-retailing (labelling, etc.), reverse logistics, retail delivery, home delivery;
6. Service parts logistics: found particularly in high-tech sectors, it involves ensuring that post-sales high value or critical parts reach a spatially extensive customer base quickly and efficiently; and
7. Reverse logistics: handling the inherently complex and inefficient processes of good returns from customers. This was estimated to be a global market worth US$35 billion in the mid-2000s.

Fourth, in what can, perhaps, be thought of as a form of functional upgrading, in certain sectors, providers have moved into activities beyond what is traditionally associated with logistics and supply chain management. Although the empirical evidence is somewhat uneven and anecdotal, leading asset-based logistics providers are entering into areas such as completing light manufacturing and sub-assembly activities and providing packing and packaging services, thereby allowing client firms to decouple product manufacture from packaging for specific markets (and also customised marketing initiatives and product combinations). DHL, for example, offers a range of assembly, kitting and packaging services to its clients in high technology sectors. Other niches may also merge; Chasen Holdings, for example, is a Singaporean logistics company that specialises in helping semiconductor companies to relocate their operations within Asia (*Straits Times*, 2012). In this way, 3PL firms may be able to penetrate into the 'core' activities of GPNs, altering the governance and value dynamics of those systems accordingly. Due to the volume and nature of information exchanged between 3PL firms and their customers, these 'deeper' forms of integration with client activities serve to strengthen the position of logistics firms in GPNs, creating longer-term relationships on a more equal footing.

Given the complexity of contemporary GPNs and their logistics requirements, it becomes apparent that, in reality, logistics needs are met by a range of different firms that are networked together or 'tiered' in particular configurations. Dicken (2007), for example, notes that the journey of one containerised shipment may involve 25 different parties and two or three different transport modes and be handled in 12–15 different physical locations. Understanding the inter-firm relationships between different kinds of logistics providers is therefore crucial to understanding economic and social upgrading dynamics. Indeed, the power and governance relationships between providers are a much under-studied area. A 3PL or 4PL lead logistics provider, for example, will often coordinate a range of different providers encompassing distribution centres, parcel services, local transport, long-distance carriers and information services (such as software providers and supply chain consultancies). Thus, it is important to consider the complex networks of inter-firm relationships that constitute the logistics industry. In reality, of course, the tiered network configurations are also differentiated across the various local, national and macro-regional markets they serve. Some logistics firms will have geographically-specific roles (such as local transport providers), while others are explicitly concerned with linking transnationally (such as freight carriers). Clearly, such systems are not only dealing with the physical requirements of logistics (such as mode transfers – sea/land, rail/lorry, etc.), but also cross political boundaries and all their associated customs clearances, tariffs, duties and bureaucracy (Dicken, 2011). As Aoyama and Ratick (2007: 159) describe it, '. . . the logistics industry serves as a critical intermediary across geographic, cultural, and institutional boundaries'. Global logistics systems hence need to combine the virtues of both strong central control and coordination and locally responsive customer-facing distribution systems. Such requirements create a range of cross-cutting functional and geographical niches for logistics providers of varying scale and scope, about which we currently know very little.

Varied regulatory and institutional contexts

These tiered networks of different kinds of logistics providers demonstrate that – the rise of certain global logistics giants notwithstanding – the *geographical divisions of labour* between logistics providers should not be played down. As Aoyama *et al.* (2006: 337) explain, 'with the exception of a few emerging integrated logistics providers (such as UPS or DHL) the overwhelming majority of logistics providers possess a geographic specialty (and even the worldwide integrated firms either have branches in, or have acquired firms with, strategic geographic locational advantage). This is because transportation is primarily a local industry that requires rich, geographically-specific knowledge, even if the industry deals with international and widely geographically dispersed transactions.' They continue: '. . . the presence of a paradox in the industry: although the logistics industry serves an integral function in the globalisation of production, it also remains one of the most localised and embedded industries of all' (p. 338). Hence, the need to conceptualise the institutionally-mediated interactions between global and local freight distribution systems is paramount. Wang and Cheng (2010), for example, provide a fascinating analysis of the different kinds of logistics service providers present in Hong Kong and their different specialisations and geographical remits, as the city develops into a 'global supply chain management centre' (see also Notteboom and Rodrigue, 2012, on the differences between local freight distribution activities and the global integration role of the leading container terminal operators).

We need to know far more about how this embeddedness in particular political–economic contexts shapes logistics provision – the impact of regulatory and institutional contexts on logistics systems is a huge lacuna in the literature. Most tellingly, discussion of the state is largely noticeable by its absence – many of the leading supply chain management texts devote only one or two pages to the topic, at best. This is a major oversight, as *state regulatory regimes* – particularly through their regulation of the cross-border movement of goods and services – can create 'a major discontinuity in the geographical surface over which distribution services operate' (Dicken, 2007: 420). The regulatory structures that affect the operation of the logistics industries can be seen to operate at a range of levels, most notably the international, the macro-regional and the national. While such frameworks are constantly evolving, by far the dominant trend in most contexts in the past few decades has been towards the *deregulation* of transportation and communication systems. However, it is important to note that the regulatory conditions affecting clients sectors can also impinge on the logistics industry. Indeed, Bonacich and Wilson (2008) go so far as to suggest that the 'logistics revolution' has ultimately been driven by neoliberalism and a regulatory context that allowed the significant build-up of retailer power.

Dicken (2007, drawing on Braithwaite and Drahos, 2000) describes how the transport and communications sectors have been regulated through a varying mix of international and national regulations developed in negotiation between international bodies (such as the International Maritime Organization (IMO) or the International Telecommunications Union (ITU)), national states and leading corporations. Key issues in terms of transport pertain to security and safety, while, in terms of communications, technological standards are a key concern. In the two pages of their text devoted to deregulation, Rushton and Walker (2007: 236–7) note the rise of macro-regional economic unions such as the European Union (EU) and the North American Free Trade Agreement (NAFTA) and the subsequent deregulation of internal markets, which have smoothed cross-border logistics in various ways, including transport deregulation, harmonisation of legislation, reduction of tariff barriers, reduction of cross-border customs requirements and various forms of tax harmonisation. Liberalisation of trucking between the US, Canada and Mexico, for example, was part of the NAFTA, although implementation has proved thorny in practice and is still not fully established. In general terms, at the national level, there is an inherent tension between states seeking to retain control over their national transport and communications spaces and corporate actors seeking the most deregulated environment possible. In most contexts, however, the transport and communications sectors have moved rapidly in recent decades towards greater deregulation and the privatisation of state-owned companies.

As the brevity of this section suggests, beyond the common-sense recognition that a general deregulation of cross-border flows has facilitated the development of GPNs and associated logistical systems, there are far more questions than answers when it comes to the regulatory and institutional dimensions of logistics. Indeed, more broadly, the interface between logistics providers and their multi-scalar institutional environments is severely under-researched. Key questions include:

1. In what ways are logistics services shaped by the regulatory and institutional formations in which they are embedded at different levels?
2. How far, and in what ways, do regulatory barriers continue to present an impediment to efficient transnational logistical operations? What border effects still exist and how are they regulated?
3. How do regulations pertaining to inward FDI shape the ability of leading transnationals to invest in particular territories? What are the associated implications for processes of economic upgrading?

Social upgrading and downgrading within the logistics industry

Earlier, it was noted that the literature on logistics and economic upgrading is thin; research into social upgrading in the logistics industry – and, indeed, labour market issues in general in the sector – is even sparser (Coe and Hess, 2010). Social upgrading is a relatively recent term coined to describe the changing working conditions within GPNs, both in terms of measurable standards (wages, benefits, etc.) and enabling rights (freedom of association, collective bargaining, etc.) (for example, Barrientos *et al.*, 2010; Milberg and Winkler, 2010). Leading supply chain management texts rarely, if ever, refer to workers, labour, training, skills and the like in any way. This is a massive oversight, given the huge numbers of people involved in transport and logistics in all economies, and means that wider developmental issues related to the expansion of logistics are commonly overlooked. Although the data is patchy, one example will suffice here: in June 2012, in the UK, 902,000 people were employed as transport drivers and operatives, 406,000 in elementary storage occupations and 156,000 as transport, distribution and warehouse managers, meaning the sector accounted for a minimum of 5 per cent of total employment (http://www.statistics.gov.uk/, accessed 19 November 2012). This lacuna is compounded by the fact that the few studies that do exist on labour conditions in logistics point towards social *downgrading* 'in the form of increased contingency for workers, weakened unions, and racialization, all of which contribute to a decline in labor standards' (Bonacich and Wilson, 2008: 21). Focusing on these issues reveals a dark side to the logistics sector that is simply invisible in the dominant business and management literatures on the topic. Bensman (2008: 3) similarly depicts a 'low-road' labour market model in which 'the impact of the logistics revolution is not only that it provides employers access to far-flung networks of cheap labor, it also enables them to hire labor in ways that reduce their responsibilities, their benefit obligations, their tax liabilities, their insurance costs, and their fixed costs for equipment and so on'.

Bonacich and Wilson (2008) – in one of the most comprehensive investigations into logistics labour markets currently available (based on research in Southern California) – diagnose four dimensions of the low-road growth model in contemporary logistics. First, cheaper and more readily exploitable labour forces are created through outsourcing, subcontracting and the use of temporary staffing agencies, leading to an increasingly contingent workforce. Such workers are vulnerable to detrimental management practices and are hard to organise collectively. Second, pressure on organised labour has been a commonplace part of the shifts in how goods are produced and transported in contemporary capitalism, leading to weakened unions. Lower rates of unionisation are clearly linked to increased levels of contingency and broader neoliberal economic and social policies. Third, there has been racialisation of the workforce, with the burden of deteriorating working conditions falling disproportionately on workers with few rights and least political power, both domestically and offshore. Employers actively seek out – often with the help of intermediaries such as temporary staffing agencies – racialised workforces to whom they can pay the lowest wages. Fourth, declining wages and working conditions are becoming a defining characteristic of logistics labour markets, resulting in a lowering of labour standards. Moreover, logistics labour is highly gendered, with male workers predominating in the sector, and heavily polarised, with decent work conditions and increasing skills as well as wages on the one side – primarily associated with transnational and 3PL/4PL providers – and a much larger domain of low wage casual labour characterised by job insecurity on the other. As these points suggest, many logistics workers find themselves caught in a 'perfect storm' of globalisation, the fragmentation of production, new logistics technologies and neoliberal deregulation of both labour markets in general and the transport industry in particular.[11] The net result is that 'the availability of low-cost labor discourages capital investment, reduces the incentive to coordinate links in the logistics chain, reduces demand for skills and skill development and raises the burden that freight movement imposes on the public' (Bensman, 2008: 15). In line with the broader argument of this article, however, it is important to realise that the ultimate driver of working conditions *within* the logistics industry may lie in the stringent demands embedded in contractual relationships with key clients, in particular large retailers (Newsome, 2010).

Perhaps understandably, given the above, sector-wide initiatives barely seem to have tackled the issue of social upgrading in the logistics industry. More attention is undoubtedly being paid to the sustainable aspects of transport and logistics, with an emerging body of literature focusing on 'greening' the supply chain, often under the wider umbrella of corporate social responsibility (CSR). Global logistics providers, in most cases, do subscribe to a code of conduct and most will comply with the UN Global Compact and International Labour Organization (ILO) schemes, among others, but firm CSR documentation often puts primary emphasis on labour conditions and the environment in the home economies, with considerably less information about their subsidiaries and networks in the Global South. Ciliberti *et al.*'s (2008) review of CSR practices in the logistics industry found that the human rights dimension was largely concerned with analysing the labour conditions of workers in supplier companies, rather than in-house. From the perspective of developing countries, social upgrading – or a switch from low-road to high-road labour markets – will necessitate coordinated action by both state and corporate actors.[12] For instance, careful labour market regulation is needed to prevent the erosion of wages and working conditions within highly competitive and contingent segments. State involvement is also of paramount importance in the domain of education and skills development and in terms of encouraging inward FDI in the logistics sector in order to bring much-needed investment and skills/knowledge. Without a solid base of research into logistics labour market conditions, however, assessments of the impacts of such dynamics will prove virtually impossible to make.

Upgrading in client sectors

The aforementioned upgrading activities within the logistics industry intersect with those within client sectors due to the powerful outsourcing dynamic that is driving growth in the sector. In general terms, efficient logistics contribute to value-adding processes in wider GPNs by providing control and coordination of the complex intra- and inter-firm material flows within those GPNs (Rodrigue *et al.*, 2006). As noted earlier, speed, flexibility and reliability have become integral to the competitive dynamics of nearly all globally-organised industry. There are important differences, however, in the precise contribution of logistics, depending on the organisational and geographical complexity of specific GPNs. We currently know relatively little about the sector-specific contributions of logistics to production network transformations and upgrading and, more specifically, (1) how the growing significance of logistics providers is transforming the power relations and governance regimes in the wider 'client' GPNs; and (2) how the growing significance of logistics providers is transforming patterns of value creation, enhancement and capture in wider GPNs. Again, as with the logistics industry itself, the manufacturing-derived categories of product, process, functional and chain upgrading are ill suited to this context, with the impacts largely reflected as different forms of *process* upgrading in client sectors. Three brief sectoral cases can be used as illustrative windows onto these dynamics – horticulture, apparel and mobile telecommunications.

Many developing economies have become increasingly reliant on export markets for horticultural products, which can be among the most important sectors for international trade. An example would be the production of fresh flowers in countries such as Colombia, Ecuador, Ethiopia and Kenya for the European and North American markets. Air freight and a reliable 'cold chain' (see Smith and Sparks, 2004) are crucial for these GPNs to function, in turn attracting logistics FDI by transnational 3PL companies. They are the only way to ensure quality, meet the standards required by international buyers and thus enhance the value in the form of higher sales prices. As illustrated by Korsten *et al.* (2008: 170), the cold chain starts on the farm, immediately after harvesting, continues through the stages of temporary storage at the farm, transport to market, and ends with storage at the place of final consumption. Compared to other agricultural supply chains, this system is more capital-intensive as it requires specific technologies and infrastructure and, therefore, the barriers of entry for local transport and logistics companies in developing economies are high, especially if production and the resulting transport volumes are low. The lack of high-quality cold chain logistics, in turn, has a negative impact on product quality, thereby reducing export opportunities, which, in turn, affects the volume, speed and frequency of international transport to market, leading to a vicious circle and severely constraining upgrading opportunities as economies of scale cannot be realised. Deficiencies in logistics systems are clearly among the most important obstacles for upgrading and development in horticulture GPNs (Joosten, 2007; Vagneron *et al.*, 2009). According to LEI (n.d.: 25), the four key areas for improving horticulture logistics in exporting countries are the generation of sufficient production volumes, longer-term and stronger collaboration between producers of different sizes, enhanced collaboration on certification and quality control procedures, and investment in refrigeration facilities to establish a fully integrated cold chain.

The challenge of economic upgrading in apparel GPNs has been the focus of many academic studies to date (for example, Abernathy *et al.*, 1999; Danskin *et al.*, 2005; Gereffi, 1999; Gereffi and Memedovic, 2003; Schrank, 2004). Like horticulture, the apparel sector is an important source of employment and export earnings in a considerable number of developing economies. Being a labour-intensive industry in search of low-cost production locations, the geographical and organisational structures of apparel GPNs have changed substantially in recent decades. Coordinating the much profiled 'triangle' manufacturing system between buyers, manufacturers and subcontractors (Antonio and Rodolfo, 2006; Gereffi, 1999) requires sophisticated logistics operations, both inbound (the sourcing of raw materials and fabric/textiles) and outbound (shipments to buyers and customers). For developing country producers, staying competitive within apparel GPNs is not just a matter of labour and production costs, but also depends heavily upon reducing lead times and ensuring timely deliveries. At the upstream end, apparel manufacturers can face difficulties when searching for reliable materials and fabric suppliers, as many of them do not have the capacity to operate their own buying offices and inbound logistics. They are also hampered by time-consuming customs and import/export procedures for materials and finished goods. Outbound logistics, on the other hand, becomes an issue when producers fail to meet the delivery deadlines set by the buyer and thereby face overtime charges. As buyers apply lean retail strategies and producers often lack the financial and organisational resources, logistics in the apparel sector has become an activity that is increasingly carried out through 3PL providers offering 'end-to-end' services, either trading companies such as Li & Fung Trading, or 'pure' logistics providers such as DHL.[13] As key intermediaries between buyers and manufacturers, 3PL providers play an important role in technology and know-how transfer, in particular through training in, and the implementation of, information technologies that enhance the visibility and traceability of orders.

Compared to the horticulture and apparel GPNs, the mobile communications sector displays an even greater degree of organisational and technological complexity, and combines manufacturing and service provisions in unique ways (Hess and Coe, 2006; Funk, 2009; Dedrick *et al.*, 2011). The main drivers of mobile communications GPNs are the branded manufacturers – such as Apple, HTC, Nokia and Samsung – which command a multi-tiered upstream, inbound logistics network, whereas mobile service providers such as Vodafone and Singtel focus on downstream logistics operations for physical products (handsets) and voice/data services (Catalan and Kotzab, 2003). Highly efficient logistics systems are again critical to the functioning of the GPN, with speed being of the essence, not only in terms of time-to-market of the finished product, but also in terms of just-in-time delivery at numerous stages of the production and distribution process. Mobile phone assembly, for instance, is geographically highly concentrated in OEM-led manufacturing clusters. In such clusters, manufacturers have implemented 'hubbing' systems in which suppliers not able to supply directly leave a minimum volume of products in a location close to the factory – the hub. In most cases, they consolidate around one or two hubs managed by third party logistics providers (*cf.* van Egeraat and Jacobson, 2005). They provide all the services at the production location, in dedicated mobile communications clusters coordinated by firms such as Nokia (*cf.* Liu *et al.*, 2004) or Flextronics. These hubs, in turn, are linked to airport logistics parks, as air cargo services have become a crucial link in electronics GPNs (Leinbach and Bowen, 2004).

As these three brief vignettes show, high quality logistics provisions are integral to the on-going dynamics of process upgrading within client GPNs. The logistics industry is not a passive service input in this context, but, at the top end, is constituted by sophisticated and knowledgeable TNCs acting strategically to expand the scope and significance of their contribution to wider GPNs. Many increasingly have dedicated global divisions offering complete logistics solutions across the whole network.

4. CONCLUSION: LOGISTICS AND GPNS IN A SHIFTING WORLD ECONOMY?

The previous section has illustrated that there is a pressing need for a research agenda that develops a deeper understanding of the role of logistics within the global economy. It is one that can be operationalised by thinking of the logistics industry both as a GPN in its own right and as a strategic and transformative input to client GPNs. The tools of GPN-style analyses – namely, a nuanced approach to shifting power and value relations within and across different institutional contexts – are ideal for unpacking the shifting intersections of the multi-tiered and highly geographically and functionally differentiated logistics industry with the equally complex inter-firm networks of client sectors. In this way, it will also be possible to move beyond firm-centric approaches and adopt a broader political–economic perspective that incorporates power and value relationships, institutional and regulatory context, and labour issues and social upgrading – all topics that are currently massively underplayed in most work on logistics. Moreover, from the perspective of particular places or 'logistics clusters' (Sheffi, 2012), the GPN framework can shine light on why some places succeed as logistics nodes, while others struggle to 'couple' with logistics circuits.

This would be a challenging enough research agenda if global divisions of labour were held relatively constant. Profound on-going shifts in the structures of the global economy, however, mean that research also needs to grapple with what in reality are highly dynamic GPNs. Inherent in many GPN-style analyses is an assumption – either implicit or explicit – of export-oriented production in developing countries for developed country markets. This, in turn, shapes understanding of the logistical requirements of GPNs, with the key task being the rapid fulfilment of orders from developed country buyers and retailers. Cool chains, air cargo systems and port/shipping operations, for instance, are often oriented towards extracting components and/or finished commodities quickly and efficiently for relatively wealthy markets. While it is too early to predict precisely what kind of global economy is emerging from the economic crisis that commenced in 2008, it is apparent that the contours of the global economy are shifting profoundly.[14] For instance, in a pioneering analysis, Cattaneo *et al.* (2010) diagnose on-going global industry consolidation, shifts in patterns of demand towards 'emerging' markets and rising levels of so-called 'South-South' trade as key elements of change, all of which will place new demands on the logistics operations underpinning constantly shifting GPNs. To draw the article to a close, I would like to point to four intersecting implications of these changes for the political economy of logistics provisions in the coming years.

First, it is likely that the *nature* of global logistics provisions will change profoundly. An increasing number of studies, for instance, point to the rapidly changing geography of the middle classes (for example, Kaplinsky and Farooki, 2010; Kharas, 2010). It is estimated that the global middle class – using a broad definition of those earning US$10–100 per day – will expand from 1.8 billion to 4.9 billion people over the period, 2009–30, with 85 per cent of this growth being accounted for by Asia. The share of middle class consumers in North America and Europe is projected to fall from 54 per cent of the world total in 2009 to 21 per cent in 2030, while the Asia-Pacific's share will expand from 28 per cent to 66 per cent. In terms of actual spending power, it is estimated that North America and Europe will fall from 64 per cent to 30 per cent of the global total, with the Asia-Pacific region rising from 23 per cent to 59 per cent. Within these shifts, two countries dominate, with China and India expected to account for almost 40 per cent of the global middle class by 2030 (data from Kharas, 2010). If these projected trends play out in reality, they will necessitate a profound reorientation of logistics systems often established to facilitate export-oriented production towards domestic consumption. The quality of domestic logistics provisions *within* the Brazil, Russia, India, China, South Africa (BRICS) economies will, therefore, become a hugely strategic issue with respect to global economic growth. Recent reports suggest that there are profound and widespread issues in each of these countries[15] – relating, for instance, to basic access to infrastructure, lack of integration between transport types and over-dependence on road transport – which are already impinging on economic growth, but the increased demand for domestic market access is likely to accentuate these challenges.[16]

Second, and relatedly, in addition to a reorientation of existing logistics channels, new corridors of growth will continue to spring up to facilitate so-called South–South trade. These maybe intra-regional, as, for instance, the spread of logistics providers in parallel with the expansion of leading South African retailers such as Shoprite across Africa – or inter-regional, as seen, for instance, in the burgeoning trade levels between China and several African economies (Carmody, 2011). Kaplinsky and Farooki (2010), for example, chart China's seemingly insatiable demand for both 'soft commodities' – such as food and intermediate inputs into manufacturing such as cotton and timber – and 'hard commodities' such as metals and minerals over the 2000s to fuel its rapid industrialisation and urbanisation. These globally significant shifts in trade flows are necessarily forging new South–South logistics channels. To give one example, between 1990 and 2007, China's share of global imports of tropical hardwood increased from 14 per cent to 68 per cent, while India's rose from 5 per cent to 17 per cent.

Third, state logistics policies within the fast-growing economies will be of paramount importance. The shifting configuration of the global economy will mean that the willingness and ability of emerging market governments to drive through logistics strategies will become increasingly significant in meeting the needs of the expanding consuming classes in the BRICS and beyond. Many of the challenges noted with respect to logistics provisions within the BRICS economies speak to the need for enhanced and coordinated government action at the national level. A 2009 Kuehne and Nagel study of logistics in China, for example, described the distribution system as 'chaotic, complex and localised' and characterised by 'restrictive, burdensome and confusing regulation'. The economic crisis has served to precipitate strategic intervention, however. In China, the State Council initiated the Logistics Industry Adjustment and Revitalization Plan in March 2009, with logistics featuring as the only service sector among 10 industry revitalisation and national investment programmes, but, more generally, a raft of legislation since the mid-2000s has made the national integration of logistics a key strategic priority (Liu *et al.*, 2011). Similarly, in Brazil, 2007 saw the release of the National Plan for Transport Logistics (Plano Nacional de Logística de Transportes) and logistics was a key plank of the Growth Acceleration Programmes, PAC1 and PAC2 (2007–10 and 2011–14, respectively), being allocated more than US$55 billion of expenditure in each programme. India is lagging somewhat, with a 2010 McKinsey report strongly advocating the need for a National Integrated Logistics Policy in response to the fact that 'India's logistics infrastructure is insufficient, ill-equipped and ill-designed to support the expected growth rates of 7 to 8 per cent over the next decade' (McKinsey, 2010: 5). The role of the state may extend beyond integrated planning and direct investment to also encompass issues of training and skills development within the domestic industry, and strategies for attracting and leveraging inward investment by foreign logistics providers. Overall, it is clear that the need to incorporate the state into the logistics literature is an increasingly urgent one.

Fourth, it seems certain that the configuration of the global logistics industry will change in accordance with the above dynamics. The entry of leading Asian firms to the top cohort of global providers was already noted in Table 1, and the process is likely to continue, especially with respect to leading Chinese operators. The internationalisation strategies of those firms will be important to chart and interpret. Changing relationships between different categories of logistics providers will also merit careful scrutiny. Many of the upgrading strategies in both logistics and client sectors are shaped by how the services of globally-connected foreign operators intersect with those of local providers in host countries. In Apapa, for instance, Nigeria's busiest container terminal run by Denmark's A.P. Møller Group butts up against a fragmented road haulage industry characterised by poor roads, congestion, low levels of investment and limited use of IT (*Financial Times*, 2011a). The story is very similar at the Accra container port, Tema (*Financial Times*, 2011b). Effectively integrating the increasingly consolidated freight and shipping arms of the global industry with fragmented local industries is a crucial developmental challenge. The changing landscape of the global economy is likely to see the continued globalisation of the leading transnational providers, but also a growth in capacity and skills among selected domestic operators, with the extent to which foreign operators are able to penetrate diffuse and locally variable markets varying from context to context. To conclude by returning to a central argument of this article, studying the intra-industry structures and strategies of the logistics sector will offer a powerful window onto the dynamic shifts within the global economy more generally. As the strategic significance of the industry continues to grow, and as independent logistics providers become increasingly central to value-creation dynamics within client sectors, they will arguably morph from reflecting changing global divisions of labour to becoming an increasingly active shaper of those patterns.

ACKNOWLEDGEMENTS

This paper draws upon a *Capturing the Gains Research Network* scoping paper entitled 'Economic and Social Upgrading in Global Logistics' co-authored with Martin Hess. Martin's involvement and the financial support of *Capturing the Gains* are both gratefully acknowledged. The paper was first presented at a workshop at the National University of Singapore in December 2011; thanks to the participants for their comments and also to the organisers Jeff Nielson, Bill Pritchard and Henry Yeung for their cogent feedback. I also appreciate the helpful guidance of two anonymous reviewers. Finally, thanks are also due to Ross Jones for his research assistance on the leading global logistics providers.

NOTES

1 This paper adopts a deliberately broad definition of the logistics industry, encompassing firms active in any area of logistics or supply chain management activity. This reflects the importance of revealing the connections between different kinds of logistics providers if we are to better understand the contemporary global industry.

2 GPN research has somewhat different origins and emphases to cognate global commodity chain (GCC) and global value chain (GVC) approaches. In the

current context, however, and in the spirit of the workshop for which this paper was originally prepared, this paper does not belabour the differences between the various approaches. Although flavoured by the author's position with the GPN approach, for the most part, the analysis does not seek to distinguish between the constituent approaches with respect to the arguments being made about logistics.

3 Upgrading is a well-established concept in GPN and cognate literatures. It seeks to capture the strategies pursued by economic actors to improve their relative position within global production systems (see Humphrey and Schmitz, 2002, for more).

4 The past 10–15 years have seen the publication of a wide range of overview texts in this vein, including, most notably, Chopra and Meindl (2009), Christopher (2005), Dornier *et al.* (1998), Rushton and Walker (2007), Skjøtt-Larsen *et al.* (2007), Voortman (2004), Waters (2010) and Wood *et al.* (2002). The field is also characterised by a broad range of some 20–30 journals aimed at both academics and practitioners. The key journals include *Asia-Pacific Journal of Marketing and Logistics; European Journal of Operations Research; Food Logistics; International Journal of Logistics Management; International Journal of Logistics: Research and Applications; International Journal of Physical Distribution and Logistics Management; International Journal of Operations and Production Management; International Journal of Shipping and Transport Logistics; International Journal of Transportation Management; Journal of Air Transport Management; Journal of Business Logistics; Journal of Supply Chain Management; Journal of Transport Economics and Policy; Journal of Transportation Law, Logistics, and Policy; Logistics and Transport Focus; Logistics and Transportation Review; Logistics Management; Logistics Manager; Logistics Research; Maritime Economics and Logistics; Outsourced Logistics; Supply Chain Europe; Supply Chain Management Review; Supply Chain Management: An International Journal; Transport Logistics; Transport Policy;* and *Transport Reviews.*

5 In the literature, an important distinction is often made between logistics and supply chain management (*cf.* Christopher, 2005: Rushton and Walker, 2007). While logistics, as already noted, refers to the movement of materials and goods through a production process to a point of consumption, supply chain management (SCM) is seen as a broader concept, which refers to the *integrated management* of all parts of a supply network from originating suppliers to end customers. It is, therefore, about the harmonisation and standardisation of supply chain practices across firms within a production network.

6 It is worth noting that there is scepticism in some quarters as to whether 4PL represents a management fad or real-world reality. Used in a slightly broader sense, however, to denote logistics providers that are able to offer a one-stop shop to demanding transnational clients, the term does capture the emergence of novel forms of partnership between client firms and logistics providers that are non-asset-based and go well beyond the usual 3PL relationship.

7 For more, see Fowler (2006), Hesse and Rodrigue (2004), Notteboom and Rodrigue (2008) and Rodrigue (2008).

8 For more, see Almotairi and Lumsden (2009), Bichou and Gray (2004), Goetz and Rodrigue (1999), Hesse (2008), Stopford (2009), Wang and Olivier (2006) and Wang *et al.* (2007).

9 As seen, for example, in the well-publicised acquisitions of Nedlloyd by Maersk (2005), Tibbett and Britton by Exel (2004) and, in turn, Exel by Deutsche Post World Net (2005) – Deutsche Post had previously acquired DHL (2003) – among many others (for more examples, see Rushton and Walker, 2007).

10 I thank one of the anonymous referees for this important observation.

11 Beyond these broad generalisations, it is important to recognise the different intersections of the above dynamics in different parts of the workforce. For example, there are important distinctions between maritime workers (see Bonacich and Wilson, 2008: Ch. 7), dockers/longshoremen (see Turnbull, 2000; Turnbull and Wass, 2007), truck drivers (see Bonacich and Wilson, 2008: Ch. 8) and warehouse workers (see Bonacich and Wilson, 2008: Ch. 9). Relatedly, Wright and Lund (2006) chart variations in labour control practices across three distribution centres within the Australian retail sector.

12 The interconnectedness of various logistics and transport sectors also allows for the possibility of inter-union cooperation (*cf.* Bonacich, 2005) at different levels: one such platform for global cooperation is the International Transport Workers' Federation (ITF), which represents 751 unions and 4.6 million workers from 154 countries.

13 For example, by February 2011, DHL had established seven Asia-Pacific Fashion and Apparel Centers of Excellence in Cambodia, Bangladesh, Hong Kong, India, Pakistan, Sri Lanka and Vietnam.

14 Although there is not enough space to discuss such issues here, for some commentators, these changes are indicative of a multipolar 'Post-Washington Consensus' global economy. As Birdsall and Fukyama (2011: 46), for instance, argue, 'in the next decade, emerging-market and low-income countries are likely to modify their approach to economic policy further, trading the flexibility and efficiency associated with the free-market model for domestic policies meant to ensure greater resilience in the face of competitive pressures and global economic trauma. They will become less focused on the free flow of capital, more concerned with minimizing social disruption through social safety net programs, and more active in supporting domestic industries. And they will be even less inclined than before to defer to the supposed expertise of the more developed countries, believing – correctly – that not only economic but also intellectual power are becoming increasingly evenly distributed.'

15 For recent overviews of the logistics sectors of the BRICS economies, see World Bank (2010) on Brazil, Capgemini (2007) on Russia, McKinsey & Company (2010) on India, Liu *et al.* (2011) on China, and CSIR (2010) on South Africa.

16 The nature of the products involved may also evolve. As Kaplinsky and Farooki (2010: 150) argue, 'low levels of per capita income mean that the nature of demand will be for cheap, undifferentiated goods with low acquisition cost, which runs against the major trends in demand in northern economies after 1970 that increasingly favoured differentiated, high-quality positional products'.

NOTES ON CONTRIBUTOR

Neil M. Coe is Professor of Economic Geography at the National University of Singapore. His research interests are in the areas of global production networks and local economic development; the geographies of local and transnational labour markets; the geographies of innovation; and institutional and network approaches to economic development. He has published over 65 articles and book chapters on these topics, and is a co-author of *Spaces of Work: Global Capitalism and the Geographies of Labour* (Sage, London, 2003) and *Economic Geography: A Contemporary Introduction* (Wiley, Hoboken, 2013).

REFERENCES

Abernathy, F. H., Dunlop, J., Hammond, J. H. and Weil, D. (1999) *A Stitch in Time: Lean Retailing and the Transformation of Manufacturing*, New York: Oxford University Press.

Almotairi, B. and Lumsden, K. (2009) 'Port Logistics Platform Integration in Supply Chain Management', *International Journal of Shipping and Transport Logistics*, 1(2): 194–210.

Antonio, E. and Rodolfo, M. (2006) *Assessment of Competitiveness and Logistics Infrastructure of the Philippine Garments Industry*, PIDS Discussion Paper Series No. 2006–08, Makati City: Philippine Institute for Development Studies.

Aoyama, Y. and Ratick, S. J. (2007) 'Trust, Transactions, and Information Technologies in the US Logistics Industry', *Economic Geography*, 83(2): 159–80.

Aoyama, Y., Ratick, S. and Schwarz, G. (2006) 'Organizational Dynamics of the U.S. Logistics Industry: An Economic Geography Perspective', *Professional Geographer*, 58(3): 330–43.

Barrientos, S., Gereffi, G. and Rossi, A. (2010) 'Economic and Social Upgrading in Global Production Networks: Developing a Framework for Analysis', *Capturing the Gains* Working Paper 2010/03, <http://www.capturingthegains.org/> (accessed 19 November 2012).

Bensman, D. (2008) 'Globalization and the Labour Markets of the Logistics Industry', Paper presented at the Sloan Industry Studies Conference, Boston, <http://web.mit.edu/is08/pdf/bensman.pdf> (accessed 19 November 2012).

Berglund, M., van Laarhoven, P., Sharman, G. and Wandel, S. (1999) 'Third-party Logistics: Is There a Future?', *International Journal of Logistics Management*, 10(1): 59–82.

Bichou, K. and Gray, R. (2004) 'A Logistics and Supply Chain Management Approach to Port Performance Measurement', *Maritime Policy & Management*, 31(1): 47–67.

Birdsall, N. and Fukuyama, F. (2011) 'The Post-Washington Consensus: Development after the Crisis', *Foreign Affairs*, 90(2): 45–53.

Bonacich, E. (2005) 'Labor and the Global Logistics Revolution', in R. Appelbaum and W. Robinson (eds) *Critical Globalisation Studies*, New York: Routledge, pp. 359–68.

Bonacich, E. and Wilson, J. B. (2008) *Getting the Goods: Ports, Labor and the Logistics Revolution*, Ithaca, NY: Cornell University Press.

Bowen, J. T. and Leinbach, T. R. (2006) 'Global Production Networks and Competitive Advantage: Air Freight Services and the Electronics Industry in Southeast Asia', *Economic Geography*, 82(2): 147–66.

Braithwaite, J. and Drahos, P. (2000) *Global Business Regulation*, Cambridge: Cambridge University Press.

Capgemini (2007) *Logistics Map of Russia*, <http://www.capgemini.com/insights-and-resources/by-publication/logistics_map_of_russia/> (accessed 19 November 2012).

Capgemini (2010) *The State of Logistics Outsourcing in 2010*, Atlanta, GA: Capgemini.

Carmody, P. (2011) *The New Scramble for Africa*, Cambridge: Polity.

Catalan, M. and Kotzab, H. (2003) 'Assessing the Responsiveness in the Danish Mobile Phone Supply Chain', *International Journal of Physical Distribution & Logistics Management*, 33(8): 668–86.

Cattaneo, O., Gereffi, G. and Staritz, C. (eds) (2010) *Global Value Chains in a Postcrisis World: A Development Perspective*, Washington, DC: World Bank.

Chopra, S. and Meindl, P. (2009) *Supply Chain Management: Strategy, Planning and Operation*, 4th edn, Harlow: Pearson.
Christopher, M. (2005) *Logistics and Supply Chain Management*, 3rd edn, Harlow: Pearson.
Ciliberti, F., Pontrandolfo, P. and Scozzi, B. (2008) 'Logistics Social Responsibility: Standard Adoption and Practices in Italian Companies', *International Journal of Production Economics*, 113(1): 88–106.
Coe, N. M. (2012) 'Geographies of Production II: A Global Production Networks A-Z', *Progress in Human Geography*, 36(3): 389–402.
Coe, N. M., Dicken, P. and Hess, M. (2008) 'Global Production Networks: Realizing the Potential', *Journal of Economic Geography*, 8(3): 271–95.
Coe, N. M. and Hess, M. (2010) 'Economic and Social Upgrading in Global Logistics', *Scoping report for the Capturing the Gains Project*, Manchester: University of Manchester.
Coe, N. M., Hess, M., Yeung, H. W.-C., Dicken, P. and Henderson, J. (2004) 'Globalizing Regional Development: A Global Production Networks Perspective', *Transactions of the Institute of British Geographers*, 29(4): 468–84.
CSIR (2010) *The Seventh Annual State of Logistics for South Africa 2010*, <http://www.imperiallogistics.co.za/event/state-of-logistics/> (accessed 19 November 2012).
Danskin, P., Englis, B., Solomon, M., Goldsmith, M. and Davey, J. (2005) 'Knowledge Management as Competitive Advantage: Lessons from the Textile and Apparel Value Chain', *Journal of Knowledge Management*, 9(2): 91–102.
Dedrick, J., Kraemer, K. L. and Linden, G. (2011) 'The Distribution of Value in the Mobile Phone Supply Chain', *Telecommunications Policy*, 35(6): 505–21.
Dicken, P. (2007) *Global Shift*, 5th edn, London: Sage.
Dicken, P. (2011) *Global Shift*, 6th edn, London: Sage.
Dornier, P.-P., Ernst, R., Fender, M. and Kouvelis, P. (1998) *Global Operations: Management and Logistics*, Chichester: Wiley.
Erker, P. (2008) *The Dachser Logistics Company: Global Competition and the Strength of the Family Vusiness*, Frankfurt am Main: Campus.
Fernie, J. and McKinnon, A. (2004) 'The Development of E-tail Logistics', in J. Fernie and L. Sparks (eds) *Logistics and Retail Management*, London: Kogan Page, pp. 188–208.
Fernie, J. and Sparks, L. (2004) (eds) *Logistics and Retail Management*, London: Kogan Page.
Financial Times (2011a) 'No Choice but to Play a Waiting Game', 23 November, p. 10.
Financial Times (2011b) 'Terminals Struggle to Keep Pace with Trade', 15 December, Ghana Supplement, p. 5.
Fowler, C. S. (2006) 'Re-exploring Transport Geography and Networks: A Case Study of Container Shipments to the West Coast of the United States', *Environment and Planning A*, 38(8): 1429–48.
Funk, J. L. (2009) 'The Emerging Value Network in the Mobile Phone Industry: The Case of Japan and Its Implications for the Rest of the World', *Telecommunications Policy*, 33(1–2): 4–18.
Gereffi, G. (1999) 'International Trade and Industrial Upgrading in the Apparel Commodity Chain', *Journal of International Economics*, 48(1): 37–70.
Gereffi, G. (2001) 'Shifting Governance Structures in Global Commodity Chains, with Special Reference to the Internet', *American Behavioural Scientist*, 44(10): 1616–37.

Gereffi, G. and Memedovic, O. (2003) *The Global Apparel Value Chain: What Prospects for Upgrading by Developing Countries?* Vienna: UNIDO.

Goetz, A. and Rodrigue, J.-P. (1999) 'Transport Terminals: New Perspectives', *Journal of Transport Geography*, 7(4): 237–40.

Hall, P., Hesse, M. and Rodrigue, J.-P. (2006) 'Re-exploring the Interface between Economic and Transport Geography', *Environment & Planning A*, 38(8): 1401–8.

Harrison, A., Christopher, M. and van Hoek, R. (1999) *Creating the Agile Supply Chain*, Corby: Chartered Institute of Logistics and Transport.

Henderson, J., Dicken, P., Hess, M., Coe, N. M. and Yeung, H. W.-C. (2002) 'Global Production Networks and the Analysis of Economic Development', *Review of International Political Economy*, 9(3): 436–64.

Hess, M. and Coe, N. M. (2006) 'Making Connections: Global Production Networks, Standards, and Embeddedness in the Mobile Telecommunications Industry', *Environment and Planning A*, 38(7): 1205–27.

Hesse, M. (2008) *The City as a Terminal: The Urban Context of Logistics and Freight Transport*, Aldershot: Ashgate.

Hesse, M. and Rodrigue, J.-P. (2004) 'The Transport Geography of Logistics and Freight Distribution', *Journal of Transport Geography*, 12(3): 171–84.

Hesse, M. and Rodrigue, J.-P. (2006) 'Global Production Networks and the Role of Logistics and Transportation', *Growth and Change*, 37(4): 499–509.

Higginson, J. and Bookbinder, J. (2005) 'Distribution Centres in Supply Chain Operations', in A. Langevin and D. Riopel (eds) *Logistics Systems: Design and Optimization*, New York: Springer, pp. 67–91.

Humphrey, J. and Schmitz, H. (2002) 'How Does Insertion in Global Value Chains Affect Upgrading in Industrial Clusters?', *Regional Studies*, 36(9): 1017–27.

Joosten, F. (2007) *Development Strategy for the Export-oriented Horticulture in Ethiopia*, Wageningen: mimeo, <http://library.wur.nl/way/bestanden/clc/1891396.pdf> (accessed 19 November 2012).

Kaplinsky, R. and Farooki, M. (2010) 'Global Value Chains, the Crisis, and the Shift of Markets from North to South', in O. Cattaneo, G. Gereffi and C. Staritz (eds) *Global Value Chains in a Postcrisis World*, Washington, DC: World Bank, pp. 125–53.

Kenney, M. and Curry, J. (2001) 'Beyond Transaction Costs: E-commerce and the Power of Internet Dataspace', in T. Leinbach and S. D. Brunn (eds) *Worlds of E-commerce: Economic, Geographical, and Social Dimensions*, Chichester: Wiley, pp. 45–65.

Kharas, H. (2010) 'The Emerging Middle Class in Developing Countries', OECD Development Centre Working Paper No. 285, Paris: OECD.

Knowles, R., Shaw, J. and Docherty, I. (eds) (2008) *Transport Geographies: Mobilities, Flows and Spaces*, Oxford: Blackwell.

Korsten, L., Njie, D. and Sivakumar, D. (2008) *Horticultural Chain Management for Eastern and Southern Africa: A Theoretical Manual*, London: Commonwealth Secretariat.

Kuehne & Nagel (2009) *Logistics Opportunities in China*, <http://www.advantageaustria.org/cn/office/zahn.pdf> (accessed 19 November 2012).

LEI (Agricultural Economics Research Institute, Wageningen) (n.d.) *Ghana: Sustainable Horticultural Export Chain*, Wageningen: mimeo.

Leinbach, T. (2001) 'Emergence of the Digital Economy and E-commerce', in T. Leinbach and S. D. Brunn (eds) *Worlds of E-commerce: Economic, Geographical, and Social Dimensions*, Chichester: Wiley, pp. 3–26.

Leinbach, T. and Bowen, J. (2004) 'Air Cargo Services and the Electronics Industry in Southeast Asia', *Journal of Economic Geography*, 4(3): 299–321.

Levinson, M. (2006) *The Box: How the Shipping Container Made the World Smaller and the World Economy Bigger*, Princeton, NJ: Princeton University Press.

Li, F., Whalley, J. and Williams, H. (2001) 'Between Physical and Electronic Spaces: The Implications for Organizations in the Networked Economy', *Environment and Planning A*, 33(4): 699–716.

Liu, B., Lee, S.-J., Jiao, Z. and Wang, L. (2011) *Contemporary Logistics in China: An Introduction*, Singapore: World Scientific Books.

Liu, W., Dicken, P. and Yeung, H. W.-C. (2004) 'New Information and Communication Technologies and Local Clustering of Firms: A Case Study of the Xingwang Industrial Park in Beijing', *Urban Geography*, 25(4): 390–407.

McKinsey & Company (2010) *Building India: Transforming the Nation's Logistics Infrastructure*, <http://www.mckinsey.com/locations/india/mckinseyonindia/pdf/building_india_transofrming_the_nations_logistics_infrastructure.pdf> (accessed 19 November 2012).

Mei, Z. and Dinwoodie, J. (2005) 'Electronic Shipping Documentation in China's International Supply Chains', *Supply Chain Management*, 10(3): 198–205.

Milberg, W. and Winkler, D. (2010) 'Economic and Social Upgrading in Global Production Networks: Problems of Theory and Measurement', *Capturing the Gains* Working Paper 2010/04, <http://www.capturingthegains.org/> (accessed 19 November 2012).

Newsome, K. (2010) 'Work and Employment in Distribution and Exchange: Moments in the Circuit of Capital', *Industrial Relations Journal*, 41(3): 190–205.

Notteboom, T. and Rodrigue, J.-P. (2008) 'Containerization, Box Logistics and Global Supply Chains: The Integration of Ports and Liner Shipping Networks', *Maritime Economics and Logistics*, 10(1–2): 152–74.

Notteboom, T. and Rodrigue, J.-P. (2012) 'The Corporate Geography of Global Container Terminal Operators', *Maritime Policy and Management*, 39(3): 249–79.

O'Connor, K. (2009) 'Transport and Globalization', in R. Kitchin and N. J. Thrift (eds) *International Encyclopaedia of Human Geography*, Oxford: Elsevier.

Ojala, L., Andersson, D. and Naula, T. (2008) 'Linking to Global Value Chains: An Imperative for Developing Countries', *International Journal of Technological Learning, Innovation and Development*, 1(3): 427–50.

Rodrigue, J.-P. (2006) 'Transportation and the Geographical and Functional Integration of Global Production Networks', *Growth and Change*, 37(4): 510–25.

Rodrigue, J.-P. (2008) 'The Thruport Concept and Transmodal Rail Freight Distribution in North America', *Journal of Transport Geography*, 16(4): 233–46.

Rodrigue, J.-P., Comtois, C. and Slack, B. (2006) *The Geography of Transport Systems*, 2nd edn, London: Routledge.

Rushton, A. and Walker, S. (2007) *International Logistics and Supply Chain Outsourcing*, London: Kogan Page.

Schrank, A. (2004) 'Ready-to-wear Development? Foreign Investment, Technology Transfer, and Learning by Watching in the Apparel Trade', *Social Forces*, 83(1): 123–56.

Sheffi, Y. (2012) *Logistics Clusters: Delivering Value and Driving Growth*, Cambridge, MA: MIT Press.

Skjøtt-Larsen, T., Schary, P. B., Mikkola, J. and Kotzab, H. (2007) *Managing the Global Supply Chain*, 3rd edn, Copenhagen: Copenhagen Business School Press.

Smith, D. and Sparks, L. (2004) 'Temperature-controlled Supply Chains', in J. Fernie and L. Sparks (eds) *Logistics and Retail Management*, London: Kogan Page, pp. 121–37.

Sparks, L. and Wagner, B. (2004) 'Transforming Technologies: Retail Exchanges and RFID', in J. Fernie and L. Sparks (eds) *Logistics and Retail Management*, London: Kogan Page, pp. 188–208.

Stopford, M. (2009) *Maritime Economics*, London: Routledge.
Straits Times (2012) 'Finding a Niche in the Logistics Space', 12 November, B10.
Turnbull, P. (2000) 'Contesting Globalization on the Waterfront', *Politics and Society*, 28(3): 367–91.
Turnbull, P. and Wass, V. J. (2007) 'Defending Dock Workers: Globalization and Labor Relations in the World's Ports', *Industrial Relations*, 46(3): 582–612.
UK National Statistics (2012) ', *Labour market data*, http://www.statistics.gov.uk/ (accessed 19 November 2012).
Vagneron, I., Faure, G. and Loeillet, D. (2009) 'Is There a Pilot in the Chain? Identifying the Key Drivers of Change in the Fresh Pineapple Sector', *Food Policy*, 34(5): 437–46.
van Egeraat, C. and Jacobson, D. (2005) 'Geography of Production Linkages in the Irish and Scottish Microcomputer Industry: The Role of Logistics', *Economic Geography*, 81(3): 283–303.
Voortman, C. (2004) *Global Logistics Management*, Claremont: Juta Academic.
Wang, J. J. and Cheng, M. C. (2010) 'From a Hub Port City to a Global Supply Chain Management Center: A Case Study of Hong Kong', *Journal of Transport Geography*, 18(1): 104–15.
Wang, J. J. and Olivier, D. (2006) 'Port – FEZ Bundles as Spaces of Global Articulation: The Case of Tianjin, China', *Environment and Planning A*, 38(8): 1487–503.
Wang, J. J., Olivier, D., Notteboom, T. and Slack, B. (eds) (2007) *Ports, Cities, and Global Supply Chains*, Aldershot: Ashgate.
Waters, D. (ed.) (2010) *Global Logistics: New Directions in Supply Chain Management*, 6th edn, London: Kogan Page.
Wood, D. F., Barone, A. P., Murphy, P. R. and Wardlow, D. L. (2002) *International Logistics*, 2nd edn, New York: Amacom.
World Bank (2010) *How to Decrease Freight Logistics Costs in Brazil*, Report No. 46885-BR, <http://siteresources.worldbank.org/BRAZILINPOREXTN/Resources/3817166–1323121030855/FreightLogistics.pdf?resourceurlname=FreightLogistics.pdf> (accessed 19 November 2012).
Wright, C. and Lund, J. (2006) 'Variations on a Lean Theme: Work Restructuring in Retail Distribution', *New Technology, Work and Employment*, 21(1): 59–74.

Index

Note: Page numbers in **bold** type refer to figures
Page numbers in *italic* type refer to tables
Page numbers followed by 'n' refer to notes

For Product Safety Concerns and Information please contact our EU representative GPSR@taylorandfrancis.com Taylor & Francis Verlag GmbH, Kaufingerstraße 24, 80331 München, Germany